DESIGNS FOR DEMOCRATIC STABILITY

Comparative Politics Series

Gregory S. Mahler, Editor

POWER AND RITUAL IN THE ISRAEL LABOR PARTY
A Study in Political Anthropology
Myron J. Aronoff

COMPARATIVE POLITICAL SYSTEMS
Policy Performance and Social Change
Charles F. Andrain

DEMOCRATIC LEGISLATIVE INSTITUTIONS
A Comparative View
David M. Olson

BLAMING THE GOVERNMENT
Citizens and the Economy in Five European Democracies
Christopher Anderson

POLITICAL CULTURE AND CONSTITUTIONALISM
A Comparative Approach
Edited by Daniel P. Franklin and Michael J. Baun

CORPORATISM AND COMPARATIVE POLITICS
The Other Great "Ism"
Howard J. Wiarda

THE POLITICS OF ABORTION IN THE UNITED STATES AND CANADA
A Comparative Study
Raymond Tatalovich

DESIGNS FOR DEMOCRATIC STABILITY
Studies in Viable Constitutionalism
Edited by Abdo I. Baaklini and Helen Desfosses

COMPARATIVE
POLITICS
SERIES

DESIGNS FOR DEMOCRATIC STABILITY

Studies in Viable Constitutionalism

Abdo I. Baaklini and
Helen Desfosses, Editors

M.E. Sharpe
Armonk, New York
London, England

Library of Congress Cataloging-in-Publication Data

Designs for democratic stability : studies in viable constitutionalism /
edited by Abdo I. Baaklini and Helen Desfosses.
p. cm.—(Comparative politics)
Includes bibliographical references and index.
ISBN 0-7656-0051-X (cloth : alk. paper).—ISBN 0-7656-0052-8 (pbk. : alk. paper)
1. Comparative government.
2. Constitutional history.
3. Democracy.
4. Political stability.
5. Representative government and representation.
I. Baaklini, Abdo I.
II. Desfosses, Helen.
III. Series: Comparative politics (Armonk, N.Y.)
JF51.D475 1997
321.8—dc21
96-36920
CIP

Printed in the United States of America

The paper used in this publication meets the minimum requirements of the
American National Standard for Information Sciences—
Permanence of Paper for Printed Library Materials,
ANSI Z 39.48-1984.

BM (c) 10 9 8 7 6 5 4 3 2 1
BM (p) 10 9 8 7 6 5 4 3 2 1

For my sons, Farid and Iskandar Baaklini

—Abdo Baaklini

For my son, Adam Cohn

—Helen Desfosses

Contents

Contributors

Joel D. Aberbach

Joel D. Aberbach is Professor of Political Science and Director of the Center for American Politics and Public Policy at the University of California, Los Angeles. He is the author of *Keeping a Watchful Eye: The Politics of Congressional Oversight,* coauthor with Bert A. Rockman of *The Administrative State in Industrialized Democracies,* and coauthor with Robert D. Putnam and Bert A. Rockman of *Bureaucrats and Politicians in Western Democracies.*

Abdo I. Baaklini

Abdo I. Baaklini, coeditor of this volume, is Professor of Public Administration and Policy at the University at Albany, State University of New York. He is also Director of the Center for Legislative Development at the University. Dr. Baaklini has published extensively in the area of legislatures, their roles, and their administrative needs. He is the author, most recently, of *The Brazilian Legislature and Political System*, and a forthcoming publication, *Legislatures in the Middle East: Their Role during Transition to Democracy.*

Philip G. Cerny

Philip G. Cerny is Senior Lecturer in Politics at the University of York, United Kingdom. He has been a Guest Scholar at Harvard University and the Brookings Institution. He is the author of *The Changing Architecture of Politics: Structure, Agency, and the Future of the State*, and *Plurilateralism: Structural Differentiation and Functional Conflict in the Post–Cold War World.*

Helen Desfosses

Helen Desfosses, coeditor of this volume, is Associate Professor of Public Administration and Policy and Africana Studies at the University at Albany, State University of New York. She is currently Senior Research Fellow at the

Center for Legislative Development at the University, and has consulted on legislative development in several countries. She is coeditor of *Socialism in the Third World*, and is engaged in a study titled *Agenda-Setting in United States African Policy*. She has been a Visiting Scholar at the Hoover Institution, Stanford University.

Diane Ethier

Diane Ethier is Associate Professor of Political Science at the Université de Montréal. She is the author of several works on economic liberalization and political democratization. Her most recent writings concern the process of economic adjustment and democratic consolidation in Greece, Spain, Portugal, Chile, Brazil, and Mexico. Her forthcoming publication is *Economic Adjustment in New Democracies: Lessons from Southern Europe*.

Erik P. Hoffmann

Erik P. Hoffmann is Professor of Political Science, University at Albany, State University of New York. He has written several works on the challenges to viable constitutionalism in post-Soviet Russia. He is the author, most recently, of *Post-Communist Studies and Political Science*, and a forthcoming volume, *Russian Dilemmas: Continuity and Change in Post-Soviet Russia*.

Ersin Kalaycioğlu

Ersin Kalaycioğlu is Professor of Political Science at Boğaziçi University and has taught at Istanbul University in the Faculties of Economics and Political Science. He has written extensively on political participation in Turkey and Europe. He is the author of three books: *Introduction to Political Science*, *Comparative Political Participation*, and *Turkish Politics*.

Gregory S. Mahler

Gregory S. Mahler is Professor and Chair of the Department of Political Science at the University of Mississippi. He is also Director of the Office of International Affairs. He has written or edited fifteen books focusing on institutions and political structures. His most recent book is *Comparative Politics: A Cross-National and Institutional Perspective*.

Fred W. Riggs

Fred W. Riggs is Professor Emeritus of Political Science at the University of Hawaii, where he taught beginning in 1967. He has pioneered in the study of why the American constitutional system has not broken down, even though the approximately thirty countries that have copied the United States have experienced crises leading to military or presidential authoritarianism. In 1991, Dr. Riggs received the Dwight Waldo Award for lifetime achievement in Public Administration, conferred by the American Society for Public Administration.

Bert A. Rockman

Bert A. Rockman is University Professor of Political Science at the University of Pittsburgh, where he holds appointments as Research Professor in the University Center for International Studies and Professor in the Graduate School of Public and International Affairs. He is coauthor with Joel Aberbach and Robert D. Putnam of *Bureaucrats and Politicians in Western Democracies*; he has also written several other books, including *The Leadership Question: The Presidency and the American System, The Bush Presidency: First Appraisals*, and *Do Institutions Matter? Government Capabilities in the U.S. and Abroad.*

T. V. Sathyamurthy

T. V. Sathyamurthy is a social scientist who has been lecturing at the University of York, United Kingdom, since 1968. His research has focused on political identity, and on the conflict between structures of power and resistance movements during rapid political and economic change. His most recent work, as commissioning editor, is *Social Change and Political Discourse in India since Independence: Structures of Power, Movements of Resistance*.

James L. Sundquist

James L. Sundquist has been Senior Fellow Emeritus at the Brookings Institution since 1985. He is the author of several books on government and politics, including *Constitutional Reform and Effective Government*. Most recently, he edited a Brookings volume entitled *Beyond Gridlock? Prospects for Governance in the Clinton Years—and After*. He has lectured on American government and politics in several countries. Among his honors is the Charles E. Merriam Award of the American Political Science Association, for significant contribution to the art of government through the application of social science research.

Acknowledgments

This book would never have become a reality without the teamwork and high-quality effort of the staff of the Center for Legislative Development, University at Albany, State University of New York. We particularly appreciate the role of Nan Carroll in directing the entire manuscript preparation process. We are also grateful to Peg Clement for her skillful copyediting of manuscripts across several cultures and languages. Ann Péan did a masterful job of proofreading countless drafts, while Clare Yates lent a keen and critical eye to overseeing the final editing and preparation of the manuscript. We are also indebted to Marlene Boland for her excellent—and patient—typing of these chapters and entering of revisions too numerous to count. Chuck Cornell was invaluable in the work of editing references and checking facts, while notes received special attention from David Carroll. The genius behind the formatting and generation of camera-ready copy was Linda Gould.

DESIGNS FOR DEMOCRATIC STABILITY

1

Viable Constitutionalism and Democratic Political Stability

ABDO I. BAAKLINI

The collapse of military regimes in South America in the mid-1980s, and the demise of communist regimes in Eastern Europe and the Soviet Union in the late 1980s, have ushered in a new era of constitution writing unprecedented since the end of World War II and the rapid dismantling of colonialism. Countries throughout South America, Eastern Europe, Africa, Asia, and the Middle East have embarked on a frenzy of adopting or amending the constitutional framework that will regulate the recently established democratic polities.

Constitutional scholars and legal experts were caught unprepared to render advice on viable constitutional frameworks to guarantee political stability within a democracy. Several explanations can account for this lack of readiness and preparation to define appropriate political institutions and constitutions. These explanations stem from intellectual developments in the field of political science after World War II, and from external political developments.

Following World War II, the academic discipline of political science was dominated by what came to be known as the behavioralist persuasion, or the effort to develop a science of politics modeled after the methodology of the natural sciences.[1] While the behavioral approach to the study of political phenomena enriched the field in many respects and advanced the theoretical and empirical understanding of politics, it also inadvertently undermined the study of institutions as independent variables in shaping political behavior. Although there is no theoretical contradiction between the behavioral approach in political science and the study of institutions, the discipline nevertheless opted to place more emphasis on noninstitutional variables in the study of politics. Postwar political science was intellectually influenced by theories that emphasized the individual characteristics of actors and informal structures rather than by theories that addressed formal institutions as independent variables in explaining political phenomena.

This intellectual bias against institutions was reinforced by a number of other developments. The invention of the computer and the development of statistics as tools available to researchers encouraged the collection of discrete data that could be manipulated by statistical packages. The policy needs of governments increased the funds available for researchers, thus enabling academics and research institutions to pay for the costs of conducting surveys and collecting data. Intellectually, undertaking empirical research and data collection became more rewarding for publication and career enhancement. This type of research was given the complimentary designation of "rigorous," as opposed to "descriptive," "soft," or "sloppy." Scholars involved in the empirical behavioral research agenda were rewarded not only intellectually, but financially as well. They were able to attract hefty grants to their institutions and students, and to summon premium consultancy fees for themselves.

This same bias against the study of institutions was also apparent in the emergent subfields of comparative politics and development studies. During the 1950s and 1960s, comparative politics was dominated by two fundamental concerns, one theoretical and the other utilitarian. Theoretically, the field was engrossed in the search for an encompassing model that could explain all political phenomena in general terms. The model that emerged was so abstract that political institutions were conceptualized as abstractions or ideal types, rather than as empirical phenomena. Furthermore, the abstractions were not derived from the realities of the political institutions as they existed in the developing world, but instead reflected the institutions of the Western societies that produced most of these theories.

The utilitarian concern emphasized the need to prevent certain groups from attaining power while promoting other groups to seize and maintain power. To the extent that comparative politics and development studies advocated an institutional strategy, the emphasis was on bureaucracies in their civilian and military manifestations. Development was considered to be an economic phenomenon that could be best attained through a rational and competent bureaucracy. Political stability was believed to be best attained through economic development spearheaded by the bureaucracy.[2]

Since the utilitarian goal of comparative and development studies was to promote development, many concluded that it was unnecessary to study existing institutions when the goal was to change and obliterate those institutions considered to be the main obstacles to development. To the extent that development required institutions, Max Weber had the answer in his formulation of the bureaucratic model.[3] Weber's writings about how societies develop showed that they progress from traditional to charismatic to rational-legal. The process of development, it was reasoned, could therefore be enhanced by the development of rational bureaucracies through education, training, and administrative reforms. Constitutions and other political structures were considered either unnecessary impediments or luxuries to be enjoyed once development had already occurred.

Finally, comparative and development studies were organized as separate topics within academia, and isolated from interacting with mainstream political science. Americanists, for example, who continued to explore the American political phenomenon in its various manifestations, were isolated from their comparative and development counterparts. This had the effect of weakening both groups. The comparative group developed its own research agenda, ignoring the findings of the American specialists. The American specialists continued to espouse theories and approaches oblivious of the richness of comparative political phenomena. The net result was an impoverishment of both subfields.

While the intellectual and utilitarian concerns within the political science community discouraged the study of political institutions in general, and constitutions in particular, other conditions also contributed to the decline of interest in these issues. The emergence of civilian-military bureaucratic regimes, whether by design or otherwise, and the disregard they have toward institutions, constitutions, and the rule of law, convinced many scholars and public policymakers that institutions and constitutions were irrelevant to an explanation of political behavior. Countries that fell under the sway of communist regimes after World War II displayed a similar disregard for their own constitutions. Although many of these constitutions espoused all sorts of liberties and rights, a bureaucratic, police-dominated state emerged in most of these countries. Citizens' rights were trampled on, and basic political and individual freedoms were completely absent. Military dictators abolished constitutions they did not like, and by fiat created constitutions that allowed them to legitimize any abuse they decided to commit.

American foreign assistance to developing countries since World War II can also serve to illustrate the lack of interest in studying the development of political institutions. The preponderance of all U.S. foreign assistance went for military purposes. Assistance targeted for development was allocated to the growth of bureaucratic institutions or to finance various socioeconomic projects. The need for political participation in the development process was not recognized until the amendment to the Foreign Assistance Act of 1967 that came to be known as Title IX. As a result of this amendment, the United States Agency for International Development (USAID) was instructed to encourage civic participation in the developing countries in administering its development aid. In the late sixties, a civic participation division was created within USAID to implement the congressional mandate contained in Title IX of the Foreign Assistance Act. In 1967, a group of U.S. scholars recommended that legislatures in developing countries be studied as institutions that could be relevant to development. In 1970, USAID allocated some funding to four U.S. universities to study legislatures in developing countries. A series of studies undertaken between 1970 and 1977 resulted in a number of publications from the Duke University Press on legislatures in developing countries, and their role in and contribution to development.[4] Unfortunately, these studies did not have any immediate impact on the priorities of U.S. foreign assistance.

President Jimmy Carter shifted foreign aid priorities away from formal government institutions to human rights nongovernmental organizations (NGOs). In 1982, President Ronald Reagan acknowledged the importance of political institutions and democracy as a weapon against communist totalitarianism. Reagan conceived of democracy and political development as an ideology against the Soviet "evil empire." Finally, in the mid-1980s, especially after the collapse of communism, President George Bush realized the importance of political development and political institutions as prerequisites for economic development. Since the mid-1980s, USAID has elevated democratic political development as a priority in its foreign assistance programs. Unfortunately, political scientists were ill prepared to render advice on how democratic institutions could be built, and what type of constitutional mechanism might enhance the political viability and stability deemed necessary for any sustainable economic development effort.

Transition to Democracy

By the late 1970s and early 1980s, political scientists became less fascinated with the developmental regimes and systems they had long espoused. Military regimes, the one-party system, and the communist model failed to produce the desired economic miracles that had been promised. Human rights advocates became vocal in their criticism of the bureaucratic state and the many abuses it had inflicted on the majority of its citizens. In response to this failure, political scientists in the comparative and developmental subfields shifted their focus away from the study of the state and its bureaucratic institutions, and toward the study of the factors that led to the collapse of the state. The demise of the Franco regime in Spain, the Salazar dictatorship in Portugal, and the collapse of the military junta in Greece gave this movement great impetus. Latin American scholars were among the first to notice the winds of change. As a result of the relevance of the Spanish experience to most Latin American countries and the Portuguese experience to Brazil, political scientists were intrigued by the developments in the Iberian peninsula. Many asked: Could what happened in Spain and Portugal also be relevant to Latin America?[5]

As a result of this challenge, the emphasis shifted to the study of the institutions of civil society and the economic and social conditions that might lead to the demise of the authoritarian state. During the late 1970s and early 1980s, many books were written that dealt with the institutions of civil society such as the church, the labor union movement, professional associations, societies, clubs, and neighborhood community-type institutions. The transition-to-democracy literature emphasized the role of these institutions in undermining the authoritarian state. Those who emphasized economic factors as the impetus for transition to a democratic regime focused on the role of the international economy as well as significant national and international economic actors.

Once the democratic transition began in earnest in many Latin American countries, the emphasis shifted from the factors that promoted the change to the mechanisms by which this transition was achieved. The actors involved in the transition as well as the methods used in negotiating the agreements took center stage. To the extent that the contents of these agreements were discussed, the emphasis was on the socioeconomic agreements represented by the national pact. Little attention was given to the role of institutions in these transitions and how these institutions were related to each other. This focus had to wait until the late 1980s.

Presidentialism or Parliamentarism

Very often, political realities precede academic speculation. This was certainly the case with respect to constitutions and constitution writing. The rapid collapse of the authoritarian state in many Latin American countries in the mid-1980s, and since the late 1980s in many communist countries in Eastern Europe and the Soviet Union, presented policymakers with the need to reexamine the viability of constitutionalism. The question asked was: What is the best way of adopting a new constitution that will ensure political viability and avoid the abuses that characterized authoritarian states?

Once again, Latin American scholars were at the forefront of this discussion.[6] Attributing the collapse of the democratic state that preceded the establishment of the authoritarian states to the presidential system prevailing in many Latin American countries, policymakers and scholars became interested in an alternative constitutional order. For many scholars, parliamentarism appeared to be an appropriate alternative.[7] During this period, both the political debate and the academic literature were caught in a frenzy of advocating one system or the other. Some of the policymakers and scholars suggested that parliamentarism, modeled along the Westminster pattern, was a system that consolidated both executive and legislative power in one authority and, therefore, was less likely to lead to a presidential dictatorship and the demise of legislative institutions. Some argued that parliamentary regimes, as a result of juxtaposing one institution against the other, were more stable and less prone to the destabilizing elements inherent in the presidential system. Others suggested that parliamentary systems were more conducive to the growth of disciplined political parties, and to the distribution and sharing of powers among a group of equals as represented in a cabinet form of government. Still others maintained that parliamentarism allowed for adjustment and adaptation to reflect the existing power shifts and challenges.

Advocates of presidentialism, many of whom cited the durability and viability of the U.S. system of government, challenged these assumptions and reaffirmed the superiority of the presidential system as the guarantor of individual liberty as well as the best means of preventing the dictatorship of the majority. Presidential advocates argued that the necessary conditions for a successful adaptation of the Westminster parliamentary model were absent in many developing countries, and therefore the model was not applicable.[8] It is important to note that during this period the policy debate preceded the academic debate. As in most policy debates, political actors advocated those alternatives that they believed would benefit their chances of assuming and holding power. The constitutional debate in Brazil during the mid-to-late 1980s, for example, clearly illustrates this point. Some political parties, irrespective of their ideological orientation, found themselves advocating a similar solution (either presidentialism or parliamentarism) because their focus was on which system provided their best chance of capturing power. Thus, for example, the small leftist parties joined rank with small rightist parties to advocate the presidential system against some of the larger, centrist parties that advocated the parliamentary system of government. Those who advocated the presidential system finally prevailed.

Beyond Presidentialism and Parliamentarism

This volume attempts to redress some of the imbalances that have developed in the political science literature on constitutions. All of the chapters share a recognition that political institutions are important for both political stability and development. One of the important instruments for establishing and defining political institutions is a constitution. Often, however, constitutions are drafted and adopted without adequate attention to the institutions they establish, or to the effect these institutions have on political behavior and the various values associated with democratic systems. The authors of the studies contained in this volume share a number of concerns relevant to constitutions and political viability.

The first is a renewed focus on political institutions as independent variables important to political behavior.

Political behavior is shaped by many variables. One important variable is the formal institution within which that behavior takes place. Herbert Simon's classic work, *Administrative Behavior*, convincingly demonstrated the importance of institutions in determining both the factual and value premises of decisions.[9] Since political behavior is usually based on a series of decisions made by political actors, those factors that shape decisions are also shaping behavior. Constitutions and the institutions they establish influence behavior in many ways. They set the parameters for acceptable action. They also set norms and procedures that need to be followed in transacting public business.

Often, however, these parameters are ambiguous and flexible; this allows for a variety of different interpretations. But the authorities entrusted with the interpretation are specified and are required to follow definite procedures, and to use specific norms in interpreting competing alternatives. Those in power find themselves bound by norms and procedures even when they consciously and deliberately attempt to violate the terms imposed on them by the constitution. Thus, King Hussein of Jordan, for example, when trying to undertake an act not authorized by the constitution, resorts to all the legal norms and procedures to amend the constitution in order to legitimize his action. Although he could discard the constitution and proceed with his unconstitutional act, he normally chooses to go through elaborate procedures to ensure that his acts conform to a constitution that was amended legally and constitutionally. To argue that King Hussein would have done what he intended to do with or without the blessing of a legally enacted constitutional amendment misses the main point. The act of amending the constitution forces him to act publicly and, therefore, to justify his actions both politically and in terms of legal and constitutional norms. To do otherwise would entail expending valuable political capital, normally in short supply, especially in authoritarian regimes.

The situation is similar with respect to military regimes. Although they usually come to power in violation of constitutional norms, they often either justify themselves as defenders and guardians of the constitution or, immediately after the success of their coup, resort to the promulgation of a constitution according to which they seek to justify their future behavior and actions. For example, whenever military officers in Brazil assumed power, they justified their actions as guardians and defenders of the constitution, which they charged the civilian politicians with violating or planning to violate. The leaders of the military regimes often took great pains to ensure that their coming to power as well as their actions while in power were in conformity with prevailing legal and constitutional norms. The existence of constitutional norms and procedures may not have prevented them from undertaking actions they deemed necessary for their survival; however, these norms and procedures forced them to seek their goals within certain parameters. Similarly, Egypt's Gamal

Abdel Nasser and Anwar el-Sadat found that their first order of priority when they assumed power was to adopt a constitution, with which they sought public approval of their actions.

Finally, when the transition to democracy began in many authoritarian and totalitarian countries, a major priority was not simply the nature of the new constitution, but how to adopt the new constitution without violating the existing constitution that had legitimized the very same authoritarian and totalitarian regimes. Thus, before adopting its 1988 constitution, the authoritarian regime in Brazil embarked on a series of constitutional amendments that legitimized the institutions and procedures used to create the new constitution. Similarly elaborate constitutional amendments and adoption of procedures and new institutions were undertaken in many of the communist countries to effect a transition to a democratic polity. Three of the chapters in this volume detail the processes that India, Russia, and Turkey employed as they adopted their new constitutions. Without analyzing this complex process of adopting a new constitution, political scientists tended to dismiss these actions as constitutional maneuvers of little significance. A closer and more thorough examination of the process by which a constitution is adopted has tremendous implications for the type of constitution that is drafted and the strength of legitimacy that it carries. This brings me to the second premise of this volume: dealing with legitimacy.

All the authors here share the conviction that, in many cases, the process of adopting a constitution is as important as the content of the constitution, and can therefore promote or undermine constitutional viability and democratic stability.

Constitutions are adopted in many ways and through a variety of institutional mechanisms. Many authoritarian regimes drafted and adopted their constitutions with very limited participation and debate. Typically, a group of jurists appointed by the military leadership drafted the constitution and forced it on an emasculated legislature or rushed it through a public referendum without allowing debate or alternatives to surface. Some dictators adopted their constitutions as an executive act and later forced a recalcitrant legislature, selected in accordance with the newly adopted executive constitution, to ratify what had already been adopted. Yet others resorted to elaborate institutional and procedural arrangements to ensure that significant groups of the population were present around the table to debate the draft of the new constitution, and to advocate policies and institutions they sought to establish as part of it.

To the extent that significant elements within a society are permitted to participate in shaping and adopting a new constitution that embodies their values and their agreements over dividing power and adjudicating future conflict, the constitution adopted may carry added legitimacy. My research on the procedures used and the institutions entrusted with the adoption of the 1988 constitution of Brazil showed that foremost on the minds of the leaders was the need for popular legitimacy of the new constitution to contrast it with the way previous military regimes in that country had adopted their constitutions. Erik Hoffmann, in his chapter on the Russian Constitution, raises similar points. The weakness of the Yeltsin constitution, he argues, is not in what it does or does not contain, but in the process by which it has been adopted. By muzzling the opposition and excluding it from effective participation in the process of adopting the new constitution, Yeltsin undermined its legitimacy, and seriously compromised its prospects for success.

Viewed from this perspective, a constitution is not simply a legal document, but more like a political agreement. No matter how refined the legal document and how sensitively crafted to create a smooth and balanced institutional structure, unless the significant parties to the conflict are present and have been given ample opportunities to voice their views, the political agreement will be aborted. For a constitution to be viable, it has to be shaped and accepted by the significant actors in a society, and their interests need to be reflected and protected.

As a political agreement, then, a constitution often embodies the political interests of those who participated in its drafting and adoption. Debates on the form of government—such as presidentialism or parliamentarism—and the distribution of power among various branches, or the relationship between the center and the regions, are often debates on who is likely to dominate which branch of government. Thus, during the constitutional deliberations in Brazil, the debate over the presidential and parliamentary forms of government was a political debate rather than simply a constitutional one. Certain political parties and individuals felt that they had more to gain by adopting the presidential system; their opponents favored a parliamentary system. In this political debate, advocates mobilized whatever legal, constitutional, political, and cultural arguments they could muster to support their points of view. Constitutions are not sought solely for the purpose of ensuring viability and stability, but often are above all else political conflicts where the winners are assured more chances of seeing their interests protected, now and in the future. The country cases in this book will amply illustrate this point.

To suggest that constitutions conceived as political agreements par excellence are important to political behavior and to political stability and viability does not, in any way, undermine the importance of other cultural and economic variables. It merely changes the focus of the discussion. Cultural and economic variables remain important within certain institutional frameworks. The question asked by many policymakers involved in constitution writing becomes: How can certain political structures accommodate the cultural or economic conditions prevalent in a society? Another question raised by many of those policymakers is whether the adoption of certain structures would produce changes in political culture. Thus, political policymakers and intellectuals during the Brazilian constitutional debates of 1987–88 raised the question whether a presidential system was more suited to Brazilian political tradition and culture than a parliamentary system. Supporters of the presidential system answered the question in the affirmative; opponents argued that the adoption of a parliamentary system would lead to the emergence of strong and coherent political parties that would have a positive impact on political culture and behavior in the country.

A similar logic prevails with regard to economic variables. Constitutional scholars advocating the primacy of constitutions do not deny the importance of economic factors as determinants of political behavior and political stability. Diane Ethier, in her chapter in this volume, summarizes the varied literature that highlights the importance of economic variables in the process of political democratization. The question that needs to be asked, however, becomes: Which political structure can lead to a better handling of economic issues? Indeed, a significant impetus for democratic and constitutional changes in many authoritarian and totalitarian regimes was the premise that these regimes were ill equipped to handle economic decisions in a globalized economy. Democratic regimes were viewed as more agile and more intelligent in generating, disseminating, and utilizing information needed for economic decision making. For both policy makers and scholars, the question then becomes: What type of democratic system is more conducive to meeting the challenge of formulating economic policy?

As a political process, constitution making is influenced by both internal and external variables. Internal political actors are important because they participate in the drafting, adoption, and implementation of any political agreement embodied in a constitution, including the national pact that many scholars emphasize. Whatever the national pact contains and whether the national pact is drafted and accepted extraconstitutionally or not, it has to be interpreted, developed, and implemented within a constitutional framework. In those countries where such a national pact has not been adopted, the constitution is itself the national pact.

External influences are always present in the adoption of a new constitution. These influences arise in a variety of ways: incorporated into the intellectual psyche of the internal actors, either through education or as historical examples; exercised through expert advice and technical assistance; and suggested, encouraged, or even imposed by a conquering or dominant power. Local actors engaged in reaching these political agreements are often sensitive to the pressure and interests of relevant outside actors. Carrying the argument to its logical conclusion, Philip Cerny, in his chapter in this volume, argues that constitutional viability and political stability are more and more dependent on external actors and forces, and that the notion of a sovereign state has long been obsolete.

A third concern among the authors in this book is that there are many variations of presidential and parliamentary systems. A system appropriate for one country may not necessarily be appropriate for another.

Although scholarly attention has been focused on the U.S. presidential system and the Westminster parliamentary model, presidentialism and parliamentarism have taken many shapes and forms. Indeed, the presidential system of the United States and the parliamentary system of the United Kingdom are aberrations rather than the norm. Yet, when discussing either presidentialism or parliamentarism, reference is usually to these two systems. Gregory Mahler's chapter in this book elucidates some of the variations of the parliamentary system and the deviations found from the Westminster Model. James Sundquist's chapter, on the other hand, analyzes the American form of presidentialism and some of the underlying assumptions that are often ignored by those who purport to be adopting that system. Both of these chapters caution constitution writers to be aware of both variations of constitutional design and, more important, what Fred Riggs has called "paraconstitutional" institutions that led to the stability and viability of the U.S. presidential system. There is a strong suggestion that if one is to promote stability and viability, certain democratic ideals may sometimes have to be toned down. We find similar contradictions in other constitutions. For example, how can one balance individual rights with group rights? Are they necessarily compatible or are they sometimes in conflict? Is there sometimes a need to limit political participation in order to promote stability and viability? Does the notion of equal representation, in some cases, need to be weighted in favor of viability? Experience from the U.S. case suggests that these values were historically defined and practiced in a variety of ways that were conducive to constitutional viability and political stability.

The challenge posed to political scientists and policymakers seems to be not simply a choice between presidentialism and parliamentarism, but what type of presidentialism and what type of parliamentarism. Brazil, for example, has over the years under various constitutions adopted a variety of presidential systems. During the military regimes, some of the restrictions adopted by the military leaders and incorporated into the constitution were closer to those of a parliamentary system. The president has been given powers that would enable him to break a constitutional gridlock. For example, if a budget is not adopted within a certain legal time frame, the president can promulgate the budget through a presidential decree. In certain areas, presidents were authorized to promulgate legislation as "provisional measures" and then present them to the legislature for adoption. The question one needs to ask is whether these measures, which appear to be undemocratic, were deemed necessary for the viability of the presidential system and for political stability. Proponents of these measures, even among the most ardent supporters of democratic systems, seem to suggest that these measures were and are necessary. To attain constitutional viability and democratic political stability, a political price may sometimes have to be paid. Not all the values associated with viability and democratic political stability necessarily reinforce each other. One value may sometimes have to be de-emphasized in favor of another. This is a policy choice that all political systems have to make.

Another important challenge seems to be the type of paraconstitutional arrangement needed to ensure constitutional survival and political stability.[10] Often, once a constitution is adopted, the necessary institutions to make the constitution functional and viable are neglected. Many constitutions leave significant portions of elaboration of certain articles to future legislation in the form of organic laws or ordinary legislation. These organic laws and complementary legislation that are needed to make the constitution functional are often neglected. My own chapter on legislatures in this volume argues that under a presidential system of government, the legislature needs to adopt certain structures and to develop and acquire certain resources and capabilities if it is to perform the role assigned to it by the constitution. Simply to adopt a presidential system and leave the legislature structurally and informationally ill equipped can lead to the breakdown of the system, either through the marginalization of the legislature as a rubber-stamp institution or through the deadlock that may occur as result of the legislature playing a mere obstructionist role. Rather than asking whether the presidential system or the parliamentary system is superior, the important question is how the viability of each of these systems can be enhanced to ensure democratic political stability through institutional structures and capabilities. The legislature is one of those centrally important institutions. Similar consideration should be given to other institutions, such as presidency or chief executive, the court system, and the bureaucracy.

Finally, the authors in this volume stress that a viable constitutional order is not a panacea that can resolve all internal and external challenges.

Thus far we have avoided any definition of a "viable constitution" or what the attributes and functions of such a constitution are, because it is extremely difficult to arrive at a widely accepted definition—it is like attempting to provide a universally accepted definition of beauty. During the three days of the conference at which these papers were presented, the issue of defining a viable constitution and democratic political stability was raised at various points, but no agreement seemed possible beyond some abstract generalities.

There is a general agreement that when we are talking about viable constitutionalism we are talking about the viability of *democratic* regimes, not undemocratic ones. We assume that while undemocratic regimes may survive in the long run, they cannot be considered a viable constitutionalist regime. The conference, therefore, did not focus on the survivability of undemocratic regimes.

Does this mean that democratic regimes are more viable because they are more productive and responsive to citizens' needs? Not necessarily. The conference reached a general agreement that sometimes in democratic regimes performance is hindered or delayed—especially in a complex, competitive internal environment. Even domestic issues from welfare to health services may be impeded in a democratic society. Therefore, one should not assume that democratic societies are more viable because they are more responsive, and that therefore they are more effective in their performances. It is also conceivable that a government could be responsive in the short run, but fail in its performance, taking actions that are detrimental in the long run. Thus, one should not always assume that a responsive bureaucracy or government is an effective government. Joel Aberbach and Bert Rockman's chapter in this book elaborates on this distinction with regard to the working of bureaucracies under different constitutional arrangements.

Aberbach and Rockman argue that there is no necessary relationship between government performance and economic development. They cite Italy and Thailand as cases in which the economy was performing at an acceptable level but government performance was viewed as inadequate. They conclude that performance is a matter of perception. Do people think that the administration is fair? Do they think it can be trusted? Is it essentially moral, does it have integrity, or can undue favoritism be displayed toward some group at the expense of others? In some cases, people are satisfied with the services they are getting but still think the bureaucracy as a whole is inadequate.

Professor Erik Hoffmann, basing his remarks on the constitutional debates raging in Russia in the early nineties, emphasizes that a viable constitution must deliver in various areas of public policy. Groups in society, he argues, become very concerned with the design and content of a constitution because of the public goods they expect to gain from the regime. According to Hoffmann, the constitution is not simply a process of resolving conflict, it is also a set of values and goals and objectives. Viable constitutions and viable regimes, he argues, are closely linked.

James Sundquist, based on his understanding of the viability of the U.S. Constitution, voices a word of caution, in his chapter in this volume, about equating a viable constitution with what it produces. According to Sundquist, the function of a viable constitution is not the social and economic policies that it produces or espouses, but rather the process and machinery of reaching these policies. To the extent that these processes and machinery are durable, they are also viable. Timothy Power, in his conference remarks, introduced the idea of democratic governability as a definition of viable constitutionalism. A viable constitution includes ways of managing conflict and setting public policy. Citizens judge governments by the product of their work, and not simply on how they reach that outcome. If the outcome of public policy is not considered acceptable over a period of time, elements within society may be willing to resort to undemocratic means to change the constitution and the government.

From all the discussion, one can conclude that a constitution is a political agreement par excellence. As a political agreement, it sets a series of goals and values as well as a method of resolving conflicts over these goals and values. It is viable to the extent that political participants in a society are willing to resort to it to discuss and manage their disagreements and differences. Very few of these conflicts are ever resolved. They are managed and contained until they appear later in a different form. Dealing with these conflicts is not a one-shot deal. It is a continuous process whereby participants in the conflict are given the forum and the mechanism to discuss and reach decisions, albeit on a temporary basis, on how to deal with their disagreements. If the constitution prevents resorting to sustained violence in dealing with this disagreement, to that extent it is viable. Conference participants failed to reach a universal description of viability. Perhaps there is no universal definition; it can be defined only contextually.

Occasionally, internal and external actors may pursue nonconstitutional strategies to influence the outcome of one conflict or the other. In those cases, a constitution can do very little. The recent experience of Lebanon is a case in point. The sources of internal conflict in that country preceded the constitution of 1926 and continue to the present time. Until 1975, the main Lebanese actors decided to manage their differences within the framework of the constitution. To be sure, the main issues dividing them persisted in one form or another, but were managed and remanaged on a continuous basis. In 1975, and within a conducive regional and international environment, some of the main actors found it to their advantage to resort to extraconstitutional mechanisms to resolve their problems once and for all. Sixteen years of civil war followed, and none of the problems were resolved. Finally in 1989, all the main actors decided that there was no extraconstitutional answer to the conflict. The constitution was once again upheld with only minor amendments to reflect the political practices that had prevailed in the country during the past five decades.

A viable constitution, however, is not a panacea for all of a society's problems. There are many occasions when political conflict reaches such proportions that existing constitutional arrangements cannot handle it. While one of the characteristics of a viable constitution is that it allows for necessary adjustments to accommodate and manage political conflict, many times this process may fail. Accommodating political conflict may fail because the constitution is so rigidly designed that reasonable adjustments are not permitted, and a determined and entrenched group may decide to fight it out rather than to allow changes to take place peaceably and through constitutional mechanisms. This may have been the case during the American Civil War.

There are other instances in which political actors decide to resort to extraconstitutional mechanisms in order to protect their perceived interests rather than lose constitutionally. This option becomes especially attractive when those actors who are likely to lose peaceably get assurance of external political and military support. It is common knowledge that many internal conflicts have international dimensions. This was true during the period of the Cold War and it is also true today. The conflict in Lebanon discussed above is a case in point.

Thus, a constitution is a political agreement on goals and mechanisms to resolve future conflict. The constitution, regardless of its attributes, cannot guarantee that political actors will always rely on it to resolve their conflicts. The more the actors resort to constitutional mechanisms to manage their conflicts, the more the constitution acquires legitimacy and viability; the more political actors find that their conflicts can be reasonably managed through constitutional mechanisms, the more they are likely to resort to these mechanisms.

Constitutions in Contemporary States

The present volume is an attempt to address some of the issues many newly democratized states face in designing a viable constitution. It is divided into three parts. The first part attempts to delineate some of the relevant characteristics associated with the presidential and parliamentary systems of government and their implications for the bureaucracy and the legislature. The second part deals with the experience of certain countries in designing a viable constitution. The third part explores the limitations of constitutionalism and their relationship to political stability.

Important Characteristics of Presidential and Parliamentary Systems of Government

Parliamentarism and presidentialism are treated in this volume as two political systems that allow many variations and adaptations. In Chapter 2, titled "The 'Westminster Model' Away from Westminster," Gregory S. Mahler argues that although the British system and its evolution have been thoroughly studied, there are few systematic studies of the adaptations of the Westminster Model to see what institutions and practices have evolved in those systems. It is obvious that institutions and practices that work well in Britain may not work so well in other Commonwealth countries. The institutions that have evolved in the British system are not the only options available for Commonwealth nations.

Mahler's study of the adaptations of the Westminster Model examines both structures within the legislature and those that exist outside the legislature. Inside the legislature, the study of bicameralism, relations between the two houses, party discipline, legislative staff and services, the legislative process itself, and committees reveals many variations that have appeared in the Commonwealth nations. Although they all share features such as the limited availability of staff and services and a very similar legislative process, in other areas Mahler found some obvious differences, such as the existence of single chamber or even of tricameral systems. He also found that even for those features that appear to be shared with the Westminster Model, their meaning in the political process can vary significantly from country to country.

Regarding nonlegislative factors, Mahler observed that most Commonwealth nations have adopted the single-member district, plurality voting electoral system. This, he observes, has affected the political party systems, and in many Commonwealth nations one finds two- or three-party systems such as those found in Britain and Canada. With respect to legislative-executive relations, he notes that the British prime minister is neither the weakest nor the strongest of the parliamentary chief executives.

Mahler concludes that Commonwealth legislatures are not simple duplicates of the legislature at Westminster. A wide and quite remarkable degree of variation is found among the institutions that the legislatures of the Commonwealth have adopted as their own, and in the manner in which these institutions have evolved. Certainly, many similarities are found throughout the Commonwealth, and Mahler observes that it is a truly marvelous family of nations, in which the new states have grown up and moved away from home, but resolved to keep in touch and to continue the basic family traditions. The essential institutions of parliamentary democracy are alive and well in the Commonwealth, and the many variations on the central themes and institutions of parliamentary democracy can only be regarded as a good sign.

The U.S. presidential system as a model of structuring government has been widely emulated and admired. James Sundquist's Chapter 3 of this volume, titled "The U.S. Presidential System as a Model for the World," attempts to analyze the attractiveness of this model and some of its hidden assumptions that are frequently overlooked by analysts and policymakers. Sundquist observes that while many countries were moving away from the parliamentary system and toward the presidential system in order to have a stronger and more legitimate leader, there was little evidence that outside the United States the adoption of the presidential model resulted in stable and durable democracy. The two main questions he asks in his chapter are: Why has the presidential system proven so durable in the United States and failed so often elsewhere, and what are the lessons to be learned from the United States to make presidential arrangements more viable elsewhere?

Sundquist observes that during the Constitutional Convention the framers sought to avoid both the tyranny of the king and the excessive power of the legislative bodies of the thirteen colonies. They created a "balanced" system in which each of the three powers was checked by the other two. Although at times one of the branches did increase its powers, this was always done with the acceptance of the other branches. Although the executive was always the most aggressive, the other branches were often able to thwart its efforts. The constitutional checks worked as intended, and the balance among the branches was maintained. A kind of built-in gyroscope appeared to have preserved the stability of the whole government mechanism. That mechanism, according to Sundquist, was that elusive but controlling element in a constitutional system: public opinion. The U.S. Constitution, according to Sundquist, has reached a point of near veneration. He concedes that the authority of the Constitution could not have been maintained if the structure of the government had not been able to cope with the nation' s problems. In addition other factors, such as the absence of a large military until the doctrine of civilian control of the military was deeply embedded, and the extremely difficult process of adding amendments, have helped to give the U.S. Constitution its extraordinary durability.

Nevertheless, dissatisfaction has been mounting for close to three decades. The approval rating of Congress reached an all-time low of 20 percent in 1992. When voters were asked about the reason for their dissatisfaction, they mentioned not only scandal and corruption, but also gridlock. Both parties were so deeply split internally that, even when both branches of government were controlled by the same party, governing still was not easy. The extraordinary majority needed to close debate in the Senate further dims the prospects of legislative achievement. The essential problem facing many constitutionalists, according to Sundquist, is how to restrain government while still endowing it with the capacity to act. Despite the values that derive from distributing the powers of government among separate branches, the pattern of distribution must ensure capacity, responsibility, accountability, and guard against paralysis.

Sundquist's advice to those drafting new constitutions is the following: Adopt an electoral system that prohibits, or at least discourages, ticket splitting for national office; provide a runoff presidential election whenever no candidate wins a majority in the initial balloting; either establish a unicameral legislature or limit the powers of the less representative body in a bicameral structure; avoid any requirement for extraordinary majorities in the legislature's decision making; allow elected officials a reasonable "breathing space" between elections; provide a means whereby a government that is clearly ineffective for whatever reason can be expeditiously reconstituted or replaced; and provide a workable procedure for keeping the constitution current through amendments.

In Chapter 4, Joel Aberbach and Bert Rockman tackle one of the thorniest problems concerning the role bureaucracy plays under different political systems. In "Bureaucracy: Control, Responsiveness, Performance," the authors raise three central issues: whether presidential and parliamentary systems differ in the extent to which bureaucracy (1) may be held accountable and thus controlled by legitimate sources of authority, (2) can be responsive to the policy interests of alternative elites, and (3) performs effectively. The authors argue that as a general matter, the parliamentary/presidential distinction is merely another, but less consistent, way of talking about the number of disparate authorities to whom the bureaucracy must respond and the distinctiveness of their preferences.

The basic argument made in this chapter is that the unification of political authority largely strengthens the bureaucracy, because the concentration of political authority tends to combat parochialism in the administration. The relative unity or diffusion of political authority, however, crosses the traditional boundaries of parliamentary and presidential systems. Some parliamentary systems, such as Italy's, may end up fragmenting power at least as much as the U.S. presidential system, while some presidential systems, such as France's, end up concentrating power more than most parliamentary systems.

The differences between parliamentary and presidential systems regarding the organization of governing authority are often less sharp than popular belief suggests. Indeed, both systems can generate a multiplicity of actors with authority to act on the distinctive preferences they may hold. On the other hand, each system also is capable, under certain conditions, of concentrating authority. The paper's basic argument is that the extent to which authority is concentrated or dispersed among authorities with different preferences shapes the nature of the problems of control, accountability, responsiveness, and performance.

In the case of the United States, which is characterized by a separation of powers, the electoral system results in a high degree of attentiveness to constituencies and complaints, which in turn produces a high degree of attention to casework and to writing more rules, such as earmarking. The electoral system therefore plays a role here. The distrust between the different branches of government and the importance of the courts contribute to the abundance of rules in the United States. The fragmentation of authority makes accountability important but inherently incomplete; it makes control and responsiveness incomplete, because no set of authorities is in a position to exert full control or to have the bureaucracy exclusively responsive to them.

In the British system, there are no conflictive authorities with distinctive claims on the bureaucracy; however, factors such as the alternation of authority when party control of Parliament changes introduce a different set of complications. Bureaucrats are in a much better position in Britain to advocate their own perspectives. Despite structural predispositions in the British system of majority party government in removing the ambiguities that surround the issues of accountability, control, and responsiveness, what really occurs is that these problems—most especially those of control and responsiveness—take on new forms. But this is not to say that these issues remain as complex as in the United States or as problematic; it merely is to say that the problems are not eliminated—and, perhaps, never can be.

Fred Riggs in Chapter 5, titled "Bureaucracy and Viable Constitutionalism," takes a different approach to the relationship of bureaucracy to regime types. While Aberbach and Rockman emphasize Western industrialized democracies—mainly the United States and United Kingdom—and deal primarily with the political context as it affects bureaucratic performance, Riggs's analysis pays more attention to the situation in newer states, including the developing countries, and tries to identify structural variations in the different kinds of bureaucracy as they affect both administrative performance and the political implications. Administrative performance is important for political stability, and political implication is important for constitutional democracy.

Riggs makes a distinction between mandarin and functionary bureaucracies and the degree to which retainers and transients are used. These differences, in turn, affect the amount of power bureaucrats exercise and the quality of public administration, subject to the competing norms that good administration requires bureaucrats to have real power, but constitutionalism requires the elected representative organs to be able to maintain control over the bureaucracy. For Riggs, an important advantage of parliamentarism is that it permits, by the fusion of powers, more effective control over a more powerful (mandarin) bureaucracy than regimes where the separation of power prevails. Finally, Riggs maintains that in many new states, especially those controlled by military groups, appointed officials (not elected representatives) control the polity, thus creating what may be described as bureaucratic polities.[11]

In the concluding piece in Part One, I argue in Chapter 6, titled "Legislative Structure and Constitutional Viability in Societies Undergoing Democratic Transition," that the structure of the legislature and the informational and staff resources it mobilizes affect the stability and viability of political systems. Legislatures, especially those in presidential systems, that are ill informed can play either a rubber-stamp or an obstructionist role. Both of these roles are detrimental to the survival of the system. What is needed is a legislature that has the necessary information to enable it to engage in a series of constructive encounters with the executive. An informed legislature is able to arrive at temporary compromises with the executive to avoid gridlock and impasses. The chapter goes on to explore some of the information systems that legislatures need and some of the staffing patterns that enable them to engage in this constructive dialogue with the executive.

Case Studies in Designing a Viable Constitution

Part Two of the volume consists of three case studies of actual constitutional arrangements that have emerged in India, Turkey, and Russia. India was chosen because it is considered by many the largest democracy in the world. Despite shocks and tremors, India is still an example of a stable democracy among Third World countries. Turkey, on the other hand, has experienced ups and downs. Because of its location partly in Europe and partly in the Middle East, and because of its secularist tradition and Islamic heritage, Turkey may provide a model for Islamic countries trying to adopt constitutional democracies. Russia, meanwhile, is the most important former communist country trying to adopt democratic constitutional reforms. The fate of that experiment will have reverberations in many of the former communist countries in the newly independent states and Central and Eastern Europe.

In Chapter 7, "The Constitution as an Instrument of Political Cohesion in Postcolonial States: The Case of India," T. V. Sathyamurthy argues that during the last four decades the viability of India's constitution has been severely compromised. The dominant classes and their supporters have made use of the state structure for their own benefit without meeting the needs of a heavily impoverished population. In the process, the constitution has become a site where conflicts between the different segments of the dominating classes have been negotiated. Far from representing enduring compromises, the adjustments within the elite may have seriously undermined the long-term stability of the state structure. The author argues that the majority of the Indian people have experienced greater and greater hardship under an increasingly oppressive state. Their attitudes toward the constitution at present are entirely negative.

The demand for a new constitution reflecting the democratic aspirations and the economic interests of the mass of the people has gathered momentum during the last two decades. A viable constitution for India would need to be rooted in widespread democratic discussion, debate, and consultation among the vast number of grassroots movements, nongovernmental organizations, and numerous other representative peoples' organizations that have spread throughout the country. According to Sathyamurthy, a constitution that neglects the economic well-being of the majority of its population loses its legitimacy and contributes to instability. India, the author suggests, is currently passing through such a period of instability. To its credit however, India's constitutional experiment is judged successful to the extent that it has allowed the elite to arrive at periodic compromises for more than four decades. It is yet to be seen whether it can provide those same avenues of compromises needed to meet the present challenges.

Turkey offers a different experience from India in constitutional design. In Chapter 8, Ersin Kalaycioğlu's "Constitutional Viability and Political Institutions in Turkish Democracy" describes this experience. Starting in 1946, the Turkish experiment in democracy has tested many constitutions or models of democratic regimes. Turkey came out of a period of one-party rule and nonalignment to join NATO and redemocratize itself. Turkey held its first truly democratic election in 1950, voting in favor of economic liberalism, lessening the power of the public bureaucracy, and reinstating the symbols of Sunni Islam. Under the constitution in force between 1950 and 1960, civilian technocrats asserted their authority over the military, public bureaucrats, and state entrepreneurs who characterized the Atatürk and post-Atatürk regimes. The masses gained a degree of power they had never anticipated until then. This democratic period lasted until 1960, when a petty officers' coup ended the first Turkish experiment with democracy.

The constitutional reform crisis in Turkey unfolded in 1961 and continued until 1982. The 1982 constitution did not create a presidential regime but a semiparliamentary system, in which the president is the party leader who shares power with the prime minister and competes for media attention. The president and the parliamentary cabinet, headed by the prime minister, do not always endorse or follow the same policies. The present constitution is still restrictive. It prohibits any political party that does not obtain 10 percent or more of the national vote from obtaining any seats in the National Assembly.

A clash of ideologies and opposing cultural images fostered conditions for a deep-seated legitimacy crisis between the military regime and the political party elites. Both tried to capture the parliamentary election by entering into different sorts of coalitions. According to Kalaycioğlu, six features stand out in the experience of Turkish democracy: a rupture of the authoritarian fundamentals since the war for independence and the Cultural Revolution, a perennial crisis of legitimacy, a lack of political consensus over a fair and just electoral system, the military as the cause of deinstitutionalization of the party system, little room for voluntary association due to an underdeveloped interest-group system, and the embedding of a culture of corruption in the National Assembly that perpetuates a bad image of politicians.

Erik Hoffmann, in Chapter 9, elaborates on the dilemmas facing constitution designers in Russia. In "Can Viable Constitutionalism Take Root in Post-Soviet Russia?" Hoffmann focuses on the core elements of viable constitutionalism and how to create and sustain them in post-Soviet Russia. Emphasis is placed on the national and subnational political institutions and cultures as well as on the socioeconomic and international contexts and dynamics within which Russian state building is taking place. The author also emphasizes the functions performed by President Boris N. Yeltsin's constitution of December 1993, which faced conflicting goals: a viable versus nominal constitutionalism, consensual versus confrontational policymaking, tolerant versus intolerant political cultures, and a strong, stable, and democratic state versus a weak, unstable, and authoritarian state. Hoffmann elucidates the concepts of viability and constitutionalism, in the context of post-Soviet politics, sharply distinguishing between constitutions and constitutionalism, and broadly defining the latter to include procedural and substantive as well as national and subnational elements. He illustrates how general theories of democratization and stable democracy can help to understand post-Soviet polities, economies, and societies, and how the post-Soviet experience can help to verify, refine, or reject different theories about transitions from authoritarianism and toward democratic consolidation. Later, he underscores the potential benefits of Russia's presidential system and the ways to minimize its liabilities, especially in the early stages of creating a protodemocratic polity and mixed economy, which are combining many new institutions with traditional values from their tsarist and Soviet predecessors.

Hoffmann evaluates the new constitution's text and national, regional, and local contexts, assessing the constitution's positive provisions but also its portentous ambiguities and omissions, which greatly diminish the chances of constructing a workable and accountable presidential democracy capable of fulfilling its lofty substantive aims (e.g., the protection of human rights and the natural environment) and its basic procedural goals (e.g., the establishment of a law-based policy process that divides powers among national executive, legislative, and judicial institutions and among national, regional, and local institutions). He concludes that the prospects for viable constitutionalism and democratic consolidation in the Russian Federation are not sanguine for the immediate future because (1) the constitution's legitimacy and effectiveness have been considerably reduced by the politicization of its promulgation and ratification, (2) the Russian state is weak but might restore imperial relations with other countries of the Commonwealth of Independent States (CIS), and (3) a stable democracy is a rare species with a long gestation period and will be especially difficult to create and nurture in post-Soviet Russia.

Limitations of Constitutionalism

The third part of this volume consists of two chapters. While most of the chapters emphasize the structural determinants of political viability as represented in the constitution and the political institutions it sets up, the last two chapters highlight the limitations of structural explanations and the importance of other factors.

Chapter 10 of this volume, titled "Democratic Consolidation: Institutional, Economic, and External Dimensions," by Diane Ethier, provides an overview of the literature on democratic transition and the importance of national and international economic actors. According to Ethier, the third wave of democratization raises the question of the viability of new democracies established since 1975 in Southern Europe, Latin America, Asia, Central Europe, and Africa. Due to the numerous studies carried out on this subject during the second cycle of democratization and after, researchers today have at their disposal more precise theoretical tools for evaluating the longevity of new democracies. Yet, the comparative analysis of democratic development in both Western and "peripheral" countries has demonstrated that the viability of democracies has depended on their *stability*—their capacity to avoid or resolve the social and political conflicts likely to lead to their replacement by authoritarian regimes. The stability of democracies has in turn been closely associated with their *consolidation*—the legitimacy (acceptance) and the institutionalization (effective application) of democratic values, rules, and procedures by the vast majority of elites and citizens. This transformation of opinions and attitudes has been linked mainly to the establishment of political institutions favorable to the representation and concentration of various interest groups. However, many other conditions have been judged necessary to the democratization of political institutions and culture, including the pursuit of economic and social development, the willingness of political leaders to promote democracy, a relatively weak level of politicization and mobilization within civil society, and the contagion effect of Western democratic models.

Recent evaluations of democratic consolidation in Southern Europe, Latin America, Asia, and Eastern Europe are inspired largely by these approaches. On the whole, they reveal that only Greece, Spain, and Portugal have succeeded in consolidating their democratic regimes, while the process remains problematic in most of the other regions. The democratization of political culture and institutions has been much more rapid and deeper in Southern Europe than in Latin America, Asia, and Eastern Europe during the period following the end of democratic transitions. Now, two new fields of research permit precise management of the role of these variables. Recent studies of the processes of economic adjustment show that the enactment of neoliberal reforms during or immediately after democratic transitions (the Latin American and Eastern European scenarios) constitute a significant obstacle to democratic consolidation, whereas the achievement of the latter before the launching of economic adjustment (the Southern European scenarios) favors both the success of democratization and economic adjustment. New studies on the third enlargement of the European Community (EC) show that the success of democratization and economic adjustment in Greece, Spain, and Portugal is due largely to cultural, institutional, social, and economic transformations imposed by the preparation for and the realization of entry into the EC (in 1981 for Greece, 1986 for the Iberian countries). Ethier's paper presents the main elements of the theory of democratic consolidation, summarizes the main conclusions of recent publications on comparative perspectives of consolidation in new democracies, examines the effects of economic adjustment processes upon democratization, and explains why and how entry into the EC has contributed to the success of democratization and economic adjustment in Southern Europe.

The comparative evaluation of the prospects for consolidation of the new democracies demonstrates that while their viability is not threatened in the short and medium term, their stabilization is problematic and due as much to institutional and cultural factors as to the disruptive effects of economic adjustments. Analysis of the Southern Europe cases, which constitute an exception to this rule, reveals that integration into the European Community has been a determining factor in the combined progress of democratic consolidation and economic adjustment in Greece, Spain, and Portugal during the period following the reestablishment of democracy.

This conclusion argues in favor of new enlargements of the EC, particularly in the direction of the countries of Eastern Europe. It also raises a number of questions regarding the possible political benefits of other regional integration processes, particularly NAFTA and the Initiative for the Americas project, on the consolidation of new democracies. Beyond its very specific character, the dynamic of the European Community shows that the regional integration of markets can foster democratic consolidation in three ways: (1) by stimulating demonstration or contagion effects from consolidated democracies when the regional bloc includes such states, as NAFTA does; (2) by favoring a renewal of investment and growth—circumstances that facilitate the reduction of the costs of transition inherent in economic adjustment, a major obstacle in the process of democratic consolidation; and (3) by encouraging, when the alliance includes advanced democratic states, a certain harmonization from above of labor legislation and social policies, as in the parallel accords of NAFTA, an important condition for lessening the costs of transition.

Philip G. Cerny, in Chapter 11, "Globalization and the Residual State: The Challenge to Viable Constitutionalism," argues that the state as an independent actor has lost many of its historical prerogatives and, therefore, no amount of constitutional engineering is sufficient to guarantee political democratic viability. According to Cerny, the globalization transforming the international system has fundamentally altered the structural context of collective action and, thereby, the nature of the contemporary constitutional state.

Globalization, as vague as it is, is a multilayered phenomenon that incorporates the state and sustains many of its ostensible functions, but at the same time alters its very essence and undermines its constitutional foundations. In a sense, it has undermined the sovereign character of the modern political association known as the state. The conceptual approach for a globalizing world takes into consideration a hypothetically uneven evolution of the state toward some more limited forms of association, opening the possibility of complex structural developments, internal tensions, and latent contradictions. This effectively creates a linking of uneven globalization with the emergence of a still-embryonic residual state. Collective action, in the form of political and economic structures following the Second Industrial Revolution, converged to a particular matrix of markets around and after World War II. Fundamental shifts in political economies, economic internationalization, and complex technological and organizational changes created a new matrix, in which the role of the state is being dramatically reformulated in the so-called Third Industrial Revolution. The scenario is perhaps familiar, but its significance enhances our understanding of the shift of the world economy to a global scale in trade and finance. Production structures have created new sources of divergence and differentiation between political and economic patterns, and between market and hierarchy. Accordingly, a highly problematic environment leads at first to political polarization and later to attempts to "reinvent government." In any event, crucial aspects of the public and constitutional character of the state are undermined, and the fundamental direction of enterprises is changing from public to private and from the specific to the nonspecific, threatening the very nature of the constitutional state. Stability of the international system is uncertain, and the constitutional state may decay and exacerbate a trend toward institutional precariousness, or remain a major force behind stability. The viability of constitutionalism may be reshaped by the new role toward which the state is being driven.

This volume focuses on the importance of institutions in promoting constitutional viability, a neglected field of inquiry. It is a first attempt at probing this serious issue. However, we have also laid the basis for a future research agenda. A number of questions connected to democratic constitutional viability are still to be explored. These include the relationship of electoral laws to the rest of the political system, the role of political parties in a democratic society, the problem of achieving political representation in divided societies without undermining democracy and effective governability, and the role of government bureaucracy in a democratic state. We hope that scholars in the future will address these important issues.

Notes

1. On the rise of behavioralism see, for example, David Easton, *The Political System* (New York: Knopf, 1953); Harold D. Laswell and Abraham Kaplan, *Power and Society: A Framework for Political Inquiry* (New Haven: Yale University Press, 1950); Austin Ranney, ed., *Essays on the Behavioral Study of Politics* (Urbana: University of Illinois Press, 1962); Robert A. Dahl, "The Behavioral Approach in Political Science: Epitaph for a Monument to a Successful Protest," *American Political Science Review* 55 (1961): 763–72; James C. Charlesworth, ed., *The Limits of Behavioralism* (Philadelphia: American Academy of Political and Social Science, 1962); Albert Somit and Joseph Tanenhaus, *The Development of American Political Science: From Burguess to Behavioralism* (New York: Irvington Publishers, 1982).

2. For example, see S. H. Wolin, *Politics and Vision* (Boston: Little, Brown, 1962), and C. J. Friedrich, "Political Development and the Objective of Modern Government," in *Political and Administrative Development*, ed. R. Braibanti (Durham: Duke University Press, 1969). For general accounts of the development literature see, for example, Samuel Huntington, "Political Development and Political Decay," *World Politics* 17 (1965): 386–430; Gabriel Almond and G. Bingham Powell, *Comparative Politics* (Boston: Little, Brown, 1966); Joel S. Migdal, "Studying the Politics of Development and Change: The State of the Art," in *Political Science: The State of the Discipline*, ed. Ada W. Finifer (Washington D.C.: American Political Science Association, 1983).

3. For example, see *From Max Weber: Essays in Sociology*, ed. H. H. Gerth and C. Wright Mills (New York: Oxford University Press, 1946).

4. The volumes published in this series include G. R. Boynton and Chong Lim Kim, eds., *Legislative Systems in Developing Countries* (Durham: Duke University Press, 1975); Abdo I. Baaklini, *Legislative and Political Development: Lebanon, 1842–1972* (Durham: Duke University Press, 1976); Albert F. Eldridge, ed., *Legislatures in Plural Societies: The Search for Cohesion in National Development* (Durham: Duke University Press, 1977); Michael Mezey, *Comparative Legislatures* (Durham: Duke University Press, 1979); Joel Smith and Lloyd D. Musolf, eds., *Legislatures in Development: Dynamics of Change in New and Old States* (Durham: Duke University Press, 1979).

5. See, for example, numerous references to this issue in the seminal multivolume work, Guillermo O'Donnell, Philippe C. Schmitter, and Laurence Whitehead, eds., *Transitions from Authoritarian Rule* (Baltimore: Johns Hopkins University Press, 1986).

6. See, for example, Scott Mainwaring, "Presidentialism in Latin America: A Review Essay," *Latin American Research Review* 25, no. 1 (1990): 157–79.

7. Perhaps the most influential article in this regard is Juan J. Linz, "Presidential or Parliamentary Democracy: Does it Make a Difference?" in *The Failure of Presidential Democracy*, ed. Juan J. Linz and Arturo Valenzuela (Baltimore: Johns Hopkins University Press, 1994). This article has been widely distributed in different forms since the mid-1980s.

8. See, for example, Matthew Shugart and John M. Carey, *Presidents and Assemblies: Constitutional Design and Electoral Dynamics* (Cambridge: Cambridge University Press, 1992).

9. Herbert Simon, *Administrative Behavior* (New York: Free Press, 1976).

10. See Fred W. Riggs, "Survival of Presidentialism in America: Para-Constitutional Practices," *International Political Science Review* 9 (1988): 247–78.

11. See Fred W. Riggs, "Fragility of the Third World's Regimes," *International Social Science Journal* 136 (May 1993): 199–243.

Part One

Important Characteristics of Presidential and Parliamentary Systems of Government

2

The "Westminster Model" Away from Westminster: Is It Always the Most Appropriate Model?

GREGORY S. MAHLER

Introduction

The British Parliament is often referred to as the "mother of parliamentary democracies." This metaphor refers to the fact that many parliamentary democracies around the world were at one time governed from Westminster, and as many of them attained independence and were establishing their own governments, they chose to incorporate—sometimes directly and sometimes with modifications—many of the institutions and practices referred to today as composing the Westminster Model of parliamentary government.

We know a good deal about the mother of parliamentary democracies—how Britain's political institutions and practices have evolved over the last several hundred years, and what those institutions and practices are. What has not been done with sufficient frequency over the last many years, however, is to systematically study the adaptations of the Westminster Model to note what institutions and practices have been developed in *those* legislative settings.

As the former colonies have become independent political actors, at least two very interesting phenomena have developed. First, we have seen the rise of the Commonwealth, a thoroughly unique type of political association. Second, these new parliaments, the sovereign legislatures of the many Commonwealth nations, have been faced with problems of their own, and in many cases have developed their own solutions. In some instances, the parliamentary institutions and patterns of behavior that have evolved have been very similar to those developed at Westminster. In other cases, however, entirely new institutions and patterns of behavior have evolved.

The assumption that the Westminster Model of legislative problem solving is the normative approach is easy to understand. After all, if some of the most basic concepts, political institutions, and rules of procedure of Westminster have been the foundation material in many of the Commonwealth countries, it is only logical that many of these countries should continue to look to Westminster for advice as new problems develop in the legislative arena. However, apart from the existence of the basic Westminster Model of parliamentary government,[1] it is not the case that the political institutions, practices, and behavior that have evolved and been adapted at Westminster will be, correspondingly, the best political institutions, practices, and behavior in all other legislative settings in the Commonwealth.

Political institutions work best when they are appropriate for their respective political settings. The United Kingdom is a unitary state, covering a small geographical territory (especially when compared with, say, India, Canada, or Australia). Also, the United Kingdom has had more than three hundred years of generally stable political history, time to industrialize and develop economically, time for the Westminster political traditions and practices to develop. It is easy to see that political practices that might work very well indeed in the United Kingdom might not work so well in a newer, nonindustrialized, and perhaps federal political system lacking the British history of political stability and the ensuing legitimacy of government.[2]

This essay is concerned with the operation of the legislature, and with the institutions and procedures developed by political systems affecting the operation of the legislature in non-British settings. This is not to suggest that the practices developed in the United Kingdom are of no value, or that they should not be taken as lessons or as models by other political systems. This simply suggests that many of the institutions that have evolved in the British legislative context are not the only options available to newer parliaments looking for solutions to their institutional problems. These new parliaments might do as well to look to other legislatures in the Commonwealth, or even to some non-Commonwealth legislatures for that matter, for possible solutions.

The Structures under Examination

By structures we mean those institutions and patterns of behavior thought of as being part of the legislative arena. The structures with which we are concerned here can be broken down into two groups: those within the legislature, and those existing outside the legislature.

Vast numbers of books have been written on legislative structures and the legislative system in general,[3] not to mention the countless articles in journals. In this literature, authors distinguish between those structures within the legislature itself, such as bicameralism, legislative staff and office space, rules governing debate and the legislative process itself (e.g., who can introduce bills, under what conditions, and how often), and the like, and other structures that exist outside the legislature, such as electoral laws of the regime (e.g., proportional representation versus single-member district elections), the power of the legislature vis-à-vis the executive, and so on.

The goal of this essay is to briefly examine some of the structures existing in the legislative arenas of many of the Commonwealth nations to see how these structures have evolved differently—either slightly or significantly—from the legislature at Westminster. Clearly, many of the Commonwealth parliamentary systems are different from the parliamentary system in the United Kingdom in significant respects that go beyond the legislature itself. For example, Australia, India, Nigeria, and Canada are federal, while the United Kingdom is unitary. This has some significant implications for the legislatures in these political systems.

To take a second example, many of the Commonwealth nations have written constitutions, while the constitution of the United Kingdom is still considered unwritten. This fact, as well, can be seen to have significant implications for the legislatures in those systems. These differences notwithstanding, most of the legislatures of the Commonwealth have decided to structure themselves on the British model (e.g., being bicameral and including British legislative practices such as the question period). The issue then becomes: Is this the best thing for them to do?[4]

Intralegislative Factors

Bicameralism

The legislature at Westminster is a bicameral system. This system was developed over a period of several hundred years for reasons that were appropriate at the time.[5] The question is: Does the fact that the United Kingdom has a bicameral legislative setting mean that all of the Commonwealth legislatures should be bicameral? The answer is: No, it does not. British bicameralism developed because of the social and economic class system in England from the 1200s through the 1700s: one chamber represented the powerful landholding elite, and the other chamber represented the commoners. Eventually, but not legally until the beginning of this century, the House of Commons took on the primary legislative role, with the House of Lords becoming the secondary of the two chambers. Today, although the House of Lords does exercise varying degrees of influence in the legislative process, few would argue that it should have more power than it presently has.[6]

Many Commonwealth legislatures are, for a variety of reasons, bicameral. In some cases, as we suggested with the English Parliament in its early years, the two-house system can be justified on the grounds that it represents different social groups. In some federal systems, as in Canada, Australia, and India for example, the existence of the second house in the legislature is justified on the grounds that it provides representation for the intermediate units of government (states or provinces). Elsewhere, where there is neither a federal system nor a rigidly class-based system, the second house has been justified on the grounds that it provides "sober second thoughts" regarding the actions of the lower house.

Some nations have decided, however, that they do not need a second chamber in their legislatures, either because the population is small and does not warrant two legislative houses (such as Nauru, for example), or the system is not federal and there are no intermediate levels of government to represent (such as New Zealand, for example), or there is no strong class base to society, or it is felt that "sober second thoughts" to check the opinion of the popularly elected house of parliament are not necessary. In any event, it is clear that it is possible to have a healthy and functioning unicameral parliamentary legislature within the context of Commonwealth membership, and it does not appear to be necessary for a legislative body to be bicameral solely because that is the case at Westminster.

We should also note that tricameral legislative bodies, such as that of the Isle of Man, provide another variation on the theme of the United Kingdom. The Manx legislature has two independently elected houses that usually conduct their business independently, but occasionally sit together as a new, third, chamber—one that happens to be made up of individuals who are also members of one of the other chambers of the Tynwald, the national legislature.

Relations between Houses

With a bicameral parliamentary system, one question to be answered has to do with the relationship between the two houses of the legislature. The Parliament Acts of 1911 and 1949 helped to clarify this relationship in the British case: Although the House of Lords today may delay a bill that has been approved by the House of Commons for up to a year, if the government of the day is willing to wait a year for a second passage in the House of Commons, the bill will become law without the approval of the House of Lords. The Lords can no longer absolutely block Commons-approved legislation.[7]

Although governments may not want to wait for more than a year to have their policies enacted (and the Lords may have a great deal of leverage with the government, with amendment of a bill becoming a quid pro quo for its passage), it is still true that the lower house in the British Parliament is constitutionally supreme.

It is generally the case throughout the Commonwealth, and outside of it as well, that when there are two houses in a parliament, the lower house is the more powerful of the two; however, there are some exceptions to this generalization. Some legislatures have an upper house with equal legislative power to that of the lower house—a truly absolute veto of legislation in which failure to obtain the approval of the upper house means that a bill dies. In other legislatures, this power may exist constitutionally and legally, but in practice the upper house chooses never to "flex its muscles," and has refused to do so for so long that it is doubtful that it *could* exercise its constitutional power in a specific instance even if it wanted to.

In other cases, the upper house has only what is called a "suspensory veto"—the situation found in Westminster in which the upper house may delay a bill, but if the lower house is willing to wait for a year (or whatever the particular waiting period is in a given political system), it can circumvent the view of the upper house and enact policy in the exact form it desires. In still other cases, the upper house operates simply in an advisory capacity, and does not even have the power to block legislation temporarily.

It is clear that although the Westminster version has provided a model for bicameralism all over the world, many variations can be found. This is because political structures need to be appropriate for their respective political systems. One example will make this clear. It was appropriate in Britain at the beginning of this century that the House of Lords should relinquish much of its legislative power to the House of Commons. Because Britain is a unitary political system, with the upper house being appointed to represent aristocracy, it was perhaps inevitable that rising liberalism and populism would require the decline in power of the Lords.

Canada, however, has a different situation. There was an appointed upper house—the Senate—but earlier in this century it was perceived to be inappropriate for the Canadian Senate to relinquish its legislative veto in a gesture similar to that of the House of Lords in the Parliament Acts of 1911 and 1949. The reason for this is quite simple: Britain is unitary, but Canada is federal, and one of the justifications for the maintenance of the Senate's legislative powers was that the Senate represented the provinces of Canada. Although the Senate's appointive nature might suggest that it give up many of its powers, the Senate's federal role required it to maintain a potential for political power. This ambivalence in the Canadian political system has led many to argue in contemporary debates that the Senate as an institution should stay, but that its members should be selected differently.

Thus, we can again see that although the general Westminster Model of bicameralism may be attractive in a wide variety of legislative settings, some "fine tuning" has been deemed necessary to make it more appropriate for any given political system. This, of course, is part of the "family" nature of the Commonwealth.

Party Discipline

The Westminster Model of government is synonymous for most of the world to the notion of strong party discipline; indeed, many would say that it is difficult to imagine the existence of a parliamentary system without a highly disciplined party system.[8] However, a number of parliamentary bodies in the Commonwealth do not have highly disciplined parties, but are essentially nonparty legislatures. The legislatures of the Isle of

Man, Jersey, Guernsey, Nauru, Kiribati, as well as a number of other Commonwealth nations seem to find it quite possible to operate without disciplined political parties in a manner that puts emphasis upon—to use a senator from Jersey's word—consensus, rather than partisanship.

Recent legislation in Ghana[9] and in a number of other nations has gone in the other direction and has strengthened the influence of political party organization on individual legislators by prohibiting them from "crossing the aisle" without resigning and seeking new elections. The justification for this policy is straightforward: The voting public supports you rather than your opponent because you are a part of a specific party team; if you quit your party's team to join another, you need to receive a new mandate from the public. Here again, it is clear that many of the Commonwealth nations have decided that what is good for Parliament at Westminster may not be best for them.[10]

Legislative Staff and Services

Although most British Members of Parliament now have some access to office space, every MP does not necessarily have an individual office. Most British MPs do not have full-time professional staff assistance; legislative staff is something desired by most MPs but not likely to be provided in the immediate future. The American legislative case is often the goal in this regard: The average American senator has a staff of thirty-six, the American representative sixteen, and both have large office suites in Washington as well as in their home districts.[11]

Unfortunately, although virtually all Commonwealth legislators may agree that more legislative and administrative staff, larger travel budgets, and more research resources, would be both helpful and, ultimately, useful to the citizens (and taxpayers) of their respective countries, these are usually not high-priority expenses in the many political systems of the Commonwealth. In some Commonwealth nations, the legislators do have more office space and staff than what is afforded to individual legislators at Westminster, but more commonly legislative staff is equally unavailable and legislative office space is just as rare.[12]

The Legislative Process

The actual process of legislating varies throughout the Commonwealth, but most of the Westminster structures are well entrenched, including such well-known parliamentary institutions as Mr. Speaker, the Clerk at the Table, question time, and private members' bills. Here again, though, there are some differences in practices and procedures among legislatures of the Commonwealth.

The institution of question time, for example, is not found in identical form throughout all of the Commonwealth nations. Some of the smaller parliamentary bodies, such as the Tynwald of the Isle of Man, or the States of the Isle of Jersey, do not have an individual called a prime minister, and consequently the dramatic confrontation and debate that take place in London are not replicated in these settings. On the other hand, question period in Canada is even more of a rough-and-tumble experience than that observed at Westminster, without the rule (although it is not always observed) that questions must be submitted in writing before they are asked, and with the prime minister vulnerable to questions every day of the week rather than just twice a week as in London.

The practice of delegated legislation varies as well. In some Commonwealth nations, the legislature has an active role in the actual process of legislation, while in others this is not the case. The factors most clearly affecting the scope and degree of delegated legislation in various political systems appear to be the size of the country and the degree of opportunity for parliamentarians to participate in the policymaking process. Moreover, the larger Commonwealth members, such as India, Australia, Canada, and the United Kingdom, face a different set of problems from those faced by the smaller members, and, correspondingly, the role of the legislature varies.

The actual details of the legislative process vary on a nation-by-nation basis. Some legislative arenas require legislative proposals to lie on the table for more time than others. Some permit more debate than others. Some limit amendment more than others. Some offer more opportunity for private members' legislation than others. In all these respects, although the general Westminster Model of parliamentary government is in evidence, Commonwealth legislatures have found it both reasonable and, in some cases, necessary to adapt the Westminster structures to their particular needs.

Legislative Committees

One of the most important structures in the legislative process is the legislative committee. Although the role of committees is not very great in the United Kingdom, this is not always the case as one moves away from Westminster. Committee autonomy and power at Westminster would work against the principle of party discipline and government power.[13] Away from Westminster, especially in settings in which party discipline is not as strong, the role of committees may be correspondingly larger, permitting a system of legislative specialization to develop.[14] Parliamentary committees tend to be not very powerful or important in the realm of foreign policy[15] because this is an area that traditionally is reserved for the political executive. However, in other policy areas, such as welfare, environmental issues, education, or trade, the role of committees may be significant. An added role of legislative committees may be to provide backbench legislators with an opportunity to act in an autonomous manner.[16] In the plenum the opportunity for individual legislators to behave in an autonomous manner is severely constrained; party discipline and the viability of the government may require that private members (at least private members on the government side of the house) mask their true opinions behind government policy. In committee discussion, however, backbench legislators may have more of an opportunity to express themselves, to represent the views of their constituencies, and to perform politically.

Extralegislative Factors

The Electoral System

The British model of single-member district, plurality voting is clearly the rule throughout the Commonwealth, although in some of the Commonwealth nations we can find alternative electoral systems. For example, in the case of the Falkland Islands, multiple (two) member district elections are held for the Legislative Council. The methods of selection for members of the upper houses (where they exist) range from appointment by the head of state or the representative of the head of state (e.g., Canada, Antigua, Belize, Fiji), to election by the members of the lower house (e.g., Isle of Man), to election by the state governments (e.g., Australia), to selection by a combination of these methods including both appointment *and* election by the legislative assemblies of the states (e.g., India).[17]

The single-member district, plurality voting framework for the lower house of the parliament has some clear effects upon the results of elections, however, and consequently upon the legislatures as well. This is a topic that has received a great deal of attention from scholars.[18] Put succinctly, the single-member district, plurality voting framework overrepresents pluralities and underrepresents minorities in elections. To take one clear example from the British election of 1992, although John Major's Conservatives won less than 45 percent of the vote (42 percent, to be exact), they received more than 51 percent of the seats in the House of Commons. The Labour Party won 34 percent of the vote and received 42 percent of the seats in the House, while the Liberal-SDP Alliance won 18 percent of the vote, but received only 3 percent of the seats in the House of Commons. Thus, although 58 percent of the British voters voted against Major and the Conservatives, they ended up with a substantial majority in the House of Commons. Some have argued that a different electoral system in Britain would have resulted in a different prime minister in 1992.[19]

Several political systems have realized the implications of this electoral system for their domestic politics, and in some systems with a single-member district voting system, such as Canada—and Britain too, for that matter—leaders of political parties continue to argue that some changes in the electoral system should take place.[20] One of the alternative voting styles mentioned is proportional representation, where citizens vote for the specific political party they support, not for individuals, and the party is allotted a number of seats in the national legislature corresponding to the percentage of the public vote it receives.[21] Northern Ireland utilizes a different electoral system, the single transferable vote system, which some experts say does a much fairer job of representing the interests of the voters than does the single-member district, plurality voting system.[22] Here again, we see that the Westminster way of doing things does not always meet with universal acclaim.

The Political Party System

Most people think of Britain as a two-party political system, although the British know very well that their system has more than two parties. In fact, the Westminster system today could probably be called a three-party-plus system, because there are three national parties (Conservative, Labour, and the Liberal–Social Democratic Alliance) and a number of smaller, regional parties.

One of the clearest explanations for the existence of two dominant political parties in Britain is the British electoral system; the single-member district, plurality voting system clearly overrepresents majorities and underrepresents minorities. Richard Rose has suggested that the British electoral system usually "manufactures a majority party in Parliament from a minority of the votes."[23] This makes it very difficult for third parties, or new parties, to get a foothold in the electoral arena and to compete. The Liberal-SDP Alliance case, cited above, is an excellent example. The Liberal-SDP candidates received 16 percent fewer votes than did the Labour Party candidates—18 percent of the vote compared with 34 percent of the vote; yet they received more than 38 percent fewer seats in the House of Commons—20 seats as opposed to Labour's 271 seats. Many British pollwatchers speculated that if Britain had had proportional representation voting in 1992, the clear outcome of the election would have been a Liberal-SDP coalition with Labour.

Many of the legislatures of the Commonwealth have two- or three-party dominant systems as in Britain, Canada, Australia, and New Zealand. However, several of the Commonwealth nations have *no* political parties organizing their legislatures. Some of the legislatures operate within single-party frameworks, in which opposition parties do not exist either because there is no demand for them or because they are prohibited.

Legislative-Executive Relations

The role of the prime minister in the British system has traditionally been referred to as "first among equals," or primus inter pares. In fact, many have said that in recent times the role is considerably larger than that.[24] This is not the case in all Westminster systems, although it could be argued that the British prime minister is neither the strongest nor the weakest of the Westminster chief executives.

Some of the prime ministers of the Commonwealth occupy extremely powerful positions because of the degree of party discipline in their respective systems, combined with the number of parties represented in their legislatures. Others are in much more vulnerable positions, perhaps because their situations require political coalitions, or because they cannot effectively control backbench behavior in their caucuses. The actual constitutional roles of prime ministers in relation to legislatures vary, too, with some systems having the position and powers of the prime minister written into their constitutions; elsewhere, the position may be both undefined and not yet politically mature.

Ultimately, many would say that the real test of the relationship between the legislature and the executive can be measured in how much power individual legislators have to legislate, to debate, and to exercise some kind of watchdog role over the executive. To a very large extent, this is one of the more uniform aspects of the Westminster Model throughout the Commonwealth.

The very nature of the parliamentary model of government today suggests that the principle of legislative supremacy comes into play on only two occasions: when the legislature invests the government with a vote of confidence after an election (and in many cases this vote of confidence is assumed to have taken place even when no vote is really taken), and on those rare occasions when the legislature flexes its collective muscle and "fires" the executive, usually through a motion of no confidence. On all other occasions, we usually speak of the legislative-executive relationship in parliamentary governments to be one of executive supremacy, in which the government of the day leads, and the legislature approves its actions.[25]

In recent years, a good deal of literature has been devoted to the theme of the decline of parliament.[26] In response to the question whether the general increase of executive power—at the expense of legislative power—found around the world is inevitable, often, the answer is yes. The increasingly important role of the political party in the electoral process augments the power of the prime minister over his or her backbenchers. Also, the increasing complexity of the modern world means that more and more issues come before the government—issues that simply are too complex to resolve in a legislative forum. The response of the legislature frequently is willingly to yield to executive leadership in these matters, leading to the current increase in delegated legislation in many systems.

Some Concluding Observations

There is nothing wrong with the current British version of the Westminster Model of parliamentary government. Nor should Commonwealth members consciously avoid the Westminster Model when they are developing legislative structures and patterns of behavior for their own systems. However, it is not the case, as some would believe, that all Commonwealth legislatures are simply duplicates (perhaps slightly smaller in scale) of the legislature at Westminster. A wide and a truly remarkable degree of variation can be found among the legislatures of the Commonwealth in the institutions they have adopted as their own, and in the manner in which these institutions have evolved.

For students of legislative behavior, the Commonwealth is a truly marvelous family of nations in which the new states have grown up and moved away from home, but are resolved to keep in touch and to continue the basic family traditions. The essential institutions of parliamentary democracy are alive and well in the Commonwealth, and the many variations on the central themes and institutions of parliamentary democracy can only be regarded as a good sign.

Notes

1. The Westminster Model includes the following four characteristics: the head of the state and the chief executive are not the same person; the executive power is vested in the prime minister and cabinet, usually not mentioned in law; the government is composed of members of the legislative branch; and the government is ultimately responsible to the legislature. See Gregory S. Mahler, *Comparative Politics: An Institutional and Cross-National Approach* (Englewood Cliffs, N.J.: Prentice-Hall, 1992), 222.

2. The importance of the context within which legislatures operate is something that has been widely discussed in the literature. See, for example, Daniel Nelson, "Communist Legislatures and Communist Politics," in *Communist Legislatures in Comparative Perspective*, ed. Daniel Nelson and Stephen White (Albany: State University of New York Press, 1982); Michael Mezey, "The Functions of Legislatures in the Third World," *Legislative Studies Quarterly* 8 (1983): 511–50; Miriam Kornblith, "The Politics of Constitution-Making: Constitution and Democracy in Venezuela," *Journal of Latin American Studies* 23, no. 1 (1991): 61–89; Frank Baumgartner, "Parliament's Capacity to Expand Political Controversy in France," *Legislative Studies Quarterly* 12 (February 1987): 33–54; and W. St. Clair-Daniel, "Caribbean Concepts of Parliament," *The Parliamentarian* 66, no. 4 (1985): 211–13.

3. See, for examples of cross-national examination of legislatures, Allan Kornberg and Lloyd Musolf, eds., *Legislatures in Developmental Perspective* (Durham: Duke University Press, 1970); Allan Kornberg, ed., *Legislatures in Comparative Perspective* (New York: MacKay, 1973); David Olson, *The Legislative Process* (New York: Harper and Row, 1980); H. Hirsch and M. D. Hancock, eds., *Comparative Legislative Systems* (New York: Free Press, 1971); Albert Eldridge, ed., *Legislatures in Plural Societies: The Search for Cohesion in National Development* (Durham: Duke University Press, 1977); Gerhard Loewenberg and Samuel Patterson, *Comparing Legislatures* (Boston: Little, Brown, 1979).

4. A recent study of this is Graham White, "Westminster in the Arctic: The Adaptation of British Parliamentarism in the Northwest Territories," *Canadian Journal of Political Science* 24, no. 3 (1991): 499–523.

5. For a very good, and brief, description of the evolution of Parliament, see Sydney Bailey, *British Parliamentary Democracy* (Boston: Houghton Mifflin, 1958), especially 12–20. A good longitudinal study of British political institutions can be found in Lynton Robins, ed., *Political Institutions in Britain: Development and Change* (New York: Longman, 1987).

6. See Andrew Adonis, "The House of Lords in the 1980s," *Parliamentary Affairs* 41 (July 1988): 380–85. This does not address the question of the subcentral governments of the United Kingdom. For discussion of this topic, see R. A. W. Rhodes, *Beyond Westminster and Whitehall: The Sub-Central Governments of Britain* (London: Allen and Unwin, 1988).

7. See Michael Rush, *Parliamentary Government in Britain* (New York: Holmes and Meier, 1981).

8. See Jonathan Lemco, "The Fusion of Powers, Party Discipline, and the Canadian Parliament," *Presidential Studies Quarterly* 18, no. 2 (1988): 283–302; Robert Harmel and E. Keith Hamm, "Development of a Party Role in a No-Party Legislature," *Western Political Quarterly* 39 (March 1986): 79–91. See also my discussion of this issue in "Parliament and Congress: Is the Grass Greener on the Other Side?" *Canadian Parliamentary Review* 8, no. 4 (1985–86): 19–21.

9. See James S. Read, "Four New African Constitutions: Part I," *Commonwealth Law Bulletin* 6 (1980): 262–71.

10. See Vernon Hewitt, "The Congress System Is Dead: Long Live the Party System and Democratic India?" *Journal of Commonwealth and Comparative Politics* 27, no. 2 (1989): 157.

11. Congressional staffing is discussed in a now-classic article by Roger Davidson and Walter Oleszek, "Adaptation and Consolidation: Structural Innovation in the U.S. House of Representatives," *Legislative Studies Quarterly* 1 (February 1976): 37–65. Harold Wolman and Dianne Wolman discussed the importance of staff in the linkage process in "The Role of the U.S. Senate Staff in the Opinion Linkage Process: Population Policy," *Legislative Studies Quarterly* 2 (August 1977): 281–93.

12. Susan Hammond, "Legislative Staffs," *Legislative Studies Quarterly* 9 (May 1984): 271–317, is very helpful in this area.

13. A study of the Canadian application of this principle can be found in Paul Thomas, "The Influence of Standing Committees of Parliament on Government Legislation," *Legislative Studies Quarterly* 3 (November 1978): 683–704.

14. See Robert Zwier, "The Search for Information: Specialists and Nonspecialists in the U.S. House of Representatives," *Legislative Studies Quarterly* 4 (February 1979): 31–42.

15. A full volume is devoted to this topic; see Antonio Cassese, ed., *Parliamentary Foreign Affairs Committees: The National Setting* (New York: Oceana Press, 1982).

16. See Michael Jogerst, "Backbenchers and Select Committees in the British House of Commons: Can Parliament Offer Useful Roles for the Frustrated?" *European Journal of Political Research* 20, no. 1 (1991): 21–38.

17. See G. Onyekwere Nwanko, "Political Parties and Their Role in the Electoral Process: The Nigerian Experiment with the Presidential System of Government," *Journal of Constitutional and Parliamentary Studies* 17, no. 3 (1985): 234–42.

18. The literature in this area is massive. See, for example, Andre Blais, "The Classification of Electoral Systems," *European Journal of Political Research* 16, no. 1 (1988): 99–110; Susan Welch and Donley Studlar, "Multi-Member Districts and the Representation of Women: Evidence from Britain and the United States," *Journal of Politics* 52 (May 1990): 391–412; and one of the best articles of its type, Arend Lijphart, "The Political Consequences of Electoral Laws, 1945–1985, "*American Political Science Review* 84, no. 2 (1990): 481–96.

19. Figures come from *Facts on File* 52 (April 16, 1992), 261.

20. It has been argued by some, for example, that single-member districts made federal-provincial disputes in Canada during the Trudeau era worse than they might

otherwise have been because there was virtually no Liberal representation in Parliament from the western provinces, even though the Liberals regularly won in the neighborhood of 20 percent of the vote there. For an example of this kind of research, see Andre Blais and R. K. Carty, "Does Proportional Representation Foster Voter Turnout?" *European Journal of Political Research* 18, no. 2 (1990): 167–81.

21. This is a basic description of the Israeli application of proportional representation. There are other variations on the same theme, but the general application is that if a party receives 25 percent of the vote in an election, it will receive 25 percent of the seats (appropriately rounded off) in the legislature.

22. The best description of the single transferable vote system that I have seen is in a book distributed by the Electoral Reform Society of Great Britain, Robert A. Newland, *Comparative Electoral Systems* (London: Arthur McDougall Fund, 1982).

23. Richard Rose, *Politics in England* (Boston: Little, Brown, 1980), 256.

24. See Patrick Weller's fine book, *First Among Equals: Prime Ministers in Westminster Systems* (London: Allen and Unwin, 1985).

25. An interesting discussion of this theme can be found in Douglas Verney, "From Executive to Legislative Federalism? The Transformation of the Political System in Canada and India," *Review of Politics* 51, no. 2 (1989): 241–63.

26. See, for example, Gerhard Loewenberg, ed., *Modern Parliaments: Change or Decline?* (Chicago: Atherton Press, 1971). A more recent study of the British House of Lords also addressed this issue in Lord Ponsonby of Shulbrede, "The House of Lords: An Effective Restraint on the Executive?" *The Parliamentarian* 69 (April 1988): 83–85.

References

Adonis, Andrew. "The House of Lords in the 1980s." *Parliamentary Affairs* 41 (July 1988): 380–401.

Bailey, Sydney. *British Parliamentary Democracy.* Boston: Houghton Mifflin, 1958.

Baumgartner, Frank. "Parliament's Capacity to Expand Political Controversy in France." *Legislative Studies Quarterly* 12 (February 1987): 33–54.

Blais, Andre. "The Classification of Electoral Systems." *European Journal of Political Research* 16, no. 1 (1988): 99–110.

Blais, Andre, and R. K. Carty. "Does Proportional Representation Foster Voter Turnout?" *European Journal of Political Research* 18, no. 2 (1990): 167–81.

Cassese, Antonio, ed. *Parliamentary Foreign Affairs Committees: The National Setting.* New York: Oceana Press, 1982.

Davidson, Roger, and Walter Oleszek. "Adaptation and Consolidation: Structural Innovation in the U.S. House of Representatives." *Legislative Studies Quarterly* 1 (February 1976): 37–65.

Eldridge, Albert, ed. *Legislatures in Plural Societies: The Search for Cohesion in National Development.* Durham: Duke University Press, 1977.

Hammond, Susan. "Legislative Staffs." *Legislative Studies Quarterly* 9 (May 1984): 271–317.

Harmel, Robert, and E. Keith Hamm. "Development of a Party Role in a No-Party Legislature." *Western Political Quarterly* 39 (March 1986): 79–91.

Hewitt, Vernon. "The Congress System Is Dead: Long Live the Party System and Democratic India?" *Journal of Commonwealth and Comparative Politics* 27 (July 1989): 157–71.

Hirsch, H., and M. D. Hancock, eds. *Comparative Legislative Systems.* New York: Free Press, 1971.

Jogerst, Michael. "Backbenchers and Select Committees in the British House of Commons: Can Parliament Offer Useful Roles for the Frustrated?" *European Journal of Political Research* 20, no. 1 (1991): 21–38.

Kornberg, Allan, ed. *Legislatures in Comparative Perspective.* New York: MacKay, 1973.

Kornberg, Allan, and Lloyd Musolf, eds. *Legislatures in Developmental Perspective.* Durham: Duke University Press, 1970.

Kornblith, Miriam. "The Politics of Constitution-Making: Constitution and Democracy in Venezuela." *Journal of Latin American Studies* 23 (February 1991): 61–89.

Lemco, Jonathan. "The Fusion of Powers, Party Discipline, and the Canadian Parliament." *Presidential Studies Quarterly* 18 (spring 1988): 283–302.

Lijphart, Arend. "The Political Consequences of Electoral Laws, 1945–1985." *American Political Science Review* 84 (June 1990): 481–96.

Loewenberg, Gerhard, ed. *Modern Parliaments: Change or Decline?* Chicago: Atherton Press, 1971.

Loewenberg, Gerhard, and Samuel Patterson. *Comparing Legislatures.* Boston: Little, Brown, 1979.

Mahler, Gregory S. "Parliament and Congress: Is the Grass Greener on the Other Side?" *Canadian Parliamentary Review* 8, no. 4 (1985–86).

———. *Comparative Politics: An Institutional and Cross-National Approach.* Englewood Cliffs, N.J.: Prentice-Hall, 1992.

Mezey, Michael. "The Functions of Legislatures in the Third World." *Legislative Studies Quarterly* 8 (1983): 511–50.

Nelson, Daniel. "Communist Legislatures and Communist Politics." In *Communist Legislatures in Comparative Perspective*, edited by Daniel Nelson and Stephen White. Albany: State University of New York Press, 1982.

Newland, Robert A. *Comparative Electoral Systems.* London: Arthur McDougall Fund, 1982.

Nwanko, G. Onyekwere. "Political Parties and Their Role in the Electoral Process: The Nigerian Experiment with the Presidential System of Government." *Journal of Constitutional and Parliamentary Studies* 17, no. 3 (1985): 234–42.

Olson, David. *The Legislative Process.* New York: Harper and Row, 1980.

Ponsonby of Shulbrede, Lord. "The House of Lords: An Effective Restraint on the Executive?" *The Parliamentarian* 69 (April 1988): 83–85.

Read, James S., "Four New African Constitutions: Part I," *Commonwealth Law Bulletin* 6 (1980): 262–71.

Rhodes, R. A. W. *Beyond Westminster and Whitehall: The Sub-Central Governments of Britain.* London: Allen and Unwin, 1988.

Robins, Lynton, ed. *Political Institutions in Britain: Development and Change.* New York: Longman, 1987.

Rose, Richard. *Politics in England.* Boston: Little, Brown, 1980.

Rush, Michael. *Parliamentary Government in Britain.* New York: Holmes and Meier, 1981.

St. Clair-Daniel, W. "Caribbean Concepts of Parliament." *The Parliamentarian* 66, no. 4 (1985): 211–13.

Thomas, Paul. "The Influence of Standing Committees of Parliament on Government Legislation." *Legislative Studies Quarterly* 3 (November 1978): 683–704.

Verney, Douglas. "From Executive to Legislative Federalism? The Transformation of the Political System in Canada and India." *Review of Politics* 51, no. 2 (1989): 241–63.

Welch, Susan, and Donley Studlar. "Multi-Member Districts and the Representation of Women: Evidence from Britain and the United States." *Journal of Politics* 52 (May 1990): 391–412.

Weller, Patrick. *First Among Equals: Prime Ministers in Westminster Systems.* London: Allen and Unwin, 1985.

White, Graham. "Westminster in the Arctic: The Adaptation of British Parliamentarism in the Northwest Territories." *Canadian Journal of Political Science* 24 (September 1991): 499–523.

Wolman, Harold, and Dianne Wolman. "The Role of the U.S. Senate Staff in the Opinion Linkage Process: Population Policy." *Legislative Studies Quarterly* 2 (August 1977): 281–93.

Zwier, Robert. "The Search for Information: Specialists and Nonspecialists in the U.S. House of Representatives." *Legislative Studies Quarterly* 4 (February 1979): 31–42.

3

The U.S. Presidential System as a Model for the World

James L. Sundquist

For the past two centuries, each new country or newly democratizing country has examined two prototypical models of governmental structure. One is the U.S. presidential system created by the Grand Convention of 1787, the other the parliamentary system that evolved over several centuries as the "mother of Parliaments" in Britain. Some countries have chosen one or another variant of the former, some of the latter, while some—especially in the last couple of decades—have been trying to conceive hybrid structures that they hope will combine the best features of the two.

The U.S. system was copied most faithfully by the new states of Latin America that came into being in the nineteenth century, but some of the new African states have also looked in our direction. The European states, as they democratized, generally looked to Britain and chose the parliamentary pattern, with various modifications. Yet even among those states, France—after a series of failed experiments with parliamentary structures—designed a hybrid that has so far been tested only during a single full presidential term. Italy has been engaged in an intense debate over whether a kind of quasi-presidential system should supersede a parliamentary system that has been adjudged by the Italian people to have failed. Most of the new democracies of Central and Eastern Europe appear to have been seeking some way to combine the virtues of a strong presidency on the U.S. pattern with some of the traditions of parliamentary government carried over from their pre–World War II parliamentary structures. And Israel, which has struggled since its creation with perhaps the purest parliamentary system ever designed, has now introduced the novel experiment of a directly elected prime minister.

Perhaps the most important reasons that countries have been moving away from the pure parliamentary structure in the direction of the U.S. model are these:

- the recognized need for strong and decisive leadership, and the perception that such leadership is more likely to be provided by a single individual than by the often diffuse collective decision-making machinery set up by parliaments;
- the added governmental legitimacy that accrues when the head of the government gets his or her mandate directly from the people rather than from an inner circle of party leaders;
- the heightened sense of political participation that comes from the opportunity given to voters to make the choice among candidates for head of state and then to hold the successful candidate directly accountable rather than indirectly through a party.

The Record of Presidential Systems

Despite the attraction of the U.S. presidential model and its continuing influence in constitution making around the world, there is little in the world experience—save for the United States alone—to suggest that adoption of the presidential model results in stable and durable democracy. Virtually every country in Latin America and in Africa that adopted the presidential system degenerated, sooner or later, into dictatorship. Many of the dictatorships have now yielded to new experiments with president-led democracies, but the stability of these new democracies is uncertain.

Recent studies have found that countries that adopt parliamentary systems have a strikingly superior record at maintaining stable democracies than presidential systems.[1] Of course, quantitative studies that use countries as their unit of analysis tend to give excessive weight to island microstates—the Kiribatis and Vanuatus of the world—in their analysis. Moreover, survival is not an end in itself, and whether the stable parliamentary democracies have been more successful than presidential democracies (or dictatorships, for that matter) under comparable circumstances, has not been well researched and probably defies systematic analysis.

Yet the prototype of the presidential system—the United States—has by far the oldest written constitution in the world. Its system has survived without fundamental change for more than two centuries. Its stability is beyond question.

All of this raises the following questions: First, why has the presidential system proved so durable in the United States, when it has failed so repeatedly in the countries that have copied it? Second, are there any lessons that can be learned from the U.S. system that can make presidential arrangements in other countries more viable?

The answer to the second question depends heavily on the answer to the first. If the durability of the U.S. system can be traced to some distinctive elements in the design of the separation of powers in the United States that makes it less susceptible to instability, then those elements may be transferable. Similarly, if there is something distinctive about other institutional features of the United States (federalism or its powerful courts, for example) that tend to compensate for any inherent weaknesses in the separation of powers, then those lessons may again be transportable. (Of course, institutional adaptations have risks of their own, and may provoke opposition from parties that see their interests threatened.) If, however, it appears that U.S. institutions operate in a more favorable social environment than do most other presidential systems—for example, weaker societal cleavages, and a weaker and less distinctive, less caste-like military officer corps—any positive lessons are likely to be more difficult to copy in other countries. Similarly, if a finding that the United States faces (or faced at critical points in its history when regime consolidation was occurring) an easier governing challenge than do most other presidential systems, notably lower expectations for government action, then there is little hope that other countries can emulate the U.S. experience.

The Genius of the U.S. System

When the delegates to the Constitutional Convention met in Philadelphia in 1787, they were obsessed with the danger of tyranny. They had lived under what they felt was the despotism of King George III of England, and after the Revolution they had suffered what they felt was the often arbitrary rule by another set of institutions—the all-powerful legislatures that controlled the thirteen newly independent states. While the delegates disagreed on virtually every particular point as they put together their grand design, no delegate ever dissented from the central objective: The executive, legislative, and judicial powers would be assigned to independent branches of the government, and each branch would be given the means of self-defense against overreaching by the other branches. "Ambition must be made to counteract ambition," in James Madison's famous phrase.

Thus, those who were most haunted by the memory of King George strove to equip the legislative and judicial branches with sufficient power to prevent the American presidency's becoming the "elective monarch" against whom George Mason, among others, anxiously forewarned. So they gave the president no hint of power to rule by decree; in this government of laws, the rules would be written by the Congress, which could override even the presidential veto by a two-thirds majority. Without its prior authorization, no money could be spent. Only the Congress could declare war or raise and support armies. The president could appoint officers of the executive branch only with the advice and consent of the Senate. And the same with treaties—in this case, requiring approval by two-thirds of that body. Even in the event of a grave emergency, the Constitution provided no opportunity for a presidential takeover. Finally, the House of Representatives could impeach a president and the Senate then, by a two-thirds vote, could remove him or her from office.

Those who worried more about a prospective "excess of democracy," such as Elbridge Gerry, Edmund Randolph, and Madison himself, devised a comparable set of safeguards against the danger of legislators running wild—especially the "levelers" who would endanger the rights of property. Thus, congressional legislation would require the concurrence of two houses, a popular house patterned on the British House of Commons, and a Senate, chosen by the state legislatures for longer terms, that came as close as could be devised to a republican House of Lords. Once those two bodies had agreed, the president could still exercise a veto, subject only to an override by a two-thirds vote of each house.

And both the executive and the legislature would be required to adhere to the Constitution by the Supreme Court, insulated from political pressure by lifetime appointments. While the Constitution was not explicit that the Court could invalidate acts of Congress that, for instance, usurped authority reserved to the states, some members of the convention anticipated that the Court would possess that power and provoked no dissent from that view. When the Court did, in fact, assert that right a generation after its establishment, it encountered no public or official protest. The Court, in turn, was held in check by the other branches—indirectly, because its membership could be gradually reconstituted through appointment of new members by the president with Senate confirmation and, more directly, because its jurisdiction could be restricted, or the number of justices increased, by law.

In devising what has been called the "delicate balance" among the branches, the framers proved to be extraordinarily prescient. Over the more than two centuries of government under the Constitution, aggressions by one or another of the three branches have in fact been checked by the others. Ambition has indeed counteracted ambition.

The executive branch has been the most common aggressor, but its aggrandizement has depended on the acquiescence of the other branches, for the legislators and the courts have always had the means to impose restraint, and have sometimes used them. President Thomas Jefferson could exceed his authority in committing expenditures for the purchase of Louisiana, but only in the confidence that Congress would subsequently provide the funds; when President Gerald Ford many decades later made a no less solemn commitment to provide aid to the government of South Vietnam in its last days, Congress refused its support and the Vietnam government—not for this reason alone, to be sure—fell. While presidents have at times claimed an almost unlimited power to enter into and fight undeclared wars, they cannot continue for long without congressional appropriations. Again the best illustration is Vietnam: Presidents led the gradual escalation of U.S. involvement in the conflict there and unilaterally extended hostilities into Laos and Cambodia, but Congress finally took policymaking into its own hands and forced a U.S. withdrawal. The supreme triumph of Congress over an aggressive president was, of course, the legislators' investigations and the threat of impeachment that culminated in Richard M. Nixon's resignation.

The principal control on expansionist aspirations of the legislative branch is the presidential veto. The veto was originally conceived for that express purpose—to enable the president to defend his constitutional prerogatives. For the first few decades, presidents used their veto power on only such occasions, but since the time of Andrew Jackson, forceful chief executives have felt no compunction in vetoing measures on policy grounds alone. On only rare occasions is a president unable to muster the one-third-plus-one of either house that is sufficient to sustain a veto, so the mere threat of a veto will normally force Congress to yield, compromise, or settle for inaction. Policymaking has thus become a truly joint executive-legislative responsibility, with each branch able to thwart the other. In the nineteenth century, passive presidents often allowed Congress to dominate policy decisions; in the twentieth, the balance has often swung toward the president. But in either case, the dominating branch could attain and sustain its ascendancy only through the acquiescence of the other.

When the president and Congress, separately or together, seek to extend their constitutional authority, the judicial branch can impose its will and, in its interpretation of the constitutional limits on executive and legislative power, its word is final. Thus, the Supreme Court forced President Harry S Truman to return seized steel mills to their owners, despite his declaration that national security demanded their operation by the government. Later, the Court compelled President Nixon to surrender the tapes that incriminated him in Watergate, and lower courts rendered a series of decisions directing Nixon to release appropriated funds he had unlawfully impounded. More recently, the Supreme Court outlawed the legislative veto, a device Congress invented but presidents often accepted and even proposed, whereby the legislature, or one of its houses, or even one of its committees—depending on the wording of the provision in any particular law—could revoke an action of the executive. Yet the judiciary is a less powerful competitor in the interbranch rivalry than the finality of its decisions might suggest. By its nature, it can react only to the agendas of others; it cannot initiate. And, to disallow the actions of the other branches, it must find either an administrative misinterpretation of statutory intent—in which case the Congress can readily reverse the Court by clarifying its intent—or a violation of some provision of the Constitution. Because the Constitution, in the Bill of Rights and in subsequent amendments, is the guarantor of civil rights and liberties, it is in the interpretation of those clauses that the Court becomes a kind of superlegislature, issuing edicts on such subjects as abortion, church-state relations, and discrimination in all its forms (although some of these decisions involve statutory interpretation as well).

But outside the area of individual rights and liberties, the Court no longer finds any substantive policies embedded in the Constitution. Until the Great Depression of the 1930s, that was not the case. But then the Court challenged the power of the elective branches to enact measures designed to reform the economic system and to cope with the consequences of its collapse. That precipitated a constitutional crisis, and the Court lost. After the Court declared unconstitutional a series of New Deal economic measures on the grounds that they invaded the prerogatives of the states in the U.S. federal system, President Franklin Roosevelt proposed to "pack" the Court by expanding its membership, which could be accomplished by simple statute. Public and congressional opinion rose in defense of the Court, and the proposal failed. However, Roosevelt lost the battle but won the war. As conservative justices retired, he replaced them with liberals; the Court conceded that economic policy was the proper province of the national government, and since that time it has overruled the president and Congress only rarely and on relatively minor matters.

The constitutional checks have worked as intended, then, and the balance among the branches has been maintained. When, through the ambition of one or another of the three, the balance appeared to the other branches to be upset, the offended branch or branches have been able to assert themselves and restore an equilibrium that leaders and the populace could find acceptable. A kind of built-in gyroscope appeared to preserve the stability of the whole governmental mechanism. And the name of the gyroscope can be identified. It is that elusive but controlling element in a constitutional system—public opinion. In every contest between branches of government in U.S. history, crucial support for sustaining or restoring the constitutional balance has come from the public. The population at large has always been as fully committed to the concept of separated powers and the independence and viability of the three branches as were the framers themselves. Rarely in two centuries of national life have amendments even been proposed that would alter fundamentally the framers' design, and at no time has any been seriously considered.

The public support undoubtedly originated in the same dread of despotism that motivated the 1787 convention. That dread was evidenced by the ratification debates in the founding states, where the challenges came from those who worried that the independence of the branches might not be sufficiently guaranteed. Few if any voices were raised to suggest that the proposed new government might be defective in not being unified enough—that the branches might not merely check but might stymie and debilitate one another.

After the first few decades, however, the memory of King George had faded, and support for the government's tripartite design has to be explained by other factors. One of those factors is intangible and somewhat mystical: the veneration that came to attach to the document itself. Every nation has its institutions and symbols of authority and nationhood that transcend differences among parties and factions and ensure the unity and survival of the nation in times of deep division. Before the Revolution, that institution had been the British monarchy and its symbol, the Crown, even in the distant colonies. Those who opposed the policies of the monarch's government were and still are His or Her Majesty's loyal opposition. When the new United States rejected the British king and foreswore the creation of an "elective monarch" in his place, the Constitution that was the safeguard against any such development became itself the symbol of nationhood. It was the Constitution that the president himself was sworn, as prescribed by that document, to "preserve, protect, and defend" when he entered on his duties.

Republicans and Federalists, Democrats and Whigs, liberals and conservatives might quarrel, but they did so strictly within the bounds of the constitutional structure that none ever made a move to overthrow. When the southern states left the Union to form their own nation, they at once adopted a constitution that embodied the essential institutions of the country from which they had seceded, and when they rejoined the Union they renewed their attachment to the U.S. Constitution with the same fervor as before. Religious folk everywhere found it easy to refer to the Constitution as divinely inspired, and to this day the "intent of the framers" is invoked—regardless of how assured, or accurate, may be the interpretation of that intent—with a reverence approaching that accorded the Scriptures themselves.

The authority of the Constitution could not have been maintained, of course, if the structure of government it created had not succeeded in coping with the nation's problems. But with the single exception of the slavery issue, which for a time dissolved the Union, it did succeed to the satisfaction of the country. The nation grew and prospered, and the Constitution could be credited with making possible what patriotic Americans never tire of calling "the greatest nation on earth." Those who protested what they perceived as governmental failure expressed their dissent through political action within the constitutional system rather than by attacking the system itself. They sought to supplant the leaders in power by creating new political parties or by capturing existing ones. Elect us, they pleaded, and we will make the system work.

Other factors, too, helped sustain the Constitution. In the early days, when the document was attaining its mystical status, the scope of government was limited and the institutions of government did not have to deal with the infinite complexities of today's economy and society. Success came more easily—except for the cataclysmic failure to resolve the slavery issue peacefully. And, had ambitious or disgruntled forces had the will to overthrow the Constitution and the democracy it ordained, no ready means was at hand, for the country had no standing army. Until the close of the nineteenth century, no professional military corps existed. And by that time the doctrine of civilian control of the military was so deeply embedded in the American tradition that any conceivable military intervention would be on the side of defending the constitutional order—as when the army was called upon to drive the "bonus marchers" out of Washington, or to integrate the schools of Little Rock to enforce a Supreme Court interpretation of the Constitution.

Finally, the stability of the U.S. governmental structure can no doubt be attributed in part to the extraordinary difficulty of amendment. After two-thirds of each house of Congress agrees on an amendment, it must be ratified by three-fourths of the states, either by their legislatures or by conventions called for the purpose. Since the legislative alternative is the one usually chosen (in every instance but one), and all states but one have bicameral legislatures, today as few as thirteen of the ninety-nine legislative houses can block any proposed amendment. To put it conversely, as many as 87 percent of the legislative bodies must vote approval. Popular support must therefore be not just preponderant but overwhelming. Any amendment must satisfy Republicans and Democrats alike, liberals and conservatives, members of Congress and advocates of the presidency, nationalists and states' righters, and both sides of any other dichotomy into which the society may be divided. But changes in the structure of government that would modify the checks and balances and redistribute power among the branches by their nature produce losers as well as winners, and the losers can assuredly rally the minimal 14 percent necessary to block ratification. No one can know what structural amendments might have been seriously considered over the centuries had the amendment process not been all but impossible, but clearly the difficulty of amendment has deterred pragmatic politicians from even considering constitutional change as a possible solution to the problems of a government that may be malfunctioning.

Advice to the World: In Copying the American System, Proceed with Caution

While Americans may be satisfied with their Constitution, and even revere it—as evidenced by the absence of any serious effort, over two centuries, to change fundamentally the institutions of government it created—there is no comparable level of satisfaction, these days, with the way in which those institutions have been performing. Dissatisfaction has been mounting for close to three decades, and by the 1990s has reached the highest levels since public opinion polls came into being, sixty years ago.[2] In 1992, the approval rating of Congress reached a record low of less than 20 percent.[3] As for the presidency, once the euphoria arising from George Bush's success in the Persian Gulf wore off, his ratings fell precipitously as well.[4]

In the 1992 campaign, the most spectacular development was the rise of a massive protest movement against all the institutions of the national government and their officeholders, led by a man hardly anyone had ever heard of before his campaign began, Ross Perot. Despite some of the most erratic conduct ever exhibited by a presidential candidate—entry into the race, then withdrawal on a strange pretext, then reentry—Perot drew an astounding 19 percent of the vote. This was the highest figure for any third-party or independent candidate in eighty years and by far the highest in U.S. history for any candidate who came from entirely outside the political system and then attacked the whole establishment. The people's alienation from their government was expressed also in the highest turnover in the membership of the House of Representatives in forty years and the approval, in all of the fourteen states where the issue was on the ballot, of proposals to limit (usually to twelve years, sometimes to as few as six) the length of time that a member could serve in Congress.

When the polltakers and journalists asked ordinary voters why they were so hostile toward their government, they mentioned scandal and corruption, but the other word that cropped up repeatedly was "gridlock." The government was just not responding to the problems that the people saw—an economy mired in recession, an apparently uncontrollable growth in the nation's budget deficit, a perceived long-term decline in the country's ability to compete in the global economy, the nation's failure to establish a health care insurance system that would cover everyone, weaknesses in the educational system, an unstemmed rise in the rate of violent crime, and so on. And since the system of separated powers had for the past twelve years given the country a Republican president and a Democratic House of Representatives and, for the past six years, a Democratic Senate, they could not affix blame. The Republican president blamed the Democratic majorities in Congress for the failures of the divided government, and they in turn blamed him. But the people were tired of excuses. They just condemned both sides, rallied around the unlikely figure of Perot, and did what they could to throw the incumbents out of office, beginning with President Bush himself.

Gridlock was by no means a new problem in American democracy. It was only a new term. Previously, writers had used the word "deadlock" to identify the circumstances when, because of the separation of powers in the American presidential system, conflict between the three centers of power that have to come into agreement for legislation to be passed—the Senate, the House, and the presidency—rendered the government immobile. James MacGregor Burns, the historian, had published his classic treatise, *The Deadlock of Democracy*, in 1963, at a time when the program of a new and popular president, John F. Kennedy, was being blocked or eviscerated on Capitol Hill. He described the "cycle of deadlock and drift" as "somber and inexorable."[5] But he was writing at a time when the Senate, the House, and the presidency were all controlled by the same party, the Democrats. After 1968, when the Republicans recaptured the White House but the Congress (or at least one of the two houses) remained Democratic, the problem of deadlock was compounded by the partisan division of the government. During all of President Nixon's and President Ford's eight years, all of President Reagan's eight years, and all of President Bush's four years, the House was controlled by Democratic majorities, and except for six of the Reagan years, so was the Senate. Under those circumstances, the normal—and on occasion, perhaps salutary—rivalry between the branches was transmuted into partisan conflict, with each branch possessed of powerful political incentive to undermine and discredit the other. Thus, the popular shift of terminology from deadlock to gridlock reflected, coincidentally, an intensification of the long-standing—albeit sometimes latent—struggle between the branches for direction of the nation's course.

In the 1992 election, the voters rebelled against gridlock by the only means at their disposal, by restoring the government to unified control by a single party, in this case the Democrats, led by a new, young president, Bill Clinton. And they did so deliberately; sampling of voters on election day showed that fully two-thirds of those who supported either Clinton or

President Bush believed that a unified government controlled by a single party would work better than the divided government they were replacing. Even a majority who voted for Ross Perot agreed.[6]

But unified government did not restore public confidence, either. Some minor legislation that had been stalled by the partisan squabbling of the Bush years was enacted, and the Democrats had some success in reducing the large budget deficits that had aroused intense concern on all sides, but in the crucial battle of the 1993–94 session, President Clinton's bold proposal for universal health care went down to defeat. The satisfaction-dissatisfaction ratio improved noticeably, but in February 1994 a majority of 61 percent of those polled still termed themselves dissatisfied, compared to a satisfied 36 percent. And in November 1994, the voters vented their frustration once again. They ended four decades of continuous Democratic control of the House by giving the Republicans a twenty-five-seat margin, and turned the Senate over to the GOP as well. And once again, they seemed to have acted deliberately. A Louis Harris poll of November 1994, asking whether respondents considered it "good" or "bad" to have a president and Congress of different parties, found 48 percent preferred a divided government to 36 percent opposed.[7] Thus, that peculiar U.S. version of coalition government—unsought and unwanted by the politicians who were thrust into it, in contrast to the voluntary coalitions formed in other countries—was again decreed by the electorate.[8]

The prospects of legislative achievement even when the government is unified are now diminished by an antidemocratic anomaly that arises not from the Constitution but purely from tradition: the extraordinary majority required to close debate in the Senate. Unanimity was once demanded to bring a measure to a vote; this was later reduced to two-thirds, and later to three-fifths of the full membership of the body. Thus, whenever the minority party has more than two-fifths of the Senate—which is most of the time, including the present time—the majority party lacks the capacity to fulfill whatever promises it may have made in the election that brought it to power. Voters who may have thought in 1992 that giving the Democratic Party control of all three policymaking institutions of the government—presidency, Senate, and House—would replace partisan gridlock with unified and responsible party government found that the necessity of bipartisan agreement still pertained and accountability was still ambiguous. And, to make matters worse, the filibuster that by an earlier tradition was reserved for use only in instances of the utmost emotional intensity—primarily as the instrument by which the South could resist the imposition of civil rights legislation on its segregated society—has now come to be employed, or at least threatened, for any routine piece of legislation that the minority may wish to obstruct for reasons of principle or perceived partisan advantage. When the Senate Democrats became the minority in 1995, they used their filibuster power about as regularly, and as ruthlessly, as had the Republican minority in 1993–94.

Any discussion of gridlock requires noting one other feature of the American system that contradicts the principle that in a democracy the majority, subject to constitutional safeguards for minorities, shall possess the capacity—and accept the responsibility and accountability—to conduct the business of the government. That feature is the constitutional requirement that treaties must be approved by the extraordinary majority of two-thirds of the Senate. Transient majorities should not be able to bind the country to grave and long-term international commitments, reasoned the framers, and their rationale has a ring of plausibility. Yet the gravest commitment of all, the decision to go to war, was left to a simple majority of the Congress. And the inescapable effect of the two-thirds requirement is that when the country is divided on an issue of foreign policy, the minority rather than the majority determines the nation's course. The most notable, and probably the most profoundly consequential, exercise of this minority power in our history occurred in the rejection of the Treaty of Versailles at the close of World War I. Although the treaty was drafted under the leadership of the U.S. president, Woodrow Wilson, and commanded the support of a substantial majority of the Senate, a majority of the House, and, on the basis of what evidence can be adduced in those days before the Gallup poll, the public at large, it was defeated by a minority of the Senate. Overruling the will of what was then an internationalist majority of the country—including both major presidential candidates in 1920—the isolationist minority determined the foreign policy of the United States.

Those in other countries who may be looking to the United States Constitution as a model are already aware of its strengths. They, like our Founding Fathers, are looking for a system that will safeguard against would-be despots, and there is no doubt that the U.S. system has served that purpose well. The checks and balances have indeed worked, and none of the three independent branches of the government has ever been able, for long, to override the others and emerge supreme. Yet a system that so scatters the powers of government that no individual or group can assemble and concentrate them for ignoble purposes will also, inevitably, hinder leaders with the purest of motives to assemble and concentrate them to achieve the most worthy of endeavors. This has been the dilemma of the U.S. government for two centuries: A structure that deters bad leaders with evil motives also deters the best of leaders with the noblest of purposes and the soundest of ideas.

The essential problem, then, is how to restrain a government while still endowing it with the capacity to act. The restraints are what appeal to those who look to the United States as a model. They may be less aware of the structural features of the U.S. system that tend to inhibit its capacity for leadership, that sometimes make its policymaking processes sluggish and indecisive, that may place more emphasis on the instruments that give the minority the right and power of veto than on those that enable the majority to lead and govern, free of gridlock. I acknowledge the values that derive from distributing the powers of government among separated branches, but I also hold that the pattern of distribution must be such as to ensure capacity, responsibility, and accountability, and it must guard against paralysis. This objective leads to the following seven admonitions for writers of new presidential-style constitutions.

First, adopt an electoral system that prohibits, or at least discourages, ticket splitting for national office. In other words, require that a voter cast his or her ballot for the candidates nominated by the same party for president and legislative representative in an election held concurrently for both branches. The terms of office of the two branches would also have to coincide. Whoever won the presidency would then normally be assured, at least in those countries that develop two-party or two-coalition systems, of a supportive majority in the legislative branch, and the problems arising from "cohabitation," as it is known in France, or divided government, as it is termed in the United States, would be averted.

Second, provide for a runoff presidential election whenever no candidate wins a majority in the initial balloting. In the balloting for president, one candidate must perforce ultimately win, so if no candidate in a multicandidate field receives a majority (or other stipulated percentage) of the vote on the first ballot, a runoff election should be required. That would forestall an outcome such as that in Chile, where Salvador Allende assumed office with only about one-third of the popular vote. In the runoff, a multiparty contest would tend to evolve into a competition between two coalitions. The parties making up the winning presidential coalition would probably, in most cases, win a majority of the legislative seats as well, either in the initial balloting or in a runoff process corresponding to that used in the presidential contest. In a close election, the parties making up the losing presidential coalition might conceivably win control of the legislature, but there would appear to be no electoral system that could absolutely forestall such an outcome—short of electing the entire legislature at large. But a system such as Germany's, where half the Bundestag is elected on party lists, would appear to be a workable safeguard against divided government, assuming that the candidates on the party lists run on a single ticket with the parties' presidential candidates.

Third, either establish a unicameral legislature or limit the powers of the less representative body in a bicameral structure. In many parliamentary countries, the powers of the so-called upper house of a bicameral legislature are limited to amending and delaying legislation initiated by the larger and more representative lower house, but without the power to reject it. These restrictions, imposed in order to prevent governmental paralysis through deadlock between the houses, would appear to serve that purpose equally well in a presidential system whose designers choose, for one or another reason, to establish a bicameral rather than a unicameral legislature. A single-chamber legislature would, of course, serve the objective with greater simplicity and with finality. However, in a large country, a second chamber with restricted powers does provide the opportunity for a fresh look at each piece of legislation before enactment while still forestalling deadlock between two houses.

Fourth, avoid any requirement for extraordinary majorities in the legislature's decision making. Such provisions appear, on the surface, to be a means of ensuring widespread support before action is taken, but in practice their consequence is to allow the minority, rather than the majority, policy position to prevail. The majority should be restrained from oppressive action by constitutional guarantees of civil rights and liberties enforced by the courts, but within those limits it should make, and take responsibility for, the nation's policies. When it errs, the next election is the people's recourse. But provisions that allow the minority to establish policy destroy responsibility and accountability, strip elections of their significance as the means by which the people determine the country's course, and in so doing subvert the fundamental principles of democracy.

Fifth, allow elected officials a reasonable "breathing space" between elections. Most countries of the world have decided that a term of four or five years is appropriate to enable a government to act free of the pressures of an imminent election. One country, Sweden, has established a three-year cycle, but it may be noteworthy that a Swedish commission on economic reform has recently recommended lengthening that period to make it easier for the government to take difficult and unpopular actions that promise long-run benefits without fear of immediate retribution at the polls for the short-term losses and disadvantages that the actions may impose. The two-year cycle that is unique to the United States invites the same criticism in more emphatic terms.

Sixth, provide a means whereby a government that is clearly ineffective for whatever reason can be expeditiously reconstituted or replaced. Governments can fail for many reasons: a popularly elected president may turn out to be incompetent or corrupt or both, the legislative body or bodies may be too fragmented or ineptly led to cope with the country's problems, or the executive and legislative branches may be immobilized by gridlock on crucial policy issues. To prevent the explosion into violence that may arise from governmental failure, a country needs a safety valve. It must be able to reconstitute its government and get off to a new beginning, and to do so promptly, smoothly, and democratically. Most parliamentary governments provide a safeguard in the vote-of-no-confidence procedure, whereby the legislature can dismiss the prime minister and the governing cabinet and the issues leading to the government's downfall may be taken to the country in a new parliamentary election. Even though such votes may occur only rarely, the existence of the procedure often forces a failing government to recognize reality and to reconstitute itself by replacing the prime minister who has lost confidence with one who will restore it, and by bringing fresh leadership into lesser executive positions. But most presidential governments, to protect the independence of the separate branches, have made it inordinately difficult, or even impossible, to replace a president before his or her term ends or to dissolve the legislature and revitalize it through fresh elections.

The absence of workable mechanisms for reconstituting a failed government is no doubt attributable, in large part, to the difficulty of designing them. An acceptable process must be effective while still faithful to democratic concepts, must be seen by the people as operating fairly, must be written so as to discourage its employment for trivial reasons or purely for partisan advantage, and must not upset a carefully designed balance of power among institutions. The procedure should enable the failure of the government to be judged by political criteria rather than—as in the U.S. impeachment process—those of criminal law. To inhibit the casual, capricious, or partisan use of the procedure, those who invoke it should be subjected to some penalty—presumably, as in parliamentary governments, the penalty of having to face the voters in a new election.

Furthermore, the procedure cannot favor either branch in its competition with the other. If the legislature is simply made subject to dissolution by presidential decree, as has been proposed from time to time in the United States, the balance between the branches would be tilted toward presidential supremacy. Conversely, if the president were made removable by the legislative branch, without risk to the tenure of the legislators, the balance would be distorted in the opposite direction. The solution would appear to lie in a system that would allow either the president or the legislative branch, or a portion of that branch, to initiate the reconstitution of the government, but that would put at stake in a special election not only the presidency but also all of the legislative seats. The experience of many countries indicates that parties that take the initiative to bring down governments tend to be punished by the voters at the next election—perhaps a sufficient deterrent in itself to partisan or capricious exercise of the dissolution power.

Seventh, and last, provide a workable procedure for keeping the constitution current through amendment. Constitutions establish the rules by which the political game is played, and rules should not be subject to easy change by temporary majorities. Yet neither should the amendment process require a consensus so broad as to approach unanimity, as has been the case in the United States. One approach to striking a balance between ease and difficulty in this country would be to reduce the extraordinary majorities required for initiation of amendments by the legislative branch—from the present two-thirds to three-fifths, say; but that does not eliminate the objection that the minority will ultimately rule, as argued earlier in the case of treaties and statutory law. An alternate approach that appears to work effectively in many American states is to impose a temporal restraint—specifically, to require approval by the legislature in two separate sessions, separated by an intervening election, with subsequent approval by the electorate in a referendum. In contrast to the national constitution, state constitutions have been amended to accomplish fundamental change in government structure, yet with the opportunity for more thorough deliberation than is required for the passage of statutes.

Two other lessons emerge from the long experience of the fifty American states. One is that substantive policy—apart from the guarantees of civil rights and liberties of a nature that can be enforced by an independent judiciary—should be omitted from constitutions and left to statutory law. Economic and social policies should be the subject of political campaigns, and their determination entrusted to the winners of those campaigns. These policies should not be written into constitutions by one generation to bind the judgment of those who come later, and to force the judiciary to make policy decisions for which they are ill prepared and cannot be held accountable by the electorate, unless the judiciary itself is converted into an elective, political branch. Omission of substantive policy from constitutions will, of course, obviate the need for frequent constitutional amendment. But there is, of course, no way to write any constitutional provision that would enforce a ban on substantive amendments.

The second lesson, related to the first, is that the people should not be empowered by the constitution to take the amendment process into their own hands, through initiation of amendment by petition and subsequent approval by referendum. State experience has shown that such procedures are an irresistible temptation to interest groups to try to entrench economic and social policies within constitutions and thus place them beyond the reach of elected legislatures and into the courts instead; moreover, popularly initiated constitutional amendments may be badly drafted and, sometimes, mutually contradictory.

This list of admonitions could be extended. But these seven appear to be the most important to be learned from two hundred years of experience in the country that boasts the most durable constitution in the history of the world.

Notes

1. See Alfred Stepan and Cindy Skach, "Constitutional Frameworks and Democratic Consolidation: Parliamentarism vs. Presidentialism," *World Politics* 46 (October 1993): 1–22.

2. Asked in June 1992 whether they were "satisfied or dissatisfied with the way things are going in the United States at this time," only 14 percent of Gallup poll respondents answered "satisfied," outnumbered six to one by the 84 percent who were "dissatisfied." As late as the previous August, after the successful conclusion of the Persian Gulf War, the same poll had found more "satisfied" than "dissatisfied." *Gallup Poll Monthly* (January 1996): 27–28.

3. *Congressional Quarterly Almanac* (Washington, D.C.: Congressional Quarterly, 1992), 3.

4. President Bush's approval rating in the CBS/*New York Times* poll fell from 74 percent in May 1991 to 40 percent in September 1992. "Opinion Outlook: Views on Presidential Performance," *National Journal* (October 17, 1992): 2388.

5. James MacGregor Burns, *The Deadlock of Democracy* (Englewood Cliffs, N.J.: Prentice-Hall, 1963), 2.

6. Donald L. Robinson, "The Problem Is Constitutional," in *Beyond Gridlock? Prospects for Governance in the Clinton Years and After*, ed. James L. Sundquist, (Washington, D.C.: Brookings Institution, 1993), 56.

7. The question was, "Do you think it good or bad for the government to be divided between the parties?" Results were reported in "Opinion Outlook," *National Journal* (December 17, 1994): 2996.

8. In an influential book, *Divided We Govern: Party Control, Lawmaking, and Investigation, 1946–90* (New Haven:Yale University Press, 1991), David R. Mayhew contends that, in the period he studied, divided government proved to be just as productive of important legislation as unified government. The research, however, covered a period when the "unified" Democratic government was deeply divided between its conservative and liberal wings and the majority party could not fulfill its theoretical responsibility of unifying the government. See my critique of Mayhew's findings and conclusions in James L. Sundquist, *Constitutional Reform and Effective Government*, revised edition (Washington, D.C.: Brookings Institution, 1992), 101–10.

4

Bureaucracy: Control, Responsiveness, Performance

JOEL D. ABERBACH AND BERT A. ROCKMAN

Bureaucracy under Presidential and Parliamentary Systems

The central questions of this paper are whether presidential and parliamentary systems differ in the extent to which bureaucracy (1) may be held accountable and thus controlled by legitimate sources of authority, (2) can be responsive to the policy interests of alternative elites, and (3) performs effectively. None of these concepts—control and accountability, responsiveness, and performance—is self-evident. All of them need to be discussed and explained. Not all of them, it should be added, can be jointly optimized.

Some believe the parliamentary/presidential distinction is important in framing the questions dealing with the control, accountability, responsiveness, and performance of bureaucracy. As a general matter, the parliamentary/presidential distinction is merely another, but less consistent, way of talking about the number of disparate authorities to whom the bureaucracy must respond and the distinctiveness of their preferences (Weaver and Rockman 1993: 22–29; Tsebelis 1993: 447–53).

Often, when the parliamentary/presidential distinction comes to mind, the two counterposed models are the Westminster system of majority party government prevalent in the United Kingdom, and the separation-of-powers system most visibly characterized by the United States. The former system is highly centripetal; the latter highly centrifugal. They represent polarities in the distribution of authority. Because there are many more parliamentary systems than presidential ones, parliamentary systems are quite variable in their nature. Obviously, multiparty governments distribute power more widely than do majority party governments. Minority governments need to be more cautious than do majority party governments. Even systems that apparently have had hegemonic party control have often been rent with factions and with faction-driven patronage that makes the concentration of authority more illusory than real (Kernell 1991: 1–13).

Although fewer in number, presidential systems also vary considerably. The American system might better be thought of as a separated-powers system than a strictly presidentialist system (Jones 1992). In Europe, the French system of the Fifth Republic is a hybrid presidential and parliamentary system, characterized by a weak parliament and a strong president who, in turn, has the power to dissolve the government. Under most, but not all, conditions, the power of the French president can be quite spectacular (King 1993: 446–48). In both parliamentary and presidential systems, real power may be lodged with party patrons who have constructed networks of support and dependence around them. Such party bosses are interested mainly in patronage and divvying up the goods generated from public works. This practice is notable in parliamentary systems, such as Japan and Italy, and in presidential systems, such as Brazil.

The differences between parliamentary and presidential systems in the organization of governing authority are often less sharp than popular lore has it. Indeed, both systems can generate a multiplicity of actors with authority who also hold distinctive preferences. However, each system also appears capable, under certain conditions, of concentrating authority. Our basic argument is that the extent to which authority is concentrated or dispersed among authorities with different preferences shapes the nature of the problems of control and accountability, responsiveness, and performance.

The Concepts of Control, Responsiveness, and Performance

In 1959, Charles Gilbert wrote about the nature of administrative responsibility. He argued that administrative responsibility covered a wide variety of concepts including accountability and responsiveness. Such features were commonly perceived, he noted, as part of a total package of traits making up responsible administration. Gilbert believed that such traits were not congruent, and that, indeed, they came wrapped in distinctive theories of administrative responsibility, which he then subjected to review. No theory of responsible administration could jointly optimize all of the values deemed to be components of responsible administration.

We begin here by discussing a key set of concepts—control, responsiveness, and performance—that similarly cannot be jointly optimized. We will then determine where these ideas may be congruent and where they may be antagonistic. In succeeding sections, we will look at how the organization of authority within political systems shapes the nature of the issues of control, responsiveness, and performance. To conclude, we will note both the role and the limits of structural explanations.

The Control and Accountability Problem

Accountability presumably is a means of controlling bureaucracy. But what do we mean by this term? The best way to think of this problem is as a principal/agent problem. The bureaucracy is an agent—quite literally the source for the word agency. It is responsible to a principal or perhaps to more than one principal. A vintage formulation of the problem of democracy from a principal/agent perspective is that the people are the ultimate principal. Electoral results render legitimate a delegation from the ultimate principal (the people) to elected political leaders. Those leaders, legitimated by public approval, then delegate authority to bureaucrats to manage the state on their behalf. It is thus assumed that the elected leaders speak in unison. Someone has control of the government, which is then able to direct those to whom authority has been delegated (the bureaucrats).

The assumption underlying this argument is that administrative authority must ultimately be grounded in popular sovereignty vested in the elected political leadership. This means that accountability is to the elected rulers, a thesis that emanates from a mandate theory of legitimacy. In this formulation, accountability can be little distinguished, if at all, from total administrative responsiveness to the present set of rulers, assuming that the latter are able to speak in the proverbial single voice.

From the classic perspective of Weberian bureaucracy, laws, rules, and precedents are the critical determinants of expected bureaucratic behavior. It is, after all, the regularity of rules that makes bureaucratic behavior predictable and fundamentally accountable. An environment in which rule-drivenness totally dominates (the rule of law taken to its logical extreme) would be one in which the bureaucracy has no discretion. Its accountability is to the law, and not necessarily to the lawmakers or the law enforcers. By way of contrast, a bureaucracy existing in an environment of few rules or precedents, or at least in an environment in which these are considered of little importance, is capable of considerable discretion, favoritism, and arbitrariness.

The problem of controlling the bureaucracy is the mirror image of the problem of accountability. Does control mean that bureaucrats are required to adhere to the laws, rules, and precedents extant in the system or does it mean that those who hold the reins of government at the moment are free to tighten their grip over what the bureaucrats do? The notion of a government of laws implies the former. But, in reality, it is hard to imagine control being exerted by law in the absence of the articulated desires of the lawmakers and law enforcers. Indeed, this distinction goes back to a debate more than fifty years ago between two eminent scholars of constitutional theory and public administration, Carl Friedrich and Herman Finer. Friedrich (1940: 3–24) claimed that administrators versed in the ways of democracy could be expected to adhere to the law and thus also exercise a necessary level of discretion in the absence of tight supervisory controls by political leaders. Finer (1941) contested this view, believing that without direct controls over the operations of the bureaucracy, the discretion given to bureaucrats could be exercised capriciously.

Of course, one way that politicians can seek to gain greater control over the bureaucracy is by writing laws or issuing directives so precisely defined that they drastically curtail the ability of administrators to exercise discretionary judgment. Such laws and directives are frequently referred to pejoratively as micromanagement. Charles Goodsell illustrated how such regulations affected the ability of lower-level state social welfare bureaucrats to deal creatively with their clients. Goodsell (1981) called this process one of "bureaucratic compression."

There is no doubt that there is always some disjuncture between what the law says and what the prevailing set of politicians might like it to say. In a majority party parliamentary government, the remedy seems obvious: change the law. In other settings, that might prove to be more difficult. Multiparty coalition governments may well have veto groups within them that object to changes in the law. Minority parliamentary governments risk being brought down should they seek such changes. And the separation-of-powers system is apt to have different perspectives emerge from those who hold authority within the three branches of government. Majorities, in other words, can change the law to coincide with changed preferences, but majority governments in parliamentary systems are actually not common (Weaver and Rockman 1993: 445–61).

The fundamental point is this: Control through the rule of law limits the discretionary capacity of bureaucracy and its responsiveness both to changing conditions and to changes in the preferences of the rulers, at least until they enact their preferences into law. Control through the idea of a political mandate, alternatively, requires a clear source of political authority—a principal to whom the administrative agent unequivocally must respond. According to this latter conception, control is vested in the power of superior office rather than through legal precedent and procedure. Thus, it is important to distinguish between the law and the office as sources of accountability and control. The former limits the degree of responsiveness to the present authorities; the latter exalts responsiveness, yet can be unequivocal only when the source of authority also is unequivocally lodged. This, necessarily, brings us to a discussion of the concept of responsiveness.

The Responsiveness Problem

Charles Gilbert (1959) defined responsiveness in terms of prompt action to popular demands. But because bureaucracy operates within a legal context and one of subordinate-superordinate relations, the bureaucracy cannot be expected by itself (outside of managerial adjustments) to initiate responses to popular demands without legal or authoritative grounding. Presumably, the political authorities in a democratic system are those whose role requires them to be sensitized to popular currents (Aberbach, Putnam, and Rockman 1981). Accordingly, for bureaucracy to be responsive to such changing currents, it must be responsive to the results obtained at the ballot box.

How responsive the bureaucracy will or can be is conditioned by a number of factors. Among these are the durability of a prior regime, the magnitude of change between regimes, and, not surprisingly, the clarity of authority. One might also add to this list the power of ideas and the changes (or continuities) in policy stance they imply. The power that ideas have, though, is generated by currents of political change (Aberbach and Rockman 1990: 190–93).

When regimes are highly durable, they tend to shape the bureaucracy increasingly in their image. The coincidence between regime and the bureaucracy is never one of perfect overlap, but over a period of time, whether through manipulation from above, anticipation from below, or otherwise, the career bureaucracy at the top takes on more and more the coloration of the regime it serves. At a minimum, it comes to know what the rulers want and, therefore, knows how to respond (Anton 1980). A likely conclusion is that the longer a regime has been in power, the more responsive the bureaucracy is. It is, of course, also likely that the more durable the relationship, the more any regime is likely to develop perspectives associated with the bureaucracy—namely, caution and skepticism toward abrupt change.

Since the bureaucracy represents continuity, sudden change and shifts in political direction provoke uncertainty within it. Unless a regime that represents such change is able to imprint its mission on the bureaucracy (often by radical shifts in personnel), the bureaucracy may be unable or unwilling to cope with nonincremental change. It may be unable to do so because its commitments have been to a past set of policies that render it incapable of conceiving how to operate differently. It also may be unwilling to adapt because its own commitments are to the status quo. The first option suggests limits to the bureaucracy's competence, whereas the second suggests limits to its neutrality.

As with the issues of accountability and control, the absence of clearly located authority makes responsiveness continually problematic. The separation-of-powers case, especially in its American version, does not confer ultimate political and policymaking authority on a single source. It invites competition between the branches of government. Just as this system entangles lines of accountability and makes control by any single authority elusive, it also makes full responsiveness to a single authority unlikely. In the peculiar American case, because of the coequal constitutional status of the branches of government, there is no single regime even when the same party controls the executive and legislative branches of government. The implication is that responsiveness can be only partial and never complete toward any given source of political authority. A further implication is that while the various authorities may not feel fully dissatisfied, they are also unlikely to feel fully satisfied with the responsiveness of the bureaucracy toward them. Both the complicated system of control and accountability and the ambiguities inherent in responding to different authorities with different preferences make it likely that the U.S. bureaucracy will be distrusted by one or more sets of political authorities at any given time. The level of distrust, it is reasonable to infer, affects both the functions with which the bureaucracy is entrusted and its performance (Polsby 1981: 7–31; Aberbach and Rockman 1985).

The Performance Problem

Performance is undoubtedly the most controversial criterion for judging bureaucracy, yet possibly the most important. But just exactly what performance means is itself subject to varying interpretations. Obviously, one thinks in this regard of a bureaucracy that is honest and committed to upholding the rule of law. Does that mean, however, that it will be regarded as uncontrollable and unresponsive by some?

It also is likely that a bureaucracy that performs well will be efficient, neutral, competent, and independent. Efficiency and the restrictive nature of legal controls, however, are likely to be inversely related. The more such controls abound, the less managerial discretion can be employed, and the lessened likelihood that "common sense" can be used to enhance efficiency. Neutrality may be seen by the present rulers as obstinacy, or at least reluctance to enthusiastically commit to the policy program of the present rulers. Although it is fair to assume that all rulers want competence, what they mean by that can be quite different (Aberbach and Rockman 1994: 461–63). While some political leaders may see bureaucrats as wielders of advice, able to speak with the voice of experience and whatever wisdom that may bring, others may desire only competence in management. Still other political leaders want from their bureaucrats only competence in strictly obeying orders from above (so-called responsive competence).

Independence, like most values, is a double-edged sword and, ultimately, leads to discontinuity in the bureaucracy. Without it, the bureaucracy can be wholly politicized and rendered incapable of resisting corruption. In the absence of independence, the bureaucracy will be seen merely as part of a system of patronage. Furthermore, there is likely to be little expectation that the bureaucracy will treat all fairly, especially those not linked to the existing regime.

Alternatively, with too much independence the bureaucracy can circumvent elected political authorities or their emissaries. With too much independence, the civil service can create its own Kafkaesque web of rules to distance itself from civil society. It can be capricious and, above all, it can generate a system of credentialization (entry of new members into the civil service elite) and a myth of indispensability that gives the higher civil service a powerful lever in protecting its status (Suleiman 1974). Bureaucrats, like others, can be self-serving. Independence, after all, is the other side of the accountability coin.

There is, of course, a different sort of consideration in accounting for the perception of bureaucratic performance. That is whether the policies the bureaucracy is charged with implementing are themselves popular or not. Unpopular policies, however they are carried out, are likely to affect popular perception of bureaucratic performance negatively, if for no other reason than that the bureaucracy is the most immediately identifiable link to those policies (Lynch 1990: 118–32).

If the bureaucracy is discredited for carrying out unpopular policies, it may not be given credit for performing effectively. Studying clients who had encountered public bureaucracy directly, Kahn and his colleagues (1986) discovered that even when clients were overwhelmingly satisfied with their treatment, they continued to hold negative stereotypes about public bureaucracy. The inference that Kahn and his colleagues drew was that there was a powerful antipathy toward bureaucracy deeply implanted in the American culture and essentially unmoved (or perhaps unmovable) by empirical evidence to the contrary.

In sum, as with the other concepts, performance often lies in the eye of the beholder. And, as with the other concepts, the conditions that may lead to optimizing performance may also be destructive of other values. It is worth noting here the language of one early critique of the National Performance Review of federal management practices in the United States under the direction of Vice President Al Gore. A chief part of that report emphasizes unshackling managers from what is perceived to be an excess of legally imposed constraints on managerial flexibility. Similarly, the report emphasizes the need to satisfy the "customers" of the federal bureaucracy:

> The administrative management paradigm with its emphasis on the Constitution, statutory controls, hierarchical lines of responsibility to the President . . . and the need for a cadre of nonpartisan professional managers, ultimately responsible not only to the President but to Congress as well is depicted as the paradigm that failed. This paradigm is the cause of the government being broken in the eyes of the entrepreneurial management promoters. It has not proven flexible enough to permit change to occur at the speed considered necessary in the new, information-driven technological world. . . . While political accountability may have once been prop-

> erly the highest value for government executives, this is no longer true. The highest value in the entrepreneurial paradigm, to all accounts, is customer satisfaction. . . . [The] precedence of economically-based values over legally-based values is evident throughout the report's recommendations. (Moe 1994: 128)

Performance, in other words, is not a value to be isolated from other concerns.

Management Functions and Advisory Functions

The language of accountability, control, and responsiveness seems peculiarly fit for the management tasks of the civil service rather than its advisory tasks. The terms above imply some form of principal/agent relationship wherein the bureaucratic task is to implement and carry out wishes expressed in law or by the political authorities. They seem to apply less to the idea of rendering advice to the policymakers themselves. It seems as though a sine qua non for the higher levels of the bureaucracy to play an advisory role is that the bureaucracy itself must be thought to perform well and to be essential to the well-being of the state.

The distinction between management and advice, at least formally, represents, among other things, different conceptions of the role of bureaucracy and its relationship to political authority. Clear lines of authority are likely to bring civil servants into closer contact with the political authorities. The civil servants represent the immediate pool of intellectual resources on which politicians depend. Where authority is convoluted or where the political authorities have disparate preferences, there is concern about the allegiances of the civil servants. Consequently, there is less likelihood that they will be relied on for advice or for political mediation (Polsby 1981; Aberbach and Rockman 1985). Politicians may bring in experts for advice, but they are likely to want to make sure to bring in "their" experts.

The heyday of the U.S. civil service appeared to have been during the New Deal years of the Roosevelt administration. The New Deal and later the war were exercises in state building. The Roosevelt presidency, endowed with large congressional majorities and a less feisty Congress than today's, created a bureaucracy in accord with its policy mission. The Johnson administration, with a handsome majority in Congress, expanded the bureaucracy and its policy mission. Each administration, arguably, brought civil servants unusually close by American standards to the action. Each, of course, was characterized by an intense, if momentary, degree of high political energy and substantial political majorities—conditions that allowed the U.S. government to resemble for a time a parliamentary majority party government.

While the "Next Steps" reform in British public management also seems to separate the management from the advisory function, it does so in a fashion exactly opposite to that of the United States. (Wilson 1993). The British reform allows managers to come in from the outside while holding the advisory function of the higher civil service inviolate. Americans use outsiders as advisers (and also, to some degree, as managers) while often thinking of civil servants purely as managers. These habits undeniably conform to very different traditions of government, but certainly also to different forms of government. These differences in governmental form have a considerable impact on the concepts of accountability and control, responsiveness, and performance.

Separation of Powers—The U.S. System

American bureaucracy, James Q. Wilson notes, is characterized by access and rules (1989: 377–78). These very same characteristics apply equally to the political system as a whole. So it is not surprising that the bureaucracy reflects the political system in that regard. Access is afforded by the tangled lines of authority and accountability that run throughout the American system. Most particularly, access is promoted by competitive authority that runs horizontally (the separation of powers) and vertically (federalism). It is hard to exhaust appeals in the American system.

The fact that members of Congress are elected in a first-past-the-post system by district promotes a high degree of attentiveness to constituencies and to complaints.This, in turn, promotes a strong concern with casework and, ironically, with writing more rules, such as earmarks. There is evidence that electoral rules and the system of representation are important here. Cain, Ferejohn, and Fiorina, for instance, noted that British MPs, elected in a first-past-the-post system, spent a good bit of effort on administrative casework (1987: 27–117; 212–29). Aberbach, Putnam, and Rockman discovered that German legislators elected by district were a great deal more oriented toward casework than were their colleagues elected from the party list through proportional representation (1981: 101). This, at least, is one case where logic and evidence seem to be compatible.

The rule-drivenness of the system stems from many of the same factors that promote access. The competition between authorities who hold equal constitutional standing leads each to so aspire to leadership of the two other branches that they have ignored precedents and laws meant to be applied whether or not the present politicians so wish. The courts themselves also become players in restricting administrative discretion by interpreting provisions of statutory law and administrative regulations more generously than at least the agencies often prefer. R. Shep Melnick (1994) has recently shown how the courts have poked between the lines of statutes to generate edicts for welfare agencies to follow.

To some extent, there is a specialization among agencies in the American system as to where their primary loyalty lies. Some agencies—or more precisely, specific programs within the agencies—tend to be heavily executive-centered, and the key political overseers are the president and the president's minions. Others tend to be legislative-centered, and although the executive sometimes tries to eliminate or alter some of them, it is not often successful because of the sense of proprietorship that Congress exerts. One way of thinking about the executive-centered and legislative-centered agencies or programs is to consider whether they come from what Thomas Cronin (1980: 253–96) called inner and outer departments of government. The basic, inner, state-maintenance departments (external relations, finance, justice, and defense) tend to be relatively less rule-driven and more responsive to the president, whom their heads get to see with greater frequency than do the heads of the outer departments.

By contrast, the outer departments involved in regulatory, social welfare, and development activities tend to be more driven by statutory law, and thus they are the ones over whom Congress is likely to claim a greater control. When the Democrats controlled Congress and the Republicans controlled the Presidency, programs such as vocational and continuing education in the Department of Education had strong external clienteles and powerful support within Congress. In the face of extreme executive-centered efforts to shape and even to eliminate such programs, Congress wielded the ultimate authority. Naturally, neither branch wishes to cede authority readily. Clashes over the organization of programs, the performance, responsiveness, and accountability of the agencies, and funding levels are frequent, especially when government is divided as well as separated.

Rules abound because distrust between the governing authorities is prevalent. Rules also abound, ironically, because Congress, among its other traits, tends to be hyperresponsive to its varied constituencies and often seeks to write protective details or earmarks into legislation. Finally, rules abound because of the importance of the courts in the United States and the supposition on the part of all the actors, but certainly the agencies, that whatever they do may wind up being contested in court. The American bureaucracy is rule-driven, in part because the reins are not held exclusively by any single authority. The fragmentation of authority makes accountability important but inherently incomplete; it makes control and responsiveness incomplete because no set of authorities is in a position to exert full control or to have the bureaucracy be exclusively responsive to them. These are old truths of American government. And like the system of government in which the bureaucracy is situated, accountability and responsiveness have traditionally been regarded as more important virtues than efficiency.

Majority Party Government—The British System

Unlike the convoluted American system, the British or Westminster system of government is a paragon of simplicity. In theory at least, the question of "who is boss" is answerable, unlike the situation in the United States. Without the presence of a written constitution as well, the accountability problem seems to be solved. There are no conflicting authorities with distinctive claims on the bureaucracy.

Other complications, however, beset the relationship between bureaucracy and political authority even in such seemingly straightforward conditions as those present under the Westminster system of government. The first has to do with the clear alternation of authority when party control of Parliament changes—which it has not done, as we write, for seventeen years. The Westminster system of majority party government is susceptible to radical shifts in policy when governments change along party lines. The absence of a third party to modulate those swings, such as the Free Democrats (FDP) in Germany since 1969, has often made for stop-and-start government. If governments do alternate with some regularity, the bureaucracy may experience precious little of the continuity for which it is to be a repository.

Moreover, the inevitable problem of maintaining vastly different courses of policy is likely to set any bureaucrat's gyroscope awry. In view of the possibility of relatively sudden shifts, bureaucrats are apt to become skilled practitioners of shaping policies in more moderate ways so that they may be acceptable with amendment to the next government. On the one hand, sculpting the details and translating politicians' soaring goals into plausible programs is one of the invaluable services that skilled bureaucrats play in modern governments. On the other hand, the belief—prevalent during the Thatcher government—that civil servants should be enthusiastic about the program of the government, whatever the government, makes nuance and subtlety difficult. Bureaucrats maintain the appearance of neutrality and generate continuity not by bursts of enthusiasm for programs but by making it appear that they can live with any government's programs, secure in the knowledge that they will have the opportunity to mold them through means more subtle than those employed in party manifestos and political speeches.

This, of course, leads to the responsiveness problem captured by the BBC television show, *Yes, Minister,* in which the bumbling minister is in fact the agent of his civil servant adviser. In real life, ministers, like full-time politicians elsewhere, tend to possess major attention deficits. The job is demanding, and dependence upon senior civil servants is considerable. No doubt, civil servants everywhere seek to persuade or manipulate their political superiors toward their own perspective of what it is possible to do. But some are better positioned than others to do just that. In Britain, ministers themselves have relatively fewer resources and less experience than in many other Western systems; in contrast to their French or German counterparts, for example, none have had a career in the civil service. In Britain, where the cult of cleverness has reigned, civil servants have benefited less by being experts reeling off lists of statistics (as their U.S. counterparts might) than by being shrewd all-around actors.

Thus, despite structural predispositions in the British system of majority party government to remove the ambiguities that surround the issues of accountability, control, and responsiveness, what really occurs is that these problems, especially those of control and responsiveness, take on new forms. While these issues are not as complex or as problematic as in the United States, they certainly are not eliminated—and, perhaps, never can be.

It is difficult to know whether the British civil service has performed better than its American counterparts. The concept of performance is laden with ambiguity and has a highly subjective component. In addition, the performance of the bureaucracy is often viewed as part of the broader performance of government, which in turn is often a function of macroeconomic performance. Whether a well-honed bureaucracy actually creates the conditions for excellent or poor macroeconomic performance is another matter. Whether real or mythological—and we suspect mostly the latter—the policy role of the civil service in Japan, and for that matter in France, has at times been credited with providing the basis for effective economic performance. There is finally a differentiation between the arenas in which various bureaucracies may excel. The British civil service, until recently, has disdained management in favor of policy influence. The U.S. system emphasizes far more the role of technical expertise and proficient management (even while the political system makes the latter virtually impossible) and far less the role of policy advice.

In the end, it is extremely difficult to separate the performance of the bureaucracy from that of the political system itself unless, of course, the bureaucracy enjoys a level of autonomy that gives it a privileged position above politics. Ultimately, however, it is important to remember that even this privileged position has been granted by politicians. Nonetheless, simplicity of authority structures encourages intimacy between political authorities and civil servants; complexity discourages it. Put differently, it is not surprising that the bureaucracy plays the advisory role that it does in Westminster-style systems, most pristinely exemplified by the United Kingdom. It would be surprising were it to do so under normal conditions in the United States. The American system, however, more frequently taps other sources of advice outside of government, such as think tanks and professional policy experts. But even if these sources are more expert, they are often perceived as less neutral.

Structure is by no means a determinant of these outcomes. Rather, it represents a predisposition. Traditions and culture are vitally important and so too is the commingling of bureaucratic and political careers among a nation's governing elite. There is no doubt that the status of the civil service lends an aura to its performance, but it is important to remember that the two are not the same. A lesser-status bureaucracy may perform well but will be more limited in its range of opportunities than a bureaucracy of higher status. The origins of the status of public bureaucracy, however, are deeply woven into the developmental fabric of societies (Armstrong 1973).

Political Fragmentation and Bureaucracy in Parliamentary Systems

Majority party government is a rare outcome in parliamentary systems; fragmented politics is more common. Most frequently, fragmentation flows from coalition government, which typically results from proportional representation voting. The more pure the proportional representation system, the greater the number of parties that arise (Rae 1967).

Fragmentation is reflected most frequently but not exclusively in multiparty coalition governments. Governments in Italy over the last thirty-plus years (since the inclusion of the Socialists in 1962) and the French government of the Fourth Republic were coalition governments, yet each had different patterns of bureaucratic performance. The bureaucracy of the French Fourth Republic was given considerable authority by default and used it to generate a number of developmental projects associated with the successor regime (Wright 1974; Ashford). By contrast, the Italian bureaucracy evinced a pattern of political penetration and patronage (reflecting the traditional terms for joining governing coalitions) such that entrepreneurial developmental initiatives have had to circumvent the ministerial bureaucracies (Sbragia 1979).

The structural condition of political fragmentation certainly should lead to fragmented control of the bureaucracy and particularized responsiveness. Nonetheless, the actual performance of the bureaucracy does not appear to be significantly determined by the nature of political structures. When the bureaucracy has achieved an independent status, political fragmentation does not seem to have raised hurdles to its role in advancing policy innovations. Such seems to have been the case with the Fourth Republic. When the bureaucracy is tethered to political patrons, however, as had been the case through successive postwar Italian governments, it is likely to act only in the interests of those patrons. The important point here is that political fragmentation and fragile regimes are indeterminate in accounting for bureaucratic performance. The real explanations for performance necessarily lie beyond these conditions.

Factionalized politics often tends to characterize hegemonic governments led by a dominant single party. In the Italian case, the factionalization of the ruling Christian Democratic Party (DCI) of pre-1962 postwar governments continued unabated after the opening to the left brought forth multiparty coalition governments. Factionalization across all parties penetrated the bureaucracy with patronage networks reaching out from Rome. Who were the relevant patrons and clients? Responsiveness to political patrons was high but accountability to the government as a whole or to the rule of law was low. Performance suffered to the extent that the bureaucracy became a tool of political party bosses, loyal only to its varied political patrons, remote from citizens, and an object of popular derision.

Addressing the ills of the Italian government almost always begins with an inquiry into the state of its bureaucracy, though the state of the Italian bureaucracy is itself attributable to, while also contributing toward, the country's poor political performance. To be fair, whatever the dysfunctions of the Italian government, they have been accompanied incidentally by generally impressive economic performance. This outcome, whatever else one concludes, should induce modesty among political reformers.

The hegemony of a single party lasted much longer in Japan than in Italy, which despite a brief hiatus, was soon reinstated. Like the Italian parties, those in Japan are highly factionalized. The factions are sufficiently formalized that, at least during the long hegemony of the Liberal Democratic Party (LDP), the factions were clearly recognized by the party: their leaders occupying offices situated in the LDP headquarters. Despite the high degree of factionalization that has persisted within the traditional Japanese ruling party, the reputed performance of the bureaucracy has been considerably different than in Italy. Indeed, the Japanese bureaucracy has been given much credit for steering the country to its miraculous postwar economic prosperity (Muramatsu and Krauss 1984: 126–46). The Japanese civil service has been invested with great prestige and policy influence. Factionalization or politicization has apparently left untouched the key ministries such as Finance (MOF) and International Trade and Industry (MITI). But the pork-barrel ministries (Transportation, for example) appear to have greater political interference in their operations (Aberbach, Krauss, Muramatsu, and Rockman 1990: 475–80).

Parliamentary systems per se do not produce greater accountability, responsiveness, or better performance from the bureaucracy than do presidential systems. Nor does the extent to which the governing elites are fragmented or factionalized seem to directly affect the quality or responsiveness of the bureaucracy, although it does seem to cloud the accountability issue. Fragmentation and factionalization provide opportunities for political colonization of the bureaucracy, but these same conditions can also allow initiatives and leadership to default to an inventive bureaucracy. How the bureaucracy responds and the extent to which it is politically penetrated or independent are outcomes generated more by developmental forces than by institutional structures.

Another Presidential System—The Case of the French Fifth Republic

Unlike the American case, the Fifth Republic of France contains both parliamentary and presidential elements. Yet, the French legislature is weak and the French president powerful. The president's ability to dissolve parliament, among other things, makes his office unusually strong. Typically, but not always, the president and the parliamentary majority come from the same party bloc. In the early 1990s, as well as from 1986 to 1988, the presidency was held by the left while the government was in the hands of the right. Under such circumstances, the Fifth Republic resembles a divided government much like that which has frequently prevailed over the last four decades in the United States. Most of the time, however, the constituted powers of the French president give the system a remarkable unity in comparison with its predecessor regime or, for that matter, nearly all other democratic regimes. One scholar observes that the most internally powerful democratically elected leader is the French president, while the British prime minister runs second (King 1993: 446–48).

This unity of regime (when it is unified) makes for enhanced accountability and probably enhanced overall responsiveness too. When political authority is unified, the bureaucracy is more likely to be subordinated to it. Of course, the illusion of political unity is always greater than its reality. On a daily basis, relations between politicians and bureaucrats are mostly segmented. A favorite saying of an American politician, the late Speaker of the U.S. House of Representatives, Thomas P. O'Neill, was that all politics is local. Not only was he right about that, the observation may hold for administration as well. Abstractions such as "the bureaucracy" and "the government" boil down on a daily basis to particular relationships between individual politicians and individual civil servants.

Still, when power is unified, the bureaucracy may be both harnessed to political authority at a systemwide level and entrusted with the mission of providing policy advice at high levels. These are the conditions that obtain in the British model. Yet, the French system is by no means a purely parliamentary one. In fact, it can be reasonably argued that under most circumstances the driving force in the system is the president. Structurally, in other words, France and Britain do not differ all that greatly despite the fact that one is a hybrid presidential system and the other a parliamentary one. In each case, accountability and control when defined in relation to superior office are enhanced, as is responsiveness. The greater integration between politics and bureaucracy that exists in France than in Britain likely increases the capability for control by French ministers. After all, the model career pattern of French ministers is through the civil service (Birnbaum 1981: 65–71; Suleiman 1978: 95–108). Unlike their British counterparts, French ministers are not members of parliament. They can devote more attention to ministerial issues and may have more substantive knowledge of those issues than do British cabinet members.

Accounting for bureaucratic performance is likely to lead primarily to factors that are exogenous to structure. The early professionalization of the French civil service and its role in developing the state (leading back to the reign of Louis XIV) certainly contributed to its present prestige and expansive role as servant of the state. The myth of *l'état* in France and the role of the higher civil service in building it generates considerable leeway for the bureaucracy. The British system has emphasized the role of the clever and shrewd adviser with sensitive political antennae. The French system emphasizes all-around political astuteness as well, mixed, however, with doses of technical training, especially in economic matters. One bureaucracy has been adept at restraining politicians from the excesses of their passions; the other has been skilled at guiding politicians to envision future possibilities.

The Structure of Political Authority—Lessons

The unification of political authority strengthens the bureaucracy because, in the main, it also strengthens and concentrates the sources of political authority, thus combating parochialism. But the relative unity or diffusion of political authority crosses the traditional boundaries of parliamentary and presidential systems. Some parliamentary systems wind up fragmenting power at least as much, and perhaps more than, the U.S. separation-of-powers system. At least one other presidential system—the French—winds up concentrating power more than most parliamentary systems do. The fact is that the performance of bureaucracy is remarkably varied across systems exhibiting different formal and informal arrangements of political authority. The search for what makes bureaucracy accountable, responsive, and effective may begin, but cannot end, with political structures.

Despite the obvious variability of developmental processes that influence the role of a nation's bureaucracy and its prestige, status, and autonomy, we can conclude that Luther Gulick (1937: 10) was at least partially correct when he analogized the separation of powers to a condition of a slave having two masters. Under a separation-of-powers system, no authority is likely to consider itself the master of the bureaucratic machinery. Competition to control bureaucratic turf can be fierce (Aberbach and Rockman 1976; Moe 1985, 1990). As a result, accountability and responsiveness are always likely to seem incomplete. To the political authorities, especially when they hold different policy views, that is likely to be an unsatisfactory condition—and it is likely to lead to a relative absence of confidence in the bureaucracy above and beyond that which cultural predispositions might predict.

Does this mean that the separation-of-powers system is lacking in the expertise that bureaucracies can provide in settings of more concentrated power? In one sense at least, probably not. The U.S. bureaucracy does not have the monopoly of expertise that gives it dramatically superior resources to those available to politicians. Rather, the bureaucracy itself is merely one supplier of ideas in an environment rife with policy ideas, neutral and partisan. Think tanks supply much of the debate. Academicians in universities are intimately involved with the civic culture to an extent that is rare elsewhere. Congressional and White House staffs are both thick in number and in policy creativity. There is simply no shortage of ideas to feed American public policy. The emphasis on accessibility applies not simply to the bureaucracy but to the political system as a whole, meaning that the bureaucracy is but one supplier in a veritable marketplace of ideas. Where power is diffused, there is incentive to create external sources of knowledge and expertise, such as those just mentioned. As a general observation, and with tremendous variation in pace and degree, all democratic societies have generated more sources of competitive policy expertise outside of the traditional state bureaucracy. But there is no doubt that the United States is foremost among these. The absence of a highly protected and prestigious bureaucracy has hardly led to an equivalent absence of policy ideas and analyses. Of these, there is a rich abundance.

The lack of insulation around the bureaucracy, however, makes it less likely that policy ideas will have a chance to develop slowly through experimentation and evolution. Whatever liabilities of imagination are incurred by the bureaucratic incubation of policy, these are likely to be offset by the virtues of patience, vetting, and evolutionary development. A multitude of ideas now flows into the public agenda from many directions. America, the land of instant coffee, also has bred instant ideas, highly and immediately exposed to public scrutiny. The influence of the bureaucracy is thus limited by the clash around it.

There can be little doubt that bureaucracy functions best in the midst of consensus and is likely to become a source of controversy when the policies or proposals of governments are themselves controversial. In Britain, the policies of the Thatcher government were frequently surrounded by great controversy, though there was little doubt that the government could carry them out. In the United States, the equally controversial proposals of the Reagan administration fared less well. Many more of Reagan's proposals than of Thatcher's were rejected. The quest to control the bureaucracy and to make it as responsive as possible to the executive authorities was greater in the United States than in the United Kingdom because control and responsiveness to presidential administrations is only one part of the accountability and responsiveness puzzle in American government. In the long term, however, a bureaucracy that is associated with unpopular or controversial policies, regardless of the system of government in which it operates, will have its stature diminished, and that may be the key to how we measure its performance.

References

Aberbach, Joel D., Ellis S. Krauss, Michio Muramatsu, and Bert A. Rockman. 1990."Comparing Japanese and American Administrative Elites." *British Journal of Political Science* 20 (October): 461–88.

Aberbach, Joel D., Robert D. Putnam, and Bert A. Rockman. 1981. *Bureaucrats and Politicians in Western Democracies.* Cambridge: Harvard University Press.

Aberbach, Joel D., and Bert A. Rockman. 1976. "Clashing Beliefs within the Executive Branch: The Nixon Administration Bureaucracy." *American Political Science Review* 70 (June): 456–68.

———. 1985. *The Administrative State in Industrialized Democracies.* Washington, D.C.: American Political Science Association.

———. 1990. "From Nixon's Problem to Reagan's Achievement: The Federal Executive Re-examined." In *Looking Back on the Reagan Presidency*, edited by Larry Berman. Baltimore: Johns Hopkins University Press.

———. 1994. "Civil Servants and Policymakers: Neutral or Responsive Competence?" *Governance* 7 (October): 461–69.

Anton, Thomas J. 1980. *Administered Politics: Elite Political Culture in Sweden.* Boston: Martinus Nijhoff.

Armstrong, John A. 1973. *The European Administrative Elite*. Princeton: Princeton University Press.

Ashford, Douglas E. *Social Democratic Visions: Interpreting the Postwar Welfare States.* Unpublished manuscript.

Birnbaum, Pierre. 1981. *The Heights of Power: An Essay on the Power Elite in France.* Chicago: University of Chicago Press.

Cain, Bruce, John Ferejohn, and Morris Fiorina. 1987. *The Personal Vote: Constituency Service and Electoral Independence.* Cambridge: Harvard University Press.

Cronin, Thomas E. 1980. *The State of the Presidency.* 2d ed. Boston: Little, Brown.

Finer, Herman. 1941. "Administrative Responsibility in Democratic Government." *Public Administration Review* 1 (summer): 335–50.

Friedrich, Carl J. 1940. "Public Policy and the Nature of Administrative Responsibility." *Public Policy* 1: 3–24.

Gilbert, Charles E. 1959. "The Framework of Administrative Responsibility." *Journal of Politics* 21 (August): 373–407.

Goodsell, Charles T. 1981. "Looking Once Again at Human Service Bureaucracy." *Journal of Politics* 43 (August): 763–78.

Gulick, Luther. 1937. "Notes on the Theory of Organization. " In *Papers on the Science of Administration*, edited by Luther Gulick and L. Urwick. New York: Columbia University Institute of Public Administration.

Jones, Charles O. 1992. "The American Presidency: A Separationist Perspective." Paper presented at the Conference on Presidential Institutions and Democratic Politics, Pittsburgh.

Kahn, Robert L., Barbara A. Gutek, Eugenia Barton, and Daniel Katz. 1986. "Americans Love Their Bureaucrats. " In *Bureaucratic Power in National Policymaking*, edited by Francis E. Rourke. 4th ed. Boston: Little, Brown.

Kernell, Samuel, ed. 1991. *Parallel Politics: Economic Policymaking in Japan and the United States.* Washington, D.C.: Brookings Institution.

King, Anthony. 1993. "Foundations of Power." In *Researching the Presidency: Vital Questions, New Approaches*, edited by George C. Edwards III, John H. Kessel, and Bert A. Rockman. Pittsburgh: University of Pittsburgh Press.

Lynch, Edward J. 1990. "Politics, Nonpartisanship, and the Public Service." *Public Interest* 98: 118–32.

Melnick, R. Shep. 1994. *Between the Lines: Interpreting Welfare Rights.* Washington, D.C.: Brookings Institution.

Moe, Ronald C. 1994. "The 'Reinventing Government' Exercise: Misinterpreting the Problem, Misjudging the Consequences." *Public Administration Review* 54 (March/April): 111–22.

Moe, Terry M. 1985. "The Politicized Presidency." In *The New Direction in American Politics*, edited by John E. Chubb and Paul E. Peterson. Washington, D.C.: Brookings Institution.

———. 1990. "The Politics of Structural Choice: Toward a Theory of Public Bureaucracy." In *Organization Theory: From Chester Barnard to the Present and Beyond*, edited by Oliver E. Williamson. New York: Oxford University Press.

Muramatsu, Michio, and Ellis Krauss. 1984. "Bureaucrats and Politicians in Policymaking: The Case of Japan." *American Political Science Review* 78 (March): 126–46.

Polsby, Nelson W. 1981. "The Washington Community, 1960–80." In *The New Congress*, edited by Thomas E. Mann and Norman J. Ornstein. Washington, D.C.: American Enterprise Institute.

Rae, Douglas. 1967. *The Political Consequences of Electoral Laws.* New Haven: Yale University Press.

Sbragia, Alberta. 1979. "Not All Roads Lead to Rome: Local Housing Policy in the Unitary Italian State." *British Journal of Political Science* 9 (July): 315–39.

Suleiman, Ezra N. 1974. *Politics, Power, and Bureaucracy in France: The Administrative Elite.* Princeton: Princeton University Press.

———. 1978. *Elites in French Society: The Politics of Survival.* Princeton: Princeton University Press.

Tsebelis, George. 1995. "Decision Making in Political Systems: Veto Players in Presidentialism, Parliamentarism, Multicameralism, and Multipartyism." *British Journal of Political Science* 25 (July): 289–326.

Weaver, R. Kent, and Bert A. Rockman, eds. 1993. *Do Institutions Matter? Governing Capabilities in the United States and Abroad.* Washington, D.C.: Brookings Institution.

Wilson, Graham K. 1993. "'Next Steps for the British State: The Significance of Reform." Paper presented at the Conference on the Changing Role of the State in Comparative Perspective, Chiang Mai, Thailand.

Wilson, James Q. 1989. *Bureaucracy: What Government Agencies Do and Why They Do It.* New York: Basic Books.

Wright, Vincent. 1974. "Politics and Administration under the French Fifth Republic." *Political Studies* 22 (March): 44–65.

5

Bureaucracy and Viable Constitutionalism

FRED W. RIGGS

The Systemic Perspective

Viable constitutional democracies have two major components: a representative system focused on an elected assembly, and an administrative system organized as a bureaucracy. The former is needed to assure political responsibility and the latter, managerial capability. A politically responsive government that cannot manage public policies effectively soon discredits itself and loses credibility, becoming nonviable for administrative reasons. Similarly, an effective governmental regime that is not politically responsive becomes, in fact, authoritarian and oppressive. A head of government who is both politically responsive and managerially effective is needed to provide a bridge or linkage mechanism between the representative and bureaucratic organs of government.

I have examined the representative and executive components of viable constitutional democracy elsewhere (Riggs 1994a). A theoretical discussion of the balance between polyarchic (representative) and hierarchic (bureaucratic) substructures found in all modern organizations, both governmental and nongovernmental, can be found in Riggs 1995b, where the concepts found here have also been summarized.

In this chapter, by contrast, I focus on the bureaucratic aspects of this equation, considering the political and the administrative functions of appointed public officials in their reciprocal interdependence. We confront a kind of double bind, or Scylla versus Charybdis dilemma: Without enough power bureaucrats cannot administer effectively, but with too much power, they endanger the viability of representative institutions. In the classic myth, Charybdis was a whirlpool or black hole that liquidated its victims, whereas Scylla was a monster or nymph who swallowed (or charmed) its victims. To extend the metaphor, powerless bureaucrats have been dissolved by a political Charybdis, whereas dominant officials smack of a transfigured Scylla.

Without pressing the analogy too far, consider its reverse image: For viable constitutional democracy to survive, its elected officials need to be able to keep the state bureaucracy under effective control. However, these officials must also permit their bureaucrats to exercise enough power—based on expertise and experience—to be able to administer public policies effectively, to share in formulating policies to cope with the increasingly complex problems of postindustrial societies. The representative system, therefore, also needs to steer a middle course between Charybdis and Scylla.

In order to see how these reciprocal aspects affect each other, we need to look at two aspects of any system of governance, the internal and the external. The external aspect of any bureaucracy is its political context—the rules and structures that impose accountability and that constrain bureaucrats to work in a responsible and efficient way. The internal aspect includes all the practices and features involved in recruiting, maintaining, and motivating bureaucrats in their day-to-day operations.

A comparative perspective on both the internal and external aspects of bureaucratic performance would be needed to understand all the major variables determining the viability of constitutional democracies. It would also be useful to cover other factors affecting the outcome, including the social, economic, and cultural features of any society and the international pressures that impinge upon it. Moreover, the time and space (historical and geographical) aspects of any such system should also be considered.

Unfortunately, it is not possible to discuss all of these factors here. We must give priority to the political context and internal arrangements of any bureaucracy because they have not yet been adequately studied and because they provide the framework needed to understand all the aforementioned variables. In the rest of this chapter, I will look first at the political context and then at the internal arrangements of any bureaucracy as the most decisive factors affecting its behavior and influencing the delicate balance of power between it and elected officials.

The Political Context

The political context of any bureaucracy includes all the structures of power that determine how and to what extent a bureaucracy is controlled by the holders of sovereign authority. In a constitutional democracy, these are the elected representatives of the people, as found in legislative bodies and, in some regimes, an elected chief executive (president) or a dominant political party. In traditional polities, hereditary monarchs often held this authority. Unfortunately, in too many contemporary polities, sovereign authority has been usurped by appointed officials under the leadership of military officers or an autocrat. In any comprehensive treatment of this subject, we need to take all these possibilities into account. Collectively, they enable bureaucracies to exercise a wide range of variability in the degree to which they hold real power, and the effectiveness of their administrative performance.

The Variability of Bureaucratic Power

In a much quoted sentence, Max Weber wrote, "Under normal conditions, the power position of a fully developed bureaucracy is always overpowering" (Weber 1946: 232). Probably, Weber could not have explained the "abnormal" conditions under which bureaucrats actually dominate a polity, nor those in which they are powerless, because, historically speaking, both extremes manifested themselves only after he wrote. Bureaucrats today often constitute a ruling class in countries where military groups, with the support of civil servants, have seized power by means of a coup d'état. The revolt by appointed officials against the absolutism of the king of Siam in 1932 was certainly one of the first good examples of such a bureaucratic polity—it took place over a decade after Weber's death in 1920. By contrast, bureaucrats are politically weakest when a dominant single party holds power. Although such a regime first appeared in 1917 with the Bolshevik Revolution in Russia, its capacity to dominate the bureaucracy only gradually evolved subsequently.

What Weber had in mind was what he called "modern" officialdom, an administrative system based on "fixed and official jurisdictional areas," the performance of "official duties," hierarchic authority, reliance on written documents, expert training, full-time work, and the observance of general rules (Weber 1946: 196–98). The word "modern" is questionable here: Officials have been appointed by governments for thousands of years and in some cases, as in the mandarinate of Imperial China, the basic Weberian principles were well established centuries ago. Although the mandarin system has been widely adopted in many contemporary democracies, it is not distinctively "modern" (Riggs 1994b, and 1994c: 102).

Many contemporary bureaucracies do not manifest all the behavioral characteristics Weber described. Since many writers equate bureaucracy with the criteria included in Weber's ideal type, we need a distinctive term to identify it as a particular kind of bureaucratic system. We might call it Weberian bureaucracy. However, a more distinctive term would be a mandarinate, because that is almost exactly what Weber had in mind.

However, if we are going to understand the political role played by bureaucrats throughout the world today, we need to consider several types of bureaucracy that are not mandarinates. This includes the truly exceptional type of bureaucracy that has evolved in the United States, and also the bureaucracies in virtually all other presidential regimes where, as I will try to show, a real mandarinate would inevitably become so powerful that it would dominate the state. Consequently, only nonmandarin bureaucracies are compatible with the maintenance of democracy in presidentialist regimes. There are two important kinds of nonmandarin bureaucracies—including retainers and functionaries—which are discussed in detail below.

We need to develop a prior understanding of why bureaucratic power in its various forms is not a focus of systematic comparative study in contemporary political science or public administration. The subject falls between the range of attention of both of these fields.

When political scientists think about ruling groups in contemporary societies they focus on elected politicians—as found in legislatures, cabinets, and elected chief executives—largely disregarding appointed officials. Exceptionally, they sometimes focus on military officers as though they were not also appointed officials—that is, "bureaucrats." Some political scientists also focus on the top echelon of appointed officials—those whose primary functions involve policy formation and advice giving, notably the "superbureaucrats" in parliamentary systems, or cabinet members and their transient advisers in presidential regimes (Aberbach, Putnam, and Rockman 1981; Campbell 1986; Campbell and Szablowski 1979; Heclo 1977; and Pfiffner 1991).[1]

Some political scientists and sociologists also pay attention to the exercise of power by the nongovernmental elite, especially business entrepreneurs and industrialists, professionals, journalists, and church leaders, while many Marxist writers focus on the "bourgeoisie": if they speak of "bureaucrats," it may be in the context of their "class" interests as members of the middle class.

By contrast to political science, where the exercise of power by nonbureaucrats takes center stage, the field of public administration tends to focus on the managerial (i.e., nonpolitical) and routine functions of appointed officials as public servants. In some countries, undoubtedly, bureaucrats are powerless and most low-status appointed officials everywhere have little or no power. However, this bias is unfortunate because it not only neglects one of the most important institutional foundations for the exercise of power in contemporary societies, but it also unnecessarily handicaps our understanding of administrative problems. In fact, high-ranking bureaucrats (military and civil) often exercise great influence within a state, and sometimes constitute the dominant ruling group. In any comparative study of political systems we need to take into account the political roles played by bureaucrats.

Bureaucratic Powerlessness

To set the stage for a discussion of bureaucratic power, we might well begin by looking at the negative case, the Charybdis of powerlessness found under single-party domination. Illuminating insights into such a system can be found in Fainsod 1958, reprinted in 1963. Because of the blanket of secrecy thrown over the operations of the Soviet bureaucracy by the Communist Party, we know very little about how it really worked. However, captured archives from the Smolensk oblast give us a rare peek inside this hidden world. What appears clearly enough is that party officers infiltrated every branch of the government bureaucracy to observe its activities, report deviations, and bring prompt and drastic punishment for offenders.

Bureaucratic submissiveness was the result, although sometimes it led to local conspiracies known as family circles (Fainsod [1958], 1963: 85), which engaged in antiparty plots to make life easier for their members by sabotaging official plans. Such conspiracies ended badly when they were eventually exposed and their organizers were punished by brutal Stalinist methods. Remember that when the party came to power, it was necessary to sustain governmental operations by reliance on established czarist officials and institutions. Although new personnel gradually replaced the old, many of the holdover bureaucrats remained, creating a mood of deep suspicion and anxiety among party leaders. Ruthless measures used to maintain effective control of holdover imperial bureaucrats were perpetuated as normal.

Within Smolensk oblast, as the captured documents revealed, "The supreme power in the oblast was concentrated in the hand of the obkom bureau [composed mainly of party secretaries], and within the bureau there existed an interlocking directorate of Party and government" (Fainsod [1958], 1963: 93). The sharp distinction between party officers and government officials blurred as many individuals came to play roles in both of these parallel structures. Nevertheless, it is clear that, to use the more recent Chinese expression, the Reds prevailed over the experts. Engineers, accountants, teachers, and health workers all found that whenever the party line and the technical requirements of a task conflicted, the line would prevail.

I lack comparable data on other countries under Communist Party domination but I well remember a fleeting impression from the congress of the Eastern Region for Public Administration I attended in Beijing a few years ago. Many papers on Chinese public administration were presented, but I could not help feeling that most of them were written to please participants from other countries rather than to report with realism on existing problems and practices. However, during a free period, I had an opportunity to visit a government personnel information center at which we were proudly shown how modern computer technology was used. Full biographical information on every government official was being collected at the district level, funneled by computer to the provincial headquarters, and from there to Beijing. This meant that whenever any question about a particular bureaucrat anywhere in China—millions of them—was raised, it would be possible almost instantaneously to secure relevant background information on a computer screen. The oral reports and handwritten documents on which Soviet party officers had to rely in Smolensk had been replaced, in China, by an advanced technology that now permits secretaries of the Chinese central committee to oversee the performance of millions of government employees throughout a vast domain.

I have no direct knowledge of how that information is used, but my guess is that it serves not only to enhance public administration but also to assure compliance with party guidelines should any clashes arise between the needs felt by "experts" and the policies promulgated by party loyalists. Much more research would be needed to verify this hypothesis, but a single episode in the former Soviet Union throws some light on the question. In April 1991, a serious coup attempt failed despite the deep crisis into which the holdover Soviet party-based system had fallen. Military leaders and civil servants in other countries where similar types of political catastrophes occurred would almost surely have been able to take power. No doubt Boris Yeltsin's ability to rally resistance to the coup was, historically, an important factor. Nevertheless, his ability to fracture the forces supporting the coup reflected the essential weakness of the Soviet bureaucracy. However, following the collapse of the Communist Party, bureaucrats in Russia and other former Soviet republics are beginning to develop their own new foundations for exercising bureaucratic power.

Bureaucratic Domination

The capacity of military cabals, with the support of key civil servants, to destroy existing governments, suspend congresses, and revoke constitutional charters in many other countries provides evidence for the potential power of a bureaucracy. In any bureaucratic polity, the lack of a center of power outside the bureaucracy that has the capacity to monitor or discipline public officials when they violate laws or abuse their authority permits them to act irresponsibly. They may be corrupt, lazy, or incompetent, and they can enrich themselves by various means at the expense not only of their own peoples, but also of foreign powers and international organizations willing to provide economic and technical assistance to them.

Their inability to enforce public policies effectively—including the enforcement of tax laws—not only means that such regimes are chronically underfinanced but also administratively ineffective. Typically, this aggravates public anger and permits the rise of revolutionary movements designed to transform the regime. It also provokes ethnonational rebellions through which minority communities seek autonomy or independence (Riggs 1995a). Moreover, the prevalence of political anarchy enables illegal gangs or syndicates to flourish and enrich themselves, sometimes even in collusion with corrupt government officials. Frequently a group of younger military officers, smarting under these conditions and confident that they could govern more effectively (or more advantageously for themselves) conspires to seize power and stage follow-up coups. Consequently, bureaucratic polities are fragile and likely to be short-lived.

Ideally, bureaucrats in power should be able to see that the only way to solve the problems facing such regimes is to surrender power to a popularly based democratic and constitutional government. Sometimes, indeed, they are willing to do so, but more often bureaucratic domination leads to bad public administration and the corruption of anarchic-authoritarian (anarchian) quasi governments from which everyone involved ultimately suffers. Catastrophic results, often accompanied by much violence and bloodshed and the exodus of refugees, are more likely to provoke new coups and continued bureaucratic domination without creating viable constitutional democracies.

In short, both bureaucratic powerlessness and bureaucratic domination—the extreme opposites of each other—reflect and generate socioeconomic disasters. Their widespread existence in many countries may be understood as one of the untoward results of the collapse of modern empires, a process that had just begun when Max Weber was writing about bureaucratic power. Fortunately, in many countries, and especially in the industrialized democracies, both extremes have been avoided and we still find, as Weber did, bureaucracies that are indeed powerful but neither dominant nor submissive.

Degrees of Bureaucratic Power

Years ago Brian Chapman noted that the dividing line between "politics and administration" was largely fictional: Politics was used to characterize the somewhat dirty games of partisanship and electioneering, while policy had come to mean "nothing more than the political activity of civil servants" (Chapman 1959: 275) that is, what Americans would call *administration*. With important variations in style and structure, the same can be said of virtually all European bureaucracies. Similar remarks apply to Canada's "superbureaucrats," as Campbell and Szablowski characterize them (1979). Indeed, there is now an extensive literature on public bureaucracy that examines both the political impact and the administrative performance of appointed officials; for a good sampling of these writers see Farazmand (1991).

For the most part, however, this literature is more descriptive than analytical—it does not help us understand variations in the extent of bureaucratic power nor how these variations relate to the viability of democratic regimes. To accept Weber's conclusion that bureaucratic power is "overtowering" gives us no basis for assessing the relationship between different degrees of bureau power and the relevant properties of the regimes in which they exist. I make a distinction between "bureaucratic power" as the power of individual officials and "bureau power" as that of organized government agencies (Riggs 1993b). In order to make such an analysis, we need a vocabulary that can more precisely distinguish different degrees of power. To say that officials are more or less influential, dynamic, or forceful might characterize their roles more accurately than to say that they are simply powerful. As noted above, bureaucrats who dominate a bureaucratic polity are more powerful than "powerful." Appointed public officials who influence policymakers in many countries are powerful but not dominant.

Ironically, our vocabulary has no convenient terms for the intermediate levels of power between domination and submissiveness. We can easily speak of powerful or powerless, but how should we speak of intermediate degrees of semipower that, surely, are the norm for bureaucracies? They need to be powerful enough to administer effectively, and to utilize the expert knowledge and extensive experience they have acquired over years of training and administrative work; but at the same time, they need to be willing to accept the control and oversight that democratic governments can organize through institutions based on popular elections.[2] A semipowered posture may, indeed, be the requisite condition for any bureaucracy to achieve the delicate balance needed between the Scylla of domination and the Charybdis of powerlessness.

Bureaucrats must not become a ruling group, but neither should they become so dependent that they cannot use their own good judgment and experience when administering public policies. Students of government and the state need to recognize our complementary needs for political responsiveness and for effective public administration. This is a circular process: Ruling circles need to be responsible to the people whom they govern, and bureaucrats also need to be accountable to the institutions for political decision making. Ideally speaking, bureaucracies need to be semipowered, that is, strong enough to be capable of implementing complex policies that, typically, also provoke serious resistance, but also not so powerful that they dominate a polity, thereby encouraging all kinds of corruption and abuse of power.

The electorally based political institutions designed to legitimize public policies need to be capable of exercising effective control over public bureaucracies. The vigor and effectiveness of the elected officials whose institutions represent the citizens of a polity center themselves around an electoral and party system, an elected assembly (legislature), and a governing group, the president or prime minister in cabinet. This is the constitutive system of any modern government (Riggs 1969: 243–46).

The Internal Arrangements

This political context needs to be supplemented by an understanding of the internal arrangements of dissimilar bureaucracies—that is, the composition and prevailing rules of different kinds of administrative system. In this section, I shall talk only about those internal arrangements that affect the relative power position of public bureaucracies. Many related factors that determine their administrative or managerial performance are already well covered in the vast literature of public administration.

Mandarins

The overtowering position of modern bureaucracies Max Weber described is rooted primarily in the development of a mandarin or quasi-mandarin class of top administrators. This class can be found in many countries today, especially in the parliamentary regimes found in Western democracies. Much has been written about it already (Dogan 1975; Suleiman 1984; Aberbach, Putnam, and Rockman 1981) and it is unnecessary to comment on these and other such works. Rather, it is enough just to note the essential basis for their power and the depth of their historical antecedents.

Modern mandarins are, indeed, modern, but the historical roots of the mandarin system are ancient and traditional. We often forget that the Chinese were the first to establish a bureaucracy whose elite members were recruited by examinations oriented to classical, philosophical, literary, legal, or other components of a general education. Moreover, after having entered the government service, bureaucrats were given many opportunities, by rotation, to participate in governance at different levels and in various departments.

Although mandarin systems were well known in China and other traditional empires, Westerners were slow to learn about them.[3] Under strong centralizing monarchs, as in Prussia and in France, especially after the Napoleonic reforms, well-trained, elitist, and powerful public servants (i.e., mandarins) representing an administrative state rather than just a monarch and royal favorites, came into existence in Europe. The Napoleonic system "was one of nomination, not co-optation, and nomination could be effected by objective tests of merit. Pupils at the Ecole Polytechnique, for instance, from which came many of the most prominent administrators gained entrance on the strength of their intellectual merit in science and mathematics." The lure of appointments to the "highest posts in the state" attracted "not only the brightest of the middle class but also those members of the upper class who happened to be both ambitious and able" (Chapman 1959: 29). Gradually, throughout the nineteenth century, carefully trained and recruited public officials, typically with a generalist rather than a specialist orientation, came to prevail almost everywhere in Europe.

Mattei Dogan tells us that, "like their Chinese ancestors, these modern mandarins are cultivated and talented men. Very seldom are they technicians with purely scientific backgrounds" (Dogan 1975: 4). Quoting T. Anton, Dogan cites the Swedish case in which bureaucrats administer large and complex programs: "Their leaders have come to play an increasingly prominent role in national policy making. The bureaucracy is thus inherently political which means that, strictly speaking, it is silly to talk about an 'administrative' elite" (Dogan 1975: 5). Modern mandarins, therefore, are not only able administrators . . . but inherently capable of exercising great power. Only regimes whose popularly elected institutions are politically effective and well coordinated can maintain control over a mandarin bureaucracy. Weaker constitutive systems cannot sustain their mastery over a mandarinate indefinitely and they readily succumb to a coup d'état led by military officers.

Even in parliamentary regimes, top officials of the mandarinate are often viewed as the real power behind the throne. An interesting clue to the difference between the British and American conceptions of public administration arises from this fact. In England, "public administration" and "public policy" are virtually the same because top career administrators, as advisers to cabinet ministers, are able to manipulate top political decision makers. By contrast, their counterparts in the United States are transient appointees and their role as policy advisers is viewed as "political," whereas the role of career officials, working at a lower level, is viewed as essentially managerial, giving "administration" a nonpolitical character. This enables some specialists in America to claim public policy as a "political" process whereas in Europe it is more easily viewed as an "administrative" function.

Retainers

Since Weberian mandarinates developed in Europe really only during the nineteenth century and the Chinese antecedents of the system were muted—because of the ill repute into which Chinese governance had fallen after the Opium War—we need to be clear about the characteristics of premandarin European bureaucracies. For the most part, public officials had typically been patronage appointees, selected and appointed by monarchs who built a personal apparatus of government staffed by their friends and relatives, clients whom they trusted. It was always risky to wear a crown, and for most hereditary rulers being surrounded by dependable retainers was always more important than knowing that they were well qualified to serve.[4]

At the end of the eighteenth century, virtually all Western governments still relied exclusively on retainers to administer public affairs. Brian Chapman tells us that traditionally, in Europe, "the public services provided by the prince were administered on his behalf by officers of his own household. No clear distinction could be drawn between the private and public personalities of the monarch. His palace officials were in law and practice his personal servants [retainers]. Household officers of high standing such as the chancellor, the chamberlain, the marshal, doubled in the role of personal attendant and advisor on special aspects of public affairs" (Chapman 1959: 15).[5] Although they could not benefit from secure tenure, systematic rotation in office, or in-service training and regular promotion, many retainers became experienced and competent public officials.

Most parliamentary regimes, after they replaced autocratic with democratic institutions, also replaced retainers with mandarins. So successful were the reform movements that we have virtually forgotten about the existence and properties of a retainer bureaucracy. Nevertheless, they were important historically and they survive in almost all presidential regimes to the present day. During its first century, they also prevailed in the American bureaucracy; the framers of the Constitution assumed that all public officials would be retainers. This institution persisted in the United States until the rotation system became institutionalized under President Andrew Jackson after 1830. Actually, many officials were able to retain their posts after rotation had become entrenched.[6] Growing dissatisfaction with the abuses of the rotation system finally led to the introduction of a nonmandarin type of career service as authorized by the

Pendleton Act of 1883. Thus, for fully one half of its existence, the American government relied mainly on retainers, and some can still be found in secure niches of government service—primarily at the state and local levels. The mandarin system that virtually all other contemporary industrial democracies have institutionalized never gained a foothold in the United States.

Strangely, contemporary political science has little or nothing to say about retainers, and public administration, as a discipline, ignores or condemns them—in fact, it doesn't have a term for them. Nor, in fact, does it have a distinctive term to distinguish the exceptional type of career bureaucrat found in the United States from those that prevail in other polities. We can, however, find many works on mandarins as administrators in contemporary parliamentary governments (Dogan 1975; Aberbach, Putnam, and Rockman 1981; Chapman 1970; Suleiman 1984).

Mandarins have not replaced retainers in any of the older presidentialist regimes. Had they done so, they would soon have become politically dominant, creating bureaucratic polities without any need for a violent coup. Throughout the nineteenth century, the relatively weak representative systems found in all presidentialist regimes were able to retain control over their retainer bureaucracies.[7] However, during the twentieth century, these bureaucracies gained more and more power while their administrative performance declined in relation to the growing needs for effective management of public policies in an increasingly complex industrializing world. Writers on Latin America have emphasized these administrative deficiencies, but they have scarcely noted their underlying causes based on the continuance of retainerism.

Historians have, by contrast, recorded the decisive steps taken in the 1830s and 1883 to replace the retainer system in the United States. However, without a comparative context, they could not recognize how exceptional this experience was. Actually, throughout the Western Hemisphere, including the United States, retainers staffed all the public services when these successor states gained their independence.[8] Prior to the development of political parties, appointees were the relatives and friends of appointing officers. As parties emerged and began to gain power, partisanship became an increasingly important criterion but it has never replaced personal connections, which still remain a potent factor.

The most important question for retainers has always, I think, involved their security in public office. Could they count indefinitely on the income, security, and status that their positions conferred, or were they mere transients who had to worry about the occupations and income they would need after their public employment had been terminated? Clearly, able and intelligent transients would not passively await such a fate if they could prevent it. Accordingly, we may expect all retainers to organize, however secretly or informally, to prevent their eviction from public office and to take advantage of the opportunities it opened to them. The dynamics of this system, as found today in Brazil, are well captured in the following sentences quoted from Abdo Baaklini:

> The civil service is continuously preoccupied with playing musical chairs. Instead of professionalism that is encouraged, it is clientelism. Those who lose are not dismissed from their jobs; they remain lurking in the corners of the hallways, working to undermine whatever innovations the new administration is likely to introduce. Even those appointed from outside the bureaucracy find it appealing to remain even after their benefactors have left. The security and perks of a civil service job are irresistible in a country where the government dominates and controls the economy. Furthermore, by belonging to the bureaucracy, one changes places from being a victim of its actions to becoming a beneficiary of its largesse. (Baaklini 1992: 28–29)

No doubt the secrecy involved in such organization—whether or not it was illegal—would hamper research. I suspect, however, that the main reason so little has been written about retainers in public office arises simply from our lack of the concept and a good term for it. Even works on public administration in Latin American republics, where retainerism still prevails, ignore the subject. Much has been written about the abuse of public office, and the prevalence of corruption, incompetence, and laziness. All of these are, I think, predictable consequences of retainerism and ineffective or powerless institutional mechanisms for assuring bureaucratic accountability. The literature, however, ignores the source of these problems and looks, instead, at measures that will, supposedly, overcome the symptoms.[9]

When retainers feel seriously threatened, should we not expect them to organize to support radical action, even when it involves the violent overthrow of constitutional governments? No doubt initially and, assuredly, for a long time, organized retainers struggle to protect their security and income, to keep their posts in the public domain. So long as governments govern acceptably, there is no reason for retainers to do otherwise. They were disinclined to organize politically during the first forty years of the American democracy, and actually for the first century of virtually all the Latin American republics.

Domination of government by aristocratic elements and the prevalence of conservative political parties, plus their own social status as, for the most part, members of upper- or middle-class families, assured at least a moderate level of satisfaction by retainers. Moreover, although serious problems arose, they were by no means as complex and unsettling as the issues that have arisen in all these countries during the twentieth century. As these problems grew, so also did the size of the bureaucracy and its potential for exercising power.

One predictable consequence of retainer power in any bureaucracy is, surely, its disposition to resist reforms that would replace incumbents with newcomers recruited through a merit system based on the recruitment of well-trained people to occupy long-term career posts in public service, with guarantees of tenure, status, and income as rewards for good performance. New recruits to government service who enjoy the benefits of a merit system would quickly displace most retainers. Surely this explains why reformers have experienced serious obstacles in their efforts to accomplish administrative reforms by means of new civil service laws and training programs; entrenched retainers are simply powerful enough to sabotage such reforms or to render ineffectual any laws promulgating them.[10]

Another result of retainerism during the twentieth century can be attributed to the increasing complexity of life that has resulted from the industrial revolution, environmental pollution, population growth, social mobilization, deteriorating living conditions in the inner cities, increasing political pressure for social justice, and external costs imposed by modern imperialism, wars, and trade imbalances. In the face of all these and other complications attributable to modernity, bureaucratic roles have become increasingly demanding and the need for effective administrative performance has escalated. In this context, retainers who lack the requisite training and skills are unable to meet the needs of governance; as a result, crime, corruption, pollution, poverty, disease, and social disorders of all kinds tend to increase. Governments find that they need to make increasingly complex and costly decisions but lack the administrative resources needed to implement them. Popular discontent grows exponentially. Paradoxically, poor public administration and the power position of retainer bureaucracies are directly correlated—as administrative performance declines, the power potential of public officials increases.

Finally, in our times, bureaucratic revolts explode in coups that bring public bureaucracies to power. Their continuing insecurities are magnified by their own inability, as public administrators, to deal effectively and efficiently with the growing problems faced by all modern societies. Faced with calamities and growing public dissatisfaction—even with revolutionary movements, often directed explicitly against increasingly unpopular public officials—threatened and angry retainers have nevertheless been able to expand their informal organizational networks to unite in support of a coup.

Military Officers

In this connection, another widely held misperception contributes to our failure to recognize the bureaucratic basis for modern coups d'état. Almost universally, students of political conflict and revolutionary action have attributed coups to military officers, as though they were an independent force and not part of the public bureaucracy. All appointed officials are dependent on the state for their positions and the rewards they get from them.

Modern bureaucracies, by contrast with premodern ones, depend almost exclusively on salaries and various other perquisites of office for their support. By contrast, the stipends or prebends available to premodern bureaucrats were normally insufficient to support their recipients and they depended heavily, therefore, on external sources of income. These sources were, of course, considered legitimate and proper—they were not bribes and carried no connotations of public corruption.

All modern appointed public officials—military and civil—share a common interest in the maintenance of their salaries and perquisites (housing, uniforms, travel funds, food allowances, honors and status, etc.). When these are threatened, they have a shared reason to revolt. All too often their own failures in office—for example, corruption in tax and customs collection—undermine the fiscal basis for government and, thereby, contribute to the inadequacy of their own incomes. A vicious circle develops: The more a retainer bureaucracy expands and its members are underpaid, the more disgruntled and restive they become. They are already organized initially to protect their positions but, under pressure, they extend their power to control the government. According to Baaklini, under both authoritarian and liberal regimes in Brazil, efforts "to create a professional and efficient bureaucracy under acceptable political control" have all failed. Instead, "What had been created, especially since the Estado Novo, was a tenured, salaried, and interdependent bureaucracy at the helm of political power" (Baaklini 1992: 33).

When appointed officials cannot control the elected politicians or when serious crises arise, they can shift the focus of their activities to support a revolt. Any such revolt, carried out by violent means, requires the leadership of bureaucratic specialists in the use of violence: military officers who can command the support of obedient subordinates. However, no military group can run a country unaided—they also require the support of civil servants. If civil servants were, unitedly, to resist military rule, they could surely bring about its collapse. The fact, however, is that military ruling juntas establish cabinets through which to direct government agencies, and they typically include civil servants in addition to military officers. They are either members of the conspiratorial group that staged the coup, or technocrats coopted to help the new regime govern.

Once a ruling junta has been established, moreover, only the bravest and most independently minded civil servants will oppose them. The alternative to continuation of their careers is not only discharge or demotion but even worse punishments. Sometimes leading civil servants are referred to as technocrats, a term that implies specialists without a power base or organizational home.[11] In fact, I believe, all technocrats are, or become, civil servants whose specialized training and experience are valued by the leaders of any government, including both elected presidents and the military officers who play leading roles in a coup d'état. Less frequently, technocrats may be outsiders brought into the government from business or academic life—they may be "engineers" or "economists" or "diplomats," but these terms describe their professional skills, not the organizational context from which they are drawn and within which they have to work. Despite their efforts, however, any bureaucracy that is not under effective political control is almost certain to administer more corruptly and incompetently than it did before the coup. A bad situation will deteriorate. Under bureaucratic domination, public administration deteriorates and the overall condition of a country becomes worse than ever.

Functionists and Transients

The historical events that enabled the United States to institutionalize functionists as a special type of career-based, nonretainer and nonmandarin bureaucracy have contributed to the exceptional administrative capabilities of this type of public official while limiting their capacity to organize for political action. The simultaneous maintenance of transients as occupants of top-echelon key positions linked partisan loyalty with an inherent inability to coordinate efforts to support a "bureaucratic" interest. Their limited tenure in office compelled transients to think more about their job prospects after leaving government service than about how their temporary posts in government might be used to enhance their long-term security or power.

The term "transient" refers to a public employee who expects to leave his or her position after a few years—normally between two and three years in the U.S. government today. The word "spoils" has been loosely linked with transiency, but the term is not only pejorative, it is also misleading. President Andrew Jackson (1829–37) is falsely credited with starting the spoils system in the American bureaucracy; the truth is that he perpetuated the well-established system of making patronage appointments, so all the retainers in office in 1829 were already spoilsmen and women.

Jackson's real innovation was to convert many retainers to transients by discharging incumbents and replacing them with his own appointees: He introduced rotation and thereby institutionalized transience in public office. Spoils is a derogatory term for patronage appointees; it derives from the cliché that the right to make appointments is one of the "spoils of office." Consequently, both retainers and transients are beneficiaries of spoils (patronage). However, whereas the former expect to keep their jobs, the latter do not—and the former can organize to exercise power while the latter cannot.

Because transients in the United States are expected to leave public service after two to three years, they have neither the necessary time nor the motivation to collaborate with any organized effort to take power; Heclo (1977) aptly characterizes them as "a government of strangers." Because they are, indeed, strangers to each other, they also lack the mutual trust based on long-term acquaintance needed to establish powerful and dangerous informal organizations.

When Jackson became president, no one questioned his right to make patronage appointments. The issue, rather, was whether or how long political appointees could keep their posts. However, the retainers then in office had not organized themselves to resist any basic change like the rotation system, nor could they have anticipated its consequences. No doubt Jackson's new appointees also expected to become retainers, so no fundamental structural changes were expected.

In fact, however, subsequent presidents institutionalized the rotation system and transients learned that their careers ultimately depended as much on the arrangements they could make for employment in the private sector after leaving government service as it did on whatever they could do within the bureaucracy. They had little reason, therefore, to be interested in schemes to enhance their power as bureaucrats. Moreover, the fact that they knew they had only a short time in public office gave them an incentive to maximize their income by unrestrained corruption. Consider also that bribes offered by private companies and accepted by transient officials could pave the way for subsequent jobs in the private sector. In short, transients are inexperienced administrators, often corrupt, and also disinterested in bureaucratic power.

There is a substantial literature on the role and background of contemporary in-and-outers in American government (Heclo 1977; Mackenzie 1987), but not much discussion of their postpublic careers in the private sector, or of their inability to exercise bureaucratic power. Ever since the Jacksonian revolution, transients have filled thousands of top positions in the American bureaucracy, from the cabinet level on down. Their intrinsic inability to organize themselves to seize power, augmenting the political limitations of functionists in the bureaucracy, contrasts strikingly with the ability of any retainer-based bureaucracy to mobilize power.

In the short run, retainers are unable to organize effectively. In 1828, the relatively small number of retainers in the U.S. national government could not have realized how much rotation in office would undermine their potential for exercising power, giving them no reason to mobilize against the Jacksonian reforms. In the long run, elsewhere, retainers have acquired both the capacity and the motives to organize themselves informally to resist changes that undermine their privileges and also to resist both the rotation principle and the establishment of a career system. Moreover, in a crisis, they are able to seize power through a military coup and transform themselves into a dominant ruling class.

These facts help us understand why the transition from a retainer to a career bureaucracy is so difficult. Its unique occurrence in the United States can be accounted for by the historically extended two-stage sequence of its evolution. The first stage involved the introduction of transients and it paved the way for the second, the institutionalization of careerism, which could not have taken place without the first. American and other international efforts to promote one-stage transitions from retainerism to career bureaucracy, whether in the functionist or mandarin mode—as described in Ruffing-Hilliard 1991—could not succeed. Because both retainers and transients are patronage appointees, there is not much reason for entrenched retainers to resist the introduction of a rotation scheme—especially if they do not expect that many incumbents will be discharged to pave the way for new appointees. By contrast, career systems always pose a much greater threat to retainers because they mean substituting examinations and impartial merit criteria for the prevailing patronage system in making appointments.

Countervailing factors may also explain the lack of popular support for reforms that replace retainers with careerists. First, retainers often gain enough experience to be able to administer public policies reasonably well even though not expertly; and second, their long-term job outlook moderates their greed, reducing their efforts to make quick "profits" through corruption. By contrast, in the United States, the time limits imposed on a growing number of transients proved historically decisive. Not only were they blatantly corrupt, but they lacked enough time in office to become competent administrators or to organize themselves to exercise power. Were it not for the persistence in the bureaucracy of many retainers—sometimes referred to as workhorses—whose experience and dedication made them so indispensable that they were retained in office, the American administrative system would probably have collapsed during the mid–nineteenth century.

Although the persistence of workhorses in the American bureaucracy helped the system survive, it could scarcely overcome the growing hostility and alienation generated by the transients whose incompetence and corruption fueled a growing movement for administrative reform. This movement, after several false starts, led to the Pendleton Act in 1883 (Van Riper 1958; Hoogenboom 1961), which supported the uneven transition that eventually produced a large and distinctive new class of bureaucrats, the functionists.

The unintended consequence of introducing rotation in the American bureaucracy, therefore, was that by lowering the level of administrative efficiency and increasing the burdens imposed by widespread corruption, the basis was laid for a political movement that, after a half century, replaced most retainers with functionists, and reduced the number of transients to those who held politically sensitive or important positions. The new brand of career officials established by the Pendleton Act was not formed as a mandarinate. Instead, its distinctive features were those of functionists. The fact that their careers were, for the most part, anchored to a specific functional field of governance meant that functionists oriented themselves primarily to their own domain and its problems; they did not identify with the whole bureaucracy as mandarins so easily do. Moreover, the fact that top echelon posts in the U.S. bureaucracy remained in the hands of transients meant that careerists were rarely given opportunities to acquire an overview of the political system.

Why, one might ask, did the American administrative reformers not copy the British mandarin system that, in fact, provided the starting point for their efforts? As Van Riper (1958) and Hoogenboom (1961) have clearly shown, when members of Congress thought about the need for a career service in the American bureaucracy, they easily agreed that it should differ significantly from the British model in which administrative class officers were recruited primarily among graduates of the most prestigious universities—Oxford and Cambridge.[12] It was easy for them to see that, with such a system, graduates of the Ivy League colleges, concentrated on the Eastern seaboard, would monopolize positions of power and prestige in the American bureaucracy. To prevent such a result, they stipulated that the examinations must be practical, not classical or humanistic, and that recruits must be drawn equitably from all the states, not from just a few. Actually, the principle of geographical representation was already well recognized in the method of recruiting cadets for the military academies through reliance on nominations by members of Congress.

A new group of vocationally oriented state colleges funded by federal land grants had already been established and it provided an ideal educational basis for the pre-entry training of future civil servants and, later, of professionals. Another basic point in the legislation involved a system of "position classification" and open recruitment; it blocked the recruitment of young graduates to become members of a privileged administrative class, as in the British model. Instead, the legislation established the principle that the qualifications needed to perform a specific set of tasks would first be established, and then anyone, regardless of age, who had the requisite skills and knowledge could be appointed to the post where these qualifications would be needed.[13]

To sum up, both transients and retainers often lack the training and administrative expertise of career officials who have been recruited through a merit system. This helps explain why countries that still rely on retainers in public office have been increasingly unable to cope with complex modern problems. They then experience revolutionary discontent. Since these countries usually also have an inherently fragile presidentialist constitution that imposes a radical separation of powers between the executive and legislative branches of government, it is not surprising that they frequently experience military coups and the suspension of their constitutions and legislatures.

By contrast, the emergence of the functionist career services authorized by the Pendleton Act in the United States permitted an increasingly effective bureaucracy to emerge—one that could analyze and cope with many of the acute problems of a postindustrial era, but that could not effectively organize itself to exercise political power over the whole polity. This bureaucratic weakness was reinforced by two related factors: the retention of the rotation system for top-echelon partisan appointees, and the gradual emergence of professionalism.

Professionals

As the functionist bureaucratic system evolved, it became increasingly professionalized. Again, a conceptual distinction is needed: by "professional" I do not mean a career civil servant whose profession it is to perform administrative tasks as a government official. Rather, the word is used in a specialized sense to refer to the independent professions outside of government, such as law, medicine, engineering, agriculture, and economics. Moreover, the word also refers to the external orientation professionals bring with them when they enter the public service. This is the sense in which the word is used by James Wilson (1989). The criteria for pre-entry examinations set forth by the Pendleton Act, and the ambitions of the new state colleges that aspired to become full-fledged universities containing professional schools combined to support this development.

In America, many career officers (functionists) in government service came to see themselves as externally oriented "professionals" who happened to be working for the government rather than in private practice, private-sector organizations, or academic posts. The provision for open entry to classified positions also enhanced opportunities for professionals to become nonpartisan transients—to enter and leave the government service in response to changing opportunities. In short, they did not think of themselves as permanent government officials: their loyalty could often be split between their roles as professionals inside or outside of government.

Functionists in the U.S. bureaucracy specialize in restricted areas of expertise over long periods of time. Increasingly, functionists have become professionals—or, conversely, professionals in private practice have become bureaucrats. Thus, although the concepts of functionist and professional are distinctly different, in the American bureaucracy a growing number of bureaucrats are concurrently functionists and professionals. This not only inhibits them from participating in any pan-bureaucratic projects to gain power, but it also reduces their dependence on government jobs—they can typically take up private employment if, for any reason, they are disappointed with their life as public officials.[14]

The opposite side of this coin involves the relatively high capacity of career officials in the United States to administer well; certainly, by contrast with the retainers and transients whom they replaced, they have been better administrators. The main limitation of American public administration arises from this virtue. Precisely because they are functionally and professionally oriented, specialist bureaucrats cannot achieve the overview of interrelated problems that generalists—such as the mandarins found in most other modern democracies—can achieve. Although transients are sometimes charged with responsibility for such coordination, their very status as transients means that they tend to leave office just when they are beginning to master the complexities of their novel and demanding assignments. This serious handicap makes it almost impossible for the American bureaucracy to manage very complex programs that require close cooperation between a wide variety of public agencies; the long-standing failure to establish comprehensive health care (which mandarinates are able to manage quite well) may be seen as an example of this limitation.

Conclusion

The main focus of this chapter has been an analysis of how external context and internal arrangements affect the exercise of power by any public bureaucracy and its capacity to implement public policies. The capacity of bureaucrats both to administer policies and to exercise power are, I believe, intimately related to the viability of constitutional democracy, that is, whether or how regimes that are responsive to popular needs and demands can be administered well without surrendering power to appointed officials. In order to understand how to maintain such a Scylla/Charybdis balance, we need to understand also how ruling groups and elites are constituted in various political systems. We also need to remove the blinders that block our understanding of the fact that, among the various classes, castes, institutions, or groups whose interactions shape the distribution of power, one that is present in all contemporary governments and should always be taken into account is the public bureaucracy, including both its military and civil personnel.

This is not to say that bureaucracies are always powerful. Indeed, under exceptional circumstances, bureaucrats can be almost powerless. In countries dominated by a single party and a communist ideology, provided we do not think of party officials as part of the "bureaucracy," we can see that the ruling party is able to dominate economic enterprises, representative institutions, and the bureaucracy—which really means, of course, all salaried workers. In such regimes, the viability of the ruling party and its leadership is crucial for regime survival—and, no doubt, for the perpetuation of bureaucratic powerlessness. Shortly after the collapse of any single-party regime, I would expect a combined bureaucratic/party structure of power to emerge that may easily devour whatever new democratic institutions may be created.

By contrast, in countries whose representative institutions are fragile, especially when crippled by an institutionalized "separation of powers," the likelihood of bureaucratic domination is greatest. This is clearest where mandarin traditions preceded the creation of such regimes, as in South Korea, South Vietnam, and Nigeria. No doubt, in the older presidential regimes, mainly in Latin America, it was possible for representative institutions to maintain control over their retainer bureaucracies throughout the nineteenth century; but during the twentieth century, virtually all of them have succumbed to military coups. The only important exception is the United States, where, as noted above, a relatively weak form of bureaucracy based on a combination of functionists, professionals, transients, and retainers has permitted moderately successful public administration to coexist with an inherently fragile presidential (separation of powers), representative system.

By contrast, in the democratic governments whose elected leaders have been able to organize power most effectively (notably in parliamentary regimes where executive and legislative powers are fused in a cabinet), higher-level bureaucrats have played extremely influential roles while refraining from efforts to dominate the regime. Their ability to administer public policies reasonably well also contributes immensely to the success of these regimes, thereby undermining the support that potential rebels or revolutionaries need in order to succeed. These regimes have been able to maintain enough control over their mandarin bureaucracies to perpetuate constitutional governance, while preserving a level of administrative performance high enough to deal nonviolently with domestic crises. Clearly the linkages between political context and internal arrangements are complex. These linkages must be understood as a framework within which we can analyze and evaluate the additional impact of cultural, economic, and social forces, as influenced also by the external pressures and resources from neighboring countries and international organizations.

Notes

1. One American political scientist who studied the political role of appointed officials carefully was Charles S. Hyneman. He wrote, after spending an extended leave of absence from his university in government service, "Government has enormous power over us, and most of the acts of government are put into effect by the men and women who constitute the bureaucracy. It is in the power of these men and women to do us great injury, as it is in their power to advance our well-being. It is essential that they do what we want done, the way we want it done." The main message of Hyneman's book was to discover how the politically responsible organs of governance could, in fact, impose "direction and control" so that bureaucrats would be compelled "to conform to the wishes of the people as a whole whether they wish to do so or not" (Hyneman 1950: 38).

2. Traditional monarchies in which a small ruling group based on the inheritance of royal authority and its supernatural sanctions also faced acute problems in maintaining effective control over their state bureaucracies. I have offered some comments on the theme elsewhere (Riggs 1991, especially on 491–92 and accompanying notes). The Chinese experience is especially relevant and is described in Kracke 1953. Max Weber refers to the "constant struggle of the literati [bureaucracy] and sultanism [imperial power]." "Numerous literati," he wrote, "who took a stand against this form of absolutism had to give their lives in order to maintain their status group in power. But in the long run and again and again the literati won out" (Weber 1946: 442). For a discussion of comparable situations in other traditional empires see Carney 1971 and Eisenstadt 1963.

A major difference between modern and traditional mandarinates can be explained by their political contexts rather than their internal arrangements. Modern governments are able to mobilize vast monetary resources not available to traditional monarchies, giving them a far greater capacity to control appointed officials. The most notable difference involves the ability to pay salaries large enough to permit public employees to live on them. By contrast, even the Chinese mandarinate was essentially prebendary—mandarins had to supplement their meager stipends by income in the form of "gifts" from those who needed their services. The prebendary status of traditional mandarins made them relatively independent of the political authorities, whereas the salaried status of modern mandarins gives their governments far more effective instruments of control (Riggs 1994c: 102).

3. The British experience in India provided one bridge for the introduction of mandarinism to the West. How the British East India Company adapted the mandarin system—with which its officers working in Canton were quite familiar—to the needs of imperial control over a far-flung empire is described in Teng 1943, and how the

fundamental principles of the Indian Civil Service were introduced to English public administration is explained in Chapman 1970.

4. Because Chinese emperors had many wives and did not suffer the constraints imposed on European monarchs by formal monogamy, they needed a large personal staff and usually trusted eunuchs to serve as harem attendants. As the mandarin bureaucracy in China evolved, the imperial household often utilized some of these eunuchs to provide a countervailing power (together with the more important Censorate) to help assure the loyalty of the empire's vast mandarinate; this expedient sometimes failed when powerful eunuchs betrayed the trust of an emperor (Kracke 1953: 56). In Europe, even kings who notoriously had mistresses could not afford to institutionalize their status by appointing eunuchs to guard them.

5. The word retainer has rather quaint connotations suggesting an antiquated aristocratic system in which family retainers (from butlers and chefs to chambermaids and gardeners) held long-term, even hereditary, appointments. Royal retainers as public servants sustained many of these characteristics and, I believe, we may justifiably use the term today for a particular type of bureaucracy. All the public officials named by the first American presidents, from Washington to John Quincy Adams, relied exclusively on retainers. According to Leonard White, "The spirit of the Federalist system favored continuity of service from the highest to the lowest levels. . . . No property right in office was ever established or seriously advocated, but permanent and continued employment during good behavior was taken for granted" (White 1951: 369).

6. The radical change Jackson introduced involved rotation—the president's right not only to make appointments but also to discharge incumbents. This claim violated the well-established retainer tradition of continuity in public office. Actually, the Jacksonian revolution did not involve total rotation: if many retainers had not kept their posts, the Federal bureaucracy would have collapsed. The experience and knowledge of these workhorses permitted public administration to continue despite the inexperience of the newcomers typically brought in over their heads.

Even today, after tenured career officials have replaced patronage appointees in a host of positions in the American bureaucracy, a substantial number of retainers are able to remain in office—some have been blanketed into the career services to legitimize their status. Both political science and public administration, as disciplines, persist in ignoring the existence of retainers, as revealed by their lack of an accepted term for the phenomenon.

7. The exceptional situations can be found in a few twentieth-century presidentialist regimes where the effort to create a workable control structure based on the separation-of-powers principle proved impossible. Three such regimes—in South Vietnam, South Korea, and Nigeria—inherited mandarin traditions from the past; this quickly led to the rise of powerful bureaucracies when presidentialist regimes were established in these countries. Shortly thereafter, in each case, the bureaucracy seized power by means of a coup d'état.

By contrast, some fifteen African regimes, plus some new states in Asia, the Pacific, and the Caribbean, have been able to maintain democratic institutions and also to control their mandarin bureaucracies—all have parliamentary constitutional regimes. Not all such regimes in the newer states have succeeded; obviously, therefore, parliamentarism cannot guarantee a country's ability to control a mandarin bureaucracy. However, it seems to have a better prospect for doing so than regimes based on the separation-of-powers principle.

8. Twenty-five years ago Rudolph Gomez published a report on Peru in which he reported on the lack of a merit system and fear of rivals as a reason "why nepotism is implicitly encouraged by the system; there is less to fear from a member of one's own

family than from a stranger." Loyalty to relatives need not imply obedience to authority, however. "Employees in government bureaucracies," Gomez reports, "use the security afforded by their positions to set their own work pace, to interpret the rules in their own way, and to do whatever will free them from supervision and control" (Gomez 1969: 54–55).

There appears to have been little change during the succeeding quarter century. As described by Karen Ruffing-Hilliard, in Venezuela, patronage appointments prevail: "The traditional bureaucratic system accorded the president the right to appoint and remove top ministerial executives, who in turn exercised great discretion in the appointment and removal of their subordinates. There was no pressure to relate work and compensation, least of all from the employees who were acutely aware of their vulnerability" (Ruffing-Hilliard 1991: 306). I suspect that, in practice, very few were actually removed—they were retainers more than transients. While emphasizing that appointments tend to be based on "nepotism, friendship, and most commonly, political affiliation," Jack Hopkins tells us that in "Latin America bureaucrats tend to be survivors and . . . their careers, if not completely orderly and stable, are at least long" (Hopkins 1991: 700–701).

9. Ruffing-Hilliard has given us a depressing picture of noble and continuing efforts to promote administrative reforms in Latin America. She reports that despite earnest internationally sponsored projects in many countries, only seven had actually established a central personnel agency, and that early optimism regarding the potential success of programs in "Brazil, Colombia and Ecuador may have been unfounded. . . . If merit reform programs in Latin America have failed or had only mixed success, it has not been for lack of trying. In fact, many countries succeeded in passing or decreeing civil service laws." Unfortunately these systems break down in "the implementation phase" (Ruffing-Hilliard 1991: 301–2).

Typically, I believe, formalism dictates polite acceptance of prestigious advice offered by foreign agencies and governments—together with various practical inducements—but entrenched forces threatened by such changes are strong enough to nullify them in practice. Ruffing-Hillard acknowledges this reality when she writes: "Adherence to laws and administrative rules is formalistic. Agencies give lip service to merit system provisions while they are busy devising ways to circumvent them" (310).

Costa Rica is often mentioned as perhaps the most successful presidential democracy in Latin America. In that country, according to Andranovich and Riposa, "public bureaucracy has contributed to the current crisis . . . through its semi-autonomous and overly self-protective practices." These have "allowed public bureaucrats to pursue their own agendas to the detriment of government wide policy." Nominally, "the bureaucracy is a public servant, yet in practice it plays varying roles in the political processes of regime transition, advancing, retarding, or helping maintain the extant regime" (Andranovich and Riposa 1991: 694).

10. The capacity of retainers to resist reforms prevails against domestic dictators as well as against foreign advisers. In Brazil, for example, Getúlio Vargas, who ruled as an autocrat from 1930 to 1945, pressed hard for fundamental reforms in the bureaucracy. Under such authoritarian regimes, however, "bureaucratic conflicts were either suppressed or expressed in the form of intrigues or conspiratorial associations and actions. . . . The president can either liquidate the opposition or co-opt it. . . . The preferred option is normally co-opting. Co-opting involves transforming the bureaucracy into independent fiefdoms. Each feudal lord exercises broad and arbitrary control over his domain and engages in expanding his prerogatives and jurisdictions for self aggrandizement and to keep his subjects satisfied. This situation leads to the ex-

pansion of the bureaucracy. . . . Under the authoritarian presidentialism, instead of the politicians being the main source of political appointments, the bureaucrats became the main conduit for political appointments" (Baaklini 1992: 30).

11. Catherine Conaghan describes how presidents of Ecuador relied on technocrats to plan economic policy during critical periods without consultations in Congress or with political parties. She refers to "the technocratic approach of the economic ministers who believed that the solution to the economic crisis involved the discovery and application of technically 'correct' policies. . . . They believed that economics was a science that should lie outside of the realm of politics" (Conaghan 1994: 276). There are no hints about who these technocrats are. If they were not bureaucrats to start with, they become bureaucrats by virtue of their governmental appointments. Even when highly skilled technocrats determine policy, their failure to win political support makes them vulnerable to attack when these policies fail.

Our tendency to partition wholes and treat their parts as distinct entities not only affects our perception of technocrats, but also the way we think of the military. In volume 2 of Linz and Valenzuela 1994, we find articles dealing with the experience of seven Latin American countries: Chile, Uruguay, Brazil, Colombia, Ecuador, Peru, and Venezuela. No index entry for bureaucracy is offered in this book, and I was unable to find any discussion in these essays of the bureaucratic role in extending or destroying democracy. There is also no entry for technocrats, but there is one entry guiding readers to Conaghan's chapter, which reads, "technocratic approach to economic policy." The author seems to have imagined a process without thinking about who did it. However, there are fifteen references under the entry for "military." In each case, the "military" is treated as an autonomous force, and virtually no information is provided to suggest that it is part of a bureaucracy or to indicate why military officers should have wanted to seize power or been able to succeed. The way we compartmentalize our understanding of polities leads us to think of technocrats and "the military" as isolated political actors but not as components of a state bureaucracy that is able, under certain conditions, to dominate a state and abuse its population.

12. In addition to the overt goal of replacing inefficient retainers with more highly qualified people in the administration of British government, as recommended in the Northcote-Trevelyan report, expediency also played a role in the English case. Consider, for example, the following quotation from a letter written in 1854 by W. E. Gladstone, then a member of Parliament, in which he endorsed the proposal as likely to "strengthen and multiply the ties between the higher classes and the possession of administrative power." He went on to claim an "immense superiority" for "all those who may be called gentlemen by birth and training," and to endorse a separation of roles between the "mechanical and intellectual" that would "open to the highly educated class a career and give them a command over all the higher parts of the civil service, which up to this time they have never enjoyed" (Chapman 1970: 28).

As the use of "administrative power" in this quotation illustrates, the British have long associated public administration with the exercise of political power, a reflection of the dynamics of their political system. Members of the U.S. Congress, clearly, wanted something quite different. They intended to bar the children of affluent parents from career posts in government and to distribute these opportunities among the middle or lower middle class recruited from all the states. By contrast, the higher-level posts where administrative power might be concentrated were to remain in the possession of political appointees, but they were to be transients, not retainers. Subsequently, some political scientists have studied the role of these transients, leaving to public administration the task of analyzing the role of lower-level career officials. By compartmentalizing the bureaucracy between its (high-level) transients and its (lowly) careerists, they have blinded themselves to the systemic bonds that closely link their counterparts in virtually all countries except the United States.

13. Exceptionally, under American domination, a parallel type of bureaucracy was institutionalized in the Philippines. However, as the system evolved after independence in 1946, so many "eligible" candidates were certified for government jobs after they had taken civil service examinations that patronage and "pull" became major factors in the subsequent appointment of career officials. De facto, this produced a kind of retainer-merit hybrid that may have accentuated the worst features of both systems.

14. The relation of professionalism in the American bureaucracy to academia is worth noting. It arises from an important provision in the Pendleton Act that created the illusion that career officials (functionists) should be nonpolitical. The act stipulated that career appointees should not help to finance political party activities or involve themselves in campaigning. This came to be known as a barrier to political activity, even though the clear intent was only to exclude partisan activity. Nevertheless, as the field of public administration developed, it sought its autonomy from political science by stressing concepts drawn from other disciplines, notably from "management science" as taught in business schools. The nonpartisan political activities of bureaucrats and the political implications of their successes or failures as administrators were largely ignored. Some specialists in public administration also hoped to gain recognition for their discipline as one of the professions whose members could be appointed as functionists within the bureaucracy. Afraid that an overt interest in politics would handicap these efforts, they backed away from the study of bureaucratic power and tried to understand administration as a nonpolitical managerial science.

American political scientists reacted by largely excluding the study of bureaucracy from their purview, limiting themselves either to the overtly "political" institutions in which elected politicians play a role, or to the political implications of economic, social, and class forces, cultural practices, and other extragovernmental forces. To the extent that they have included bureaucrats within the scope of their work, they tend to focus on transients, especially noncareer appointees, in the U.S. government. Hyneman (1950) is an exception to this generalization, but it is difficult to find others in the mainstream of American political science who have followed his example.

Because career positions in the American bureaucracy are nominally nonpolitical, political scientists see no role for themselves as specialists on politics in the public service, nor do they see any useful way to prepare themselves or their students for noncareer posts as transients in the bureaucracy. These diverse considerations appear to have contributed to the inattention of both public administration and political science in the United States to the political implications of bureaucracy. Paradoxically, many contemporary American students of both public administration and political science protest the artificiality of the politics/administration dichotomy. Nevertheless, the institutionalized pressures that maintain the rift between these two fields of study reinforce the split and penalize those on either side who dare to cross its boundaries.

References

Aberbach, Joel D., Robert D. Putnam, and Bert A. Rockman. 1981. *Bureaucrats and Politicians in Western Democracies*. Cambridge: Harvard University Press.

Andranovich, Gregory D., and Gerry Riposa. 1991. "Bureaucratic Politics and Political Regimes: A Comparison of Nicaragua, Guatemala, and Costa Rica." In *Handbook of Comparative and Development Public Administration*, edited by Ali Farazmand. New York: Marcel Dekker, 687–96.

Baaklini, Abdo I. 1992. *The Brazilian Legislative and Political System*. Westport, Conn.: Greenwood.

Campbell, Colin. 1986. *Managing the Presidency.* Pittsburgh: University of Pittsburgh Press.

Campbell, Colin, and G. J. Szablowski. 1979. *The Superbureaucrats.* Toronto: Macmillan.

Carney, T. F. 1971. *Bureaucracy in Traditional Society.* Lawrence, Kans.: Coronado Press.

Chapman, Brian. 1959. *The Profession of Government: The Public Service in Europe.* New York: Macmillan.

Chapman, Richard A. 1970. *The Higher Civil Service in Britain.* London: Constable.

Conaghan, Catherine M. 1994. "Loose Parties, 'Floating' Politicians, and Institutional Stress: Presidentialism in Ecuador, 1979–1988." In *The Failure of Presidential Democracy,* edited by Juan Linz and Arturo Valenzuela. Vol. 2. Baltimore: Johns Hopkins University Press, 254–85.

Dogan, Mattei, ed. 1975. *The Mandarins of Western Europe: The Political Role of Top Civil Servants.* New York: John Wiley.

Dogan, Mattei, and Ali Kazancigil, eds. 1994. *Comparing Nations: Concepts, Strategies, Substance.* Oxford, U.K.: Blackwell.

Eisenstadt, S. N. 1963. *The Political Systems of Empires.* London: The Free Press of Glencoe.

Fainsod, Merle. 1958. *Smolensk under Soviet Rule.* Santa Monica, CA: Rand, reprinted by New York: Vintage Books, 1963.

Farazmand, Ali, ed. 1991. *Handbook of Comparative and Development Public Administration.* New York: Marcel Dekker.

———. 1994. *Handbook of Bureaucracy.* New York: Marcel Dekker.

Girling, John L. 1981. *The Bureaucratic Polity in Modernizing Societies.* Singapore: Institute of Southeast Asian Studies.

Gomez, Rudolph. 1969. *The Peruvian Administrative System.* Boulder: University of Colorado Bureau of Governmental Research and Service.

Heclo, Hugh. 1977. *A Government of Strangers: Executive Politics in Washington.* Washington, D.C.: Brookings Institution.

Hoogenboom, Ari. 1961. *Outlawing the Spoils: A History of the Civil Service Reform Movement, 1865–1883.* Urbana: University of Illinois Press.

Hopkins, Jack W. 1991. "Evolution and Revolution: Enduring Patterns and the Transformation of Latin American Bureaucracy." In *Handbook of Comparative and Development Public Administration,* edited by Ali Farazmand. New York: Marcel Dekker.

Hyneman, Charles S. 1950. *Bureaucracy in a Democracy.* New York: Harper and Brothers.

Kracke, E. A. 1953. *Civil Service in Early Sung China, 960–1067.* Cambridge: Harvard University Press.

Lewis, Eugene. 1977. *American Politics in a Bureaucratic Age: Citizens, Constituents, Clients, and Victims.* Cambridge, Mass.: Winthrop Publishers.

Linz, Juan, and Arturo Valenzuela, eds. 1994. *The Failure of Presidential Democracy,* vol. 2. Baltimore: Johns Hopkins University Press.

Mackenzie, G. Calvin, ed. 1987. *The In-and-Outers: Presidential Appointees and Transient Government in Washington.* Baltimore: Johns Hopkins University Press.

Peters, Guy. 1988. *Comparing Public Bureaucracies.* Tuscaloosa: University of Alabama Press.

Pfiffner, James. 1991. *The Managerial Presidency.* Pacific Grove, Calif: Brooks/Cole.

Riggs, Fred W. 1966. *Thailand: The Modernization of a Bureaucratic Polity.* Honolulu: East-West Center Press.

———. 1969. "The Structures of Government and Administrative Reform." In *Political and Administrative Development,* edited by Ralph Braibandi. Durham: Duke University Press, 220–324.

———. 1981. "Cabinet Members and Coup Groups: The Case of Thailand." *International Political Science Review* 2, no. 2: 159–88.

———. 1991. "Bureaucratic Links between Administration and Politics." In *Handbook of Comparative and Development Public Administration,* edited by Ali Farazmand. New York: Marcel Dekker, 485–509.

———. 1993a. "Fragility of the Third World's Regimes." *International Social Science Journal* 136 (May): 199–243.

———. 1993b. "Bureau Power in Southeast Asia." *Asian Journal of Political Science* 1, no. 1. (June): 3–28.

———. 1994a. "Conceptual Homogenization of a Heterogeneous Field: Presidentialism in Comparative Perspective." In *Comparing Nations: Concepts, Strategies, Substance,* edited by Mattei Dogan and Ali Kazancigil. Oxford, U.K.: Blackwell, 72–152.

———. 1994b. "Bureaucracy and the Constitution." *Public Administration Review* 54, no. 1: 65–72.

———. 1994c. "Bureaucracy: A Profound Puzzle for Presidentialism." In *Handbook of Bureaucracy,* edited by Ali Farazmand. New York: Marcel Dekker, 97–147.

———. 1995a. "Ethno-National Rebellions and Viable Constitutionalism." *International Political Science Review* 16, no. 4: 375–404.

———. 1995b. "Viable Constitutionalism and Bureaucracy: Theoretical Premises." *Journal of Behavioral and Social Sciences.* Tokyo: Tokai University Research Institute of Social Sciences 2: 1–35.

Rourke, Francis E. 1984. *Bureaucracy, Politics, and Public Policy.* Boston: Little, Brown.

Ruffing-Hilliard, Karen. 1991. "Merit Reform in Latin America: A Comparative Perspective." In *Handbook of Comparative and Development Public Administration,* edited by Ali Farazmand. New York: Marcel Dekker, 301–12.

Suleiman, Ezra, ed. 1984. *Bureaucrats and Policy Making: A Comparative Overview.* New York: Holmes and Meier.

Teng, Ssu-Yu. 1943. "Chinese Influence on the Western Examination System." *Harvard Journal of Asiatic Studies* 7: 267–312.

Van Riper, Paul A. 1958. *History of the U. S. Civil Service.* Evanston, Ill.: Row, Peterson.

Weber, Max. 1946. *From Max Weber: Essays in Sociology.* Edited and translated by H. H. Gerth and C. Wright Mills. New York: Oxford University Press.

Wilson, James Q. 1989. *Bureaucracy: What Government Agencies Do and Why They Do It.* New York: Basic Books.

White, Leonard D. 1951. *The Jeffersonians.* New York: Macmillan.

6

Legislative Structure and Constitutional Viability in Societies Undergoing Democratic Transition

ABDO I. BAAKLINI

Introduction

Constitutional viability in countries undergoing democratic transition depends on many structural and nonstructural variables.[1] This chapter explores the importance of structures and procedures of legislatures, and the resources available to these institutions, as well as the manner in which these resources are allocated among the various political groups within the legislative arena.

In an open and democratic political system, the elected legislature is usually the highest forum in which political groups in society wage their political battles. Regardless of which system of government prevails (presidential or parliamentary or any variation in between), political actors need structures, processes, and resources to conduct the various roles that a constitution assigns to the legislature. Research on the U.S. Congress has amply demonstrated the importance of these variables to the survival of the institution and to the policy outcomes that it produces.[2] Yet in designing new constitutions, the variables associated with the legislative institution—how it is internally structured, what procedures it adopts, how it transacts its business, what resources are available to the various political actors—are topics rarely explored by either scholars or policymakers.

It is beyond the scope of this chapter to address the entire range of issues associated with the legislative institution building required for a stable democratic regime. In this paper, only two important issues will be addressed. The first is how to build a legislature that is active in discharging its various constitutional powers within a democratic state, without causing an impasse with the executive. The second challenge for the legislature in a society undergoing transition to a pluralistic democratic system is how to provide enough incentives to newly legalized political parties (especially minority political parties) to participate constructively in the legislative process and to abandon the secretive and conspiratorial role they may have developed during a dictatorial regime.

The first dilemma is especially acute in presidential systems. It concerns the proverbially thorny executive-legislative relationship and the appropriate checks and balances, not merely from a constitutional perspective, but to facilitate day-to-day working relationships. The second dilemma is especially prevalent in parliamentary systems.

This chapter discusses these two dilemmas as they affect the executive-legislative relationship in countries where presidential and parliamentary systems are undergoing democratic transition, political parties in societies undergoing democratic transitions, and the role and the institutional needs of legislatures. In each section, I make recommendations as to how these dilemmas can be ameliorated and managed.

Legislatures in Presidential and Parliamentary Systems

Legislatures in many countries undergoing a transition to democracy operate under one variation or another of a presidential or parliamentary system. This is true in Central and South American countries, the Middle East, Eastern and Central Europe, Africa, and Asia. While the powers and functions of those legislatures vary from one country to another, they nevertheless share some common characteristics.

Unlike the parliamentary form of government in which one finds a degree of unity between the executive and the legislative powers, the presidential system of government maintains the principle of separation of powers between the executive and the legislature. In general (and subject to many refinements that vary from one parliamentary system to another), in a parliamentary system an impasse between the executive (the prime minister) and the legislature is resolved through a vote of confidence in the legislature. If the cabinet loses the vote of confidence, it tenders its resignation and a new cabinet is formed.[3] In extreme cases, if the impasse continues and the formation of a new cabinet is not possible, the legislature can be dissolved and a new election is scheduled. Those who emerge as winners, either alone (if they have an absolute majority), or in coalition with other parties, are called upon to form the new cabinet. To come to power and to maintain themselves in power, political parties try to formulate winning coalitions, and seek to maintain them after acquiring power. A cabinet form of government, even when it is constituted from one political party, is still a coalition among the various political wings within the party. The members and political groups within a cabinet stand or fall together. For reasons of political survival, cabinets continuously engage in strategies and actions intended to cement the coalition.

In presidential systems, only one executive position is filled by election—the presidency. The competition among the various political parties is characterized by the "winner takes all" approach.[4] To win an election, the president needs to build a winning coalition. As soon as the election is over, the coalition that elected the president begins to disintegrate over priorities, programs, and benefits. Impasses between a popularly elected president and a popularly elected legislature are difficult to resolve, since the president in principle cannot dissolve the legislature, and the legislature cannot withhold the vote of confidence from the executive to force a change in policy, a cabinet modification, or a resignation.[5]

To prevent the emergence and persistence of impasses inherent in the presidential system, presidents and legislatures resort to a series of constitutional, political, and coercive measures, which, taken separately or in combination, end up weakening and delegitimizing the political system. Constitutionally, many presidential systems (especially those in Central and South America) limit their leaders to one term in office, with no possibilities of immediate reelection. The moment a president is elected, he or she becomes a lame duck. To balance this inherent weakness of the president, the constitution places a number of constraints on the legislature. In the case of Costa Rica, for example, members of the legislature are eligible to run for only one term. In many other states, legislative leaders can serve for only one term. Legislative and committee chairs are therefore in constant rotation. Unfortunately, this leadership instability both in the executive and in the legislature prevents the emergence of stable expectations and constructive working relationships between the two branches.[6]

In addition to this constitutional limitation and leadership instability, presidents in presidential systems come to power riding on high expectations and promising to solve a variety of economic and social problems. Once in power, however, they soon realize their constitutional and political limitations. They have only one term in office, no broad political and party base in the legislature, and are presiding over a permanent bureaucracy that they can do very little to control or change. Their principal allies are transients who have little understanding of the workings of the bureaucracy, or who have an independent power base of their own and therefore have no allegiance to the president.[7] They are appointed because of their personal loyalty to the president or as a quid pro quo for campaign support. Their capacity to manage an entrenched and legally protected bureaucracy is limited, and as outsiders their political support, if it exists at all within the legislature, is personal and does not extend to the president's whole team. Managing the intricate relationship between a weak presidency and a disorganized and unstable legislative institution becomes a formidable task.

Added to this political and institutional weakness is the contradictory role that a president is called upon to play. As a nationally elected officer, the president is supposed to represent the entire nation and to symbolize its aspirations, integration, and common goals. However, electoral imperatives and the need for political survival as head of government force the president to behave in a partisan way. While the president, as a symbol of national unity, expects respect, cooperation, and compliance from his political opponents, the opposition sees him as a partisan trying to monopolize resources and consolidate his power to benefit his supporters and friends, to the exclusion of his opponents. The opposition considers it a duty and a right to oppose the president's policies and programs. The stage is thus set for a legislative-executive impasse.

Historically, this impasse was temporarily resolved either through a military coup—to remove the president from power or to strengthen him against his opponents—or through a popular uprising, or the threat of one, which in turn might invite the military to intervene in the name of law and order to protect the integrity and sovereignty of the state. Authoritarian regimes often came to power to rid the state of the impasse between the executive and the legislature.[8] Employing a combination of national security and economic imperatives, they dissolved legislatures, restricted political activities, and resorted to coercion and abuse of human rights. If legislatures were allowed to exist, they were stripped of many of their powers and prerogatives. To maintain their majority status in those weakened legislatures, authoritarian regimes resorted to massive electoral manipulations, outright fraud, and falsification of the electoral process. In both cases, authoritarian regimes soon lost the legitimacy and support they may have initially enjoyed. A new legislative-executive confrontation that might peaceably or through violent means lead the political system to a new cycle of legislative-executive impasse would soon develop.

In a presidential system of government, therefore, the constitutional imperative of separating powers gives the legislature a role to play in the policymaking process separate from the executive. Legislatures in presidential systems—even those controlled by the party of the president—are expected to participate in the policy process and formulate their own proposals.

Uninformed legislatures that do not have the institutional capability to study, assess, and amend executive-initiated proposals, or to initiate and formulate their own solutions to societal problems, can play two roles—both dysfunctional to the political system. They can endorse executive initiatives without deliberation or amendment, and be seen as playing a rubber-stamp role—a perception that causes them to lose their own political legitimacy, without affording any additional standing to the executive. Or, they can oppose executive initiatives without coming up with their own amendments or solutions; here, they are seen as obstructionist and parochial, losing their legitimacy and inviting the retaliation of the executive in the process.

To play a constructive role in contemporary societies, legislatures in both presidential and parliamentary systems need to be properly structured and informed, and institutionally capable of tackling complex issues with the executive. An informed legislature should be able to participate constructively in the evaluation of alternative public policy proposals, and perhaps avoid the pervasive impasse between the two powers. An informed legislature should have the necessary ingredients to hammer out agreements, to avoid these fatal confrontations and impasses. Later in this chapter I provide a general framework for enhancing the legislature's ability to play this constructive role.

Consolidation and Democratization of Political Parties

One of the most important but difficult functions that regimes undergoing transition to democracy have to contend with is how to deal with political parties that until recently have been illegal and operating surreptitiously. Parties that have spent most of their existence operating illegally develop a certain style of political behavior and elevate a certain brand of political leadership. The need to operate illegally forces political parties to be suspicious and distrustful of government and of outsiders. Their operating style becomes less open and more conspiratorial. Throughout their existence, these illegal parties develop a hostile orientation toward the state and its political and security institutions.

The leadership of these parties normally consists of individuals who have mastered the skills of hard-line resistance, and developed a ruthlessness in dealing with internal and external opponents. To keep the allegiance of the party's hard-core supporters, the leadership often adopts simplistic and rigid positions that set the party apart from outsiders and especially from the regime in power.

For transition to take place, the regime in power attempts to establish dialogue with those parties that were previously outlawed. This causes a strain within the leadership of the outlawed parties, between those who want to compromise and those who want to continue adhering to the simplistic and extremist logic of the party. As the transition process moves along and agreements on the general outlines of the transition are reached, hard-line leaders feel threatened. The moderate elements, as a result of participating in the negotiating process and developing a more accommodating position, begin to gain prominence. Those more moderate members who win election find themselves in an unenviable position within the legislature; to maintain their influence within the party, they need to continue to use the old unyielding rhetoric. To gain influence within the legislature, they need to master the art of compromise and appear reasonable to their fellow parliamentarians.

The manner in which legislatures are structured can play a major role in reinforcing the authority of the emerging moderates. If the authority and influence of the moderate opposition members are undermined, the hard-line party leaders outside the parliament (who usually continue to be influential among the hard-core party members) may regain influence and disrupt the transition process. This is true in both presidential and parliamentary systems of government, but especially true in the parliamentary system. In a parliamentary system of government, the majority party in the legislature ends up forming the cabinet either alone or in coalition with other parties. Normally, it is expected to support the policies advocated by the cabinet. Minority parties outside the cabinet, if they are to play a constructive opposition role, need to have the necessary structures and capabilities to play such a role. If denied such an opportunity, these parties may resort to negative or destructive tactics, and radical elements may take control of the party.

Legislatures are the most appropriate forum for the development of responsible and transparent political parties. Legislatures, as open political forums, can encourage the development of party leadership that is accountable and sensitive to others. Legislative work by committee or in plenary, if properly structured and equipped, can encourage both cooperation and debate. It can also allow political parties to refine their positions and, at the same time, to seek acceptable solutions. Legislative parties should be given the forum and resources to formulate their programs, communicate them to the public, and compare them to other platforms. All of these factors can be addressed through the structure of the legislature, the processes it adopts, and the resources it marshals.

Unfortunately, the importance of legislative structures and resources is not well understood by constitution drafters or by policymakers. Most scholarly work on political parties in transition focuses on political culture, and ignores the structural and resource dimension of political party behavior in the legislature. Internal rules governing the structure and operations of the legislature are often adopted without attention to the political realities of a particular place and time. Structures and procedures that governed the operation of a legislature under an authoritarian or totalitarian regime are resurrected and adopted for the operation of a multiparty legislative institution. It is quite often the case that legislatures in societies undergoing democratic transition continue to be hierarchically structured and that resources are unilaterally controlled by the Speaker and ruling majority party. Opposition parties have no specified role, nor are they provided with resources necessary to perform their varied constitutional roles.[9]

Functions of Legislatures

Legislatures perform different functions under different political systems. Even those performing similar functions perform them differently. In this section, I will analyze briefly the main types of functions that legislatures play in societies undergoing democratic transition.

Public Policy

Most constitutions empower the legislature as a whole and through its committees to propose bills in all areas of public policy. The practice, however, has been that all major legislation originates in the executive and is transmitted to the legislature for approval. Once in the legislature, it is considered pro forma by the whole body and is immediately referred to one of the subject-matter committees for consideration. The report of the committee is then submitted to the whole assembly for approval. Both within the committees and in the plenary, bills are scrutinized and debated. Ministers and their representatives appear before the committee or the plenary to defend their proposals. Members present suggestions and occasional amendments to proposed bills. It is up to the cabinet to accept those proposals and amendments. Quite often an accommodation is reached with the executive to accept certain changes that the legislature deems necessary. Proposed legislation referred to the legislatures often deals with general policies and directions. The ministers are left to draw up the details and to provide implementation guidelines and standards. These are often issued through executive or ministerial decree and are not subject to legislative approval.

Review of the Budget

Most legislatures are authorized to study and approve the budget. Once the budget is received by a legislature, it is often referred to a budget committee. Most legislatures have no authority to change the budget without the agreement of the cabinet. They can, however, reject it with an absolute majority, although that rarely happens. If it did, it would be considered a major confrontation with the executive and might lead to the dissolution of the legislature.

Normally, legislatures study the budget and comment on many of its components and then recommend changes and general policy guidelines to the cabinet. The cabinet is free to accept or reject those suggestions. Quite often it accepts some of the general principles but sticks to its own proposals on the specifics. It promises to take the members' suggestions into consideration when implementing the budget. Because the budget document is based on general estimates and guesswork, and because it does not represent what the government eventually implements, the whole process of debating the budget appears, in many legislatures, to be ceremonial.

The executive budget usually provides general principles but very few specifics. The executive is left with a wide margin of discretion in determining what actually happens at the implementation stage. Most legislatures have no capability to study the budget's various components or to follow up on its implementation. To rectify this weakness, legislatures need both the analytic capability to study the budget once it is presented, and an oversight capability to evaluate its implementation.

Oversight

Closely related to the budget function is the oversight function. Legislatures are usually authorized to exercise oversight of the executive. Usually this function is not systematically performed. The auditing and evaluation function necessary to undertake systematic oversight is normally dominated by the executive even though it is under the nominal supervision of the legislature.

Constituency Services

Serving constituents is a well-developed function of most legislatures, because it fits within the accepted political and social norms and because it utilizes informal political and social structures already developed in many countries. Through a variety of means, constituents forward their demands to the members and expect services in return. Indeed, many legislatures have developed a standing committee to consider suggestions and complaints. While constituency services is considered an accepted function, few formal resources are dedicated within most legislatures to it. Normally, each member uses his or her own means and network to respond to demands from the electorate. No staff or system of information is in place to handle this function. Instead, the informal network of families, friends, and the goodwill of bureaucrats are still the accepted means of serving the citizens who call upon their members for help.

Strengthening this function would not only serve to tie the citizen to the government and ameliorate the insensitivity of the bureaucrat to the concerns of the citizen, but it might also allow the legislature to begin exercising some oversight of the bureaucracy, although in a limited and personal manner. Undoubtedly, one has to be careful not to inadvertently foster corruption and special favors. Unless this function is appropriately handled, it can result in abuses and a sense of dependency and clientelism by the member vis-à-vis the bureaucrat.

Educational Function

A legislature can perform the important function of educating both its members and the public at large. Decades of legislative experience in many countries have led to the formation of a class of politicians well versed in the art of negotiation and compromise, and well informed about the public policy issues they confront. Sometimes, legislative debates are televised on a delayed and abridged basis. In addition to television, radio and the print media provide regular coverage of the debates.

One important source of information relevant to public education is the work of committees, which is usually not well publicized. A modern information system where committee agenda and committee work are recorded and made public may help to address this weakness and strengthen the educational function of many legislatures. Resources, such as publication and press capability, need to be allocated so that this function is performed adequately.

Information Needs of Legislatures

The information needs of legislatures to perform the above five functions and to manage their operations fairly and effectively can be conceptualized under three categories: management information needs, centralized legislative needs, and member and political party needs.[10]

Management Information

Like any institution, a legislature needs a management information system to operate well. The management information system includes a personnel database for both members and staff (containing salaries and payroll, employment history, fringe benefits, medical services and benefits), as well as purchasing, inventory, legislative budget and accounting, and other databases.

Legislative Information Systems

Information systems to help legislatures perform their functions have seen many improvements in recent years. A legislative information system includes a number of databases intended to serve the whole parliament.

1. Constitutional and legislative documents: This is a system that would include the full text of the constitution and major legislation. It would be available on-line and accessible by subject matter, title, and date of legislation. The system could be expanded to include a summary of major executive decrees and administrative regulations.
2. Major court decisions: Decisions of the supreme court and other high-level specialized courts would be entered into this system.
3. Legislative debates: This system, once established, can be used to publish the official journal of the legislature and for legislative reference. Access to the system is normally open to all members and their staff and to other government units.
4. Bill status: This application is concerned with the work of committees. It is a system that identifies the bills being considered by various committees and the action taken on each of the bills. It allows various amendments to be incorporated as the action proceeds.
5. Budget information system: This system incorporates the yearly budget of each of the government agencies, and shows the way the budgets are presented by the government, approved by the legislature, and then spent by the various agencies. It can also include revenues by source and expenditure, by purpose, and by geographic distribution.
6. Structure of government system: This system includes the basic government structures, their principal functions, and the names, addresses, and telephone numbers of the senior staff.
7. Issue briefs: This system gives a short summary and analysis of important issues of interest to the legislature.
8. Subscription to external databases: A number of external databases of relevance to the legislature are already available in many countries.
9. Voting system: This system enables members to vote electronically on matters discussed during the general sessions. The sys-

tem identifies each member present and the way the member votes on a particular measure. The vote is recorded as "yes," "no," "abstain," or "absent." It also automatically tallies the total number of votes in each category.

System for Members and Parties

Individual members and political parties usually use, develop, and maintain a number of databases. With some technical assistance from information specialists and the availability of a personal computer, members and parties can develop their own mailing lists, labels, correspondence with constituents, and other types of specialized applications. Four centrally managed systems may also be useful.

1. Electronic mail system: This allows communication among members themselves and between members and various other bodies.
2. Dissemination of information: This system includes a profile of each of the members and of the political parties and the areas of special interest to them. Using this profile, selected information from the other systems (especially those operated by the legislative library) could be collected and sent periodically to the member.
3. Socioeconomic data: This system provides a socioeconomic profile of each of the electoral districts. It can be developed and maintained by political parties and used during elections.
4. Election results: Perhaps the most important database for members and political parties is the set of election results by district and the socioeconomic characteristics of the voters. If such a system is developed, political parties can undertake statistical analysis of their strengths and weaknesses and then devise strategies to address those weaknesses in future elections.

Components of Legislative Development

A viable strategy to develop the above legislative resources and capabilities involves the interplay of several key elements to ensure its success. Legislative development is often confused with legislative modernization, in which emphasis is placed on the acquisition of modern equipment and information systems. While this facet may be important, it is not the critical variable in a successful legislative development program. Other factors must be present so that equipment and modern information systems are truly relevant to legislative development.

In this section I outline the elements of a successful strategy to ensure that the legislature plays a constructive role in the political system while avoiding impasses with the executive, and builds a responsive party system without exacerbating partisan conflict within the legislature.

A Vision

The assembly needs to develop both a vision and a committed leadership. In a legislature characterized by leadership and membership continuity, such as the U.S. Congress, such vision and commitment are not as crucial. The continuity allows the legislature to resort to an incremental approach where the leadership develops its priorities and builds consensus around these priorities as it moves along. However, in legislatures where such leadership continuity is lacking, structural mechanisms may be needed to ensure that attention to legislative institution building (involving the structure, the process, and the resources of the institution) is provided.

Appropriate Structures and Relationships

A successful strategy of legislative development rests on the provision of appropriate structures and relationships within the legislature and the availability of qualified people to occupy them. The emphasis on structures and relationships is as important as the emphasis on qualified individuals. Quite often qualified staff members are not appropriately and fully utilized. It is important to determine the right type of staff and, more important, what type of structures and relationships need to be developed so that the staff is properly utilized by the elected members. A legislative development strategy should also address a whole array of issues connected with the structure of the institution—prerogatives of leaders, minority and majority parties, and committee chairs; staffing and structural patterns of staff; information systems and organizational development. These issues pertain to both staff and members and to the relationship between the two. Such relationships also take into consideration the needs of each member as an individual, as a member of a political party, and as a member of a committee within the legislature.

Appropriate Linkages

A legislature is a forum in which all public issues relevant to a polity are debated, formulated, and decided. By its nature, a legislature is an open, amorphous institution. It is constantly interacting with its environment. For a legislative development strategy to succeed, the legislature must systematize these relationships. This is particularly true of relationships with those institutions that may provide the legislature with needed information, and with those institutions that shape the public's image of the legislature. (In many cases, the same institution may perform both functions.) There is a need to elaborate a plan for the development of relationships with universities, research institutes, professional associations, and the media. The universities and the research centers socialize and train future generations of leadership and the public. Jointly with professional associations, they generate a lot of information relevant to the public debate within the legislature. The media have a similar function. They generate valuable, timely information, articulate the concerns of significant groups within society, and shape the public's image and appreciation of the legislature's work.

Good Management

While modern and efficient management practices are not a necessary function of a strong legislature, a legislature in the process of development needs at least credible and efficient management practices. These require a symbiotic relationship between the legislative and the administrative functions of the institution. The legislative development strategy articulated in this paper involves a change in the work culture of the institution. One cannot modernize the legislative culture without changing the administrative culture. In most countries, this is especially so because the administrative bureaucracy is permanent while the elected members are transient. A legislative development plan should articulate a series of activities and steps intended to create a modern and efficient management system in the legislature.

Decent Physical Facilities

Physical facilities and equipment become a strategic variable only when the above conditions are in place. Members and staff need appropriate work space and equipment to discharge their functions. The complexity and rapid pace of modern information systems require equipment that can store, manipulate, access, and retrieve information quickly and in the appropriate format.

Conclusions

Any conclusions in this area of inquiry have to be tempered by many qualifications. There are few, if any, systematic studies, and the process of democratization is a recent phenomenon. It is too early to predict how it will proceed and what factors will influence its progress. Singling out one factor for analysis and drawing conclusive evidence of its centrality is at best closer to informed judgment than to scientific conclusions.

Yet in spite of these glaring limitations, and based on empirical experience of the past quarter century, some tentative guidelines can be posited.

Structure the Legislature Horizontally Rather than Vertically

Horizontally structured legislatures are those where all members of parliament have the same legal and constitutional powers; vertically structured legislatures are characterized by a hierarchy among the staff and enormous power given to the leaders. Vertically structured legislatures play one of two roles: The leadership of the legislature either uses its control to support executive initiative with little debate, or it can confront the executive on every issue and thereby cause executive-legislative impasses. Neither of these roles is conducive to the positive image and legitimacy of the legislature, nor do they contribute to the stability of the regime.

Horizontally structured legislatures allow for sharing of power among various political groups in the legislatures. They also allow for much needed flexibility for the institution to deal with its various political groups. In a horizontal legislative institution, the executive has many points of entry to the legislature and is not limited to negotiating with one leader. This multientry capability allows the executive to forge coalitions with political forces in the legislature that vary from one issue to the next.

A horizontally structured legislature allows many initiatives to be generated and debated. The enrichment of the legislative agenda and the multiplicity of actors allow the executive and the legislature to avoid the politics of polarization in favor of compromise, without either of the two institutions losing face. Horizontally structured legislatures allow the emergence of mediators and compromisers and then elevate them to the forefront of political influence.

Decentralize Authority and Resources along Functional Lines

A horizontally structured legislature without a commensurate delegation of authority is not able to respond easily to policy initiatives or to display accountability. These weaknesses can be rectified by dividing the work along functional lines and by providing those in charge with adequate authority and resources to act. A decentralized structure can lead to an energized legislature; it also encourages innovative solutions, minimizes partisanship, and promotes substantive debates.

Provide Party Leadership with Prerogatives, Authority, and Resources

To encourage the emergence of moderate, democratically oriented party leadership, it is important that members of political parties elected to the legislature be given a meaningful role to play. This can be accomplished by changes in the internal rules to recognize the existence of political parties and their role in the legislative process. It can also be achieved by allocating institutional resources (staff, information, equipment, and funds) for parties to exercise their legislative role. Finally, it can be achieved by integrating party leadership and legislative position to enhance prestige and moderate partisanship.

Mobilize All Resources

Resources made available to the members and parties should be provided through the institution itself, rather than through the political parties. Although members and political parties should be allowed to choose their advisers and staff, these individuals should be recruited by the legislature and be subject to its rules and regulations. Staff recruited through the normal procedures of the legislature tend to identify with the institution and its goals. They can then promote agreements among the various political forces in the legislature rather than exacerbate partisan conflict.

Notes

1. This paper is based on the experience of the author over the last twenty-five years assisting legislatures in more than two dozen countries in Latin America, Africa, Asia, the Middle East, Eastern Europe, and the United States in building institutional capabilities.

2. For example, see Walter Oleszek, *Congressional Procedures and Policy Process*, 3d ed. (Washington, D.C.: Congressional Quarterly, 1989); Richard Fenno, Jr., *The Power of the Purse: Appropriation Politics in Congress* (Boston: Little, Brown, 1966); and Richard Fenno, Jr., *Congressmen in Committees* (Boston: Little, Brown, 1973).

3. In some countries to minimize the risk of forcing cabinets from power by a temporary coalition that has little in common, the constitution stipulates that a vote of no confidence can only be taken if the opposition forces can agree on a replacement cabinet. Barring such an agreement the cabinet can continue in power, although it may not have won approval for its proposed policy. This is a deviation from the Westminster Model. It is intended to provide some stability and continuity in divided legislatures that do not have a single majority party, but are ruled by a coalition of parties of divergent political agendas. This is the case in Hungary.

4. For information about the difference between presidential and parliamentary systems, see Fred W. Riggs, "The Survival of Presidentialism in America: Para-Constitutional Practices," *International Political Science Review* 9 (1988), and "Presidential or Parliamentary Democracy: Does It Make a Difference?" in *The Failure of Presidential Democracy: Comparative Perspectives*, ed. Juan J. Linz and Arturo Valenzuela, vol. 1 (Baltimore: Johns Hopkins University Press, 1994).

5. I argue that the intrinsic problems of presidential systems of government are associated with the high expectations of both the public and the president and the typically restricted power of the presidency. This contradiction usually leads to severe constitutional constraints on the ability of the president to deliver on what he and the public actually expect of him, which eventually leads either to paralysis or confrontation. In the case of paralysis, the urgent affairs of the government are often left unattended and unresolved. A confrontation is normally resolved through a coup d'état by the military or a popular revolt. If the president emerges victorious, the democratic order is often suspended in favor of an authoritarian, undemocratic regime. If the legislature emerges victorious, the powers of the president are further diminished, and his ability to meet public expectations is further eroded. See Abdo I. Baaklini, *The Brazilian Legislature and Political System* (Westport, Conn.: Greenwood Press, 1992), 17–24.

6. In the Brazilian case, there were numerous ways in which the authoritarian regime that gained power in 1964 fostered congressional leadership instability that in turn weakened the legislative institution. One was by instituting a rotating leadership policy whereby leadership in the Congress was given to temporary figures who were unable to succeed themselves and whose selection for these positions was highly influenced by the military. Second, the military succeeded in isolating party leadership from control of the political, informational, financial, material, and staff resources available to Congress. The institutional leadership of the Congress was instead entrusted to the Mesa (Board of Directors). For additional information, see Baaklini, *The Brazilian Legislature and Political System*, 39–56.

7. The role of transient bureaucrats has been adequately elaborated by Fred W. Riggs, "Bureaucracy and Viable Constitutionalism" in Chapter 5 of this volume.

8. In many respects the authoritarian regime that came to power in Brazil in 1964, for example, tried and failed to structure the political system to remove some of the contradictions in the presidential system of government. See Baaklini, *The Brazilian Legislature and Political System*, 15–17.

9. This is the case one finds in most legislatures of Third World countries undergoing transition to democracy. Recently, through technical assistance programs sponsored by the United States Agency for International Development, some attention has been given to building the staff and information capabilities of legislatures and to encouraging the policy analysis function of these institutions through the provision of centralized staff capabilities. In some countries, such as Costa Rica, Panama, Hungary, and Brazil, political parties were given staff and information resources to advance their own legislative agendas. Most of the literature on this topic is still in the form of reports and project papers commissioned by USAID. For example, see Abdo I. Baaklini, "Privatization Policies and Parliamentary Intervention in Hungary," paper presented at the annual meeting of the American Political Science Association, Washington, D.C., 1991; Abdo I. Baaklini, "The Legal, Political, and Information Dimensions of Yemen's Transition to Democracy" (Albany, N.Y.: Center for Legislative Development, 1992); Abdo I. Baaklini, "The Peoples' Assembly in Egypt: Its Staff and Information Needs" (Albany, N.Y.: Center for Legislative Development, 1993); Baaklini, *The Brazilian Legislature and Political System*, Chapter 3; and Abdo I. Baaklini, "Prodasen: The Congressional Information System of the Federal Senate of Brazil," *Government Information Quarterly* 11, no. 2 (1994): 171–90.

10. For works addressing the information needs of legislatures, see John A. Worthley, ed., *Comparative Legislative Information Systems* (Washington, D.C.: National Science Foundation, 1976); Abdo I. Baaklini, *Science/Technology Information Sources and State Legislatures: A Manual* (Albany: New York State Assembly and Comparative Development Studies Center [Center for Legislative Development], 1979); Baaklini, "Prodasen."

References

Baaklini, Abdo I. *The Brazilian Legislature and Political System*. Westport, Conn.: Greenwood Press, 1992.

———. "Prodasen: The Congressional Information System of the Federal Senate of Brazil." Government Information Quarterly 11, no. 2 (1994): 171–90.

Fenno, Richard, Jr. *The Power of the Purse: Appropriation Politics in Congress*. Boston: Little, Brown, 1966.

———. *Congressmen in Committees*. Boston: Little, Brown, 1973.

Linz, Juan J. "Presidential or Parliamentary Democracy: Does It Make a Difference?" In *The Failure of Presidential Democracy: Comparative Perspectives*, edited by Juan J. Linz and Arturo Valenzuela. Vol. 1, Baltimore: Johns Hopkins University Press, 1994.

Oleszek, Walter. *Congressional Procedures and Policy Process*. 3d ed. Washington, D.C.: Congressional Quarterly, 1989.

Riggs, Fred W. "The Survival of Presidentialism in America: Para-Constitutional Practices." *International Political Science Review* 9 (1988): 247-78.

Worthley, John A., ed. *Comparative Legislative Information Systems*. Washington, D.C.: National Science Foundation, 1976.

Part Two

Case Studies in Designing a Viable Constitution

7

The Constitution as an Instrument of Political Cohesion in Postcolonial States: The Case of India, 1950–1993

T. V. SATHYAMURTHY

The political history of postcolonial nations is heavily influenced by the constitutional arrangements that they make at the time of independence. Written (and heavily amended) constitutions were invariably viewed as much needed panaceas, placebos, or political healers, or as a combination of all three. Constitutions were expected to fulfill a dual role, enabling a smooth and orderly transition from anticolonial struggle to independent self-rule, and at the same time securing for the new regime the political fruits of nationhood, new state structures, legitimacy (domestic and international), and sovereignty (free from challenge from regional, ethnic, and other quarters). Yet, within a few decades (as in Asia), if not years, of independence (as in many parts of Africa, especially during the 1960s and 1970s), political tensions ranging from nonviolent challenges to civil war surfaced. These undermined and, in a number of instances, swept away the aims and goals claimed by the new regime.

The nexus between a country's constitution and its internal political cohesion has thus been tenuous in the extreme in many parts of the Third World. In this sense, then, there is a sharp contrast or divergence of concrete experience between the more stable countries of Western Europe and North America on the one hand, and those of Asia, Africa, the Caribbean, and Latin America on the other. This general picture, however, is in need of qualification. In certain countries of the Third World, constitutional political behavior has not only survived, but has also spread to political movements that often began their careers of protest by rejecting its commonly accepted canons. The cases of Sri Lanka and India in South Asia, and of Zimbabwe and South Africa (since the introduction of majority rule and the ending of apartheid in April 1994) seem to go against the grain of ready resort to unconstitutional means by the forces of opposition, a common phenomenon in the Third World.

This chapter will explore the relationship between the constitution and certain aspects of sociopolitical change that characterize the Indian case. During the 1920s, the internal differences between the "gradualists" and the "militants" within the Indian National Congress (INC) were resolved. Its profile was raised under new leadership by Mohandas K. Ghandi. The INC was projected as a mass movement embracing the whole of India and seeking to unite, politically, different communities, regions, languages, castes, and religions. It claimed to speak for all groups with a single, united political voice. The demand for total independence *(purna swaraj)* from colonial rule became the political slogan of the INC during this phase. Behind this general reorientation of strategy was the idea, not of sweeping differences under the carpet, but rather of providing a single, democratic, secular, political umbrella in the form of a united national state of independent India under which real differences could be worked out to the mutual satisfaction of divergent forces.

The integrated and unified nationalism engendered in the Congress movement was challenged from three quarters. Of these, the most serious was the Muslim League, which by the beginning of the 1940s had become a solidly entrenched political force demanding partition of the country and the establishment of a Muslim state of Pakistan. Less strident than the Muslim League, but no less ardently committed to the interests of their religious and caste communities, were the leaders of the Sikhs, "Master" Tara Singh, and the untouchables, Dr. B. R. Ambedkar. They expressed doubts about the democratic, secular, social reformist, and egalitarian protestations of the INC, and the dangers to which their political constituencies would almost certainly be exposed under Congress rule in independent India. Their challenges were low-key—for a time the INC was able to co-opt them into an uneasy partnership, at least during the visit of the Cabinet Mission and the negotiations leading up to Partition.[1] Moreover, the emergence of the Dravidar Kazhagam, or Self-Respect Movement, under the leadership of E.V. Ramasam Periyar, represented a powerful challenge to the INC's commitment to the idea of an undifferentiated Indian nation on a cultural level.

The only ideological alternative to the INC's vision of the political future of India[2] was provided by the Communist Party of India (CPI). Notwithstanding several serious errors of judgment, the importance of the CPI's role in Indian politics was out of proportion to its size or the largely uneven character of its influence. Despite Gandhi's implacable opposition to communism, and the almost visceral animosity of the socialists under the leadership of Jaya Prakash Narayan, the CPI succeeded in building up a great popular following among the working classes in major cities as well as in rural Travancore, Malabar, Bengal, the Telugu districts of the Madras Presidency, and Hyderabad State.

The CPI's intervention in the debate on Indian nationalism focused on the question of the "nationality" status of religious minorities—a question on which there was considerable divergence of view between the CPI Central Committee, which laid down the broad principles, and the leadership, which was responsible for the implementation of party policy. In actual fact, the latter edged closer and closer toward the acceptance of Partition as the Muslim League became more determined. Another issue related to the CPI's ideological subservience to the CPSU/Comintern (Communist Party of the Soviet Union/Communist International), and its consequent inability to think independently about the question of the Indian nation and state. For this reason, the CPI incurred the odium of the mainstream of the Indian nationalist movement. After independence, the CPI made somewhat confused attempts to redefine the question of nationalities (mainly as linguistic regions) without upholding the principle of self-determination. This placed the communists squarely in the camp of the secularist segment of the INC on this particular question.[3]

Constitution making in India (1948–50) was profoundly influenced by these ideological and theoretical viewpoints. Of equal importance was the question of what kind of state structures should take the place of the colonial state in India after independence. The answer can be gleaned from the behavior of the Congress Party in the by no means democratic power-sharing experiment of the period 1937–39, in which it took part under the provisions of the Government of India Act of 1935. The organizational wing of the INC eagerly participated in the process of establishing limited provincial (and ever so minimal) self-government under the control of the governor. Gandhi was skeptical, and even marginally hostile, because of a general animus he felt toward colonialism and large conglomerations of political power (of which an Indian Province or presidency was a good example). Jawaharlal Nehru, characteristically, stood equidistant between the Congress government and Gandhi.

Far from using the opportunity to control the power of day-to-day decision making to improve the living conditions and political status of the poor, and to enact legislation to help them, the Congress-ruled governments invariably assumed postures clearly indicating that they saw themselves as representatives of a populist party serving the interests of organized groups of landlords, industrialists, and the social elites (communally or otherwise defined) rather than as representatives of the mass of the Indian people.

Although unavoidable political compulsions precipitated the demise of these governments in 1939, the leadership of the Congress in the various provinces had savored the aroma of colonial power, for which they developed an immediate liking. The aim of the Congress, then, was to achieve a transfer of power that would leave intact the colonial power structures (including, and especially, the civil service bureaucracy) and embody them in a constitution in which the INC's vision of politics would be enshrined.

Throughout the 1930s and 1940s, the INC vacillated on the question of the political form that independent India should assume. Should it be a federal (in the classical Western sense of the word) union of States?[4] Or, should it be so structured that the power of the Indian state[5] would be expressed through a central, unitary government, with its writ always ready to overrule any form of provincial or regional dissent? The prospect of Pakistan quickened the debate within the INC, bringing the two opposing tendencies, federal and centralist, face to face. The preference of the constitution makers—or Founding Fathers, as they are fond of referring to themselves, after the American fashion—generally shifted toward the "unitarists" or "centralizers," and away from the "autonomists" or "federalists."[6]

In order to establish a democratic, secular, integrated, monolithic Indian nation-state, under the political control of a powerful central structure, the Constituent Assembly as well as the first central cabinet formed at independence incorporated a number of disparate forces from outside the INC, with the singular exception of the CPI, which was in a state of revolutionary confusion until its 1964 split.

Thus, B. R. Ambedkar, leader of the untouchables and radically opposed to the Congress Party's line on the *harijan* question, became India's first law minister and one of the chief architects of the Indian Constitution. Representatives of industry, commerce, insurance, and speculative finance, such as T. T. Krishnamachari, C. H. Bhabha, John Mathai, and R. K. Shanmukham Chetty, who had never publicly opposed colonial rule, played an important role in the formation of the overall economic strategy of independent India. This conformed to the general economic orientation of the INC despite the apparently left-leaning political postures of Prime Minister Jawaharlal Nehru, and was reflected in the debates of the Constituent Assembly.

To a smaller but by no means negligible extent, the political forces that were to become prominent during the 1960s and 1970s were already noticeable by the time of independence. In particular, these included the rich- and middle-peasant classes that would gather strength under the aegis of the Green Revolution, fragments of the Indian national bourgeoisie who would seek privileges and protection from powerful State governments, and, most important, Hindu movements and political parties whose aim was and still is to recast the political foundations in a new idiom of Hindu (as opposed to the INC's Indian or polyglot) nationalism.[7] The visibility of these groups contrasted with the neglect of the mass of the poor and disadvantaged sections of the oppressed castes, the *Adivasis* (officially the Scheduled Tribes), poor peasantry and agricultural or landless labor, and above all women. These constituted vast populations for which there was no direct or indirect representation in the Constituent Assembly, which was established on the basis of a severely restricted franchise.

In sum, the constitution of India was the product of deliberations among like-minded representatives of the powerful segments of society (including a small number of token women), who, for all practical purposes, ignored the political voice of vast swaths of the population. Furthermore, their appreciation of the political potential of the rising agrarian classes, in a rural economy that was due to enter an era of relatively sharp differentiation and acutely uneven modernization, left a great deal to be desired.

The political vision of these "Founding Fathers" of the Indian Constitution was thus greatly narrowed by the leadership's simplistic goal to rapidly industrialize the modern urban and national economy. Nor, indeed, did the constitution makers anticipate the strength of regional identity or the powerful sway that ethnicity would exercise during the decades to come. These forces were embedded in an extremely complex relationship between fundamental sociological categories, such as caste, religion, culture, region, and gender, that penetrated the economic and class divisions.[8] They affected and continue to affect, increasingly, not only the vertical divisions between dominant and oppressed classes, but also conflicts of a horizontal character between different segments of the bourgeoisie as well as among the working classes. The symbolic inclusion of Ambedkar, the leader of the untouchables, in the power structure merely served to underline the total inadequacy of the INC's response to the profound contradictions of Indian society already prevalent at the time of independence.

The political history of the democratic-socialist republic of united India, functioning under the aegis of the constitution that came into force on January 26, 1950, can be divided into three broad phases.

Phase I: 1950 to 1967

During the first period, between 1950 and 1967, the Congress Party remained unchallenged not only at the center but also in almost all the States (with the singular exception of Kerala, which returned a CPI-led government in 1957), and the Indian polity was guided by the assumption that this state of affairs would prevail indefinitely. Political opposition took the form mainly of peasant discontent in certain regions and unrest among certain sections of the urban working class. With the brutal crushing of the Telangana insurrection, the center embarked on a strategy of taming the CPI into a docile parliamentary opposition party. This strategy was largely successful even after the party split in 1964, resulting in the emergence of a radical but still parliamentary (rather than revolutionary) party to the left of the CPI, the Communist Party of India (Marxist), known as the CPI(M).

Within the Congress Party itself, dissidence took the form of demands for a reorganization of States in accordance with the principles of linguistic and cultural pluralism and regional cohesion. Such reorganization would involve a move away from colonial administrative boundaries of provinces and toward political boundaries between States with more or less homogeneous cultural identities. Prime Minister Nehru, who regarded such a change as retrogressive and potentially antithetical to the unity and integrity of the Indian nation, however, overcame to a certain degree his aversion to regional pressures.

The reorganization of States[9] was accomplished despite some resistance from the center. Even so, the center stopped short of resolving satisfactorily and democratically the question of regional cultural, linguistic, and communal identity, especially regarding India's far-flung periphery—particularly the disputed States of Jammu and Kashmir (which have been governed, to this day, under the special Article 371 of the Indian Constitution), Punjab, and the vast and varied northeastern region of India, now comprising seven different States known as the "Seven Sisters."

Phase II: 1967 to 1977

During the decade from 1967 to 1977, the Congress Party, and subsequently the Congress-R, after the party split in 1969, found itself increasingly on the defensive as a widely varied assortment of opposition forces attacked the ruling party at the hustings. The disparate and fragmented character of the forces of opposition would, eventually, be mirrored in the Congress Party itself as its internal cohesion and ideological mold developed cracks and gradually broke, leading to endemic intraparty conflicts.

The general strategy adopted by the Indira Gandhi government prior to the Internal Emergency consisted of two main elements: suppression of dissidence within the party, and a severe strengthening of the central government and party control.

The suppression of dissidence was achieved through gross interference from party headquarters and the prime minister's office in the day-to-day affairs of Congress governments in the States. The main casualty of this interference was democratic decision making at the regional and State levels and the reduction of the State legislative assemblies to the status of marketplaces for defection, invariably engineered by the powers that be, with the copious use of money and threats. This general tendency reflected the extraordinary degrees to which corruption had taken hold of the ruling party and the government with the active encouragement of the prime minister herself.

The strengthening of the center took place by means of various subterfuges, all of which undermined the constitution simultaneously on a number of important fronts. These included the politicization of the president's office (especially after the 1969 split); the weakening of center-State relations (and therefore the "federal" character of the Indian system of governance) by means of promiscuous recourse to presidential rule and the arbitrary dismissal, on flimsy grounds, of democratically elected governments led by coalitions and parties opposed to the Congress Party (Sathyamurthy 1989); the application of political pressure on the bureaucracy, which spread fear among civil servants while systematizing and deepening corruption throughout all layers of government; the enfeeblement of the judiciary by interfering in the procedures affecting its smooth operations at the center and in the States, and attempting to politicize it by robbing it of its independence; and last but not least, under the cloak of populist rhetoric, the attempt to tinker with the constitution in order to undermine the fundamental democratic and civil rights of the people.[10]

The Internal Emergency, imposed suddenly by Mrs. Gandhi on June 25, 1975, represented the denouement of this phase. The Internal Emergency, declared in the name of safeguarding the unity, integrity, and cohesion of the Indian regime, can be appropriately described as an attempt by the central government to subvert the Indian Constitution in order to impose an authoritarian regime. The decision to call a general election in 1977 in order to legitimize the changes that had been wrought under the Emergency was as much a happy accident as the imposition of the latter had been an embattled prime minister's deliberate act of will.

Phase III: 1977 to the Present

The third phase, from 1977 on, has been characterized by an intensification of socioeconomic conflicts and a simultaneous accentuation of political fragmentation, which will profoundly affect the balance between the constitution and the cohesive polity envisaged by its authors. Since 1977, political changes have gathered pace and have affected cohesion at different levels in different ways. The extent of restlessness within the various social, economic, and political forces competing for control over structures of power and participation in governance has been so great that it is unlikely that single-party dominance will ever be reestablished at the center.

Coalitions embodying interparty arrangements or intraparty agreements have become normal; no party can expect, for the foreseeable future, to take power as an exclusive democratically elected political force. Ruling elements have become coalitional rather than single-party in character since the disappearance of the Nehru dynasty from center stage in Indian politics. In the immediate aftermath of the Emergency, a genuine and largely successful attempt was made by the Janata coalition, which took power after the 1977 general election, to restore the constitution.

The success of the Janata government could by no means be deemed irreversible for two major reasons.

First, the very nature of coalition politics being as it is, governmental stability at the center was at risk. This was amply demonstrated not only by the rapid disintegration of the Janata government (1977–79) but also by the brief interlude provided by the National Front administration (1989–90), each of which was followed by a lame-duck ministry pending a mid-term general election. In effect, this means that the Congress (I) Party is able to exercise control over the forces of state power either by default (as in the 1979 election), or by taking advantage of some event of magnitude (as in the 1984 general election), or, as at the present time, simply by being the party with the largest number (oscillating between a minority and a majority) of members of the Lok Sabha, the lower house of the federal legislature, with a president who showed himself to be partisan in essential ways (Guhan 1994). The crux of the matter, therefore, lies in the fact that the centralizing tendency of the Congress (I) Party will continue to undermine the federal principle in the absence of a clear alternative.

Second, over the years, two contradictory perceptions of the Indian state have developed, largely due to the different experiences of the dominant elites and their supporters on the one hand, and on the other, the vast mass of the Indian people belonging to the "subaltern" or underclasses and living at or below the poverty line. The Indian state has acted during the past four decades largely in the economic and political interests of the elites. Despite the tensions and conflicts between different segments of the dominant classes—between the agrarian rich and the industrial bourgeoisie, between upholders of national capital and supporters of international capital, between small regionally based industrialists and big capitalists, and between productive and nonproductive elites—political disputes challenging the center have always been resolved in such a way as to reinforce rather than undermine the broad assumptions of the constitution makers.

Changes in the relationship between the center and the regions have been changes of style rather than of substance. The ideology of national cohesion has been furthered in the interest of benefiting from a growing middle class and an ever expanding market, at the present time catering to the needs of anywhere between 300 million and 400 million consumers. Contrast this with the steady impoverishment, marginalization, and relentless socioeconomic and political oppression of a similar number of people (any figure between 360 million and 500 million can be reasonably justified). To these people terms such as national cohesion, integrity, and unity have an altogether different and hollow ring. Nevertheless, they have shown a determination to survive and protest with whatever help they might be able to obtain from political forces and even parties that rhetorically support their betterment and the removal of social barriers.

Contemporary Indian political organizations, for the mass of the poor people, operates on two levels. The first concerns resistance movements, which have become a common feature during the past two decades, and are invariably directed against the state—as in the huge Narmada Andolan, of which even the World Bank has been compelled to take note. Even though they take the form of agitations with a specific target, they also have a cumulative effect, as in the case of the Chipko movement, as well as an imitative dimension, as in the agitations over the building of huge dams displacing vast numbers of people from their habitats.

The second level of political activity for the poor concerns political parties. In certain States of India, as well as centrally, political parties have arisen during the past ten years or so that emphasize changing the balance of power in favor of the lower and lowest castes.[11] Thus, in Uttar Pradesh and Bihar, there has been a shift in the social base of political power at the local level, with the lower-caste leaders of the Yadav having replaced the upper- and middle-caste leaders in positions of regional political power. This pattern has been replicated in elections to the three lower tiers of local governance—the *zilla*, the *samiti*, and the *panchayat*). Even though their assumption of power has by no means initiated a fundamental transformation of the elitist character of power-wielding in the States,[12] the lowest social strata,[13] whose interests are still without effective representation, tend to support new parties embodying an ideology of populism in their political propaganda.

Populist appeals by new parties to minorities that have become alienated from the Congress (I) have been accompanied by suggestions, which over recent years have become more and more vociferous, that India needs a new constitution based on contemporary reality.[14] In other words, the current constitution is seen by the poorer half of India as inappropriate to its needs.

The Congress (I) has been challenged from yet another force, much bigger in size and of much further reach than the parties of the poor and movements of resistance. The Bharatiya Janata Party (BJP), itself the political vehicle of the much more widely dispersed but highly influential Sangh Parivar (literally, the "family of the Hindu community"—in actual fact, a "family of Hindu political and social organizations"), is a populist party that has never been in sole control of the Indian state except during the fortnight following the 1996 general election. It has been propagating a concept of India at variance with the spirit of the constitution in one important respect. Its aim is to put Hindu nationalism in the place of Indian nationalism, while claiming to leave intact the democratic character of the polity and leaving the position of minorities (in concrete terms) unaltered.

In practice, the Congress (I) has, in recent decades, pandered to the Hindu angle of electoral calculus in election after election while claiming to be a secular party. A major segment of the Indian intelligentsia—English educated and Western oriented—has been fulminating against the "populist," "totalitarian," and indeed "fascist" character of the Hindu parties, without appreciating the fact that, as an opposition force, these parties are bound to attract support from the vast mass of Hindu electorate, as in the case of the Ayodhya episode leading up to the demolition of the Babri Masjid mosque on December 6, 1992. An increase in the power of the BJP to govern nationally or regionally will inevitably result in demands to rewrite the constitution to reflect the "true" character of the Indian polity. Whether this would necessarily result in an end to the secular state in India remains an open question.

In two fundamental respects, the populism of the BJP offers a stark contrast to secular parties of the poor and movements of resistance. While the latter have as their principal constituency disadvantaged sections without any reference to communal or other divisive social identification marks, the BJP's base is centered chiefly in religious identity. At the same time, the economic program of the BJP by no means favors the poor in any significant way. Despite its newfound slogan of self-reliance, or *swadeshi*, the BJP is committed to an overall economic program essentially identical to that which has prevailed since the late 1970s: liberalization and privatization are its main features.

The Constitution under Congress Rule

Three specific aspects of Indian politics have a central bearing on the nexus between the constitution and national cohesion in postcolonial India: the institutional structure of power, with special reference to the judiciary and the office of president of the republic; center-State relations; and fundamental human, civil, and democratic rights guaranteed under the constitution.

It is essential to grasp that the Indian Constitution is an amalgam of several ingredients. They constitute, in the metaphor of elementary chemistry, a mixture rather than a compound. Among the ingredients brought together were the Government of India Act, adopted by the British in 1935 to expand the franchise and cover provincial elections, and incorporated more or less intact in the constitution, with minor omissions and modifications;[15] elements of British parliamentary practice, in particular parliamentary sovereignty, as reflected in an elected parliament and an executive provided by the party with a majority of seats; principles embodied in the U.S. Constitution, especially those relating to the judiciary; and several French and German legal and constitutional ideas relating to the state (the "Preamble, the Chapters on fundamental rights and the Directive Principles of [s]tate policy"), thrown in for good measure. The specific problems posed by features unique to Indian society, with its peculiar cleavages of caste and linguistic variety and conflicts over communal and religious plurality, were dealt with in a more or less ad hoc manner under appropriate rubrics. The "state" envisaged in the Indian Constitution was not a product of study of the historical and cultural features of Indian society, but instead was based on the intellectual predilections of a narrow band of the Indian social spectrum consisting of Westernized middle-class intellectuals who saw themselves as pragmatists par excellence.

Yet, at a different level, it must be stressed that the text of the constitution reflects certain values and ideals that go "beyond its instrumental use" in the hands of the wielders of state power and the judicial organs. Thus, even though those who wrote the constitution were imbued with a political vision based on the tacit assumption that the Congress Party would remain in power in perpetuity, in actual practice it has been put to unintended use as in the words of Sudarshan, "a valuable weapon and shield from the perspective of dominated classes."[16]

The intellectual framework of the constitution was rooted in a contradiction. Those who were to wield power in the Indian state represented certain more or less clearly articulated economic interests of the propertied classes, while at the same time playing a crucial role as mediators between the propertied classes and the impoverished masses. The Congress Party saw itself as the only legitimate political force; all other political parties were viewed as led by self-seeking and half-baked politicians whose democratic credentials and commitment to the rule of law were suspect, to say the least. The lawyers and other intellectuals who played a crucial role in writing the constitution paid very little attention to ensuring the democratic character of civil society in India,[17] but a great deal of attention to how best to steer a middle course between revolutionary programs of the left and conservative, procapitalist authoritarianism of the right. "The framers were more inclined to trust the judiciary and the civil service because these institutions were expected to remain aloof from politics. . . . Therefore, they conferred on the Supreme Court and the High Courts one of the widest jurisdictions in the world" (Sudarshan 1994: 67).

Yet the Constituent Assembly took great pains to word the provisions of the constitution to avoid disputes of jurisdiction between the executive, legislature, and judiciary regarding interpretation. In practice, however, such a neat compartmentalization led to the opposite of what had been intended. While assuming a position of supremacy in the sphere of lawmaking, the legislature expected the courts to "supply what is, in fact, a missing tradition" (Sudarshan 1994: 69). The missing tradition here is the centuries-old evolution of British parliamentary practice that no written constitution could encapsulate (Kothari 1994: 58–60). Furthermore, the reasoning behind the Indian Constitution conflates the British tradition of constitutional proprieties and procedures with that implied in a written constitution, "which seeks to supply binding norms and substantive goals for political conduct. It further confuses a continental Rousseauistic idea of the will of the people, or the collective will, with the decisions of a parliamentary majority, rather than identify the collective will with the idea of the state" (Sudarshan 1994: 70).

As long as the power of the state was wielded without challenge from the regions or political parties and forces opposed to the Congress, the cases that came before the Supreme Court dealt with questions on which the latter found no need to raise its profile.

However, as the Congress Party became more and more embattled and the parliamentary majority proved to be increasingly problematic, the blurring of sovereign authority between Parliament and the Supreme Court gave way to conflict between the two organs of the Indian state. Several cases brought before the Supreme Court resulted in decisions regarded by the government as going far beyond the reach of powers given to the court under the Constitution.

In the Golaknath case of 1967,[18] the decision of the Supreme Court that fundamental rights could not be amended by Parliament was seized by the government as an important factor in undermining its land reform policy. In fact, Mrs. Gandhi gave as one of the reasons for the imposition of the Internal Emergency in 1975 the need to suspend fundamental rights in order to speed up agrarian reform, which the Supreme Court had obstructed in its antiegalitarian judgment.

But even before the Emergency was declared, Subba Rao, the former chief justice whose court had delivered the Golaknath judgment, had put himself forward as a presidential candidate in the 1969 election.[19] As the conflict between the government and the Supreme Court gathered momentum, the prime minister became more and more enamored of the opportunities provided by populist politics, while the august body at the head of the judiciary appeared to be so rarefied in its arguments as to project the impression that it had no convincing and clear blueprint to offer on what it saw as "a proper form of political rule" (Sudarshan 1994: 73).

The decision in the Golaknath case, followed by others in which the court ruled that the Congress government's hastily passed populist economic measures violated the Constitution, revealed a conservative cast to the Supreme Court. The Congress election campaign of 1971, with Mrs. Gandhi's newfound radical populist mood, held the judiciary up to ridicule. It was as though the ruling party had become disenchanted with the state that it had itself fashioned on the anvil of the constitution. In an act tantamount to a denial of the very legitimacy of the state, the ruling party lurched toward the politics of personality cult and dynastic appropriation of state power.

If the Golaknath decision gave a powerful boost to ideas about property entrenched in the constitution, the historic judgment of the full bench of the Supreme Court on the Kesavananda Bharathi case illustrated a much more profoundly political dimension of the working of the court as interpreter of the constitution. It laid down the principle that the basic structure of government as embodied in the constitution could not be altered by the government. Its political impact was bound to be of considerable significance. The case highlighted a clash of ideas, if not wills, between the prime minister, who saw herself as the champion of social justice in India (despite being already surrounded by litigation over her alleged corruption), and a court anxious to curtail the government's tendency to exercise power in an arbitrary manner. Its judgment, despite the variegated arguments it contained, laid down a dictum of far-reaching political importance, that the Parliament's power to amend the constitution did not extend to altering its "basic structure and framework" (Sudarshan 1994: 74).[20]

The government's determination to resist the imposition of constitutional limits on its power crystallized in its declaration of the Internal Emergency in June 1975. In the same breath, the central government attempted to amend the constitution within a few weeks of the Emergency taking effect.[21] Even before the ink had dried on the approval by the Rajya Sabha (the upper house of Parliament) of this bizarre amendment, the government entered a plea in the Supreme Court that the latter's judgment in the Kesavananda Bharathi case be annulled.[22]

The government's attempt to alter the constitutional foundation of the Indian state rested on the notion that, in order to centralize power and make its arbitrary exercise easy, the British-style cabinet system of government should be replaced by a presidential system in which a president, elected by direct franchise, could overrule intermediate tiers of government with impunity. Furthermore, a serious attempt was made to introduce profound alterations in the different lists of jurisdiction (central, State, and concurrent) with a view to undermining the relative autonomy of State governments in crucial areas, such as education, agriculture, and home and police (Palkhivala 1984: 195–98).

Just as events, with the imposition of the Internal Emergency, overtook the regular constitutional evolution of the Indian political system in one direction, so, too, events gathered momentum in the opposite direction with the accidental ending of the Emergency in February 1977, followed by a general election. Happily, the hastily cobbled together amendments to the constitution, intended to pave the way for the replacement of an indirectly elected, ideally nonpartisan president, with reserve powers, by a directly elected executive president, with a vast reservoir of power at his disposal, was consigned to the dustbin of history (Palkhivala 1984: 204).

However, it is important to note that even without an amendment to the constitution, the office of the president had been severely compromised in a political sense even before the Emergency. Even though Rajendra Prasad, the first president of the Indian Republic (a congressman who had also been the president of the Constituent Assembly), made no secret of his unhappiness with a crucial piece of legislation relating to Hindu family law, his role was neither obstructive to, nor politically supportive of, the elected government. The political behavior and general orientation of subsequent presidents, Sarvepalli Radhakrishnan and Zakir Husain, were constitutionally unexceptionable.

A qualitative change did occur in the character of the presidency from 1969 onward. In that year Mrs. Gandhi split the ruling party over the very question of the undivided Congress Party's preferred candidate (Sathyamurthy 1969) for election to replace Zakir Husain.[23] Claiming to give a new look to the administration by overhauling the party with the help of Young Turks (a group consisting of young pseudoleftist political arrivistes), Mrs. Gandhi made the issue of voting for N. Sanjeeva Reddy, the ruling party's official candidate, one of conscience. With the prime minister's encouragement and support, V. V. Giri, the incumbent vice president, offered himself as an independent candidate in opposition to Reddy. Giri became the fourth president of India. He was also the first occupant of the office who completely subordinated himself to the will of the prime minister.

Fakhruddin Ali Ahmed, Giri's immediate successor, had the misfortune to hold office when the Internal Emergency was imposed, a measure to which he was believed to have given reluctant presidential assent. But any constitutionally required independence of spirit of which he might have been capable had already been thwarted by the diminution of scope that the office of the president underwent during Giri's tenure. Ahmed, too, like Husain (in 1969) died halfway into his term of office.

The Janata government's coming to power was swiftly followed by a presidential election.[24] Sanjeeva Reddy, a member of the rump of the Congress Party at the time of the split, was elected. For the first time in the history of the Indian Constitution, a weak coalition ministry took power at the center. As an experienced Congress leader and former chief minister of one of the largest States of the Indian union, Reddy was able to interfere in the working of the government in ways not altogether salutary to the maintenance of healthy, parliamentary democratic norms. After nearly three decades of relatively low-key incumbents of the presidency, the contrast between Giri's submissive role and Reddy's domineering style could not have been sharper.

Reddy allowed his personal predilections and caste prejudice to stand in the way of presidential objectivity. When the Janata government went into crisis and Prime Minister Morarji Desai lost a vote of confidence in Parliament, President Reddy, ignoring well-worn constitutional procedures, appointed a minority government without even inviting the deputy prime minister Jagjiwan Ram, (arguably the most experienced parliamentarian in the history of independent India), to try to form a government (Palkhivala 1984: 218–20). This was widely believed to have been motivated by caste prejudice, which the president shared with the Janata government's prime minister and his senior cabinet colleague, Chowdhury Charan Singh.[25]

After Reddy's term came to an end, Mrs. Gandhi and her son Rajiv Gandhi reverted even more blatantly than in 1969 to the practice of installing her henchmen. Zail Singh blew hot and cold as president. Under Mrs. Gandhi he was content to remain tame and voiceless. During his last year in office, however, he tried in vain to take advantage of the corruption in which the Rajiv Gandhi government had mired itself to carve out a political niche for himself. In both incarnations—Zail Singh the meek, and Zail Singh the defiant—he, like Giri, Ahmed, and Reddy before him, acted in a way that did not reflect creditably on the office of the president.

Singh was followed by the worst of all incumbents to the post of president of India. Ramaswamy Venkataraman was a dyed-in-the-wool party functionary whose career in the secondary ranks of Congress politics dated to the 1930s. Rajiv Gandhi chose him as a safe candidate after Singh's belated attempt to be "his own man." Old and wily, Venkataraman's mark on the presidency was distinguished by his partisanship on behalf of the Congress (I), whether it was in power or out, serving mainly to demean the constitutional nature of the office by reducing it to a party instrument.

With the coming to power of a minority Congress (I) government in July 1991, and the assumption of office soon afterward by Shankar Dayal Sharma as president, the role played by those who have occupied this high constitutional position so far has come full circle. Starting from a neutral, titular role, aloof from the rough-and-tumble of parliamentary politics, the presidency was transformed by Mrs. Gandhi into an office robbed of its independence and objectivity. From being a creature of Mrs. Gandhi, the presidency suddenly became a weapon in the hands of experienced incumbent politicians who attempted to exploit the inherent political weakness of coalitions that have, on occasion, taken power at the center. All in all the presidency, already a weak link in the chain of institutions spawned by the constitution, may have been weakened to such an extent that the capacity to intervene in crises affecting the democratic values enshrined in the constitution may have been all but fatally impaired.

The conduct of politics in India and the development of the Indian state under the aegis of the Congress Party have departed considerably from the political order envisaged in the constitution. However, despite systematic attacks against democracy on the part of the Congress administration, the enthusiasm and highly developed consciousness of the mass of the people with respect to fundamental civil, human, and democratic rights have largely prevented the center from exercising arbitrary authority beyond certain limits.

Of profound significance is the gulf between the role of civil society envisaged in the constitution and its reduction, if not attempted elimination, in practice by the state throughout the three phases I have described. Thus, for example, the constitution guarantees freedom of speech, which in effect means that the state can be interrogated as to its conduct in the public sphere. Until 1962, a regional movement such as the Tamil Dravida Munnetra Kazhagam (DMK) could openly articulate demands for autonomy (including secession); although, it must be added, even at this stage the CPI was not free to propagate its views. Starting with the Preventive Detention Act (1950), a steady accumulation of increasingly draconian laws in the name of internal security (e.g., Maintenance of Internal Security Act of 1971) and preventing terrorism (e.g., Terrorist and Disruptive Activities [Prevention] Act of 1987) has resulted not only in an extension of police powers to the private and personal sphere, such as legal sanction to arrest and detain persons at will for indefinite periods of time, but also in arbitrarily curtailing even the most elementary freedoms.

At another level, that of the dominant classes and elite segments of society, the original consensus appears to have held, by and large, despite the eruption of conflict in various regions against the center's authoritarianism, and painful readjustments and agonizing reappraisals of how much power each of the major segments of the ruling classes should appropriate to itself. Such reorientations of political power have been brought about by means of shifts of authority between the different organs of the state under the constitution. National unity as viewed from the perspective of the nationally and regionally dominant classes has been largely maintained and, in the process, the president's office has been distorted; the judiciary's position was severely imperiled during the decade from 1967 to 1977, and has only been fully restored during the last few years (Palkhivala 1984: 221–34).

Center-State Relations and the Indian Constitution

The shaping of the Indian union was marked by frequent shifts of emphasis in the relationship that was envisaged between the center and the States.

As long as it was believed that Partition could be averted or circumvented, the Constituent Assembly favored a loose federation of relatively autonomous States. By April 1947, however, with the inevitability of Partition, the Constituent Assembly shelved the original proposal favoring a hybrid between a confederal and a federal structure. Instead, a union of States, with a powerful center entrusted with legislative authority and preponderant financial powers, was proposed and accepted. Under the powers that the center thus arrogated to itself, the union Parliament was empowered to alter the boundaries of States by a simple majority "without necessarily obtaining the consent of the States concerned" (Sudarshan 1994: 75). The template for this centrist orientation was provided by the Government of India Act. Despite the linguistic reorganization of States that the center implemented against Nehru's wishes, and the rise of regional consciousness and the spread of subnational political identities in different parts of the country, the center resisted the clamor for greater autonomy for States on the grounds that the "unity and integrity" of India would be threatened.

The arena of center-State relations has witnessed major political conflicts from a very early stage in the history of postcolonial India. The enormous range of restrictions imposed on the power of provincial governments, and the practically unlimited authority vested in governors during the colonial period, resurfaced in the form of presidential rule under Article 356 of the Indian Constitution, "with ominous consequences for the functioning of federalism in India. The Constitution thus mimics the colonial state where the center controlled the periphery" (Sudarshan 1994: 76).

The two instances of summary dismissal of democratically elected governments in PEPSU[26] in 1951 and Kerala in 1959, were followed, during the decades since the 1960s, by a promiscuous rash of States being brought under presidential rule on the flimsiest of pretexts. To date, the total number of such cases has far exceeded a hundred.

The most sustained protest against the center's arbitrary rule over the States was organized by regional parties, movements, and struggles—especially, but not only, in the Punjab since the 1950s, in Tamil Nadu since the 1960s, and in Andhra Pradesh, the northeastern States, Assam, Jharkhand, Uttarakhand, and Darjeeling since the 1980s—and by the CPI(M) from the mid-1960s onward (Sathyamurthy 1985, 1989). Between 1967 and 1971, numerous coalition governments, formed of parties on the left and right in opposition to the Congress, took office in several States. In Madras (subsequently rechristened Tamil Nadu), the

DMK, a regional Tamil party, rode to power after winning a huge majority of seats in the State legislative assembly. Tempering its original demand for complete autonomy from the center, the DMK government initiated a wide-ranging debate on the question of center-State relations. It took the form of a report submitted by a specially appointed commission under the direction of Justice P. V. Rajamannar.[27] The Rajamannar Report represented the first major interjection of a State government in a dialogue between the two unequal sides that was to extend over a period of two decades.

The CPI(M) played an important role in organizing opposition throughout the country against presidential rule. Since 1977, with its impregnable majority in West Bengal, it has been a powerful regional political force against arbitrary central rule. Thus, apart from the period 1971–77, during which the writ of the center ran high and strong throughout the country, and even Congress chief ministers trembled for their fates, the past twenty-five years have been fraught with numerous tensions and conflicts. The net result of these confrontations has been to increase gradually the influence of the States, even though in important matters such as fiscal autonomy they have not yet made significant progress.

The politics of the struggle between the center and the States has followed two distinct lines over the decades. Until the end of the Emergency, the social base on which political power rested in India was more or less homogeneous in character. Any social contradictions surfacing during this period did not signify serious conflict of interest or rift between regional elites and the national bourgeoisie. Apart from its antipathy toward the communist parties in general and the CPI(M) in particular, the ruling Congress Party was in a position to accommodate intra–ruling class rivalries in a more or less satisfactory manner (Sathyamurthy 1983). However, as the rich- and middle-peasant classes acquired greater and greater regional strength, the power of the Congress Party (especially in the States) was subject to erosion. Even in such States as Uttar Pradesh and Bihar, where the Congress Party's dominance was more or less taken for granted, its power was challenged by new political formations often led by powerful rural caste leaders of the newly emergent rich- and middle-peasant classes (Das 1992).

The center-State conflicts of the 1960s and 1970s thus represented no more than political adjustments, within constitutionally permitted limits, of differences along horizontal lines, between various segments—industrial and agrarian, big industrial and small industrial, productive and nonproductive, regional and national—of the bourgeoisie. Starting with the reorganization of States in the 1950s and ending with the Emergency, the center followed a policy of insisting that it had preeminent responsibility for maintaining national cohesion and that the political demands of subsegments of the bourgeoisie would be partially met by appropriate financial and administrative measures, as long as they did not extend to formal devolution of powers from the center to the States (Sathyamurthy 1985).

The demands of the CPI(M), which by the mid-1960s had joined the mainstream of Indian politics as a party beginning to attach much greater importance to its parliamentary than to its revolutionary agenda, were more harshly dealt with by the center for two reasons. First, the CPI(M) was the only major cadre-based party that focused on the vertical contradiction between the oppressed working classes (rural and urban, but organized) and the ruling classes (represented in the control of state power by the center under the aegis of the Congress administration). The vertical line of conflict has also been anathema in the eyes of the parties not only of the national bourgeoisie but also of the regional bourgeoisie and petit bourgeoisie. Second, Mrs. Gandhi, as a radical populist leader, saw herself as the champion of the poor, the cleanser of the Congress, and the slayer of the idle rich. As such, she would not tolerate any political party claiming to address political questions relating to the equitable economic and social development of the poorer sections of the country.

The major conflicts in the sphere of center-State relations that erupted anew or that reached new levels of militancy after the Emergency were of a different ilk from those prior to the Emergency. In the Punjab, Assam, northeast India, Kashmir, and more recently in sub-State regions such as Darjeeling (in West Bengal), Jharkhand (in Bihar), and Uttarakhand (in Uttar Pradesh), new movements arose, challenging the center and demanding autonomy.[28] The struggle was no longer confined to the sphere of administrative and fiscal devolution; it aimed to forge a new political identity around the crystallization of unique ethnic characteristics that had a "national" ring to them.

The movements in the northeast, Assam, Kashmir, and the Punjab (Sathyamurthy 1986), which had been troubled areas even during the peaceful interludes, stressed their particularities without linking them to the threads that bound the region to the center. Thus, the theme of complete secession was advanced by those favoring Khalistan and independent Kashmir, and the language of Partition (of the late 1930s and 1940s) favoring statehood based on religious cohesion was once again revived. Resort to political militancy and civilian violence by religious separatist movements (e.g., the Khalistan movement in the Punjab, and the Jammu and Kashmir Liberation Front in Kashmir) on the one hand, and the police forces of the States concerned and the Indian military on the other, have imparted a sharper edge to the tension between the Congress brand of monolithic cohesive nationalism and the movements of ethnic self-determination based on radically different definitions of "nationality" (Sathyamurthy 1983, 1985).

However, it is important to note that this larger form of struggle spills well beyond the confines of center-State contestations, let alone constitutionally contained formulations of the issues at stake. Thus, for example, in the Punjab, despite the undoubtedly more serious resonance of this conflict during the 1980s than that of the center-State conflicts of previous decades, an unwritten consensus did prevail between the center and the dominant classes among the Sikhs. These elites included urban traders, capitalist investors in the State and in other parts of India, certain segments of the intelligentsia, the working-class segments under the leadership of the CPI, and those segments of the agrarian rich entering other arenas of enterprise, such as trucking. All were able to agree with the government on the desirability of limited rather than complete autonomy, even though the center, until the Rajiv Gandhi–Longowal agreement of 1985 (Sathyamurthy 1986), chose to give the Anandpur Sahib Resolution a narrow rather than a broad interpretation. The resolution, originally adopted by the Shiromani Akali Dal in the early 1970s, embodies Sikh demands of a political, economic and cultural nature which could only be met by increasing the autonomy of the State of Punjab within the federal State of India.

At the level of the oppressed masses, however, militant autonomy movements were no longer satisfied with the consensus embraced by the dominant classes and elite. In 1983, the central government appointed a Commission on Center-State Relations with Justice R. S. Sarkaria as chairperson. The Sarkaria Report, published in 1987, recommended that the continuation of a strong center should be combined with a system of decentralization of power and local government, under which an Inter-State Council (already provided for in the constitution but never established in practice) would be expected to generate a consensus on critical issues of federalism and decentralization,[29] and elected assemblies would be extended to cover all five tiers of government, including zilla, samiti, and panchayat (Mukarji 1994; Bandyopadhyay 1994). The Sarkaria

Report represents the closing of a chapter in the constitutional history of India, of which the opening gambit was provided by the Rajamannar Report.

Even without considering the political options open to the vast mass of the Indian people under the present system of government, it is clear that the consensus on national unity is not nearly as strong now as it was prior to the Emergency. The constitutional discussion of this question has not been matched by the political discussion, which has been stifled by a center—increasingly ruled by heterogeneous coalitions including the Congress (I)—no longer able to respond effectively to social conflicts in States ruled by less heterogeneous political forces. The judiciary, grossly impaired by decades of manipulation at the hands of the government and subject to interference in its day-to-day administration was, at least until 1944, slow to step into the breach "to provide 'relief' to an impotent political process by converting into constitutional discourse critical issues that are best handled in terms of political discourse." Nor was it capable of handling "grave problems arising out of the assertion of 'Hindu nationalism' and Muslim 'fundamentalism,' or the claims of Other Backward Classes for employment quotas, or, for that matter, inter-State riparian disputes" (Sudarshan 1994: 84).

The following assessment strikes at the heart of the question of the tension between national integrity and regional interests based on a rival brand of cohesion reflecting local realities.

> Unfortunately, the terms of political discourse . . . have been corrupted, first by colonial practices, and later by the Congress culture. Even though we may praise India's Constitution for having survived several crises, it still remains . . . a Constitution fashioned by the colonizer and the Congress. Independence, and several relatively free democratic governments have failed to give India's political leadership the maturity to be self-conscious about the moral content of a constitutional order. Nor have they made much difference to the intensity of poverty and exploitation in the country. The "people of India" can truly give a Constitution suited to their "genius," and rid it of its unfortunate legacies, only in the course of prolonged political and democratic struggles. (Sudarshan 1994: 84)

The Constitution as a Site of Struggles over Fundamental Rights

An important strand in the debates surrounding the constitution, and the discourse generated by it, is concerned with the larger promises embedded in the chapter of the constitution entitled "Directive Principles of

State Policy" (Kothari 1994). These embody high aspirations with respect to the standards of democracy, citizenship, and cultural, economic, and social freedoms to which all Indian people are entitled. The directive principles were, however, deliberately not made an operational part of the Constitution, their status being merely hortatory in character.

Political practice was vitiated by the vertically divided nature of Indian society (Dumont 1986), and by the potentially antagonistic contradiction contained in it (Dutt 1940). A majority of the population, consisting of the lower classes, the rapidly expanding underclass, uprooted peasantry and landless labor, women, marginalized workers, Scheduled Castes, Scheduled Tribes, and minority communities, such as Muslims, have not been well served by the constitution. At the same time, the postcolonial Indian state, which has made use of its relative autonomy to adjudicate between the conflicting claims of established and newly arisen segments of dominant classes (and the associated sociological strata, based on caste, regional, and communal identification marks), has not been entirely successful in its effort to bend the constitution and the institutional structures established under its aegis to accommodate the multiplex, mutually (though not yet antagonistically) contradictory interests across the horizontal lines dividing different segments of the dominant classes and the ruling elites.

The role of the judiciary in relation to the citizen needs to be seen in a dual light. The Court has dealt with cases involving property rights in a generally conservative spirit, even though the regime's populist measures, especially during the 1970s, represented at best a feeble effort to score propaganda points against the Supreme Court rather than addressing the dire economic straits of the 40–50 percent of the Indian people below the "poverty line."

At the same time, the Court has offered itself as a useful site for unraveling disputed issues relating to constitutionally guaranteed fundamental rights to individuals. To this effect, an extensive and impressive edifice of case law has been built up during the last four decades. All this no doubt adds up to a spirited and vigilant defense of the constitution against political attacks of the ruling party, which have the effect of undermining the countervailing power and influence of the judiciary in postcolonial India.

Furthermore, certain judges of the Supreme Court (e.g., V. R. Krishna Iyer) and organs of public opinion have made notable contributions to the constitutional discourse and debate surrounding "public interest litigation".[30] These debates have breathed new life into the "Directive Principles", to which a number of politically conscious citizens and grassroots organizations and groups have returned from time to time pressing home the social objectives of law and legal instruments, and . . . . asking for new instruments . . . . aimed at social justice—all the way from "right to work" and the "right to information" to statutory status to the rights of Scheduled Castes and Tribes, implementation of the Mandal Commission Report,[31] the setting up of the National Commission on Women . . . . all of these equipped with juridical teeth (Kothari 1994: 40).

Yet, in another and very different light, the political impact of the Court has been slight and insubstantial. The reason for this lies in the fact that access to its ministrations and intervention is restricted to those who command the resources required to make use of its services. For the vast majority of the people who live under severe conditions of deprivation and oppression (not least, the oppressive behavior of the instruments of state power), "struggle" rather than court cases is the only option left.

During the last twenty-five years or so, numerous democratic struggles have been waged by different segments of the Indian people (the most impressive of these being those launched during the Emergency to regain civil and democratic rights which were arbitrarily rubbed out of the Constitution by the fiat of a dictatorial Prime Minister). The nature, scope and impact of these struggles are directly linked to questions of development, class, human rights, representative and participatory politics, and democratization of the economy by means of a systematic devolution of fiscal and political power.

The remit of "viable constitutionalism", with reference to postcolonial India, looks very different depending on whether one situates it in the political perspective of the dominant classes and their supporters, *or* in the viewpoint of those segments of the Indian masses which the Constitution has by-passed or ignored. That the gap between these two broad orientations is difficult to bridge is clearly evident from political developments leading up to the Emergency (Rajagopalan 1977) and those since its ending. I consider below the problem posed by "viable constitutionalism" from these two contradictory angles.

With the proliferation of the bourgeoisie (Patnaik, Chandrasekhar and Sen 1995), the divergence of interests between the industrial bourgeoisie, on the one hand, and the newly arisen (post-Green Revolution) rich- and middle-peasant classes (Sathyamurthy 1995), on the other, and the acute competition between all these rival segments of the dominant classes for the limited surplus generated by the Indian political economy (Sathyamurthy 1994), the development of capitalist relations of production in India has by no means followed a path of smooth and linear ascent.

The growth of capitalism in India has been marked by alternate phases of spurts and stagnation, unevenness, persistence of precapitalist modes of production (and social oppression that go with them, especially in agriculture), acute dependence on the state during the first three decades of independence, a permanent and almost parasitic psychological and financial dependence on international capital as well as on the governments of the industrially advanced countries of the world, and above all by a lack of capacity to fire the engines of production to the extent needed to cater fully to the needs of a rapidly expanding domestic market, with simultaneous promotion of export of goods abroad.

The conflicts to which horizontal divisions between different segments of the dominant classes gave rise were not anticipated by the Founding Fathers. Their linear view of India's future did not permit any unforeseen undulations in the path of development, while the political assumptions on which the constitution was based imparted to the postcolonial state a quality of inflexibility. Translated into practice, the Indian state, after the first two decades of independence, found it increasingly difficult to cope with the numerous nuances that appeared in the course of the development of the dominant classes and the elite. In other words, the new state was not ready for the challenges posed by the inherent and inescapable distortions to which the development of capitalism under Indian conditions was subject.

The conflicts engendered in such an uncharted course of development—between the different institutions of state power blueprinted in the constitution, between the center and the States, and between the dominant and subordinate classes—had the effect of reducing the constitution to a plaything in the hands of a dominant one-party state, and of eventually preventing it from offering itself as a site on which sociopolitical conflicts of such enormous magnitude could be debated and even resolved.

The voices demanding an altered or radically amended or even an entirely new constitution, belonging to the dominant elite, do not represent any serious differences over the question of the "Indian nation" and its "cohesion" or "integrity" or "unity." Rather, such demands constitute, in effect, a confession that the constitution of 1950 has been disappointing in the light of actual developments affecting the ruling classes and dominant elites, and needs a radical reorientation. The viability of the Indian Constitution of 1950 is in serious doubt among the newly arisen segments of the dominant (particularly regionally based) classes for structural, rather than ideological, reasons. The political experience of the poorer classes and oppressed segments of society points to an altogether different kind of dilemma. Their sense of belonging to a civil society in which their fundamental democratic civil rights as citizens were guaranteed instilled in them a higher degree of political consciousness than they had been credited with. This level of political awareness was, however, not matched by their concrete experience with Indian democracy, which became engulfed, in certain regions of the country, in a miasma of violence and corruption.

To a large extent, the social and political history of the vast mass of the Indian people has been one of steering a dangerous course between the Scylla of arbitrary state power and the Charybdis of social violence and intimidation perpetrated with increasing fierceness by the upper and middle castes, slumlords and agents of violence whose services are eagerly sought by politicians belonging to various parties—none more than the Congress (I). The high ideals of "secularism," "democracy," "civil society" at peace with itself, equality of opportunity, free participation in elections as a right, and respect for human dignity have been severely eroded in the marketplace of everyday politics.

The injured masses of India have been in no position to turn to the Constitution for enablement to exercise their just rights enshrined in that very document. Thus, an aroused populace found the Indian state so unbearably oppressive that, during the two years or so before the Internal Emergency was declared, it looked to the leadership of alternative political forces—chiefly to Jaya Prakash Narayan, who flew the banner of the Nav Nirman movement.

The viability of the constitution, for the vast majority of the Indian people, is imperiled by the widening gulf between constitutional idealism and corrupt political practice. The failure of the Indian Constitution to deliver on any of the fundamental "value goods"—such as democracy, socialism, equality, fundamental and civil rights—that it claims for the republic is at the root of the widespread rejection of constitutional channels and methods of protest in favor of direct political action. Viable constitutionalism in this context would entail an entirely new approach to constitution making, based on a recognition of the political maturity and discriminating capacity of a vast electorate with, by now, long experience in making informed political choices.

The precise ingredients of such an alternative constitution must await widespread public discussion, debate, and consultation. It would have to involve a much more complex and diversified procedure than the highly undemocratic method adopted in 1946–49 to dictate to the people a constitution from above. But it is entirely within the realm of possibility to design a new framework for defending and disseminating democratic political values. The lessons of the past fifty years can be summed up in a single statement. The authoritarian segments of the elite have shown greater eagerness than the mass of the people to transgress constitutional boundaries, while the majority of the people (especially the "weaker sections") have, through various political movements (grassroots and other), reached the conclusion that the country needs a new constitution to breathe life into a state capable of delivering the chief value goods—namely, democratic, civil, and fundamental human rights in a political sense, and a decent standard of living.

Notes

1. The question of Sikh autonomy had been raised often during the nationalist movement. But the extreme hostility that prevailed between the Muslim and Sikh populations (the history of which goes back to the seventeenth century) made it possible for the Congress to reach a political compromise with the Sikh leaders. By the same token, Ambedkar had fundamental differences with the Congress on the question of the untouchables. The Congress saw this question in terms of "jobs and "reservation"; Ambedkar's view was based on a root- and branch- opposition to the Hindu caste system.

2. A caveat must be entered here. The stream of nationalist thought, originally developed within the folds of the Congress Party under Bal Gandaghar Tilak's leadership, was picked up and given a specifically Hindu ideological content by the Hindu Mahasabha (the political party claiming to represent the interests of the majority Hindu community). However, important leaders with a specifically "Hindu" political orientation on the future of India were also highly placed in the INC hierarchy, at least until the 1940s. The ideological mainsprings of Hindu nationalism must be located in the Hindu Mahasabha; at the same time, it must be noted that the INC included a segment, by no means negligible in size or organizational influence, that was not nearly as secular in its commitment as the mainly Western-educated following of Nehru. Vallabhbhai Patel, Rajendra Prasad, and Purushottam Das Tandon were examples of the tendency counter to secularism that prevailed at the heart of the Congress movement.

3. Alam 1994 has developed this point in an important contribution.

4. Throughout this paper, the term "State" is used to refer to the States of the Indian union or federation.

5. Throughout this paper, the term "state" is used to refer to the Indian state, the power of which at any given time is controlled by the government at the center.

6. These debates and discussions are documented extensively in Rao 1965–71.

7. However, in his eagerness to accommodate divergent political tendencies in his cabinet, Nehru appointed Dr. Syama Prasad Mookherjee, the Hindu Mahasabha leader, as industries minister during the 1950s. Mookherjee's death coincided with the departure from government of non-Congress elements and the complete political homogenization of the central cabinet.

8. Sathyamurthy 1994–1995 explores, through sixty-one contributions by a number of interdisciplinary social scientists, the complexities of Indian society during the postcolonial phase. The four volumes composing *Social Change and Political Discourse in India*, explore the tensions and contradictions between structures of power and movements of resistance directly relevant to the issues addressed in this paper.

9. Consequent to the self-immolation through fast unto death of Potti Sriramulu, a Telugu leader, Nehru was under pressure to appoint a high-powered commission to report on the reorganization of States. Even though its recommendations were largely accepted, the actual redrawing of the boundaries of the new States left much to be desired.

10. Even though the Internal Emergency (1975–77) witnessed the worst excesses in this respect, repressive legislation dates back to the early years of independence. Moreover, the numerous instruments of police repression and paramilitary formations the state created from the early 1950s onward were intended primarily for the purpose of intimidating the people, often, as in rural areas, by giving support to social oppressors such as the high- and middle-caste rich peasantry and middle peasantry.

11. It must be remembered, however, that the "lowest" castes have not yet experienced the beneficial effects of such initiatives. From a sociological point of view, a clear distinction between "upper," "middle," "lower," and "lowest" castes is necessary for analytical purposes; equally essential is the "class" differentiation within each of these caste categories. Oppression is not confined to the relationship between higher and lower castes. Gradations of oppression apply to the relationship between "superior" and "inferior" castes throughout the caste hierarchy. Likewise, a relationship of oppression prevails between different segments of the same caste depending upon their relative power and affluence. Roughly speaking, in historical terms, the upper castes had their day under colonialism, the middle castes during the first thirty years of Congress rule and since the ascendance of certain regional parties, and the lower castes have come into their own in certain States since the mid-1980s.

12. This is due mainly to the fact that as soon as a new elite captures power, its main aim is to corner all the avenues to enrichment for its own caste members. In the process it is interested not only in displacing the higher-caste elite but also in keeping up the pressure on castes lower down the hierarchy.

13. Despite a number of efforts since the Mandal policy of the National Front government in 1989, neither the center nor the State governments have yet recognized their responsibilities toward the lowest castes (see Mandal 1980). Minority communities in general, and Muslims in particular, have fared badly; more specifically, rural Muslims have suffered as much oppression at the hands of the local elite and bureaucracies as have the *Adivasis,* OBCs, *Dalits*, and women.

14. The distinction is drawn in a subsequent section between initiatives from those in authority to change the constitution in the direction of even greater authoritarianism, and those actively involved in political movements for the poor in the direction of democratization of state power.

15. Colonial law was reformulated to fit the requirements of establishing the hegemony of the Indian bourgeois ideology of property and capital to which labor and skill would be subordinated. "In 1947 the colonial state apparatus was transferred to an Indian elite comprising those representing agrarian interests, Indian industry, and middle-

class professionals. A liberal order legitimized by democratic consensus, remained an aspiration of the nationalist movement" (Sudarshan 1994: 60–61).

16. For an elaboration of this point, see Sudarshan 1994: 58; see also Austin 1966: 1–25.

17. Notably, Ambedkar circulated a detailed draft incorporating principles of state socialism and "economic democracy," advising the Constituent Assembly to insulate these basic principles from the vagaries of fickle simple majorities in Parliament by incorporating them in the constitution (see Rao 1965–71, vol. 2). Sudarshan (1994: 64) has noted that the "Congress majority accepted Ambedkar's argument for expanding the scope of constitutional law, but rejected the principles he had submitted."

18. The Golaknath case represents an important milestone in India's constitutional history. At issue was the question of whether the government could legitimately interfere with a citizen's right to own property by imposing a ceiling on landholdings. The court ruled that the right to property was a fundamental right, and fundamental rights could not be amended by Parliament. It took the government nearly a decade, during which several amendments were made to the constitution, finally to cut the Gordian knot by removing, in 1978, the property right altogether from the chapter on fundamental rights to another part of the constitution (Sudarshan 1994: 70–71).

19. The 1969 presidential election, which precipitated the split in the Congress party, took place after the Golaknath decision of 1967 and before the decisions of the government on bank nationalization and privy purses (1970–71). Both were challenged in the Supreme Court and struck down. The way was thus paved for a head-on collision between the prime minister and the Supreme Court.

20. For perceptive, if narrowly focused, comments on the Kesavananda Bharathi case, see Palkhivala 1984: 183–89. The importance of the case can be gleaned from the following observation: "Kesavananda's case was heard by the largest Bench ever constituted. . . . It took the longest time . . . any case ever occupied in this Court; and the vastest materials ever brought together in a single case formed the record" (Palkhivala 1984: 187).

21. For an account of the political background of the government's attempted amendment of the constitution in the wake of the Emergency, see Sudarshan 1994: 77–82; for a spirited and impassioned discussion of the juridical aspect, see Palkhivala 1984: 199–202.

22. For a critical discussion of the government's reasoning, see Palkhivala 1984: 183–89.

23. In 1962, Nehru attempted to revitalize the ruling party by urging Congress leaders to give up ministerial office in favor of party work. The "Kamaraj Plan" resulting from this initiative was widely viewed as a scarcely veiled attempt on the part of senior leaders (known as "the Syndicate") to keep political power in their hands and not let it pass to a more dynamic and younger cohort. Mrs. Gandhi was able to exploit the discontent among the younger and more radical segment of the party in her effort to wrest power from the Syndicate.

24. The Janata government was sworn in to office by Vice President B. D. Jatti, a former congressman from Karnataka, who acted as president during the interval between Ahmed's death and the election of a new president.

25. Jagjiwan Ram belonged to the Scheduled Castes, had served as a central minister from 1946 onward, and was the only minister who enjoyed a reputation for knowing the government inside out.

26. PEPSU was the Patiala and East Punjab States' Union, an interim formation that disappeared in the reorganization of States with the formation of Himachal Pradesh.

27. The Rajamannar Report remains a most comprehensive document on the subject of center-State relations (Rajamannar 1971).

28. The Telugu Desam movement, which defeated the Congress (I) in the 1983 Andhra Pradesh State Assembly election, belonged to the earlier category of opposition rooted in the State even though it attained a high degree of militancy. The center feared Tamil Nadu to a much greater extent because of the overlap of Tamil identity between southern India and northern Sri Lanka and the presence, since 1983, of Tamil liberation fighters on "Indian soil" (Sathyamurthy 1983, 1985).

29. Based on the Sarkaria Report recommendations, two amendments to the constitution were enacted during the early 1990s. Even these were bedeviled by accusations from the opposition that devolution and decentralization could be used by the center as instruments of patronage reaching down to lower levels of society. The United Front Government, which assumed office in 1996, has pledged to restructure center-state relations further along the lines laid down in the Sarkaria Report.

30. The sphere of "public interest litigation" is a matter of acute political contention. See Sudarshan, 1994: 72–73; Kothari, 1994: 40 ff.

31. In this respect, the contrast between the Indian Constitution and the American Constitution—both written, unlike the British Constitution—could not be greater. Other written constitutions in this century, especially the Weimar Constitution, which have failed or only been partially successful, can be said not to have annealed properly through a "fair" competition between the different arms of state power.

References

Alam, J. 1994. "Nation: Discourse and Intervention by the Communists in India." In *Social Change and Political Discourse in India, Structures of Power, Movements of Resistance*, edited by T. V. Sathyamurthy. Vol. 1, *State and Nation in the Context of Social Change*. Delhi: Oxford University Press.

Austin, G. 1966. *The Indian Constitution, Cornerstone of a Nation*. London: Oxford University Press.

Bandyopadhyay, D. 1994. "We, the People." *Mainstream* 32 (January 15): 21–22.

Das, A. N. 1992. *The Republic of Bihar*. New Delhi: Penguin Books.

Dumont, L. 1986. *Essays on Individualism: Modern Ideology in Anthropological Perspective*. Chicago: University of Chicago Press.

Dutt, R. P. 1940. *India Today*. London: Gollancz.

Guhan, S. 1994. "The Blotted Copybook." *Economic and Political Weekly* 29 (August 27). 35: 2283–88.

Kothari, R. 1994. "Fragments of a Discourse: Towards Conceptualization." In *Social Change and Political Discourse in India: Structures of Power, Movements of Resistance*, edited by T. V. Sathyamurthy. Vol. 1, *State and Nation in the Context of Social Change*. Delhi: Oxford University Press.

Mandal, B. P. 1980. *Report of the Backward Classes Commission*. New Delhi: Government of India.

Mukarji, N. 1994. "Self-Government and Its Instrumentalities." *Economic and Political Weekly* 29 (April 2). 14: 789–91.

Palkhivala, N. A. 1984. *We, the People*. Bombay: Strand Book Stall.

Patnaik, P., C. P. Chandrasekhar, and A. Sen. 1996. "The Proliferation of the Indian Bourgeoisie." In *Social Change and Political Discourse in India: Structures of Power, Movements of Resistance*, edited by T.V. Sathyamurthy. Vol. 4, *Class Formation and Political Transformation in Post-Colonial India*. Delhi: Oxford University Press.

Rajagopalan, R. 1975–76. "Background to India's State of Emergency." *Black Liberator* 2 (January/August): 313–19.

Rajamannar, P. V. 1971. *Report of the Centre-State Relations Inquiry Committee.* Madras: Government of Tamil Nadu.

Rao, S[hiva] B., ed. et al. 1965–71. *The Framing of India's Constitution.* New Delhi: Indian Institute of Public Administration.

Sarkaria, R. S. 1988. *Commission on Centre-State Relations: Report.* 2 parts. New Delhi: Government of India.

Sathyamurthy, T. V. 1969. "The Crisis in the Congress Party: The Indian Presidential Election." *World Today* 25 (November): 478–87.

———. 1983. "Maturity at the Polls: Contradiction, Dissent, and Dissidence." *Statesman* (February 16): editorial page.

———. 1985. "Indian Nationalism and the 'National Question.'" *Millennium: Journal of International Studies* 14 (summer): 172–94.

———. 1986. "India's Punjab Problem: Edging Towards a Solution?" *World Today* 42 (March): 46–50.

———. 1989. "Impact of Centre-State Relations on Indian Politics: An Interpretative Reckoning, 1947–87." *Economic and Political Weekly* 24 (September 23): 2133–47.

———, ed.1994–96. *Social Change and Political Discourse in India: Structures of Power, Movements of Resistance.* 4 vols. Delhi: Oxford University Press. Vol. 1, *State and Nation in the Context of Social Change*, 1994; vol. 2, *Industry and Agriculture in India since Independence*, 1995; vol. 3, *Region, Religion, Caste, Gender, and Culture in Contemporary India,* 1996; vol. 4, *Class Formation and Political Transformation in Post-Colonial India*, 1996.

Sudarshan, R. 1994. "The Political Consequences of Constitutional Discourse." In *Social Change and Political Discourse in India: Structures of Power, Movements of Resistance*, edited by T.V. Sathyamurthy. Vol. 1, *State and Nation in the Context of Social Change.* Delhi: Oxford University Press.

Venkataraman, R. 1994. *My Presidential Years.* New Delhi: HarperCollins.

8

Constitutional Viability and Political Institutions in Turkish Democracy

ERSIN KALAYCIOĞLU

Introduction

The world is again going through a cycle of democratization. Almost every regime on the globe is making some modifications in its design to express its allegiance to democracy (Huntington 1991: 3, 13–30). The former states of the Warsaw Pact, Albania, and Yugoslavia, as well as the new members of the Commonwealth of Independent States, have shown interest in democracy. Even though their records look complicated, some Middle Eastern countries have begun to introduce seemingly democratic institutions such as representative or deliberative assemblies to their previously authoritarian or monarchic systems.

Concomitantly, Turkey has begun to look interesting as an experiment in democracy that has relevance to a host of countries with large Muslim populations from the Atlantic Ocean to China. The popular press in the West has suggested a Turkish model of democracy, and has referred to Turkey as a regional democratic power in the Balkans, Transcaucasus, and the Middle East (for example, *The Economist*, September 21, 1991: 15–16). In fact, Turkey has been trying to consolidate democracy since 1946, and has a relatively lengthy record of democratic politics. However, it is not clear whether there is a Turkish model of democracy, or whether it should be replicated elsewhere. Because of the increasing interest in the Turkish experience with democracy, we will examine its characteristics, its success, and its desirability.

Constitutions, Models of Democracy, and the Institutional Linkages in Turkish Politics

In 1946, Turkey came out of a period of one-party rule that had lasted for a total of twenty-three years. The single-party regime of the Republican People's Party (RPP) was a pragmatic authoritarian regime, founded as the mass mobilizing organization of the successful political elites of the Turkish War of Independence of 1919–22. The RPP elite inherited a well-established tradition of political rule from the Ottoman Empire (Mardin 1975: 7–32; Zürcher 1984: 68–105; Tachau 1984: 223). The pivotal sociocultural cleavage of the Ottoman Empire was between an autonomous, compact, culturally distinct, internally homogeneous, patrimonial "Center" that represented the interests of the "Palace/State," and a culturally heterogeneous "Periphery," which was often defined by parochial idiosyncracies of the localities of the Ottoman Empire. From the early 1920s to the late 1940s the RPP elite represented such a compact, unified, culturally homogeneous elite who shared the fundamentals of the same political program of secularization and modernization (Mardin 1975: 7–32).

The RPP elite, under the leadership of Müstafa Kemal Atatürk, carried out a cultural revolution of secularization and modernization in Turkey. The Cultural Revolution of Turkey was indeed welcomed by the majority of the urban population, the educated stratum of the society, and the local notables of the small towns. However, the economic policies of the RPP during World War II, under the leadership of İmet İnönü, who replaced Atatürk after his death in 1938, hurt many sectors of the Turkish economy. The economic policies of the RPP severely disturbed the pattern of income distribution and precipitated the emergence of a new class of the war rich. When the RPP moved to tax the wealth of this new class and to consider land reform, it was perceived as a class enemy of the upper and middle classes.

During the same period, Joseph Stalin demanded territory from Turkey, and rebuffed the offer of the Turkish government to renew the Treaty of Non-Aggression and Friendship between the Soviet Union and Turkey in 1945 and 1946. Turkey refused the former demand, and it was the

British, but most vehemently the Truman Doctrine, that came to Turkey's rescue. The RPP government started to veer away from a nonaligned stance in foreign policy toward an alliance with the West and eventually to NATO membership. Joining the club of democratic countries required democratization, which was also advocated by the threatened upper and middle classes in Turkey. The coincidence of domestic and international pressures in 1945–46 started the process of transition to democracy in Turkey.

The first multiparty elections of the republican era took place in 1946. Two major political parties participated in that election: the ruling RPP and the challenging Democratic Party (DP). The DP was also founded by some of the ex-RPP elite, who emerged as the representatives of the threatened urban middle classes and the rural upper classes (landlords). The ruling RPP won the 1946 elections; however, the DP accused the RPP of rigging the elections.

Turkish democratization did not start with an overhaul of its 1924 constitution in 1946; rather, a series of ad hoc decisions determined the process of democratization in the mid-1940s. No major compromise emerged over the essence of the model of democracy, or the rules of the political game, such as the design of new electoral laws, a new Standing Order of the Turkish Grand National Assembly (TGNA), or the amendment of the 1924 constitution that had been debated before the 1946 elections. Some were of the opinion that if Turkey had discussed and amended the 1924 constitution in 1945–46, most of the problems and crises of the 1950s could have been avoided (Erim, quoted in Soysal 1969: 11). Mumtaz Soysal argues that the political elites of the 1940s believed either that they would still be in control after multipartyism was introduced, or that the Westminster-type of parliamentarism that the 1924 constitution had provided for was without problems in the Turkish political and cultural context. In fact, the first constitution that Turkey devised and adopted during the multiparty era was the 1961 constitution.

A period of two-partyism, operating in the form of a Westminster-like political regime provided by the 1924 constitution, unfolded in the 1950s. May 14, 1950, is often referred to as the day of the "white revolution" in Turkish politics. It was the first time the Turkish voters were asked to cast their votes to make a real choice between different political parties. They were given a clear choice between the RPP, the symbol of the Center and the major force behind centralism, bureaucratic rule, statism, and secularist modernization, and the DP, which presented itself as the representative of the Periphery, promising to follow a policy of economic liberalism, to end the rule of the public bureaucracy, and to uphold traditional Islamic values (Mardin 1975: 7–32; Heper 1987: 52–64; Tachau 1984: 113–64; Karpat 1959: 387–441). The Turkish electorate favored the latter, and ended the one-party rule of the RPP, effectively handing the government over to the Democratic Party.

Economic liberalism, harnessing the power of the public bureaucracy, and the dissemination of the symbols of Sunni Islam, became the core of the policies of the DP governments. However, the organizing principle of clientelism persisted in defining political interactions between the citizens and their representatives in the 1950s (Kutad 1975: 61–87; Sayari 1975: 121–33). The masses voted for those representatives who provided them with jobs and helped them out in their relations with the public bureaucracy (Sayari 1975: 128–31). The earlier linkage between the local notables, the RPP leadership, and the public bureaucracy was slightly modified (Sayari 1975: 130). The public bureaucrats were demoted to a subordinate level in relation to the DP leaders, cabinet ministers, and the DP deputies in the TGNA. All public bureaucrats, from teachers and university professors to the directors of the state enterprises and the generals of the Turkish military, suffered a decline in power and downward social mobility. Professionals, especially engineers and doctors, rose sharply in the social hierarchy. The majority of the masses, that is, the peasants, gained an unanticipated amount of influence throughout the 1950s (Karpat 1959: 419–35; Tachau 1984: 126–45).

The DP governments were also responsive to the demands of the rural masses. The villages of Turkey received tangible benefits in the form of roads, irrigation projects, schools, and an increased ability to travel to the urban centers of Turkey. An era of social mobilization thus began in Turkey (Özbudun 1976: 60–96). However, the speed of this process, combined with the downturn of the world economy in 1956–57 and the inability of the Turkish economy to adapt to the market rules and to develop competitiveness in the international markets, resulted in a severe economic recession; a sudden and drastic 330 percent devaluation of the Turkish lira took place in 1957 (Weiker 1967: 11–13). This was followed by high inflation in 1957 and 1958, and a major loss of real income for the salaried middle classes. These dire economic conditions intensified the conflict between the DP and the RPP, its main opponent, which in turn led to the DP's harsh treatment of the RPP (Weiker 1967: 13–20). By 1959–60, the DP started to look more and more like a one-party regime. The student revolts of April–May 1960 precipitated a petty officers' coup, which not only ended the first democratic regime of Turkey, but also started a new era (Turan 1969: 123–26).

The First Constitutional Reform: The 1961 Constitution

In 1961, a new constitution and a new political regime that modified the earlier Westminster Model were instituted. The authors of the 1961 constitution believed that the most important problem of the political regime of the 1950s was the unlimited and unchecked power of the majority in the TGNA (Weiker 1967: 66–72). Certain limits, and checks and balances, were imposed on the power of the legislative majority by the 1961 constitution. A Constitutional Court was established to oversee the constitutionality of the deeds of the TGNA. An upper chamber (the Senate) of more elderly and, it was hoped, more mature politicians was instituted to review the legislation of the lower chamber. The coup leaders were also made senators for life. Although they had no veto power, the coup leaders were able to keep vigil over the populist tendencies of the majority in the lower chamber. The Turkish Radio and Television Agency and the universities were given autonomous status, and the state's administrative tutelage over them thus came to an end. The independence of the judiciary was further bolstered by enabling the higher courts to elect their own judges without state or governmental intervention. Freedom of association and human rights were also given liberal treatment in the new constitution. A new electoral law completed the deviation from the Westminster Model.

The national elections of 1961 created a novelty in Turkish politics: The country experienced four coalition governments between 1961 and 1965. However, the landslides of the Justice Party (JP) in the 1965 and the 1969 elections indicated that governability was not a problem of the new electoral law. Nevertheless, the 1961 constitution was branded a partisan document by the sympathizers of the former DP. Celal Bayar, one of the four founding fathers of the DP, and the president of the republic between 1950 and 1960, declared that, while the 1924 constitution was a document that solidly established the sovereignty of the Turkish nation, the 1961 constitution limited national sovereignty by incorporating the agents of the Center as wielders of sovereignty (Mardin 1975: 30).

It did not take long for the JP spokesmen to declare that the 1961 constitution made the country ungovernable. They also expressed their dislike of the performances of the constitutional and other high courts, which they perceived as illegitimately encroaching upon their right to govern the country according to the dictates of the "national will," which they believed they had obtained with the electoral mandate. Gradually, a legitimacy crisis unfolded. When the international wave of student revolts of 1968 reached Turkey, the legitimacy crisis deepened and contributed to increasing tension between the opposition and the government.

The student protests eventually grew into a revolt against the government and were carried into the streets of Ankara and Istanbul, and into liberation struggles in the mountains of Anatolia. In 1971, the top brass of the Turkish military declared the government incompetent and the JP government resigned. An odd combination of military rule with an elected parliament followed until 1973. The 1961 constitution was amended in ways that would partly placate the JP. It was made easier to put effective limits on liberties by the government under the auspices of "emergency measures." With these amendments, Turkey entered a ten-year cycle of political instability, military coup, and a new constitution (or a new political regime). The 1970s further corroborated this picture.

The 1973 national elections ushered in a new era. The RPP was able to devise an altered program in the 1960s. It declared itself a party at the "left of center," projecting an image of a party that cared for the interests of the traditional center in Turkish politics, while representing the landless peasants, urban lumpenproletariat, and blue-collar workers. When the JP majority in the TGNA failed to prevent another coup and also collaborated with the military rule of 1971–73, the RPP emerged as a "civilian" alternative. The RPP presented the image of a party that could placate the masses and the military at the same time (Karpat 1975: 111). (However, the RPP could not obtain a majority of seats in the TGNA in the 1973 elections. A new period of odd, short-lived, coalition governments ensued.)

The most important feature of the coalition governments was that the RPP formed a coalition with the radical Islamist National Salvation Party (NSP), and the JP formed coalitions with the NSP and the Nationalist Action Party (NAP)—an anticommunist, ultranationalist party. The smaller, radical parties of those coalitions tried their best to capitalize on their situation by infiltrating the public bureaucracy and further undermining the established order. Meanwhile, a wave of terror grew as economic hardship increased during the oil crisis of 1973. The

Marxist-Leninists and the sympathizers and militants of the NAP battled throughout the country. By the summer of 1980, a total of twenty-five people were being killed per day in acts of terrorism in Turkey. The military ousted the civilian government once more to establish law and order.

The Second Constitutional Reform: The 1982 Constitution

The cycle of the 1970s thus came to an end. A new constitution was designed in the early 1980s, and thus, a new political regime was instituted. This time, the Westminster Model was totally abandoned. In the 1982 constitution, the legislative branch of government was now relegated to a new, subordinate legal status vis-à-vis the executive branch. The main intent of the authors of the 1982 constitution was to establish law and order in Turkey. Therefore, the catchwords of the new document were "strong state," national unity, and indivisibility of the nation-state.

New powers were vested in the office of the president of the country, who also symbolizes the state. However, the president is no longer a titular head: national security, defense, and foreign policy are now partly designated prerogatives of the president. Furthermore, the president was given additional powers of appointment. The higher court judges, the rectors of the universities, and the director of the higher educational council are appointed directly by the president, and a host of top-level appointments within the public bureaucracy also require the president's approval. Finally, the president is given the right to declare war under certain circumstances. This is a total novelty, in that none of the former constitutions had such a provision. Both the 1924 and the 1961 constitutions had designated the TGNA as the sole body able to decide on matters of peace and war.

The 1982 constitution has not created a presidential political regime in Turkey. However, it has created a semiparliamentary system. In the current political regime of Turkey, a president who is elected by the parliament from among the ranks of professional politicians functions as a power broker in the game of politics. Both the last and the current presidents were party leaders and former prime ministers, who continued on with their practices of acting like party leaders when they were elected president. The president seeks media attention, and tries to do whatever is necessary to capture daily media coverage. The president is made a policymaker in some realms of government. However, the president is neither politically nor legally accountable; a prime minister and the cabinet of ministers are in fact legally and politically accountable to the TGNA and to the people. The president and the cabinet do not always endorse or follow the same policies, and even contradict and clash over certain issues. The cooperation of the president with the prime minister becomes a problem, especially when they are from different parties or even from different factions within the same political party.

Turkey now has an illiberal constitution, and an electoral law that prohibits any political party that does not obtain 10 percent or more of the national vote from getting any seats in the TGNA. Furthermore, the right to form a voluntary association is severely restricted by the 1982 constitution. A new Political Parties Act of April 22, 1983, also severely curbs the organizational activities of political parties. Party structures, relations with youth and women's organizations, and the local branches that the political parties can have are put under severe restrictions. Nevertheless, the 1983 elections started a new period of democratization in Turkey.

The 1983 national elections occurred under stringent limitations. A new political party—the Motherland Party (MP)—that purported to represent the conservative, liberal, social democratic, and religious right won the 1983 national elections. The other two parties endorsed by the military government suffered an electoral defeat that they had not anticipated. From that point on, Turkish politics became embroiled in a struggle for democratization and liberalization. The 1987 and the 1991 national elections became a severe struggle between those who were banned and those who were favored by the military government of 1983. Finally, in the 1991 national elections the old guard was able to win enough votes to oust the Motherland Party and to form a coalition government between the Social Democratic Populist Party (SDPP), which is one of the new representatives of the old RPP, and the True Path Party (TPP), which claimed to be the old JP reincarnated. The MP is now the main opposition party in the TGNA.

In the 1990s, no political party seemed to support the 1982 constitution. However, the parliamentary parties have not been able to amend it to loosen up its illiberal character. In 1993, one article of the 1982 constitution was amended to establish private radios and TV channels and end the state monopoly on audio-visual media. (Note that there has never been state monopoly on the print media in Turkey.) By summer 1995, a more comprehensive amendment of the 1982 constitution and its illiberal preamble took place, whereby articles that pertained to the right to participate in associations and political parties, voting age, the right to strike, and related articles were redesigned. The 1982 constitution has now gained a slightly more liberal character. In the meantime, the country was rocked by news of political corruption, the rising power of the Walfare Party (WP)—the new party of the former NSP leaders—in some major cities, and the terror campaign of a Kurdish organization (the Kurdish Workers' Party) in the southeastern provinces. Serious political issues pertaining to national and cultural identity emerged. The capability of the public bureaucracy was called into question after every wave of terror, which increased government expenditures to enormous levels. Various efforts to increase government revenues failed to provide a balanced state budget. The handling of the economy by different party and coalition governments failed to tackle the perennial issue of inflation in the general level of prices, which has been oscillating between 40 and 80 percent per annum since 1983. Cultural, national, and economic issues, and scandals of political corruption created conditions for a deep crisis in Turkish politics in the 1990s. These processes culminated in the June 1996 news that, for the first time, an Islamic party would head a government in secular Turkey. In July 1996, the parliament narrowly approved a government led by Necmettin Erbakan, head of the Welfare Party.

The Overall Pattern of Constitutional Design and Democratic Consolidation

Basic problems of Turkish democratization persist. Turkish democracy is still under the spell of a political and economic crisis, caused by the lack of democratic consolidation that has prevailed through the last half century. The main political actors simply cannot agree upon the ground rules of a model of democracy for the Turkish Republic. Turkey's political actors have never managed to agree upon a written constitution that spells out the basics of a democratic political regime. The opportunity to adopt a constitution suitable for Turkish democracy at the outset of the initial phase of transition to democracy in the 1945–46 period was not exploited. The constitutions of 1961 and 1982 were both designed without the full participation or cooperation of all the major political forces in the country. Thus, they contributed mainly to a crisis of political legitimacy.

Two different and irreconcilable views of the electoral mandate were propagated by the government and the main opposition parties between

1950 and 1980. The DP and the JP argued that they represented the "national will" that was declared on the day of elections when a majority or plurality of the electorate supported them. They believed themselves to have the seal of popular approval to rule the country according to their party platforms, and to be able to design and execute policies in accordance with their ideologies. The RPP, as the main opposition party, argued that the rule of the DP and the JP could not contradict the stipulations of the constitution, and that the ruling party did not receive a mandate to rule the country with total disregard for the constitution and laws of the land.

The RPP observed that the DP and the JP were intending to tamper with the Cultural Revolution of the 1920s and the 1930s. The most critical issue was the role of religion in public life and, more specifically, in politics. The DP and the JP tried to exploit religion to gain votes, a strategy the RPP considered a severe breach of the 1924 and the 1961 constitutions. The DP and the JP considered those constitutions documents designed and imposed upon the people of Turkey by the forces of the traditional Center. They considered the Center their opponent and sought to conquer and destroy it, in the name of the Periphery, which they purported to represent. The DP and the JP saw no moral obligation to abide by a constitution they considered a political and partisan statement of an "image of a good society" belonging to the Center, and which they vehemently opposed. Hence, a clash of ideologies and opposing cultural images gave rise to a far-reaching legitimacy crisis.

The 1980s and 1990s have been somewhat different. What the military regime of 1980–83 managed to do was antagonize all the political party elites. Now, no party elite wishes to identify with the current constitution, nor try to uphold it. In fact, violations of the constitution are considered legitimate, if not encouraged, by the political elites. Consequently, political legitimacy has become more of a complex problem. Political rule became arbitrary in the 1980s, in the style of Turkish neo-patrimonialism, with the same basic features of arbitrary rule in the Ottoman Empire under Abdülhamid II, 1876–1909 (Kalaycioğlu 1992: 111–13).

Today, the institutions of political participation and representation function in a milieu of uncertainty, with every aspect of the political regime—from the vertical and horizontal distribution of political power to electoral laws and political party structures—under debate. Uncertainty over the ground rules of democratic contests, government instability, plus a lack of consensus over abiding by the laws of the land breed an environment of corruption of local and national public bureaucracies and their political bosses. The legitimacy of, and support for, the current democratic regime and the political elites of the country starts to erode. Opinion polls indicate an unprecedented increase in electoral support for the antisystem religious Welfare Party (WP) (*Sabah*, February 20, 1994), sweeping it to power in 1996.

The post-1980 political legitimacy crisis of Turkish democracy did not emanate from the traditional confrontation of Turkish politics between the secular, modernist, centralistic, statist Center versus religious, traditionalist, decentralist, market-oriented Periphery. Rather, it arose from a lack of agreement on the rules of the political game and disenchantment with the 1982 constitution. However, the overall confrontation over the "images of a good society" between the parties of the left and the right has continued and has deepened the legitimacy crisis. The acts of political participation and representation occur within institutions that have been deeply influenced by the underlying legitimacy crisis. The political institutions of elections, parties, interest groups, and legislature will now be examined from the perspective of democratic consolidation in Turkey. My aim is to identify those political factors that have contributed to the crisis of political democracy in Turkey since 1946.

The Electoral Laws and Politics of Uncertainty

The national elections were carried out according to a majoritarian electoral formula in Turkey from 1950 to 1957. The opposition parties, that is, the DP between 1946 and 1950 and the RPP from 1950 to 1960, always criticized this formula. In the 1960s, the electoral formula was one of the first rules of the political game that was thoroughly revised. This time, Turkey adopted a form of proportional representation for the National Assembly elections and the majority formula for the newly established Senate elections (Weiker 1967: 109; Özbudun 1985: 267).

Proportional representation led to coalition government in the 1961 elections. It was not only the electoral formula that caused it, but also the lack of clarity in the minds of the electorate as to which new party was the genuine successor to the DP (Weiker 1967: 109–15). When the doubts of the electorate were clarified, the JP obtained the majority in the TGNA after the 1965 and 1969 elections (see Table 8.1). However, social mobilization and urbanization, as well as the ease with which the new political

Table 8.1

Election Results and the Distribution of Seats in the TGNA, 1950-1995 (in percent)

		Political Parties											
Year		DP	JP	RPP	NAP	NSP	MP	PP	NDP	SDPP	TPP	WP*	DLP
1950	Vote	53.3	---	39.9	---	---	---	---	---	---	---	---	---
	Seats	83.8	---	14.2	---	---	---	---	---	---	---	---	---
1954	Vote	56.6	---	34.8	---	---	---	---	---	---	---	---	---
	Seats	91.6	---	5.6	---	---	---	---	---	---	---	---	---
1957	Vote	47.3	---	40.6	---	---	---	---	---	---	---	---	---
	Seats	69.6	---	28.7	---	---	---	---	---	---	---	---	---
1961	Vote	---	34.6	36.7	---	---	---	---	---	---	---	---	---
	Seats	---	35.1	38.4	---	---	---	---	---	---	---	---	---
1965	Vote	---	52.9	28.7	---	---	---	---	---	---	---	---	---
	Seats	---	53.3	29.8	---	---	---	---	---	---	---	---	---
1969	Vote	---	46.5	27.4	3.0	---	---	---	---	---	---	---	---
	Seats	---	56.9	31.8	0.2	---	---	---	---	---	---	---	---
1973	Vote	---	29.8	33.3	3.4	11.8	---	---	---	---	---	---	---
	Seats	---	33.1	41.1	0.6	10.6	---	---	---	---	---	---	---
1977	Vote	---	36.9	41.3	6.4	8.5	---	---	---	---	---	---	---
	Seats	---	42.0	47.0	3.4	5.3	---	---	---	---	---	---	---
1983	Vote	---	---	---	---	---	45.1	30.5	23.3	---	---	---	---
	Seats	---	---	---	---	---	52.8	29.2	17.7	---	---	---	---
1987	Vote	---	---	---	---	---	36.3	---	---	24.4	19.9	---	---
	Seats	---	---	---	---	---	64.9	---	---	22.0	13.1	---	---
1991	Vote	---	---	---	---	---	24.0	---	---	20.6	27.2	16.7*	---
	Seats	---	---	---	---	---	25.7	---	---	19.7	39.7	13.1*	---
1995	Vote	---	---	10.7	---	---	19.7	---	---	---	19.2	21.3	14.7
	Seats	---	---	8.9	---	---	24.0	---	---	---	24.5	28.7	13.8

Source: Kalaycioğlu 1994: 404-405; TGNA, 1982: 13-46; *Official Gazette*, January 3, 1996: 2-3.
Note: Only those parties with coalition or government capability are included in this Table.
(*) This column refers to the Welfare Party Alliance, which includes WP, Nationalist Work Party, and Reformist Democracy Party. NSP = National Salvation Party (Islamic); NAP = Nationalist Action Party (ultranationalist, anticommunist); WP = Welfare Party (Islamic); DP = Democrat Party (liberal/right); RPP = Republican People's Party (left-of-center); NDP = Nationalist Democracy Party (praetorian, right-of-center); TPP = True Path Party since 1984; SDPP = Social Democratic Populist Party (left-of-center); PP = Populist Party (praetorian, left-of-center); JP = Justice Party (right-of-center); MP = Motherland Party (right-of-center); DLP = Democratic Left Party.

parties could enter the TGNA, enabled the emergence of new parties on the left and right in Turkish politics (Ergüder 1980–81: 50–52). Furthermore, it became clear that the splinter groups from the two main parties could survive in the national political arena. The Reliance Party (RP) and the Democratic Party were formed by deputies who resigned from the RPP, in the former case, and from the JP in the latter. The 1961 constitution and the liberal judges of the Constitutional Court enabled the socialist, religious radical, and ultranationalist, anticommunist parties to enter the electoral contest in the 1960s and the 1970s. A pluralist multiparty system emerged in Turkish politics by the 1970s (Ergüder 1980: 52–59).

Finally, Turkish politics became ideologized in the post-1960 period. It was not only the intrusion of the smaller left- and right-wing parties that precipitated it, but also the RPP which decided to declare itself a left-of-center party, emerging as the party of the Center while also representing the interests of the urban poor and landless peasants (Kalaycioğlu 1992: 104–9). This twist in the RPP program enabled it to form a coalition with the religious National Salvation Party, solely because both parties were bent upon changing the established order, and not because they had anything in common with respect to the "image of a good society" they had envisioned. That was the first of a series of coalitions in the 1970s. None of them lasted for longer than two years, and Turkey slid into a period of governmental and political instability (Kalaycioğlu 1992: 105–10).

The spurious correlation between coalition governments and political instability seen by the authors of the 1982 constitution and of the other laws that shaped the new game of democracy in Turkey led to another electoral formula in the 1980s. The current electoral system of Turkey looks like proportional representation, but works as if it were a majority formula (Ekşioğlu 1983: 203, 218–19). The marriage of the two principles of representativeness and governability by means of a deception was considered a cure for the search for the "golden electoral formula of turkish politics." A threshold of 10 percent of the national vote was required for earning seats, to keep the "unwanted" parties of the far left and the far right out of the TGNA (Özbudun 1985: 276–77). Then, those parties that managed to obtain more than 10 percent of the national vote had the seats of the TGNA distributed among them according to a proportional representation formula in the 1983 elections. However, in the 1987 elections an additional district-level quotient was established on top of the 10 percent national threshold (Kara and Özdoğan 1988: 19–23).

This system provided Turkey with party governments, namely Motherland Party governments, after the 1983 and 1987 elections. However, in 1991, with a slightly different version of the same electoral law, the vote was so distributed in the national elections that no party was able to gain control of the majority of seats in the TGNA. Consequently, Turkey has returned to the experience of coalition governments. Furthermore, the right-wing radical Islamic and ultranationalist, anticommunist parties united under the WP banner in the 1991 elections, and won 13.1 percent of the seats in the TGNA. The Welfare Party, an Islamic party, earned the right to form a coalition government in 1996.

There are only a few electoral formulas that Turkey has not yet tried. Lack of stability is a major feature of the Turkish electoral system, since Turkish political elites have not been able to agree on an electoral system that would marry the double goals of representativeness and governability, and also be accepted as fair by all the major political parties.

So far, there has not been a period in which an electoral formula was used without any perturbation by the governing party for more than two elections. Most recently, the 1983 and the 1987 national elections were declared unfair and unjust by those parties that lost the elections. The 1991 elections were carried out according to a slightly different version of the same formula; however, those political parties most critical of the electoral formula of the 1980s, the TPP and the Social Democratic Populist Party, were able to form a coalition government. They stopped criticizing the electoral formula, and the MP, having lost the national elections in its own game, could not be critical of those rules.

Just before the December 24, 1995 national elections a new electoral law was put into effect. Previously, during summer 1995, the 1982 constitution was also amended to increase the number of seats in the unicameral TGNA from 450 to 550. Ten percent national threshold for election was preserved, but most electoral districts were expanded to hold up to 20 seats. Proportional representation's d'Hondt formula was employed for the convergence of the votes to parliamentary seats. The result was unfair for those parties that could not score up to 10 percent of the national vote, but quite fair for those that went over the threshold. However, the results were also detrimental to governmental stability. Consequently, between the day of the elections, December 24, 1995, and October 1996, Turkey experienced three different coalition governments.

Political Parties and the Party System

The political party system of Turkey has also been in flux. During the period 1946–60, Turkey was somewhat able to establish a two-party system (Özbudun 1981: 228–31). The DP was banned once and for all following the coup of 1960. The JP emerged as its successor. The main contest occurred between the JP and the RPP in the 1960s. Therefore, the 1960s may be considered a continuation of the same bipartyism of the 1950s, within a new context of left- and right-wing parties. However, in the 1970s the Turkish party system started to incline toward a moderate pluralist structure (in the sense employed by Sartori 1976: 173–85). In the post-1983 period the party system continues to exhibit signs of limited pluralism, especially following the 1991 elections. Although the structural aspects of the party system from the 1970s to the 1990s look similar, the names of the parties demonstrate the changes that occurred in the party system (see Table 8.1). The underlying sociopolitical reality of the party system seems to indicate that limited pluralism is likely to persist under these circumstances.

In 1990 and during the 1991 national elections, the electorate was divided into three blocs. As Figure 8.1 indicates, the one on the far left was the smallest with about 5 to 10 percent of the electorate. The one in the middle spans from center of the left to the center of the right, and holds about 75 percent of the electorate, and the last bloc, which appears on the far right has about 15 to 20 percent of the electorate. However, all that started to change by the mid-1990s. Under the accumulated influence of the rapid social mobilization of the 1980s, with the rising tide of various forms of chauvinism (i.e., Turkish, Kurdish, Abkhaz), and a surge of xenophobia in the post-Cold War era, which was further exacerbated by a sense of political stalemate and inadequate government performance, an identity crisis was triggered. As people searched for their cultural origins, political affiliations, and ethnicities, it did not take long for the radical Islamic pressure groups and political party (the Welfare Party) to exploit the sentiments of the masses. They argued that the new world order rested on double standards. There was one standard for "Muslim" Iraq's act of aggression, and other standards for the Armenian and Serb aggressions against Muslim peoples of the Caucasus and the Balkans. The previously minor radical political parties began to gain political support by leaps and bounds.

The Welfare Party (WP), which negates the established secular basis of republicanism and proposed to substitute an Islamic "just order," a return to the glorious Ottoman past, and an anti-west foreign policy that called for Islamic solidarity against the Zionist conspiracy of Israel and the United States, started to emerge as a major political force in the early 1990s. However, the WP is hardly a newcomer to Turkish politics. It was established as the National Salvation Party (NSP) in the 1960s. Its pre-

Figure 8.1

Left-Right Continuum, Voters, and Parties

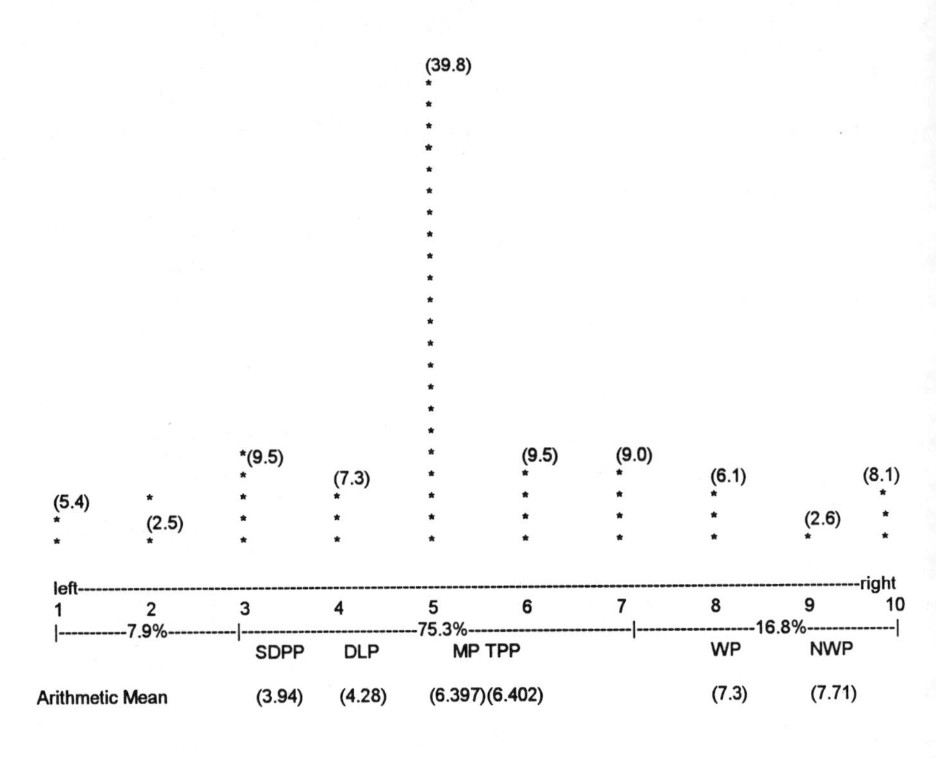

Source: Kalaycioğlu 1994: 415.

Note: Values are calculated from the data of the Turkish Values study (1990). Number of observations = 636. The values of the histogram in parentheses indicate the percentages of respondents who reported the corresponding answer. The percentages underneath the scale scores indicate the percentages of respondents who placed themselves in the middle, at the far right, or at the far left of the scale. The values that are presented just below the party titles in parentheses indicate the arithmetic means of the left-right scale scores of the respondents, who indicated that they would vote for the corresponding party if the elections were held the next day. Only those respondents who registered a preference for the above-mentioned six parties are incorporated. "Don't know yet" responses and "no answers" are treated as missing values.

decessor had obtained about 11 percent of the national vote in the 1973 national elections. Furthermore, it had participated in the National Front coalition governments with the moderate right wing Justice Party (TPP's predecessor), and the ultra-nationalist Nationalist Action Party (NAP) between 1975 and 1980. When all of the political parties of the 1970s were banned by the military government in the early 1980s, the NSP was also closed for good. After the national elections of 1983, the old guard of the NSP started to organize a new political movement, which culminated in the Welfare Party. The WP managed to get 21 percent of the national vote by the 1995 national elections, and to form a coalition government with the conservative True Path Party (TPP) by summer 1996.

Similarly, the Nationalist Activity Party, which recently adopted its earlier title as Nationalist Action Party (NAP), has also gained political clout since the beginning of the 1990s. The NAP has been an ultra-nationalist anti-Communist party that supported a pan-Turkish foreign policy, and an ethnic nationalism for the population of Turkey. It was also formed in the 1960s, participated in the coalition governments of the 1970s, and was banned in the early 1980s. The WP and the NAP established an electoral alliance in the 1991 national elections and were able to get a total of 17 percent of the national vote. Previously, the WP had received 7 percent, and the NAP had obtained 3 percent of the vote in the 1987 national elections. In the local elections of March 1994, the WP was able to receive 19.8 percent and the NAP obtained 8.8 percent of the national vote in the provincial council elections and 8.5 percent of the national vote in the 1995 national elections (Sertel and Kalaycioğlu 1995: 23–30).

In the meantime, the traditionally secular parties are going through a period of relative decline. The RPP seems to have lost ground to an unprecedented extent in its seventy years of existence. As the party that established the republican regime of Turkey, the RPP seems to have lost its pivotal position in Turkish party politics. It was banned by the military government of 1980–83. In the post-1983 period, the ban continued in effect until the early 1990s. Therefore, the RPP could not participate in politics during the 1980s. The pre-1980 RPP members split into the Populist Party (PP), established by the military government to play the role of the loyal opposition, the Social Democratic Party (SDP) of the former

RPP elite, except their leader Mr. Bülent Ecevit, and the Party of Ecevit, the Democratic Left Party (DLP). The 1983 national, and the 1984 local elections clearly indicated that the PP stood no chance among the other two left-of-center parties. It dissolved itself and merged with the social democrats to form the Social Democratic Populist Party (SDPP). Finally, the RPP was reestablished by law in the 1990s; this entailed a further split of one major faction from the SDPP to form the RPP. However, the dismal performance of the RPP in the 1994 local elections resulted in a merger of the SDPP and the RPP with the new RPP. Nevertheless, the pre-1980 RPP is still split into the new RPP, which hosts most of its former elites, and the DLP, which consists of Ecevit and some of the former RPP elite.

In the meantime, the center of the public opinion in Turkey seems to be shifting toward the far right (Erder et al. 1995: 15–22). In fact, the most important determinant of the political party preferences of the Turkish voters has become religion (Kalaycioğlu 1994: 402–24). It seems as if those who espouse deep Sunni Islamic convictions tend to vote for the radical, formerly fringe parties of the system. Others tend to vote for the moderate right-of-center and the left-of-center parties. Meanwhile, all of the fringe left wing parties of Turkey seem to have lost their meager electoral support since the military coup of 1980 and the collapse of the Soviet Union (Kalaycioğlu 1994: 402–24). Consequently, the center of the left-right continuum as represented in Figure 8.1 started to erode from 75 percent to 65 percent, and the far-right began to receive more support and rose to between 30 and 35 percent of the national vote. In the 1995 national elections, a right wing swing of the Turkish voters seemed to have occurred. However, it is still too early to judge whether it constitutes the beginning of a realignment of the Turkish voters or just a temporary change in Turkish voting behavior.

Another important aspect of the Turkish party system is that the political parties, even the most established ones, are periodically banned by military governments. In the 1980s, the last military government completely banned all the existing political parties. Beginning in 1983, all of the former leaders of Turkish politics established new parties and made a comeback. A law promulgated in 1992 permitted the reestablishment of all the old and once-banned parties. Now, the DP as well as the RPP are back. A multiplicity of parties participated in the 1996 national elections. The rapid turnover of parties, mostly due to the military interruptions of 1960 and 1980, resulted in a complete overhaul of the party system twice in recent Turkish history. Hence, the party system, as much as the electoral systems of Turkey, seems to lack stability or durability. Lack of institutionalization or periodic deinstitutionalization is a major characteristic of the Turkish party system.

The deinstitutionalized nature of the party system also contributes to the volatility and fragmentation of the electoral alignments in Turkish politics (Ergüder and Hofferbert 1988: 90–99). The turnover of parties and the emergence of new parties and leaders create a state of confusion in the minds of the voters, on the one hand, and contribute to further fragmentation of the electorate on the other.

Now, the difference between most political parties is one of personalities of leaders and specific party histories. However, there is no indication that lack of ideological distance between political parties promotes agreement and consensus on fundamental issues of Turkish democracy, such as the electoral law, amendment of the constitution, human rights, and so forth. In the past, lack of ideological distance promoted tensions and conflict to an extreme degree that I have called amoral partyism (Kalaycioğlu 1988). A form of tribal affinity to a party or its leader had been emphasized to overcome the difficulty of losing support to another party that seemed to propagate a similar program, or similar ideas, such as nationalism, or Islam (Frey 1975). There seems little reason not to return to a more dissent-based politics in Turkey, especially when economic recession gets deeper, and staying in power looks more difficult.

Interest Groups and Clientelism

The interest-group system in Turkey was solidly embedded in clientelism in the period between 1946 and 1980. In a cultural environment of distrust, it is not easy to establish voluntary associations (Ergüder, Esmer, and Kalaycioğlu 1991: 19–24). Turkey is no exception to the rule. However, the liberal constitution of 1961 engendered a fertile environment for interest groups to thrive (Bianchi 1984). Local, religious, and economic interests became better organized, especially in the urban centers (Bianchi 1984: 155–66). However, the spurious correlation between interest-group involvement in politics and political terrorism that the authors of the 1982 constitution perceived encouraged them to weed out the undesired interest groups from the system by an elaborate system of bans and permission in the 1980s. Under the current system, even the strongest interest groups, such as the TÜSIAD (Turkish Industrialists' and Businessmen's

Association), find themselves pitted against a hostile state. Lack of tolerance by the political authorities for the criticisms of organized interests creates an environment that makes survival difficult for interest groups not supported by the state in Turkey.

Paternalistic control over interest associations creates an environment of corporatism for Turkish interest groups. The election of Tansu Çiller as the leader of the TPP with the active support of the Turkish Federation Union of Chambers of Commerce and Industry and Commodities Exchange (TOBB) implied a corporatist symbiosis between a partner in the governing coalition (the TPP) and organized commercial interests. The symbiosis looked like an extension of the clientelist linkages between the government and the organized economic interests of small- and medium-size economic enterprises of the 1970s. The latter delivered the delegates in a party convention, and the former delivered beneficial policies to small- and middle-size economic interests. The TOBB has been further utilized to exert control over the behavior of the organized economic interests through threats of closure for those voluntary economic associations that criticize the government's economic policy (Arat 1991: 144; Esmer 1991: 133). It has become traditional for TOBB spokespersons to accuse the TÜSIAD of being involved in politics, thereby violating the Turkish Constitution (Article 33), whenever the latter criticizes the economic decisions of the government (Kalaycioğlu 1991: 81).

Organized local and religious interests have been subject to the same stringent legal stipulations (Özbudun 1991: 41–53). Ironically, religious interests have been vocal about being harassed during the 1990s. The 1982 constitution (Article 24) provided a greater legitimacy to religious activism, especially in the public school system. Unless they indicate a threat to the national integrity of Turkey, neither local nor religious groups seem to run into any difficulties. Furthermore, *hemsehri* associations (people of the same city or region) have become increasingly active in promoting the interests of their brethren in the Balkans and in the Transcaucasus. They are now perceived as benign, even functional, groups in the eyes of the political authorities. They are given red-carpet treatment in the state-sponsored media. The same corporatist twist seems to be operating for all the interest associations.

The illiberal constitution of 1982 and the lack of associability in Turkish culture have contributed to the further deinstitutionalization of voluntary associations in the political system (Özbudun 1991: 43–49; Esmer 1991: 132–34). Except for religious associations, Turkish democracy seems to lack the vigorous voluntary associations that are so critical in organizing political participation. Even though some voluntary associations have gained stability over the years, they seem to be in the background of interest-group politics, which is dominated by institutional and nonvoluntary professional associations, such as the Chambers of Commerce and Industry, bar associations, and the Turkish Medical Association.

It seems Robert Bianchi's observations about the corporatist nature of interest groups in Turkey still holds: "a collection of growing but still weak, insecure, and manipulable associations, eager for official recognition and privilege in order to improve their political and economic positions immediately and in the long run" (Bianchi 1984: 143). The fragility and lack of support for voluntary associations constitutes a major bottleneck in the process of democratic consolidation in Turkey.

The Legislative System and the Democratic Regime

The TGNA was established in 1920 as the sole fount of political legitimacy in Turkey. The 1921 and the 1924 constitutions provide the same interpretation of the legal basis of the TGNA. However, the 1961 constitution was designed to forestall despotism of parliamentary majorities. Certain checks and balances were established, such as the Constitutional Court, to check the powers of the TGNA. The 1982 constitution was designed to emphasize law and order, and further limited the authority of the TGNA. It bolstered the powers of the executive branch of government, and most specifically the office of president of the Turkish state. The loss of status for the TGNA becomes most visible with a simple comparison of the 1924 and the 1982 constitutions.

The TGNA was a major arena of political debate and conflict in the early 1920s. However, with the advent of one-party rule, opposition became less salient within the legislature and a consensual assembly developed. The Center was a coherent body of political elites and public bureaucrats. They shared a common "image of a good society" (Yücekök 1983: 110–16), and agreed upon a common political program that was carried out under the leadership of Atatürk. The urban elites shared the same outlook as the Center. The Periphery was a heterogeneous cultural mix of the rural notables, lower middle classes, and the peasantry. It differed from the Center by means of its allegiance to traditionalism in the form of folk religion, and a conservative lifestyle (Mardin 1975). The

Cultural Revolution of the 1920s and the 1930s had little impact on the countryside. The urban population embraced it with minimal difficulty.

However, World War II brought about a new period of hardship that began to strain the happy marriage between the urban elites and the Center. The Periphery was also very hard hit by the scarcity of goods. Corruption charges and the war rich became salient in the public eye. The gestures of democratization in the 1940s ushered in new political parties that championed the have-nots, and successfully mobilized the forces of the Periphery against the party of the Center, the RPP. National elections not only ousted the RPP from most seats in the TGNA, but also brought in the representatives of the Periphery (Yücekök 1983: 123–30). The TGNA, once again, became an assembly of political debate and conflict, rather than a legitimating institution of consensual policymaking. It is still an arena of political conflict and debate. Since 1946, the TGNA has functioned as an institution in which grievances of the represented are aired, and in which legislative debate has contributed to political communication in the media. Some conflicts have been resolved, while others are simply taken up in the legislative debates.

Executive-legislative relations in Turkey are organized around the principles of parliamentarism. However, in the 1982 constitution, the office of the president is endowed with some powers that are inspired by the French model of presidentialism. Therefore, the current form of Turkish parliamentarism is mired in added conflicts between the president and the prime minister.

The TGNA is a plenary body, as opposed to a committee-dominated one, such as the German Bundestag or the U.S. Congress. The executive branch is the real power broker, and initiator of legislation. The parliamentary group that occupies the most seats in the TGNA controls the legislative process by means of its dominant position in the standing committees as well as on the floor. Although it is possible for any deputy to introduce a motion in the TGNA, the agenda priorities are determined by the dominant party group. The agenda items, even when suggested by the opposition party groups, can also be amended by the governing party deputies through joint proposals to make them fit government policies. It is virtually impossible to legislate without the consent of the majority party or coalition leadership (Kalaycioğlu 1990: 210–11).

The leader of the majority party group of the TGNA is the prime minister. Prime ministers are in a very powerful position not only because of the public bureaucracy at their disposal, but also because of the ability to sanction or reward the deputies of the majority group. The two most obvious rewards are the offer of a ministerial seat in the cabinet, and a safe position in the party list of candidates in the next round of national elections. Investments, various projects, and new jobs can be dished out to the constituents of deputies by the prime minister as rewards, or they can be withheld or redirected to other electoral districts as punishment. Very few deputies have enough autonomous grassroots support to be elected without their party leader's blessing. Therefore, since 1950 all parliaments in Turkey have been dominated by the executive branch of government.

However, the subordination of the TGNA cannot be taken for granted. The distribution of seats in the TGNA is one factor that often hinders a prime minister from acting dictatorially toward the deputies. The volatility and fragmentation of the vote also restricts a prime minister from mistreating the deputies. The splinter group of the JP that formed the Democratic Party in the early 1970s showed Süleyman Demirel the dangers of taking one's reign over a party for granted. Deputies are often as volatile as the voters (Turan 1985: 22–23). The lack of ideological differences and programmatic parties make it very easy for a deputy to hop around to different parties and seek better career prospects and rewards elsewhere (Turan 1985: 31).

A cabinet seat is not the only concern of the TGNA deputies. They participate in the game of clientelism. Their local support, and reelection, in part, depend on how successful they are in the game of trading benefits for votes, and in protecting the interests and values of their constituents. If they cannot continue obtaining benefits for their constituents from the state or local government, or if they receive clear hints that their grassroots support is under challenge, then the deputies are under pressure to make a dramatic gesture, such as to resign from the party and join the ranks of another. Article 84 of the 1982 constitution, designed to stop such party switching, failed to deter any deputy from changing party affiliations (Gençkaya 1990: 78). There is little evidence that constituents care with which party their deputy is affiliated, so long as he or she plays the clientelist game correctly.

The parliament of 1991 showed little sign of submissiveness. While the prime ministers were not embarrassed by a vote of the TGNA to adopt a proposal of the opposition not amended by a joint bill, they were stopped from legislating a variety of bills concerning education, cultural affairs, labor laws, and human rights issues. Deputies do not vote against the proposals of the government unless there are clear signs that party discipline is not being enforced. Instead, they do not attend the assembly meetings at all. Therefore, bills cannot be properly processed. Furthermore, some deputies coalesce to drastically amend the bills proposed by the coalition government when they are taken up in the committees. The government either withdraws the proposed bill, or is compelled to accept the amended form. In short, the 1991 Parliament seemed to be more effective vis-à-vis the executive branch of government than most that preceded it. It also functioned as a conservative, status quo force, often conflicting with the government's program and commitments.

In frustration, governments tend to use the power legally vested in them by the TGNA to promulgate decrees having the force of law, instead of using the regular legislative process. The TGNA's granting of the authority to legislate by means of decrees to the executive branch of government is constitutional. Furthermore, not granting that authority when it is officially requested by the government is tantamount to a no-confidence vote. Therefore, unless the majority of the deputies in the TGNA wants an early election (which means that about four out of ten lose their seats), there is always enough support to grant the authority to the executive to legislate by means of governmental decree. The problem with governmental decrees is that they are often not adopted by the TGNA (Kalaycioğlu 1990: 205), and the constitutionality of their substance may also often be doubtful. The action of the TGNA that authorized the government to issue decrees having force of law, used lavishly by the current government since July 1992, was ruled unconstitutional by the Constitutional Court (*Milliyet*, October 7–9, 1993). Therefore, the legality and legitimacy of the acts of government based on those decrees create a major problem. It seems as if the executive branch of government has lost its ability to lead the TGNA. Consequently, the current picture of the TGNA is now less and less close to what Weinbaum (1975: 40, 56) calls a "submissive" legislature. Nevertheless, the lack of cooperation between the two branches of government incapacitates, or even paralyzes, the government. Legislative-executive relations in Turkey seem to continue to produce more conflict and stagnation.

The current assembly of the TGNA has become a conservative force that protects the political regime of the 1982 constitution. It should not be forgotten that the current political regime of Turkey rests not only on the 1982 constitution, but also on a host of vested interests, which are well organized in the TGNA. Although no political party identifies with the constitution, a group of deputies from the TPP, MP, WP, and NWP consistently cooperate to amend, block, or support legislation in a highly disciplined and concerted manner. Issues pertaining to religion, culture, human rights, security, foreign policy, and financial support for certain foundations or endowments cannot be legislated without their consent. This group does not heed formal party discipline, either. An informal party organization seems to be at work behind the formal organizations of the moderate- to ultra-right-wing political parties in the TGNA (*Cumhuriyet,* November 17, 1992). The deputies belonging to this right-wing faction are effective in the standing committees of the TGNA, exerting their influence on bills during committee debate. Their power cannot be limited on the floor either. For example, on the issue of higher education, then prime minister Süleyman Demirel publicly committed himself to amend one decision of the standing committee on national education when the bill was to be taken up on the floor, and had to suffer a defeat at the hands of the conservative faction (*Cumhuriyet*, June 18, 1992).

The problem with the balance of power in the current TGNA is that the reform program of the coalition government cannot be written into law and become government policy. The TGNA matters, but in a way that the media and some of the voters do not appreciate. The TGNA becomes an effective mechanism to stop reform, to halt attempts to amend the 1982 constitution, and to promote the vested interests of the current political regime. Therefore, a dilemma emerges: Faced with a conservative TGNA, bogged down in clientelist politics and bent on defending vested interests, how can reforms that are so much demanded by the voters, and publicly accepted by all the major political parties, be carried out by the government?

Consequently, since 1991, Turkish public opinion and the mass media have been incessantly involved in an ongoing debate over the nature of the country's democratic regime. Some journalists, political pundits, and politicians suggest doing away with the current form of the republic, and establishing a totally new political system, or "Second Republic." Some desire a presidential regime; others want less presidentialism and more parliamentarism. Some want to jettison the unitary nature of the state and make it a federation; others proclaim the merits of a consociational model of democracy. Nevertheless, one matter is certain: The political institutions of the current democratic regime are not performing to the satisfaction of the voters. The electoral and party systems do not contribute to stable governments that distribute values and resources evenly. The TGNA has become a house of clientelism, and lacks a zeal for reform. The electoral system is not accepted by all the major parties as fair and just. The interest-group system is too feeble to matter for political participation. The current democratic regime of Turkey seems to be producing more corruption than sound economic growth, welfare, and security. Therefore, Turkish democracy seems to have the same Mediterranean malaise as the Italian, Spanish, and Greek democracies. There seems to be no easy way out.

Conclusions

The constitutional and institutional performance of political democracy in Turkey is obviously complex. To summarize, this chapter proposes six basic findings.

First, the Turkish transition to democracy did not occur after the collapse of an authoritarian or totalitarian regime. There was never a total disillusionment with the Cultural Revolution of the 1920s and 1930s. In fact, even today a large majority of the electorate looks back with admiration at the War of Independence, the Cultural Revolution, and the deeds of Kemal Atatürk, the founder of the Turkish Republic. At a time when contemporaries of Atatürk such as Lenin, Stalin, Hitler, Mussolini, and Mao are considered fallen dictators, a simple motion by religious fundamentalist deputies of the TGNA to denigrate Atatürk can still precipitate public uproar and mass demonstrations (*Milliyet*, November 11, 1993). The RPP and its policies throughout World War II were disliked by the middle and upper classes, and by the peasants of the 1940s. However, a complete rupture with Turkey's authoritarian past never occurred. The RPP could still attract the support of 42 percent of the electorate in the last national elections before it was banned by the military government of 1980–83.

Second, in the Turkish transition to democracy, a thorough consensus over the constitutions and the rules of the democratic game never developed. In the 1960s, the JP formed a government while arguing that the 1961 constitution was illegitimate. In the 1980s and the 1990s, all of the political parties tried to disassociate themselves from the 1982 constitution. By not agreeing on the fundamentals of the game of democracy and the specifics of the political regime, the major political forces of the country contributed to the perennial crisis of legitimacy.

Third, the Turkish political elite failed to reach a compromise over an electoral formula that would marry the goals of representativeness and governability such that no doubts over the fairness of election results emerge. Turkey, after experimenting with democracy for five decades, still needs an election system that is accepted by all the major political leaders, parties, and their followers. Lack of such an electoral system breeds a legitimacy crisis, which has contributed to breakdowns in Turkish democracy. The electoral formulas provided by the military governments have failed to perform the trick. It seems as if the first task of consolidation of Turkish democracy is a political consensus of all the major party leaders and their followers over an electoral system that they would consider fair and just.

Fourth, military rule and social mobilization have contributed to deinstitutionalization of the party system in Turkey. Banning and outlawing political parties, together with a rapid rate of urbanization and industrialization, contributed to the volatility and fragmentation of the vote. The proportional representation formula used in the elections of the 1960–80 period further enabled the major political parties to split, and new groups to organize their parties and participate in elections. A participation crisis emerged with the establishment of the parties of the far left and the far right in the 1960s, which could not be resolved within the democratic regime of that period. Co-opting them in the governing coalitions further exacerbated the participation crisis and eventually led to the breakdown of the democratic regime in the 1980s. A similar crisis is in the making with the emergence of a Kurdish party in the 1990s. Again, a legitimacy crisis emanating from the electoral formula, a participation crisis surfacing from the inclusion of a Kurdish party in the elections, and rapid social mobilization are converging to put an excessive amount of stress on the democratic regime. Furthermore, the challenge of the Islamic, antisystem Welfare Party has not been routinized in Turkey, for example, in a way similar to the antisystem communist parties of the Western European democracies during the Cold War era. Ethnic and religious parties are not permissible according to the 1982 constitution, but both exist in the TGNA as a matter of fact. The Turkish democratic regime has produced no solution to the incorporation of such participatory challenges of radical parties.

Furthermore, no imminent solution to any of the three factors (the legitimacy crisis, participation crisis, and rapid social mobilization) that contributed to democratic breakdowns in the past is being produced by the democratic political institutions. Ad hoc treatments of such developments have been the basic response of the political system so far; they have not produced any tangible results.

Fifth, the fragile interest-group system of Turkey is still overwhelmingly paternalized by the corporatist policies of the state. Voluntary associations are still viewed with great suspicion by the state elites. Even the strongest of those voluntary associations finds its survival at risk. It is important to remember that only approximately 6 percent of Turkish voters have any affiliation with voluntary associations, according to a recent Turkish Values Survey (for more information see Ergüder, Esmer, and Kalaycioğlu 1991). Consolidating democracy with an underdeveloped interest-group system that leaves little room for voluntary associations is very difficult, if not impossible.

Sixth, and finally, the TGNA is embedded in a clientelist format, which provides the have-nots of Turkish society with some of their most desired values of respect, security, and welfare. However, the TGNA seems to be an institution of stagnation in Turkish politics, which frustrates governments seeking reform. The media project images of the TGNA as a political elite embedded in a culture of corruption. Clientelist politics often breeds corruption. The recent developments in Italian and Japanese politics indicate that clientelist systems can also multiply corruption to levels found intolerable by the public. Turkey seems to be trespassing on the same territory, and corruption is likely to contribute to a further erosion of political trust not only in the legislative system, but also in the democratic regime.

Under the influence of rapid social mobilization and democratization, which provided opportunities for political participation to the members of the former Periphery, the traditional confrontation between the Center and the Periphery has changed dramatically. The party system that was constructed around the pivotal role the RPP played, as the party of the Center against which all the parties of the right and left were lined up, no longer exists. The split of the former RPP into three political parties symbolizes the change taking place in the Turkish party system. If there is a Center in Turkish politics now, it comprises the security establishment, which includes the military, and some of the civilian bureaucracies such as the Ministry of Defense, the prime minister's office, the National Security Council, the Ministry of Foreign Affairs, and the Ministry of Finance. It is also possible to include those intellectuals who are motivated by the will of the state rather than the will of the nation, and the deputies of the TGNA who share the same ideological bent. The Kemalist Center of the 1920s through the 1940s was to be a coalition of the public bureaucracy, the deputies of the TGNA, and the intellectuals. It has since diminished to include the security establishment, some deputies of the TGNA, and some intellectuals—mainly those organized through Aydinlar Ocagi, a voluntary association well connected with the center of Turkish politics, Yuksek Ogretim Kurulu (YOK–the Higher Educational Council), and a host of other cultural organizations and endowments. They are not all Kemalists. What unites them is their belief in anticommunism, Turkish nationalism, and their zeal to serve the state.

This contraction of the Center has made room for other major groups to emerge. Perhaps the most noteworthy among them are those representing the economic interests of the middle classes, and the upper middle classes formed by the new industrialists and owners of big business. They are globalists, motivated by profit maximization and the free-market economy. They seem to consider the new Center as a facilitating mechanism for most of their activities. They are represented in the TGNA (Kalaycioğlu 1995: 58), and they are also inclined to develop relationships with intellectuals who think along their lines.

The Periphery of Turkish politics has also been changing dramatically under the influence of rapid social mobilization. It is now much more urban than it used to be. It was able to benefit from the game of democracy, which enabled its members to use the facilities of the state to legitimize their ideas, to get financial support for their endeavors, and also to gain access to upper echelons of the public bureaucracy. It can no longer be assumed that a top-level bureaucrat speaks Turkish with a "proper" Istanbul accent. In fact, because 62 percent of the inhabitants of Istanbul were born in villages of Anatolia (Kara and Köksal 1989: 1), it is doubtful that there is any Istanbul accent, or *Istanbul efendisi* left to talk about. Therefore, the sharp divide between the Center and Periphery makes little sense in the 1990s. It is necessary instead to focus on the organization of the security interests and economic interests, on the one hand, and on the great fragmentation and flux due to social mobilization, on the other, in order to explain developments in Turkish politics in the 1990s. The interplay of these new forces will determine whether Turkey will have strong interests that contribute to the consolidation of democracy in the country.

The 1996 election, which give the Welfare Party the power to form a coalition government, demonstrated a continuing struggle to find a compromise between the Center and the Periphery. On the one hand, an Islamic party is heading a government in secular Turkey for the first time. On the other hand, Necmettin Erbakan, the prime minister, has promised a standard center-right economic program, chiefly focusing on fighting inflation and promoting foreign investment. It remains to be seen how long his ruling coalition based on compromise and moderation will survive.

References

Almond, Gabriel A., and G. Bingham Powell, Jr. 1978. *Comparative Politics: System, Process, and Policy*. 2d ed. Boston and Toronto: Little, Brown.

Arat, Yesim. 1991. "Politics and Big Business: Janus-Faced Link to the State." In *Strong State and Economic Interest Groups: Post 1980 Turkish Experience,* edited by Metin Hepir. Berlin and New York: deGruyter.

Bianchi, Robert. 1984. *Interest Groups and Political Development in Turkey.* Princeton: Princeton University Press.

Cumhuriyet, June 18, 1992; November 17, 1992.

Economist, September 21, 1991.

Ekşioğlu, Kani. 1983. *Siyasal Yasalar*. Istanbul: Yasa.

Erder, Necat, Tüzün, Sezgin, Kardam, Ahmet, Kardam, Filiz. 1995. *Türkiye'de Siyasi Partilerin Seçmenleri ve Sosyal Demokrasinin Toplumsal Tabani.* Ankara: Cem Ofset.

Ergil, Doğu. 1980. "Turkey." In *Electoral Politics in the Middle East: Issues, Voters, and Elites,* edited by Jacob M. Landau, Ergun Özbudun, and Frank Tachau. London: Croom Helm.

Ergüder, Ustun. 1980–81. "Changing Patterns of Electoral Behavior in Turkey." *Boğaziçi University Journal: Social Sciences* 8–9, 45–81.

Ergüder, Ustun, and Richard I. Hofferbert. 1988. "The 1983 General Elections in Turkey: Continuity or Change in Voting Patterns." In *State, Democracy and the Military: Turkey in the 1980s,* edited by Metin Heper and Ahmet Evin. Berlin and New York: deGruyter, 119–34.

Ergüder, Ustun, Yilmaz Esmer, and Ersin Kalaycioğlu. 1991. *Türk Toplumunun Degerleri*. Istanbul: TÜSIAD.

Esmer, Yilmaz. 1991. "Manufacturing Industries: Giants with Hesitant Voices." In *Strong State and Economic Interest Groups: Post 1980 Turkish Experience,* edited by Metin Heper. Berlin and New York: deGruyter.

Frey, Frederick W. 1975. "Patterns of Elite Politics in Turkey." In *Political Elites in the Middle East,* edited by George Lenczowski. Washington, D.C.: American Enterprise Institute for Public Policy Research.

Gençkaya, Ömer F. 1990. "The Impact of Organizational Attributes on Legislative Performance." Ph.D. diss., Boğaziçi University in Istanbul.

Heper, Metin. 1987. "The State, Military, and Democracy in Turkey." *Jerusalem Journal of International Relations* 9: 52–64.

Hofferbert, Richard, I. 1988. "The 1983 General Elections in Turkey: Continuity or Change in Voting Patterns." In *State Democracy and the Military: Turkey in the 1980s,* edited by Metin Heper and Ahmet Evin. Berlin and New York: deGruyter.

Huntington, Samuel P. 1991. *The Third Wave: Democratization in the Late Twentieth Century*. Norman and London: University of Oklahoma Press.

Kalaycioğlu, Ersin. 1988. "Political Culture and Regime Stability: The Case of

Turkey." *Journal of Economics and Administrative Sciences* 2, 2: 149–79.

Kalaycioğlu, Ersin. 1990. "Cyclical Breakdown, Redesign, and Nascent Institutionalization: The Turkish Grand National Assembly." In *Parliament and Democratic Consolidation in Southern Europe: Greece, Italy, Portugal, Spain, and Turkey,* edited by Ulrike Liebert and Maurizio Cotta. London and New York: Pinter 184–222.

———. 1991. "Commercial Groups: Love-Hate Relationship with the State." In *Strong State and Economic Interest Groups: Post 1980 Turkish Experience,* edited by Metin Heper. Berlin and New York: deGruyter.

———. 1992. "1960 Sonrasi Türk Siyasal Hayatina Bir Bakis: Demokrasi, Neo-Patrimonyalizm ve Istikrar." Universite Öğretim üyeleri Derneği, *Tarih ve Demokrasi: Tarik Zafer Tunaya'ya Armaga.* Istanbul: Cem.

———. 1994. "Elections and Party Preferences in Turkey." *Comparative Political Studies* 27 (October): 402–24.

———. 1995. "The Turkish Grand National Assembly." In *Turkey: Political, Social, and Economic Challenges in the 1990s,* edited by Cigdem Balim et al. Leiden: E.J. Brill, 42–60.

Kara Nihal, and Sema Köksal. 1989. "Istanbul'da Yerel Politika ve Büyük Şehir Yönetimi." Research Report. Istanbul: Marmara University.

Kara, Nihal, and Günay Göksu Özdoğan. 1988. "1987 Seçimleri: Parti Sisteminin Geleceğine Ilişkin Bazi Gözlemler." *Iktisat Dergisi* 279: 13–30.

Karpat, Kemal. 1959. *Turkey's Politics.* Princeton: Princeton University Press.

———. 1975. "The Politics of Transition: Political Attitudes and Party Affiliation in the Turkish Gecekondu." In *Political Participation in Turkey: Historical Background and Present Problems,* edited by Engin Akarli and Gabriel Ben-Dor. Istanbul: Boğaziçi University Publications.

Kutad, Ayse. 1975. "Patron-Client Relations: The State of the Art and Research in Eastern Turkey." In *Political Participation in Turkey: Historical Background and Present Problems,* edited by Engin Akarli and Gabriel Ben-Dor. Istanbul: Boğaziçi University Publications.

Mardin, Serif. 1975. "Center-Periphery Relations: A Key to Turkish Politics?" In *Political Participation in Turkey: Historical Background and Present Problems,* edited by Engin Akarli and Gabriel Ben-Dor. Istanbul: Boğaziçi University Publications.

Milliyet, October 7–9, 1993; November 11, 1993.

Özbudun, Ergun. 1976. *Social Change and Political Participation in Turkey.* Princeton: Princeton University Press.

———. 1981. "The Turkish Party System: Institutionalization, Polarization, and Fragmentation." *Middle Eastern Studies* 17 (April): 228–40.

———. 1985. "Political Parties and Elections." In *Sudosteuro Pa-Handbuch: Türkei,* edited by Klaus-Detlev Grothusen. Göttingen: Vandenhoeck and Ruprecht.

———. 1991. "The Post-1980 Legal Framework for Interest Group Associations." In *Strong State and Economic Interest Groups: Post 1980 Turkish Experience,* edited by Metin Heper. Berlin and New York: deGruyter.

Sabah, September 22, 1993; February 20, 1994.

Sartori, Giovanni. 1976. *Parties and Party Systems.* Cambridge: Cambridge University Press.

Sayari, Sabri. 1975. "Some Notes on the Beginnings of Mass Political Participation." In *Political Participation in Turkey: Historical Background and Present Problems,* edited by Engin Akarli and Gabriel Ben-Dor. Istanbul: Boğaziçi University Publications.

———. 1978. "The Turkish Party System in Transition." *Government and Opposition* 13 (Winter): 39–57.

Sertel, Murat and Ersin Kalaycioğlu. 1995. *Türkiye için Yeni bir Seçim Yöntemi Tasarimina Doğru.* Istanbul: TÜSIAD Publications.

Soysal, Mumtaz. 1969. *Dinamik Anayasa Anlavisi: Anayasa Divalektigi Uzerine bir Deneme.* Ankara: Ankara University Faculty of Political Science Publications.

Tachau, Frank. 1984. *Turkey: The Politics of Authority, Democracy, and Development.* New York: Praeger.

TGNA. 1982. *Seçim, Seçim Sistemleri ve Türkiye'deki Uygulamalar.* Ankara: TBMM Basimevi.

Turan, Ilter. 1969. *Cumhuriyet Tarihimiz: Temeller, Kurulus, Milli Devrimler.* Istanbul: Caglayan.

———. 1985. "Changing Horses in Midstream: Party Changers in the Turkish National Assembly." *Legislative Studies Quarterly* 10 (February): 21–34.

Weiker, Walter. 1967. *The Turkish Revolution, 1960–1961, Aspects of Military Politics.* Washington, D.C.: Brookings Institution.

Weinbaum, Marvin G. 1975. "Classification and Change in Legislative Systems with Particular Attention to Iran, Turkey, and Afghanistan." Chapter 2 in *Legislative Systems in Developing Countries,* edited by G. R. Boynton and Chong Lim Kim. Durham: Duke University Press.

Yücekök, Ahmet Naki. 1983. *Siyaset Sosyolojisi Acisindan Turkiye'de Parlamento'nun Evrimi.* Ankara: Ankara Universitesi Siyasal Bilgiler Fakultesi.

Zürcher, Erik Jan. 1984. *The Unionist Factor: The Role of Union and Progress in the Turkish National Movement, 1905–1926.* Leiden: E. J. Brill.

9

Can Viable Constitutionalism Take Root in Post-Soviet Russia?

ERIK P. HOFFMANN

> Political compromise is the handmaiden to the preservation of principle in a complex world.
>
> —James Underwood

This chapter focuses on the core elements of viable constitutionalism and assesses whether they are taking root in post-Soviet Russia. Emphasis is placed on the national and subnational political institutions and cultures, as well as on the socioeconomic and international contexts within which Russian state building is taking place. Also emphasized are the functions performed by President Boris Yeltsin's constitution of December 1993, and whether it is fostering viable or nominal constitutionalism, consensual or confrontational policymaking, tolerant or intolerant political cultures, and a strong, stable, and democratic state or a weak, unstable, and authoritarian state.

Addressing five basic issues, this chapter will

1. elucidate the concepts of "viability" and "constitutionalism" in the context of post-Soviet politics;
2. illustrate how general theories of democratization and stable democracy can help to understand post-Soviet polities, economies, and societies;

3. underscore the potential benefits of Russia's presidential system and ways to minimize its liabilities;
4. scrutinize the new Constitution's text and national, regional, and local contexts, assessing the constitution's positive provisions but also its portentous ambiguities and omissions;
5. conclude that the prospects for viable constitutionalism and democratic consolidation in the Russian Federation are not sanguine for the immediate future.

The Politics and Jurisprudence of Viable Constitutionalism

Conceptual Issues

It is important to clarify the choices concerning our basic concepts of viability and constitutionalism. The meaning of these terms is quite elastic in Western democracies and is hotly disputed by politicians and analysts in Russia and in the other Commonwealth of Independent States (CIS) countries. At a minimum, we must identify and compare the various ideas of leading politicians and policy analysts.[1]

The concept of viability is highly contextual. "Capable of working, functioning, or developing adequately" and "having a reasonable chance of succeeding" are dictionary definitions with instrumental connotations. But "functioning" to serve which purposes, "developing" in what direction, and "succeeding" in fulfilling whose goals, priorities, or interests? Should viability focus on political leadership or culture, power or authority, change or stability, effectiveness or efficiency, policymaking procedures or substantive policies, and Western or non-Western types of democratization, marketization, military conversion, and ethnic homogenization? Also, can and should analysts and actors adapt to one another's conceptualizations, given their diverse goals and experiences? For example, "viability" in Russian *(zhiznesposobnost)* connotes having sufficient physical capacity for survival rather than purposefulness, feasibility, or instrumentality.

Some core elements of viable constitutionalism and some recommendations for democratic consolidation in Russia can be derived from my earlier study of federalism with Richard P. Nathan.[2] Different branches and levels of government must

1. acknowledge that they all have consequential rights and responsibilities guaranteed by the constitution, jointly safeguard their

separate rights and responsibilities, and balance clarity and elasticity in codifying their mutual obligations and conflict resolution mechanisms;

2. establish incentives that generate consensus and compromise on fundamental issues of policy and metapolicy and that reward collaboration and coalition building to cope with common problems;
3. share power in mutually advantageous ways that seize opportunities and develop potentials, and that deter political leaders from violating citizens' rights and from denying equal opportunities to all geographical regions and ethnic groups;
4. create and sustain democratic political and legal cultures that foster respect for the law and that include widely accepted procedures to amend the national and regional constitutions;
5. strengthen democratic pluralism, especially through support for competing political parties, responsive bureaucracies, independent mass media, and a myriad of associational interest groups;
6. stimulate economic performance and minimize economic inequalities, which are probably the chief nonprocedural sources of governmental legitimacy;
7. safeguard basic nonmaterial needs and wants, such as religious freedom, educational opportunities, physical safety, access to quality health care, an unpolluted natural environment, and respect for cultural diversity.

Constitutions and Constitutionalism in the Soviet Union and Russia

Specialists on constitutional law can no doubt refine the concept of constitutionalism in the current Russian context. But I distinguish sharply between "constitutions" and "constitutionalism," and broadly define the latter to include procedural, substantive, national, and subnational elements. Russia is facing a cultural, institutional, socioeconomic, and political as well as a legal and technical challenge. A respected American specialist on Russian law reportedly commented, "I'm not interested in legislatures"; this kind of technocratic and compartmentalized thinking is disappointing.

Quite helpful is Robert Sharlet's observation that in the Mikhail Gorbachev period, Soviet leaders and jurists used the concept of constitution in diverse ways and as a code word for diverse purposes. The national constitution was viewed as a "metapolicy or framework for subconstitutional policymaking," the "supreme law," a "higher symbol," or "a framework or arena for civilized forms of struggle"—all of which provided a "vocabulary for the language of political negotiation." The constitution was not an immutable legal fiction; it was the centerpiece of "a constitutional convention *writ large,* addressing strategic questions on the future shape of the political system."[3]

President Yeltsin has conceptualized the new constitution in all of these ways, but the multifaceted legacies of the tsarist and Soviet past remain powerful. Only the last tsar grudgingly accepted a constitution, after nationwide anarchy throughout 1905, although he cavalierly discarded the constitution and disbanded successive parliaments shortly thereafter. Soviet commissars from Vladimir Lenin to Leonid Brezhnev viewed the constitution as an instrument to augment and legitimize party and state power, not to limit or share it. The 1977 constitution stipulated that "the Communist Party of the Soviet Union is the leading force of Soviet society, the nucleus of its political system and state and public organizations" (Article 6). The same article added that "all Party organizations operate within the framework of the USSR Constitution." However, the official rules of the Communist Party of the Soviet Union never mentioned the constitution, nor did they promise to abide by it, until Gorbachev included in the 1986 party rules (Article 60) the identical sentence just quoted from Brezhnev's constitution.

Gorbachev, a lawyer by training, began to make serious constitutional revisions (e.g., steps toward de facto federalism and separation of powers). But Gorbachev's power, unlike Yeltsin's, was never based on a direct popular vote, and Gorbachev's avowed purpose, in contrast to Yeltsin's, was to strengthen "socialist democracy" rather than constitutional democracy. Gorbachev liberalized the legal system in order to legitimize the newly created presidency, restructure the state ministries and soviets (councils), and prevent the further fragmentation of the Communist Party as well as the disintegration of the Soviet Union and the Russian Soviet Federated Socialist Republic (RSFSR). To Gorbachev's credit, the much-amended 1991 version of the constitution obligated all party, state, and other organizations to "observe the USSR Constitution and Soviet laws" (Article 4), and the 1990 amended party rules stipulated that "the CPSU and all of its organizations operate within the framework of the USSR Constitution and Soviet laws" (Article 34).[4] The Communist Party even produced a Western-style "bill of rights" just before its demise.

A stubborn historical fact remains: Soviet constitutions were intended to serve the interests of the party and state as defined by its current top leaders, not to mediate conflicts among the bureaucratic elites or to protect individual citizens against arbitrary abuses by governmental authorities. The 1936 constitution guaranteed freedom of speech, assembly, and the press to all citizens, but only if they used these civil liberties to further "the interests of the working people" and "to strengthen the socialist system" (Article 125). "In the contrary case," explained Stalin's commissar of justice, "the Constitution does not guarantee anything to anybody." Nikita Khrushchev's chief ideologist, in a statement with equally profound implications, declared, "We have complete freedom to struggle for Communism. We do not and cannot have freedom to struggle against Communism."[5] Similarly, the 1977 constitution affirmed that individuals could exercise their constitutionally granted rights only "in accordance with the people's interests and for the purpose of strengthening the socialist system" (Article 50); the 1991 amended version granted citizens the additional right to "develop" socialism (Article 50). Citizens were also guaranteed the right to form or join public organizations "in accordance with the goals of communist construction" (Article 51), but this conditional clause was eliminated in 1990 because the beleaguered CPSU was forced to give up its "leading" role and to share power with "other political parties" (Article 6).

When a polity's core elements are hotly disputed and its most fundamental socioeconomic supports are visibly weakening, democratic constitutional principles are difficult to assimilate and legitimize, and democratic institutional relationships are difficult to create and nurture. No one understood this better than Andrei Sakharov, the great Russian democrat and Nobel laureate. In 1989 Sakharov began to write a new constitution. Witnessing the breakup of the Soviet bloc and anticipating the collapse of communism in the Soviet Union, Sakharov presciently sought to provide the intellectual and moral leadership essential to the birthing of a constitutional democracy. Had Sakharov lived into the early 1990s, he would surely have played a seminal role in crafting and promulgating a more effective and pragmatic as well as a legitimate and consensual Russian constitution. According to St. Petersburg mayor Anatoly Sobchak, "Sakharov's draft is a kind of litmus paper with which to test all other constitutional ideas and drafts for conformity with the highest principles of true democracy, true popular rule, and true humanitarianism."[6] But Sakharov's political and ethical precepts are infinitely more difficult to apply without his unique charisma and courage and with the widespread corruption and confrontation that have flourished in postcommunist Russia, especially during the constitutional crisis from 1991 to 1993. A Polish commentator starkly poses the key question confronting democratic reformers—"What is better: Disrupt the rules of democracy and chase out the totalitarian parties while they are still sufficiently weak? Or respect the democratic order and open to these parties the road to power?"[7]

Of enormous practical and intellectual significance are the obstacles to viable constitutionalism in Russia. To comprehend these obstacles, it is useful to recall the functions that Marxist-Leninist ideology played in the Soviet Union: analytical and cognitive, operational and tactical, and utopian, revolutionary, and missionary. Soviet ideology also helped to legitimize the top elites' power vis-à-vis the subelites, citizenry, and foreign communists, and sought to mold the values, upbringing, and career expectations of the diverse peoples of the USSR's internal and external empires.[8] Soviet constitutions were, of course, an important part of official ideology. Marxist-Leninist rhetoric notwithstanding, one of the chief functions of Soviet constitutions was to diminish citizens' participation in decision making and to dull their sense of political efficacy. Virtually everyone knew that liberties guaranteed to all Soviet citizens by law were flagrantly denied to most people in practice, and that rights explicitly granted in the formal constitution were strictly forbidden in the "informal" constitution—the body of Communist Party rules and popular norms that governed bureaucratic politics and everyday life.[9]

Only the democratic dissidents challenged these presumptions and practices. Andrei Amalrik contended that all members of the "democratic movement" had at least one objective in common: the establishment of a "rule of law, founded on respect for basic human rights." Some dissidents, especially those who sought to abolish basic characteristics of the Soviet system, did not believe that a just society could be created with current constitutional and federal laws. Other dissidents, especially those whose first priority was to pressure the party and state to change key national policies, repeatedly demanded that political and legal authorities abide by *existing* laws, in particular the USSR Constitution and, on occasion, international or universal law.

One of the most important oppositionist contentions was that the USSR Constitution was the highest law of the land and that the constitutionality of all other laws should be measured against this standard. Vladimir

Bukovsky, Vyacheslav Chornovil, Pyotr Grigorenko, and others advocated nothing less than the depoliticization of the Soviet legal system—that is, the significant reduction of party control of the judicial process, adherence to the constitutional principle that "judges are independent and subject only to the law" (Article 112), and the establishment of constitutionality, not party fiat, as the chief criterion of legality in Soviet theory and practice.

At issue was the role or functions of law in the polity. A handful of dissidents affirmed that what was crucial was not the structure of government but the paramountcy of law—laws that restrain both political leaders and individual citizens, laws that cannot be changed or flaunted at will, and laws that are adjudicated by men and women who are not beholden to the current government, but whose authority derives from the entire society's commitment to abide by legitimately established, usually written, rules.

In sharp contrast was the official Soviet perspective that written law is an instrument to serve the state, that the spirit of the law is more important than the letter of the law, and that individual rights can be exercised only if they further centrally determined goals. Soviet jurisprudence, in this view, was above all "a means of educating, guiding, training, disciplining, and mobilizing people to fulfill their political, economic, and social responsibilities"—as current political leaders defined those responsibilities.[10] But the private opinions of average citizens best described political realities. Laws were seen as instruments to serve the *nomenklatura* elites and to preserve their power and privileges. Laws also controlled the nonelites and repressed their unauthorized political and economic activities as well as their unorthodox social and cultural behavior. In a word, the constitutional, civil, and criminal norms applied only to ordinary people, not to the ruling caste.

This historical context reminds us of the gulf between leading Russian politicians and average citizens and helps to explain why they may be going in different directions at different speeds. Parts of Soviet ideology (minus the communist utopian component) still serve the perceived interests of entrenched industrial and agricultural elites and appeal to many workers and peasants, especially those who prefer the security of Brezhnev's "stagnation" to the insecurity of Gorbachev's *perestroika* and now Yeltsin's "marketization" and "privatization." Moreover, the response of certain prominent Russian democrats, including Yeltsin on many occasions, has documented once again that intolerance and intractability are not consigned to only one part of the political spectrum. Creative compromise is crucial to democratic consolidation and collaborative problem solving, which in turn are crucial to the dismantling of the ideological and institutional legacies of Soviet power.

It will be very difficult to institutionalize consensual thinking and behavior in post-Soviet national politics, because too few top elites have the will or ability to tolerate their political rivals and to depersonalize the policy process. Although a few of the former democratic dissidents and some of their children have become elected and appointed political leaders, the vast majority of today's officials were *nomenklatura* elites from the political, administrative, military, security, and youth league apparatuses. Especially in the current context of economic uncertainties for most white- and blue-collar workers and of huge fortunes for entrepreneurs with political clout or protection, laws of all kinds could easily become even more instrumental or irrelevant. In a word, the new Russian constitution may prove to be merely another pragmatic form of ideology, which serves as a guide to action for some politicians and as post-facto justification for most.

Transitions from Authoritarianism and Democratic Consolidation

A constitutional democracy cannot suddenly emerge in a country with deep-rooted authoritarian and autarchic traditions, which raises thorny questions about stages of democratization and means-ends relationships in different domestic and international contexts. Disintegrating authoritarian or totalitarian regimes are not necessarily emerging democracies, and disintegrating centrally planned economies are not necessarily emerging markets. Democratization and marketization depend on whether the national and regional constitutions, electoral laws, party systems, and interest groups can establish legitimate and effective metapolicies, which in turn can produce feasible substantive policies that are implemented and accepted by the citizenry, especially the voting public. These goals are proving especially difficult in the twelve CIS and three Baltic countries, because the Soviet system consisted of external and internal empires, an immense military-security-industrial complex, a centrally directed economy, and repressive structures to ensure conformity in a multinational, multireligious, and multiclass society.

In this post–Cold War period of new possibilities and dangers, an age-old question resurfaces: How do the governors and the governed minimize the abuse of political power and maximize the use of legitimate authority to benefit the masses? Separation of powers, federalism, and checks and balances are laudable institutional relationships, given the American proclivity to limit governmental power and not to rely heavily on governmental institutions. We want these democratic structures, procedures, and perspectives to fragment power in order to generate the compromises, coalitions, and comity that foster individualism. But we sometimes forget how difficult and time consuming it is to create and nurture a civil society and civic culture. Rules of fair play, legitimate political and administrative practices, interest-group access to the policy process, and citizen participation in decision making often take generations to develop. And unstable democracy is much more common than stable democracy. In brief, disparate political cultures and institutions may be essential to the viability of a mature democratic polity, but fatal to the democratization of a recently authoritarian or totalitarian polity.

Scholars have yet to develop a theory about the types of constitutions that strengthen constitutionalism at successive stages of democratization. The initial efforts to do so, especially by specialists on Russia and Eastern Europe, deserve our close attention. Sharply distinguishing between "democracy (majority rule) and constitutionalism (limitations on government and the majority)," Jerry Hough concludes that constitutionalism often precedes democratization in successful democratic consolidations. He laments that "Gorbachev and Yeltsin were both so contemptuous of the constitutional rules of the game and that both Russian and Western theories did not speak more of constitutional democracy than simply of democracy and democratization."[11] Yeltsin's adviser Andranik Migranyan, in contrast, has long argued that authoritarian leadership is necessary in the initial phases of democratization, especially to control the potentially destructive conflicts arising from new "spiritual" freedoms, ethnic identities, and economic ambitions and deprivations. He favors strong and enlightened national leadership, not constitutional restraints and divided powers.

The constitutions of nascent democracies are much more likely to be interim documents than those of long-standing democracies. Jan Zielonka affirms that "what is required in the early democratic stage is a constitution that deals mainly with the machinery of government rather than the rights of individual citizens." But the constitution's initial content should be tailored to political legacies and aspirations as well as to the reform capabilities and public accountability of the new government. If a protodemocracy has a long tradition of "welfare-state authoritarianism" (George Breslauer's apt phrase), then it is probably wise to include substantive welfare-state benefits in its initial constitution and programs, rather than heavily emphasize procedural democracy and civil liberties. The more authoritarian the postrevolutionary institutions and cultures and the more difficult it is to amend the constitution or to impeach the president, the more constitutional law should balance procedural and substantive components, in order to reduce political instability in the short run and to produce a stable democracy in the long run. As Zielonka concludes: "The experience of the post-communist countries during these first years of democratic consolidation has clearly shown that new constitutions generally have a stabilizing effect, while the lack of them has more often than not been a source of instability. Thus the new Russian constitution, imperfect as it may be, is an asset to Russia's very fragile democracy."[12]

To be sure, the authoritarian pursuit of democratic ideals has subverted many a libertarian experiment, and the decree-issuing powers of new presidencies have often been abused. But Charles de Gaulle *is* an example of a powerful president who used his charismatic authority to solve pressing socioeconomic and international problems, imposed a seemingly authoritarian constitution on the nation, and then voluntarily resigned. And many nonprofessional legislatures have exercised arbitrary power and served selfish parochial interests—especially in the absence of capitalist markets, democratic political parties, and accountable military and civilian bureaucracies. The dilemma, of course, is to generate authority through a combination of procedural norms and policy successes and to create institutions that can govern themselves and the population.

Both strong and weak presidencies, as well as the Burkean and mandate forms of legislative representation, are very difficult to institutionalize in a recently totalitarian or highly authoritarian political culture. It helps if the polity has a tradition of civilian control of the military or even a long-standing symbiosis between a ruling communist party and its military-industrial complex, as in the Soviet Union. And it does not help if the political parties and party identification are very weak, or if the legal norms for interest articulation and aggregation are virtually nonexistent. Under such conditions, a directly elected president who increasingly cooperates with his parliament and regional governments and whose sizable permanent staff reduces conflicts with its own ministers, even if not compelled to do so by the constitution, may be the least dangerous alternative or even the only hope of fostering viable constitutionalism.

Presidential Democracy and Political Culture in Russia

President Yeltsin possessed charisma, electoral authority, and international acclaim after the August 1991 putsch, and he had enormous power to exercise transformational leadership. However, democratization in post-Soviet Russia was probably impeded by Yeltsin's insufficient use of presidential power and by his premature efforts to establish a consensual policymaking process. Only the president could have ordered new parliamentary elections and commissioned a real constitution, which would safeguard individual liberties and limit the powers of governmental bodies vis-à-vis one another and the citizenry. But Yeltsin tried unsuccessfully to collaborate with the Supreme Soviet deputies who had been elected under reasonably democratic procedures in 1990. His draft constitutions differed fundamentally from the legislature's drafts, which were based on the frequently revised RSFSR Constitution of 1978 and were predicated on the fiction of a strong Supreme Soviet under Communist Party rule. Political polarization and parochialism quickly gained the upper hand and, to make matters worse, were justified in the name of "constitutionalism."

The Supreme Soviet had granted Yeltsin temporary emergency powers until November 1992, but he showed little inclination to relinquish these powers at the agreed-upon time. Parliamentary leaders held ever more tightly to the letter of the Soviet-era constitution, which they could easily amend, which minimized the importance of the elected president of the RSFSR, and which, of course, had not anticipated an independent post-Soviet Russia. The new state's popularly reelected president could not promulgate *any* constitution or disband the Supreme Soviet by "constitutional" means, nor could he politically or legally accept the inconsequential role eventually carved out for him by his parliamentary rivals. Russia's unfettered struggle over power and policy and its alarming socioeconomic and international decline weakened the democratic proclivities of almost all national leaders, including the president and top parliamentarians and judges. And the prospects for viable constitutionalism were greatly reduced by this profound governmental crisis, which was rooted in the very different legitimacy claims and increasingly incompatible power ambitions of the president and Supreme Soviet.

To help explain these events one must recall the theories of democracy that stress the need for "congruence" between a nation's political institutions and public policies, on the one hand, and its general societal values and authority patterns, on the other. One must also examine the shifting relationships between Russian political institutions and culture. For example, Viktor Sergeyev and Nikolai Biryukov conclude that "the most important single obstacle to the transition from a totalitarian to a democratic society is the incompatibility of the new forms of social life and the new political institutions with the political culture of the nation.

The lesson of Russia's history must be learned: namely, that a modern democratic society will not emerge unless the political mentality of *sobornost* is overcome." *Sobornost* refers to a political culture of organic collectivism, popular will, and quest for objective truth as well as to a model of inclusive representation and consensual decision making, which was formulated and developed in the protoparliamentary assemblies *(zemskie sobory)* of the sixteenth and seventeenth centuries and was adapted and utilized by Soviet leaders from Lenin to Gorbachev, as in the 1921 resolution "On Party Unity," and the 1989 Congress of People's Deputies. Unlike Western parliaments, which function as arenas of compromise, bargaining, and coalitions, the *zemskii sobor* "is to represent the people in its intercourse with the authorities; its function is to confirm (or deny) the latter's legitimacy. It is, therefore, convened only when this legitimacy has, for some reason, been lost and is to be re-established. In this capacity it is expected to say either "yes" or "no," thereby assuming a markedly plebiscitary character."[13]

If Sergeyev and Biryukov are right about the persistence of conservative traditions, then congruence theories may help to explain the behavior of both Yeltsin and his parliamentary adversaries. Yeltsin has wisely insisted on direct elections for the presidency of the RSFSR and post-Soviet Russia, but he has less wisely relied on plebiscites to reconfirm his authority, policies, and metapolicies and has persistently eschewed support for political parties, independent mass media, and other associational organizations common to civil societies. Consciously or subconsciously, Yeltsin may have tailored his populist theory of democracy to the legacy of *sobornost.* However, he has selectively adjusted his old priorities and predispositions to match the new political, administrative, and socioeconomic realities. For example, since the plebiscite that tepidly ratified the 1993 constitution, Yeltsin has tried to strengthen the rule of law throughout society and to institutionalize executive-legislative collaboration, but he also launched a vicious civil war in Chechnya without even informing the legislature or the mass media. Innovative Russian political institutions and traditional Russian political cultures are reshaping one another, and they are spawning innovative conceptions of procedural democracy, adapting Western ideas about presidential power, and weakening *sobornost.*

Other elements of Russian political culture may be of contemporary relevance, too. Walter Laqueur reminds us that "'society'—that is to say, the intelligentsia, much of the middle class, and even sections of the nobility—were opposed to tsarist rule."[14] Gregory Freeze impressively documents the mounting demands and complaints of most social and professional groups during the 1760s–70s, 1860s–70s, and 1905–6.[15] Peter Juviler underscores "the tsar's contempt for the constitution [but] the immense progress made toward constitutionalism at central and local levels by the time of the Provisional Government's reforms."[16] And the New Economic Policy (NEP) of the 1920s and Khrushchev's domestic and international reforms of the 1950s resisted totalitarian institutions and policies. Arguably, the NEP went underground but never died, and Khrushchev laid the foundations for Gorbachev's "socialist democracy" and Yeltsin's populist or plebiscitary protodemocracy. In any case, the growing shoots of civil society in tsarist Russia, the nascent constitutionalism manifested in the first dumas and local governments of the last tsars, and the more progressive elements of NEP and Khrushchevism resurfaced in new forms and new contexts in the late 1980s and early 1990s.

Donna Bahry has documented the continuity in political culture at the ends of the Stalin, Brezhnev, and Gorbachev eras. In each of these periods there was popular support for economic reform and welfare benefits as well as popular dissatisfaction with excessive party-government controls and privileges. Only the generational cohorts most strongly influenced by these basic Soviet values have changed considerably since they were first authoritatively documented in the late 1940s and 1950s by Alex Inkeles and Raymond Bauer of the Harvard Project. Hence, Gorbachev and Yeltsin probably enjoyed broader and deeper public endorsement of their respective reforms than is commonly recognized. And conservative opponents of both leaders gained the support of some segments of the population because of the Soviet regime's rapid and unexpected disintegration and of the widespread and jarring dislocations it produced. As Donna Bahry concludes,

> Our data show public values at the end of the Soviet era poised between the partial reforms of the Gorbachev years and the more radical platform of Yeltsin and [former prime minister Yegor] Gaidar. Most people supported political liberalization and at least limited economic change along the lines of NEP. It is not necessarily true that they were wedded to the old Soviet system, though they might welcome the stability of the Brezhnev years over the chaos of the post-Soviet transition.[17]

Are the past decade's cultural changes in Russia, such as the political, economic, social, and psychological uncertainties and the shifting mix of anticipation, exhilaration, angst, and anger, fostering democratization in the short or long run? Could it be that, because of Gorbachev's policy of *glasnost* and especially the "return of history," elite political culture is changing more than mass political culture? And could it be that the nonconformist private political culture, which thrived under the tsars and commissars, is finally displacing the conformist public political culture, which had been especially strong among the tsarist and Soviet bureaucratic elites?

The only certainty is that taking care of oneself and one's immediate family has become a much more important part of Russian culture, and that the pursuit of nationality, group, and regional interests has become more important, too. Ethnic identities, environmental lobbies, and local governments and businesses are all getting stronger. But few nonbureaucratic professional or occupational groups are well organized (miners may be the only exceptions), and the rapid pace of privatization clearly favors a reorientation toward individualism and away from collectivism. The concept of "national interest" is especially murky, because the concepts of "Russia" and "Russians" have been untied from their Soviet moorings and are being vigorously debated. Such changes and soul-searching could be constructive steps toward material, spiritual, and professional enrichment or destructive steps toward narcissism, chauvinism, and imperialism. The consequences of self-fulfillment, self-assertiveness, and self-aggrandizement depend heavily on the context.

Presidential-parliamentary gridlock, bureaucratic corruption, social injustices, economic crises, and international disappointments have made political cynicism and apathy significant parts of Russia's emerging culture. Western tutors in democratization and marketization were at first welcomed and now are selectively tolerated. Hence, it is exceedingly difficult to explain or predict the indigenous and foreign influences that are reshaping individual Russians, the Russian state, the CIS, and the post–Cold War world. Attitudinal and institutional transformations are interacting in dynamic and differentiated ways that are only beginning to be understood through public opinion polling and other empirical research.

Many analysts contend that Russians will find it difficult to alter authoritarian values, attitudes, and beliefs and hierarchical power relationships among top political leaders, political and bureaucratic elites, and citizenry. For example, most Russians have long viewed political phenomena in black and white, waited for orders from top "bosses," eschewed risk taking and innovation in their professional work, and limited frank talk to their kitchens. Russians find it difficult "to agree to disagree," to compromise on large or small matters, and to tolerate different political, social, ethnic, and religious viewpoints. And, reinforced by the constitutional crises of the Gorbachev and Yeltsin periods, Russians still view constitutions and laws as instruments that power holders use to enforce their will and that ordinary citizens do their best to evade.

But not all Russian political traditions are authoritarian, as some Russian parliamentarians have frequently underscored, citing representative institutions as far back as the Kievan period. Moreover, Russia's extraordinary sacrifices and victories during World War II can no longer effectively legitimize authoritarian rule, especially among younger people. And deeper understanding of the blood purges can evince only disdain for the perpetrators and empathy for the victims from Russians of all ages, except recidivist reactionaries. Thanks to Gorbachev's policy of *glasnost* and the disintegration of the Soviet Union, Russians (especially elites with foreign contacts) possess much more accurate information about their country's present and past and about the rest of the world. This "information revolution," together with greatly enhanced freedom to voice one's beliefs, has unleashed ethnic, religious, ecological, commercial, and territorial grievances and ambitions within the Russian Federation and the CIS. Cleavages in professional, personal, and family relations have also been exacerbated. Hence, new values, attitudes, and beliefs are mushrooming, old orientations are adapting to radically new circumstances, and the outcomes are virtually imponderable.

I would hypothesize that continuity is most likely, but hardly inevitable, in predominantly agricultural and ethnic Russian areas and among older and less educated people. And dramatic change is most likely, but hardly inevitable, in urban and ethnically mixed areas and among younger and better-educated people. Russia's short-term socioeconomic performance, not just its policymaking procedures and public policies, will have a decisive impact on the long-term viability of its nascent democratic institutions and culture.

Today, many Russians equate democratic reforms not only with greater freedom of speech and religion but also with the loss of the external and internal empires, domestic political stalemate, economic hardship, ethnic rivalry, rising crime rates, and a wide range of professional and personal anxieties. Because the breakup of the Soviet bloc in 1989 and the implosion of the Soviet Union in 1991 were remarkably swift and bloodless, many communist political structures and perspectives have survived and are thriving in the new Russian Federation. Most of the former *nomenklatura* elites have been able to preserve or increase their power and wealth in a freer and more chaotic polity, economy, and society. However, the current and future prospects of the peasantry, factory workers, and cultural, technical, and military intelligentsias are changing abruptly—mostly for the worse. The same is true for entire ethnic groups and geographical regions, their newfound "sovereignty" notwithstanding.

All these factors, especially the heightened tensions between political legacies and socioeconomic transformations, are shaping the new Russian nation and state as well as its policymaking and administrative procedures and domestic and foreign policies. Fundamental issues, such as the territorial boundaries of Russia and the meaning of being "Russian," are unresolved. Fortunately, the noun "Russian" has two distinct meanings in the Russian language—*russkii* (ethnic Russian) and *rossianin* (a citizen of the Russian Federation of any nationality). But what about the twenty-five million ethnic Russians living outside of Russia in the fourteen democratic, protodemocratic, authoritarian, and sultanistic polities of the former Soviet Union? All Russian leaders, especially ultranationalists, have taken a keen interest in the treatment of Russians in the "near abroad," and this issue may be as important as economic ties in determining the future of the CIS. Also, there is a mounting immigration problem. Countless Russians and non-Russians from the Soviet Union's successor countries, to say nothing of refugees from Third World countries, are pouring into a transformed Russia that lacks the will and ability to absorb them.

The experience of Gorbachev's Soviet Union and Yeltsin's Russia underscores the cultural as well as the institutional foundations of viable constitutional democracies. Gorbachev set loose fissiparous political, economic, and social forces and accelerated their momentum by periodically trying to rein them in with authoritarian measures. For example, ethnic aspirations and animosities greatly increased as did unrealistic expectations about economic prosperity and autonomy. Yeltsin spurred these trends, launching major anti-inflationary reforms with painful economic, social, and psychological effects for the vast majority of the population. Currency speculators, entrepreneurs selling state property, and mafiosi continue to do extremely well. They are becoming increasingly indistinguishable from, and enjoy close ties with, leading politicians and bureaucrats in the national, regional, and local arenas.

There is now a widening economic gap and a sharpening class conflict between the few newly rich entrepreneurs and mafiosi, on the one hand, and the many newly poor blue- and white-collar wage earners, on the other, including large segments of the cultural, technical, and military intelligentsias. These disparities are exacerbated by the haphazardly implemented Russian laws on privatization and commerce as well as by the power of the *nomenklatura* and criminal elements to abide only by their own norms. The cycles are vicious—the weaknesses of the constitutional, civil, and criminal codes have all undermined one another. Moreover, the content and functions of laws were in constant dispute during the first two years of the post-Soviet polity. The bare-knuckles power struggle between the executive and legislative leaders doomed any coordinated national policy initiatives, dissipated the center's control over the periphery, and fueled nationwide political instability, economic deprivation, ethnic rivalries, social turmoil, and psychological stress.

At issue was Russia's readiness for political democracy and market reforms. Consider the dramatic sequence of political events from November 1991 to February 1994: The Supreme Soviet gave the RSFSR's first directly elected president extraordinary decree powers for one year, primarily to ensure economic growth and productivity; the president signed an agreement with the leaders of Ukraine and Belarus disbanding the USSR and establishing the CIS; Yeltsin initiated the long-postponed "radical economic reform," especially industrial and consumer price liberalization; economic performance precipitously declined and presidential-parliamentary relations soured; the Supreme Soviet then attempted to strip the president of all but his ceremonial powers and to sabotage his anti-inflationary, privatization, and military conversion policies; the Constitutional Court openly sided with the parliament; the president abolished the parliament and suspended the Constitutional Court in violation of the 1978 RSFSR Constitution; the president stepped up his already tight control over television and radio; parliamentary leaders "appointed" a new president and ministers and incited the army and citizenry to take over the mass media and executive branch of government; the president persuaded the reluctant armed forces to bombard the parliament building and to jail its most conservative and reactionary leaders; the president discarded the Soviet-era constitution and ordered a constitutional plebiscite and parliamentary elections (to a bicameral Federal Assembly, whose upper chamber is the Council of the Federation and whose lower chamber is the State Duma); and the newly elected State Duma pardoned all of the former Supreme Soviet's leaders as well as the ultraconservative leaders of the putsch against Gorbachev and Yeltsin in August 1991.

As this chronology illustrates, Western democratic values were sorely lacking in Russia's national executive, legislative, and judicial leadership and the military, police, and economic bureaucracies. Russia did not have a legitimate and effective national government, a body of clear and enforceable constitutional, criminal, and commercial laws, a politically and economically independent television and radio, an adequately financed network of higher and secondary education, an ambitious program of environmental cleanup and health care reform, or a de-Sovietized ethnic identity and official democratic ideology. Hence, a transformation of public policies and institutions as well as an enlightened political and legal culture were urgently needed to avert the demise of democratization, the criminalization of capitalism, and the breakdown of the best traditional ethical values and social mores.

But what kind of transformation was feasible, and how do cultural and institutional changes influence one another? In Russia and the West, there has been a heated debate about economic and political "shock therapy" and the interconnections between economic and political development in the Soviet Union's successor countries. Disagreements about unemployment, privatization, inflation, bankruptcy, and taxation have their political counterparts in disagreements about the appropriate nature and functions of constitutionalism and parliamentarism. Russian democrats, centrists, and conservatives conceptualize "democracy" in a wide variety of ways and have diverse ideas about the phases and pace of democratic state building and civil society building. They prefer very different combinations of democratization and marketization at successive stages of development and very different institutional, legal, and cultural linkages between the domestic and international political economies.

For instance, the desirability and probability of massive Western aid and investment are vigorously disputed. Also, Russian conservatives emphasize Gorbachev's political and economic failures and China's successes, whereas Russian democrats emphasize Brezhnev's political and economic failures and Poland's and the Czech Republic's successes.

My personal view is that economic shock therapy was never attempted in Russia and that political shock therapy was not attempted until the fall of 1993. For example, major factories never faced bankruptcy, natural resources remained in the hands of *nomenklatura* officials, and the Central Bank belatedly conceded that inflation was a top-priority problem. But in 1992 rapid inflation abruptly lowered the living standards of most Russians, who experienced "shock without therapy." Also, conservative legislators were able to dominate an increasingly obstructionist Supreme Soviet and to recoup power in their constituencies, in part because citizens perceived executive authority and the president's right to dissolve the parliament to be less "constitutional" in 1993 than they did shortly after August 1991. And the intemperate rivalry between the national executive and legislature was exacerbated by intense and often irresponsible wooing of local authorities, who used this freedom from a monolithic Moscow to implement their own diverse economic programs. The president's bombing of the White House proved to be a more successful means of shock therapy vis-à-vis the independent-minded regional governments than the national legislature, as the composition of the new Federal Assembly and the tensions between Yeltsin and the armed forces clearly demonstrated. However, no kind of political shock therapy seems desirable for the foreseeable future, especially one pursuing ultraconservative "nationalist" goals and supported by dictatorial or military rule.

The fragmentation of power within the twelve countries of the CIS and the eighty-nine administrative units of the Russian Federation was not the handiwork of like-minded founding fathers committed to fundamental democratic values. Many Soviet institutions are adapting to the new political realities, and some old structures are remarkably intact on the local, regional, and even national levels in both Slavic and Muslim countries. The inconclusive struggle between the formidable Soviet legacies and their protodemocratic successors has produced much more conflict and apprehension than security and satisfaction for the vast majority of former Soviet citizens, notwithstanding the seductive appeals of international ethnic bonding, national political independence, and regional and local economic gains.

Leading democratic reformers can visualize the viable constitutionalism that might emerge from this remarkably complex and dynamic context, but few can specify how to get from existing to desired conditions, let alone mobilize the resources and forces to get there. Crafting constitutions and institutions may be the easiest and first stage; creating a successful mixed economy may be the second and more difficult stage; and consolidating a genuine civil society and civic culture may be the final and most difficult stage. But all goals and stages are interconnected in different ways in different countries. And it will probably be a prolonged and uphill struggle to adapt Western ideas and practices to the congealed remains of a totalitarian polity, which has grudgingly relinquished its external and internal empires, the former over four decades old and the latter accumulated over five centuries.

The first years of democratic strivings under Yeltsin produced irreconcilable legislative-executive gridlock and an ineffective judiciary on the national level, together with many firmly entrenched regional and local satraps. Fragmentation of power was legitimized by law and was institutionalized by experimentation under conditions of steep economic decline and sharpening ethnic conflict within Russia and most other CIS countries. Such conditions threatened to revive a military ethos and to sever the shoots of a civic culture. Political and economic reformers sought to establish new constitutional guarantees and to generate more consensual authority relationships, but ultraconservatives and reactionaries used democratic metapolicies to pursue traditional communist domestic and foreign policies and to perpetuate traditional *nomenklatura* and clientelist power bases. And an intensified struggle between the proponents and opponents of constitutional governance and capitalist economics may yet incapacitate Russia's national government and jeopardize the territorial integrity of Russia itself. The Russian state is weakened by mounting inflation, poverty, criminality, environmental decay, health crises, ethnic animosities, class conflict, demographic decline, drug trade, and other serious social ills. Ominously, the only quick way to reassert the power of the state and to ensure the unity of the country is through economic protectionism and military might.

Popularly elected but partyless President Yeltsin cannot quickly democratize traditional political and legal cultures, and his presidency may have strengthened authoritarian elements of these cultures, intentionally or unintentionally. For the authoritarian side of Yeltsin's personality, this is not a pressing problem; for his democratic side, it is a top-priority concern. In the first two years of post-Soviet Russia, there was rapidly increasing public dissatisfaction with most national political institutions and politicians. To be sure, many democrats had won seats in the Russian republic's Supreme Soviet, thanks to the unprecedentedly free election of 1990. But this body could not agree on the most basic metapolicies (e.g., the parliamentary/presidential division of labor) or on fundamental substantive policies (e.g., economic reforms), and democratic deputies gradually resigned their positions to join the executive branch or to pursue other careers. Political polarization and confrontation intensified as did the worsening socioeconomic conditions for all but the new entrepreneurs and mafiosi.

The president's decision to call for direct parliamentary elections and a constitutional plebiscite in December 1993 was probably two years too late. Yeltsin has explained this delay in a book that reveals a lot about his attitudes toward power, bargaining, and political and economic reform. For example, he asserts that "the most important opportunity missed after the [August 1991] coup was the radical restructuring of the parliamentary system," although "society might not have been ready to nominate any decent candidates to a new legislature." He acknowledges "some doubts" about not removing all former officials of the Communist Party's national and regional committees from their government positions. And he claims there was widespread public sentiment to "destroy the party" after the putsch. "It would have been possible to turn August 1991 into October 1917 with one sweep of the hand, with one signature. But I didn't do that, and I don't regret it." Why? Because Yeltsin perceived a "continuity between the society of the Khrushchev and Brezhnev period and the new Russia," especially the need to recruit experienced production executives into government.[18]

Well before the autumn of 1993, unfortunately, the context of constitutional, parliamentary, and economic reform had become revenge rather than accord, frustration rather than anticipation, and turf staking rather than groundbreaking. Not only had popular support for the president, Supreme Soviet, and Constitutional Court dropped precipitously, but so did the hopes for a viable constitutional order that would have eased the painful transition to a much less militarized and centralized economy and to a greatly reduced role in world affairs. Yeltsin and his most reformist supporters seem to have been especially surprised when these elections produced a State Duma perhaps as conservative as the disbanded Supreme Soviet and a Council of the Federation strongly committed to regional and local interests. And only the president forcefully affirmed that the constitution was a sizable first step toward viable constitutionalism.

Yeltsin's Constitution

The Text

Yeltsin's constitution is, of course, a huge improvement over its Soviet predecessors and is, arguably, the most viable of the post-Soviet drafts, including the less strong presidential version of July 1993.[19] Praiseworthy components include explicit commitments to guarantee the "inalienable" birthrights of individuals (Article 17.2) and the free activity of "interest" groups (Article 30.1) as well as to prohibit "censorship" (Article 29.5) and the instigation of "social, racial, national, or religious hatred" (Article 29.2). Moreover, the principle of the separation of powers is legitimized for the first time in Russian history (Article 10). Included are affirmations that "the right of legislative initiative" belongs to all of the top executive, legislative, and judicial bodies (Article 104.1), "deputies to the State Duma may not be in the civil service" (Article 97.3), and "judges are independent and subordinate only to the Constitution" and federal law (Article 120.1).

Furthermore, Russia is deemed to be a "federal state," which divides powers among the national, regional, and local governments (Articles 1 and 5.3). A residual powers clause gives regional and local governments "full state authority" in areas outside the sole jurisdiction of the national government or joint jurisdiction of the national and subnational governments (Article 73). A few important powers are granted solely to the regional and local governments. For example, republics can define their status with a "constitution" and provinces, territories, autonomous provinces and regions, and Moscow and St. Petersburg with a "charter." Also, "republics have the right to establish their own state languages" in addition to Russian (Article 68.2). And "bodies of local self-government independently manage municipal property; draw up, confirm, and fulfill the local budget; establish local taxes and fees; safeguard public order" (Article 132.1).

It is generally prudent not to enumerate the powers of the regional and local governments in the national constitution, because constitution writers are not political seers, policy analysts, or cultural anthropologists. Yeltsin's jurists were wise to delete the detailed Federal Treaty from the constitution's final draft. However, they included the subnational powers noted above for pressing political reasons. Center-periphery relations were deteriorating, and the country was in danger of breaking apart. The most immediate purpose of the constitution was to help preserve the Russian Federation, and, to that end, the president had rejected the claimed "sovereignty" of ethnic and territorial subnational units. Some kind of symbolic or tangible concession was surely in order, and the former was much less costly or risky than the latter, at least in the short run.

But there are serious ambiguities and omissions in Yeltsin's constitution. A pervasive problem is that it creates enormous potential for a new "war of laws" within and among the different branches and levels of government. The terms "laws" *(zakony)*, "resolutions" *(postanovleniia)*, "decrees" *(ukazy)*, "directives" *(rasporiazheniia)*, "decisions" *(zakliucheniia)*, "policy guidelines" *(napravleniia)*, "normative acts" *(normativnye akty)*, "charters" or "rules" *(ustavy)*, and domestic and foreign "treaties" *(dogovory)* all appear in the constitution. For example, after "mandatory consideration by the Council of the Federation," the State Duma adopts "federal laws" on a broad range of crucial domestic and foreign policies, including "war and peace" and "the federal budget," which is decided by the Russian government. The president issues "decrees and directives" on an even broader range of fundamental policies, and the government issues "decrees and directives" on their implementation (Articles 90, 104, 105, 106, 114, 115). The meaning, relationships, and practical applications of these terms are likely to be bitterly disputed by politicians and jurists until a substantial body of constitutional law develops or until a very strong president or authoritarian leader emerges.

Imprecise text in national constitutions and ill-defined separation of powers among national institutions invariably give subnational officials greater leeway in interpreting and administering national legislation. A disputatious and divided "center" could be especially destabilizing in protodemocratic Russia, because most of its republics and territorial subdivisions have their own constitutions and charters. Certain provisions of these subnational constitutions and charters contradict their national counterparts, and certain regional leaders insist on the primacy of their constitutions and charters. Indeed, twelve republics and ten provinces did not ratify the national constitution in the referendum of December 12, 1993.

Yeltsin's closest advisers have acknowledged the seriousness of center-periphery constitutional disputes. Then chief of staff Sergei Filatov concurred that there were many differences between national and subnational constitutions and other legislation on the following fundamental issues: "republic status; the operation of the Russian Federation Constitution and federal laws; demarcation of the jurisdiction and powers of the Russian Federation and its components; citizenship; the organization of a system of state power for the republics and local self-government; the rights of the individual and the citizen." Filatov blamed these rifts on the ambitions of regional political and economic elites, who were using new and old laws to consolidate their autonomy and authority as well as to control their region's property and other financial assets, and he warned that "if more radical forces come to power, there may be enough existing provisions in [subnational] legislative acts to threaten the unity of the Russian Federation and the political and humanitarian rights of its citizens."[20] Needless to say, the view from the provinces is very different, especially regarding Moscow's claimed right to correct "distortions" in subnational laws and its philosophical justification for so doing.

"War of laws" was a phrase originally coined to describe the crescendo of regional and local claims of sovereignty in the Gorbachev period. The post-Soviet Federal Treaty termed the republics "sovereign states," not merely "formations," and granted their inhabitants "republic citizenship," not only Russian Federation citizenship. Trying to reverse this decentralizing trend and to mollify the nonrepublic regional governments, the constitution's final draft deleted the word sovereignty from the penultimate draft's characterization of the republic governments. But the sovereignty issue cannot be resolved so easily. Giving the republics, provinces, and territories equal, though reduced, status motivates all of the regional governments to cooperate with one another vis-à-vis the national government, quite possibly through the Council of the Federation. Most republics continue to proclaim their sovereignty in their respective constitutions, yet few national executive leaders seem inclined to think seriously about divided sovereignty or dual citizenship. Also, the Federal Treaty retains some juridical authority, which is in dispute among politicians and in conflict with parts of the new constitution. And the lengthy list of "joint" jurisdictions of the national and subnational bodies (Article 72) leaves wide open questions about the relative powers of different bodies and the means of adjudicating intergovernmental conflicts.

In principle, the Constitutional Court "resolves jurisdictional disputes" between national governmental bodies, between national and regional bodies, and between the top regional bodies (Article 125.3). However, the constitution very sketchily describes the organs of the judicial branch and their responsibilities and interrelationships. For example, the Constitutional Court seems to be limited to cases concerning the constitution, not other federal statutes, whereas the one-sentence descriptions of the Supreme Court and the Higher Court of Arbitration empower the former to adjudicate civil, criminal, administrative, and "other" disputes and the latter to adjudicate economic and "other" disputes "through procedures stipulated by federal law" (Articles 125–27).

Most important, the president has immense power to rule by decree under emergency and nonemergency conditions. If the president declares a nationwide or local "state of emergency" (Article 88), specified civil rights and liberties can be suspended to the extent and for the time period he indicates (Article 56.1). But if an emergency is not declared, unspecified rights and liberties can be "restricted" indefinitely, if the president believes their exercise endangers "the foundations of the constitutional system, morals, health, and the rights and legitimate interests of other persons" or "the defense of the country and the security of the state" (Article 55.3). And if free speech is deemed to be "propaganda or agitation that instigates social, racial, national, or religious enmity," it too is "prohibited" for an unspecified period (Article 29.2).

Significantly, the president is empowered "to determine the basic guidelines of domestic and foreign policy" (e.g., Articles 56, 80, 83h, 90, and 114g). It is not clear that all presidential prerogatives are listed in the constitution and that, if the president uses his full executive powers, the national parliament and judiciary or the regional and local governments can play even a minor role in formulating public policies. Government bureaucracies, including the armed forces and security agencies, will always shape policy through implementation. But institutional checks and balances and other restraints on an aggressive or assertive Russian president are minimal. The Federal Assembly does not have the power of the purse, all regional governments do not have the power to collect and allocate important taxes, and the national and subnational courts do not have the unambiguous and enforceable power of judicial review. Although elements of all of these powers are contained in the constitution, its language is so murky or incomplete as to invite unilateral presidential decrees, deals, and appointments and to ensure rancorous interbranch, interlevel, and interregional rivalries. The president's power has been enhanced by separate treaties with more than two dozen republics and major provinces, but the creation of clear and uniform decision rules as well as the principle of fair and equal treatment under law have been undermined. Yeltsin's frequent use of this decree-issuing power and his occasional quick reversals of his own decrees are not encouraging precedents.

The National Context

President Yeltsin's leadership has been inconsistent on both substantive and procedural matters, including vision, priorities, ambition, and effort. He has periodically compromised with the legislature, including the former Supreme Soviet, and with the subnational governments, including the most autonomy-minded republics. He has influenced government officials directly through political negotiation and indirectly through public opinion. But, at times, Yeltsin has used few of his enumerated powers, even vis-à-vis his own presidential staff and government officials. At other times, he has flaunted the most rudimentary principles of the separation of powers and federalism. Both the little carrots and the big sticks often have been ineffectual in the policy arena, have destabilized the policy-making process, and have cost the president supporters in all political institutions and among the public. Neither extreme bodes well for establishment of a viable constitutional order in Russia, although both extremes can probably be legitimized by the letter of the new constitution.

Regrettably, Yeltsin has periodically demonstrated an instrumental attitude toward constitutions and constitutional law. He felt less and less bound by the much-amended 1978 RSFSR Constitution, especially when it was used by ultraconservative legislators to try to strip him of his popularly won powers and to sabotage his economic reforms. He further weakened constitutionalism by belatedly dissolving the Supreme Soviet—intransigent, ineffectual, and illegitimate as it was or principled, hamstrung, and legitimate, depending on one's point of view. Also, he seems never to have understood that the national legislature and judiciary can enhance the efficacy and legitimacy of constitutional law, and that the presidential staff cannot rewrite regional constitutions and local charters in a genuinely federal system. And Yeltsin's interpretation of the "spirit" of the national constitution has sometimes prevailed over the unambiguous meaning of its text, for example, in the omnibus anticrime legislation of 1994, which deprives suspected criminals of several constitutional rights.

To create and maintain a viable separation of powers in Russia's national government, more precise demarcation of the powers of the three branches is needed. The constitution could do much more to encourage the sharing of power, to provide checks and balances, and to construct a stable and regularized policymaking process in major issue areas. The lack of enabling legislation, the underfunding of judicial administration, and the embryonic multiparty system further weaken interbranch collaboration, bargaining, and coalition-building. Russia has a long road to travel before authoritative laws effectively limit the president and the leaders of the sizable presidential staff, the security and government bureaucracies, and to a lesser extent the national and subnational legislatures. The flexibility of national governmental structures and functions is so great as to make the personalities of top officials critical variables in state-building as well as policy formulation, implementation, and adjudication. But presidential restraint is essential to transform power into authority. Thus, it is unlikely that President Yeltsin will use his constitutional right to replace the entire cabinet and State Duma. If Yeltsin does not strive to legitimize the current constitution and institutional arrangements, who will?

Significantly, presidential patronage and loyalty to the president are strongly supported in the constitution. Yeltsin has had virtually unlimited powers to staff the national executive and judicial bodies as well as, until 1996, the upper house of the legislature, which consists of many leading regional administrators directly elected by their constituencies but initially appointed by the president (see especially Articles 77, 78, 83, 96, 117, 121, and 128). For example, if the State Duma expresses no confidence in the government, the president can either "dissolve" the State Duma or "dismiss" the government (Article 117.3). The president "appoints" the prime minister with merely the "consent" of the State Duma, and if this consent is withheld three times, the president can dissolve the State Duma and appoint the prime minister of his choice (Articles 83a, 109.1, 111.4, and 117). The president not only "presides" at cabinet meetings but can dismiss the whole government without the consent of either branch of parliament (Articles 83b and 117.2). Furthermore, the "independence" of the judiciary is seriously undermined by many corrupt judges and the intimidation, even murders, of honest judges, as well as by the power to "terminate" or "suspend" judges under "federal law," which the president could easily decree or either chamber of parliament could legislate (Articles 120.1 and 121.2).

Chief executives and legislators exercise self-restraint, especially in parliamentarian democracies, because they know that their party will eventually fall out of favor with the electorate and will benefit from a quid pro quo with competing parties. In Russia, however, neither party discipline nor other governmental bodies can effectively restrain the president's decree-issuing authority under the present constitution. As two Russian commentators observed about the separation of powers, the constitution

> will not only de-Sovietize Russia but also legislatively codify the supremacy of presidential power over representative power. . . . The [constitution] virtually precludes the possibility of forming a coalition government, a practice that many traditionally democratic countries use to attain civic harmony. Emphasis is placed not on having various political parties represented in the Cabinet—especially since Russia does not even have real political parties yet—but on having a unified, functional body that acts in accordance with the president's political will.[21]

The constitution's "amnesty" clause (Article 103.1f) illustrates the political and legal shortcomings of Yeltsin's constitution. It was the new constitution, after all, that enabled the State Duma's democratically elected conservatives, communists, and neofascists to grant "amnesty" to the president's jailed archrivals from the old Supreme Soviet and to the anti-Yeltsin and anti-Gorbachev putschists of August 1991. From the perspectives of constitutional textual analysis and elementary semantics, people accused of crimes but not convicted by a court of law cannot be granted amnesty, only a pardon or clemency. The constitution grants the former power to the State Duma and the latter power to the president (cf. Articles 89c and 103.1f). But the State Duma voted overwhelmingly for an amnesty, and the executive branch lacked the will and power to prevent its immediate implementation. Ironically, a few leading democratic parliamentarians (e.g., Sergei Shakhrai) voted for the amnesty, allegedly in the interests of national reconciliation, and some conservatives voted against it, presumably for political reasons having little to do with the intent or phrasing of the constitution's amnesty article. Thus, less than three months after the public elected a new legislature and approved a new constitution, and days after the president delivered his first State of the Union speech to the Federal Assembly calling for "real collaboration" and "trust in one another" and for "forgiveness" and "compassion" when they do not "contravene the law and moral standards,"[22] political power realities trampled the letter of post-Soviet Russia's first constitution, just as they did throughout the Soviet period.

The amnesty was a flagrant attack on the president and the presidency and, arguably, a flagrant violation of the new constitution and the rule of law. To be sure, the State Duma was trying to redress the constitutional imbalance between presidential and parliamentary powers and to prevent the executive from dominating the legislature as in the Soviet era. But the amnesty's intent and effect were to increase the compartmentalization of power, not power sharing, and to intensify interbranch and national-subnational conflict over power and policy, not cooperative problem solving. Worse still, the amnesty was claimed to be legitimate because of the recent democratic elections, the State Duma vote, and the widely acknowledged unconstitutionality of the president's dissolving of the previous parliament—not the explicit wording of the new constitution.

Another early decision by the State Duma and the president's response to it jeopardized the development of viable constitutionalism in Russia. Many newly elected legislators feared that Yeltsin's constitution would not only continue domestic and foreign policies they strongly disliked, but would also curtail their real and imagined powers and privileges. Legislators quickly squandered their popular authority with demands for ten-thousand-dollar monthly expenses, when the average wage in rubles was under fifty dollars. Prime Minister Viktor Chernomyrdin, to his credit, politely responded that the government lacked sufficient funds for the legislators' requests. Nonetheless, this incident weakened the Federal Assembly's legitimate claims for the funds needed to create a professional legislature and strengthened Yeltsin's resolve to control parliamentary perquisites. The president's staff now enjoys this responsibility, as Supreme Soviet leader Ruslan Khasbulatov did before.

National legislators' and executives' desire for personal aggrandizement and the rampant corruption in Russian society are a lethal mix. Money and power go hand in hand in virtually all political systems, but the temptations for Russian officials to use elective and appointive positions for personal gain and the opportunities for mafiosi to buy political offices and preferential treatment are enormous. Certain legislators and executives have welcomed these enticements, and others are being coerced into compliance by their underworld "protectors." Hence, democratic legislative institutions and an honest, competent, and permanent civil service are developing very slowly and in some regions not at all. Democratization and marketization often subvert one another in post-totalitarian Russia, and their interaction will perpetuate old forms of corruption and spawn new ones until a law-based constitutional order, a civil economy, and a civic culture are created.

The Regional and Local Context

To establish and preserve a viable federal system in Russia, the constitution and enabling legislation must enumerate regional and local prerogatives much more precisely. The sole powers of the Russian national government and the joint powers of the national and regional governments are defined so broadly that they may nullify the residual powers of the regional and local bodies (Articles 71–73). If so, the courts have very little power to support regions and localities that challenge the constitutionality of legislation in any sphere emanating from the executive branch or from either chamber of parliament. Although the July 1993 draft constitution deleted the concepts of republic "sovereignty" and "dual citizenship" in the nation and a republic, many subnational leaders have vowed to ignore these imposed restrictions, and some have done so explicitly in republic constitution and province charters. Such apprehension is well grounded. Articles 71–73 of the constitution virtually ensure that bilateral political and economic bargaining, rather than uniform constitutional and other federal law, will be decisive in exercising joint powers. Regional and local authorities are thereby put at a distinct disadvantage vis-à-vis the president and his cabinet as well as the national judiciary and Federal Assembly.

The constitution provides for equal representation of all subnational governments including the preeminent cities of Moscow and St. Petersburg in the Federal Assembly's upper chamber. But any concerted attempt by the Council of the Federation to strengthen the subnational governments could easily produce a constitutional crisis. The Council's powers to represent subnational interests, especially in the vitally important spheres of budgeting and taxation, are problematic. Regional and local authorities are not guaranteed the right to collect and spend the key profits and value-added taxes, nor are national authorities obliged to distribute tax revenues equally among the localities. Because President Yeltsin's apparatus and Prime Minister Chernomyrdin's government lack the extractive capabilities of their Soviet predecessors, the national, regional, and local institutions are negotiating their taxation policies on a largely ad hoc basis. Crude economic threats and forced requisitions by central authorities as well as mafia intimidation of local governments and businessmen are not uncommon. "Fiscal federalism" is the unachieved goal of the localities and an issue central to the future of the Russian Federation.[23]

If genuine federalism is to develop in Russia's polity, the constitution must safeguard the rights of individual regions and localities. They must be free to define and pursue their particular interests (cf. Article 73) and to create and preserve their own administrative and representative institutions (cf. Articles 77.1 and 77.2), and to hire and fire key personnel without presidential approval (cf. Article 78). Moreover, the constitution must unambiguously deny the president the authority to grant or revoke specific subnational powers, which Yeltsin now possesses and has periodically exercised.

The late U.S. congressman "Tip" O'Neill's favorite saying was that "all politics is local," and, with contemporary Russia in mind, one might add that "all political cultures are local." In some regions, environmental groups are working with local government officials and business leaders to cope with the horrific ecological and demographic legacy of the Soviet period, certain elements of which (e.g., health care and life expectancy) have worsened since the breakup of the Soviet Union. In many other regions, *nomenklatura* elites are gaining political power legitimately through freely contested elections in a multiparty system, and economic power not-so-legitimately through favoritism or corruption in a clientelist spoils system. Whether these conservative elites will use their authority to privatize and demilitarize industry and agriculture, as well as to improve the living standard and physical security of average citizens, is problematic. Whether they will continue to support democratic elections if they are voted out of office is even more problematic. And it is still possible that a revitalized *nomenklatura* will follow in the footsteps of the Supreme Soviet leadership and allow the KGB's and Red Army's successor organizations to write the laws defining their roles in the polity, thereby legitimizing lawlessness at home and imperialism abroad.

The evolving relationships between Russian national and regional politicians and their relationships with the constituents they share are critical to viable constitutionalism and successful market reforms. Economist Richard Ericson has suggested that the political gridlock in Moscow "might not be bad" for capitalist development in the provinces. Ironically, nonviable constitutionalism at the national level could be facilitating marketization and privatization in certain localities. This might eventually help to create a viable constitutional order in selected local and regional arenas and, over time, in the national arena. Consensual decision making may prove effective in many cities; conservatives and democrats in the parliament may find additional constructive reasons to collaborate with one another and with the powerful executive branch; the national and republic constitutions may empower but limit politicians of all political persuasions; and elected officials may respond more to their democratic proclivities and more to the enlightened instincts of the citizenry.

But for all of this to happen, *Yeltsin's* constitution will have to become the *Russian* constitution. The new or revised constitution will have to be crafted much more carefully, promulgated with much more input from diverse elites, ratified with much more public support, and thereby stand a much greater chance of fostering a democratic constitutional order.

The Prospects for Viable Constitutionalism in Russia

The Rhetoric and Realities of State Building

The most portentous pressures, tensions, and uncertainties generated by Russia's new constitution stem from the mix of its rhetoric about a strong democratic state and the political realities of a weak authoritarian state. According to the constitution, the president has more than enough power to shape his own programs, and the people have the right to hold him accountable for the consequences. In practice, the current president lacks the power to implement most of his policy initiatives and can disclaim accountability for most negative outcomes. To his credit, he has accepted responsibility for certain undesired consequences and has asserted they are short-term hurdles to long-term solutions. But Yeltsin has lost much of the credibility he earned from 1990 to 1992 and cannot convince people to make sacrifices for a common future. Valuable human and material resources are leaving Russia for good.

Powerful political forces (e.g., state security and military officials and national industrial and agricultural bureaucrats) are striving to create a strong government in the traditional Soviet mold, and powerful socioeconomic forces (e.g., rapidly rising crime rates and rapidly declining free health care services) are creating preconditions for a very authoritarian national government.

Extreme pessimists raise the specter of Adolf Hitler to warn about the rebirth of an autocratic and imperialist Soviet Union. But today's postmonolithic and postautarchic Russia is very different from interwar Germany, and today's nuclear and information age world is very different from its interwar counterpart. Already, some Russian national and regional leaders have come to understand, as their European counterparts did after two horrific world wars, that a rigid division of governmental powers does not serve their parochial interests, let alone Russia's national interest, and that an aggressive foreign policy does not serve the national interest, let alone global interests.

In post-Soviet Russia, there are greatly expanded political liberties, which are a necessary though surely not a sufficient condition for democratization. True, these freedoms of the ballot box, the press, political parties, and voluntary associations are being used to good advantage by neofascist, ultraconservative, criminal, and corrupt power seekers inside and outside the government, in the context of a breakdown of law and order and of material and emotional deprivation. But even when the president and State Duma can agree on specific legislation, they often do not have the financial resources, the civil servants, or the technical and professional means (e.g., a body of commercial law and a cohort of trained lawyers) to implement national policies. Also, many central institutions are becoming less and less relevant to the periphery, which is fending for itself by traditional or innovative methods. The vast majority of provincial cities and rural areas are clinging to authoritarian practices. Meanwhile a growing number of democratic and prosperous localities are fostering viable constitutionalism despite national institutions and laws (including the constitution) but in conformity with republic constitutions or provincial charters. In short, the relevance of national governmental bodies may depend on their ability to cooperate with one another and with their regional and local counterparts.

The breakup of the Soviet Union fragmented the communist political system vertically and horizontally in countless ways. The countries of the CIS, the regions of the Russian Federation, the old party-state bureaucracies, and the emerging political, professional, and ethnic groupings have suddenly developed new identities and cohesion and are savoring their newfound independence. But too few Russian politicians and bureaucrats understand that the exercise of power is a multiple-sum game. Many national, regional, and local leaders seem to feel they have little or no stake in the establishment of agreed-upon metapolicies or in the success of brokered policies. Hence, many metapolicies and policies are being strenuously contested in the formulation phase or circumvented in the implementation phase. Such attitudes and actions are no doubt delaying law-based competition among cohesive political parties and among associational interest groups.

It could take decades before Russian leaders view the essence of politics as procedural rather than personal, and the fruits of political compromise as constructive rather than destructive. The current ineffectiveness of the Russian state, together with its good economic and military bargaining position vis-à-vis the other CIS countries, might just speed this process. So might the perceived costs of the personal animosity between Gorbachev and Yeltsin, and between Yeltsin and Khasbulatov, when he headed the Supreme Soviet. But the political motivations and skills, as well as the organizational mechanisms and resources, needed to democratize Russia are still in short supply in the national executive, legislature, and judiciary. These normative and technical elements of viable constitutionalism must be developed by leading officials and citizens in diverse governmental and nongovernmental arenas. And democratic orientations and behaviors might be learned primarily by negative example, especially as intransigent politicians learn that self-interest includes self-restraint.

Two comparativists (not specialists on Russia) have argued that "providing the president with limited legislative power, encouraging the formation of parties that are reasonably disciplined in the legislature, and preventing extreme fragmentation of the party system all enhance the viability of presidentialism."[24] Russian constitutional theory and practice do not meet any of these criteria. President Yeltsin, of course, has enormous decree-issuing powers under the new constitution. But he has few decree-implementing powers in the de facto multiconstitutional polity and extraconstitutional society. Yeltsin's weakness stems primarily from the legal, budgetary, and ethnic "wars" that are preventing democratic consolidation and from the Hobbesian struggle for power, property, and survival that is transforming Russia's socioeconomic foundations. Also, the plethora of weak parliamentary parties is of little help to the president in formulating, implementing, and mobilizing support for feasible policies. Furthermore, some members of the popularly elected Federal Assembly and regional governments are striving to undermine the presidency by compartmentalizing rather than coalescing policymaking powers. Finally, the prospects for a democratic judiciary and bureaucracy are greatly reduced, because the rule of law and a professional civil service were virtually nonexistent in the Soviet political system.

Yeltsin was slow to comprehend the constitutional ramifications of Russia's deteriorating economic and social conditions and its upsurge of ethnic and territorial aspirations, all of which have been fueled by worldwide scientific, technological, and information revolutions and by more permeable borders with new and old neighboring countries. Also, Yeltsin has not entirely resisted the pressures and temptations to use the Russian Army and economic sanctions to protect Russian citizens and to help or hinder ethnic separatist movements in the "near abroad." But the president seems to understand quite well the foreign policy implications of domestic power struggles, and of Russian citizens' reluctance to accept their country's reduced status in the world. Indeed, a weak president is more likely than a strong president to try to bolster his personal power by recouping parts of the USSR's internal and external empires. A weak authoritarian state is more likely than a stable democratic state to revive imperial ambitions for largely domestic reasons. And a weak president and state will probably be less willing and able to strengthen diplomatic and economic ties with the United States, Western Europe, and Japan.

Gorbachev's seminal ideas about international politics (e.g., interdependence, mutual security, military sufficiency, joint economic ventures, and global and panhuman interests) are now exceedingly pertinent to domestic politics and to relations among all countries of the former Soviet Union. "Pacts or formal arrangements for sharing power" and "an accommodating and civil tone for political life" are necessary but not sufficient conditions for democratization. Larry Diamond rightly concludes:

> Above all, [competing party elites] must manifest a faith in the democratic process and a commitment to its rules that supersedes the pursuit of power or other substantive goals. Building among political competitors such a system of "mutual security," as Robert Dahl calls it, of transcendent respect for the rules of the game, may demand not only faith but a leap of faith from political leaders. They must believe that whatever results from the democratic process will, in the long run, serve their interests better than an intransigence that risks the breakdown of democracy. Among the manifold uncertainties that attend the founding of all new regimes, probably nothing is more important to democracy than the presence of party leaders with the courage and vision to join hands in taking this leap.[25]

Arguably, Yeltsin took this leap of faith not on a tank defending the White House in August 1991 but after witnessing the charred shell of the same White House he bombed in October 1993. Even more jolting to the president may have been the violence in other parts of Moscow, especially at the Ostankino television station, and the hundreds of casualties who evoked the specter of civil war. Understandably, most conservative leaders of the new Federal Assembly, state bureaucracies, and regional governments have yet to take this leap and will not do so with the current president, because of the drastic measures that triggered his "conversion," or vented his vindictiveness. Nonetheless, conciliatory attitudes can be learned and consensual practices can be institutionalized, even if the initial aims are predominantly authoritarian, the initial methods coercive, and the initial motivations revenge or retribution. The worldwide resurgence of democracy since the mid-1970s documents these contentions, and the evidence includes unlikely achievements as well as setbacks.

The Fitful Emergence of Constitutionalism

Some of the core elements of a viable constitutional order have begun to take root in Russia, but none is flourishing. Democratic political institutions are in the early stages of development at the national level, and democratic governance is progressing very unevenly in the regions and localities. Although the disintegration of the Soviet Union has brought Russians considerable freedom from the law and governmental intrusiveness, it has barely begun to bring them freedom within the rule of law and a democratic policy process. Moreover, the precipitous decline of socioeconomic conditions has significantly weakened the state, and has destabilized virtually all physical and psychological elements of daily life. The fragmentation of the polity and the stratification of the society are fueling one another, and a tragic conflagration is still a possibility.

Most of the institutional and cultural factors discussed in this chapter are combining to render the national constitution nominal rather than real. Yeltsin's constitution seems to be an interim document because of the questionable legitimacy of its promulgation and the president's unlimited decree-issuing powers. But the constitution is difficult to amend, the president is virtually immune to impeachment, and the president's de jure powers are much greater than his de facto powers. It is unlikely that future presidents will refrain from using the immense formal powers of the office, especially if economic hardships, ethnic rivalries, criminal activities, and pressures for a reconstituted Soviet Union intensify. And yet it is possible that Yeltsin's successor will institutionalize the executive-legislative and center-periphery cooperation that has developed sporadically since 1994.

Checks and balances among governmental institutions—not merely separation of powers and federalism—are essential to the rule of law in Russia and other democratizing countries. Without permanent checks and balances, arbitrary legislation and staffing are quite likely, as are a disproportionately powerful president or national legislature and an insufficiently legitimate or effective political system as a whole. Stable and reciprocal restraints on policies and personnel can foster power sharing at any governmental level or among levels, while preserving the authority of national and regional institutions to make unilateral decisions on specific issues, to influence joint decisions in overlapping spheres of jurisdiction, and to share responsibility for policy outcomes. Regrettably, both the theory and practice of post-Soviet Russian politics have minimized the importance of such checks and balances, and have echoed traditional claims to Moscow's omniscience and omnipotence.

Russia's "nonparty system" and weak party identification among the citizenry undermine constitutional governance, too. Without political parties, the concept of loyal opposition is unlikely to permeate in governmental institutions and popular culture and plebiscitary democracy is likely to stunt the development of independent interest groups, trade unions, bureaucracies, judiciaries, and mass media. Also, a viable constitutional order and a prosperous mixed economy depend more on predictable metapolicies, especially the rule of law and governmental checks and balances, than on the dismantling of traditional formal and informal organizations. Jerry Hough underscores that Gorbachev and his closest advisers feared "all-powerful bureaucratic resistance to economic reform," and that "rather than try to establish a predictable institutional framework in which individuals could act, they deliberately destroyed old institutions and saw the market as something which would be unleashed rather than as something that needed to be created."[26] Yeltsin continued these practices in post-Soviet Russia, at first gingerly (vis-à-vis the Supreme Soviet), then intensely (vis-à-vis the Communist Party, some ministries, and most soviets), and then with a vengeance in the October 1993 bombing of the parliament's White House.

Ironically, the violent end to Russia's deepening constitutional crisis seems to have had several positive consequences. The efficacy of the Russian government is increasing (e.g., inflation has declined considerably, and the legislature has approved a comprehensive budget); the chief national governmental bodies are becoming institutionalized (e.g., the Federal Assembly is developing a workable committee system, and the Constitutional Court has been reconstituted); and the benefits of collaboration are becoming apparent to more and more national and regional governmental officials (e.g., legislative leaders have become members of Yeltsin's National Security Council, and bilateral treaties between the national government and regional governments have dampened economic and ethnic independence movements, with the tragic exception of Chechnya).

But, as Chechnya and Yeltsin's health problems amply demonstrate, Russia's constitutional difficulties are far from over. The crisis management and institution building since 1994, especially the tentative strengthening of the separation of powers and the decidedly asymmetrical form of federalism, have yet to be reflected in the text of the constitution. Although progress toward constitutionalism in the national arena has exceeded the expectations of virtually all foreign analysts, many of these accomplishments are informal and highly dependent upon personalities, and the current or next president can easily reverse them by constitutional means. For instance, Yeltsin created permanent staff bodies to work directly with parliamentary committees and began to meet with more parliamentary leaders. It is to be hoped that a much better balance among executive, legislative, and judicial authority will be achieved in Moscow, and that it will be written into the Russian Constitution and into the growing body of constitutional law.

Progress toward genuine federalism, however, is much more problematic and varies considerably by region. The Russian Ministry for Nationalities Affairs and Regional Policy concluded in October 1994 that most subnational constitutions contradicted the national constitution in important respects. Only sixteen of twenty-one republics had constitutions and four republics were still using Soviet-era constitutions from the late 1970s. Ministerial officials maintained that "nearly all" republic constitutions had declared state sovereignty directly or indirectly, contravening a basic tenet of the national constitution. All republics except Komi and Karelia "proclaimed land, mineral resources, water, flora, and fauna the property of the peoples living on the territories of these republics," ignoring the constitution's economic provisions. Many republic constitutions had allegedly infringed on the rights of ethnic minorities, while the constitutions of Yakutia and Tuva "violated the federal authorities' exclusive rights in matters of war and peace." Moreover, diverse regional leaders seem to think that their territory's laws on taxation are primarily their own concern and that they can nonetheless cut advantageous deals with Moscow. Some government analysts argue that these parochial attitudes can be changed and these constitutional discrepancies can be removed through bilateral treaties, whereas other analysts insist that the republic constitutions must be altered to conform with Russia's "supreme legal force," the constitution. Both groups of ministerial specialists agree that "today the most meticulous analysis of the Russian Federation components' constitutions is necessary because if no chance is given to implement the new Russian Constitution, there is a possibility of either sliding into a rigid centralism or of undermining the country's state integrity."[27]

President Yeltsin has alarmed some Westerners with his heightened appeals for "a strong Russia" and "the strengthening of the state." Moreover, Russia's executive branch leaders and many citizens do not seem to comprehend or care about the crucial distinction between "rule *by* law" and "rule *of* law." But Yeltsin has affirmed the need to create "a fully democratic and lawful state." And such a constitutional order will probably respond to Russian values, attitudes, and beliefs insufficiently understood in the West. For example, the Russian people may intensify their support for a mixed economy, as they have done since the late Stalin era (and probably did during NEP in the 1920s and the reforms of Alexander II in the 1860s). Also, most Russians never strongly supported the Stalinist industrialization model, the extreme violations of civil liberties, or the *nomenklatura's* disproportionate wealth and privilege that continued throughout the Khrushchev and Brezhnev periods.

Russian elite and mass political culture are not immutably authoritarian, and the trend is toward values supportive of a civil society and civic culture. But the cultural shifts under Gorbachev and Yeltsin have been differentiated or selectively combined with tsarist and Soviet orientations. Conservative Russians favor strong presidential or modified Communist rule, because they still accept or embrace traditional authoritarian ideas about a powerful government and an acquiescent citizenry. Even the most reformist Russians may never accept a reduced Russian role in world politics. Also, many Russians hope that the rebuilding of a strong state will curb the new mafiosi and entrepreneurs, and will continue Soviet welfare-state benefits while equalizing public access to them. Significantly, Yeltsin has warned about "the rapid stratification of society" and the emergence of "a new alienation between the authorities and the everyday needs of the people. . . . If bureaucracy previously stood between them and the *nomenklatura* caste, then today money must be included as well. It is precisely the disgrace of corruption that is increasingly often the gulf preventing a solution to many issues."[28] This affirmation calls to mind Robert C. Tucker's concept of "dual Russia," the dramatic political and economic power imbalance between the ruling elites and the ruled masses under both tsarist and Soviet polities. In the post-Soviet era "dual Russia" is taking new forms, and "democratic Russia" is struggling to develop.

The proverbial jury is still out on all of the issues crucial to the future of viable constitutionalism in Russia. Democratic governance is a challenge of immense proportions, and there are immense obstacles to it. A stable constitutional democracy is unlikely to emerge in the current decade and is problematic thereafter. The costs of confrontation and the benefits of cooperation are not yet comprehended by most politicians or citizens, and these lessons will probably continue to be learned the hard way. Everything hinges on judicious leadership, intragovernmental collaboration, improved socioeconomic conditions, the institutionalization of a civil society, and the emergence of a civic culture. There has been progress and regress on all these fronts. But given the formidable obstacles to a constitutional order and a mixed economy, Russian democrats should expect periodic setbacks and not lose heart. And Russian authoritarians might well ponder the wisdom of the aphorism with which we began this chapter: "Political compromise is the handmaiden to the preservation of principle in a complex world."

Notes

An earlier version of this paper was published in *The Harriman Review* (November 1994), Columbia University. Reprinted by permission.

1. See, for example, Frederic J. Fleron, Jr., and Erik P. Hoffmann, eds., *Post-Communist Studies and Political Science: Methodology and Empirical Theory in Sovietology* (Boulder, Colo.: Westview Press, 1993); and Frederic J. Fleron, Jr., Erik P. Hoffmann, and Edward W. Walker, "Whither Post-Sovietology?" *Harriman Institute Forum* 6 (February–March 1993): 2–28.

2. Richard P. Nathan and Erik P. Hoffmann, "Modern Federalism: Comparative Perspectives and Lessons for the Commonwealth of Independent States and Russia," in *Government Structures in the USA and the Sovereign States of the Former USSR: Power Allocation Among Central, Regional, and Local Governments,* ed. James Hickey and Alexej Ugrinsky (Westport, Conn.: Greenwood Press, 1996), 53–62.

3. Robert Sharlet, *Soviet Constitutional Crisis: From De-Stalinization to Disintegration* (Armonk, N.Y.: M. E. Sharpe, 1992), 105–10 (emphasis in original); and Robert Sharlet, "Russian Constitutional Crisis: Law and Politics under Yeltsin," *Post-Soviet Affairs* 9 (October–December 1993): 314–36.

4. Robert Sharlet, *The New Soviet Constitution of 1977: Analysis and Text* (Brunswick, Ohio: Kings Court Communications, 1978), 93. Included is the full original constitution. The final version of the constitution, with amendments through Au-

gust 1, 1991, is in Gordon Smith, *Soviet Politics: Struggling with Change,* 2d ed. (New York: St. Martin's Press, 1992), 348–79. The party rules, with amendments through March 28, 1990, are in Donald Barry and Carol Barner-Barry, *Contemporary Soviet Politics: An Introduction,* 4th ed. (Englewood Cliffs, N.J.: Prentice-Hall, 1991), 373–85.

5. Cited and discussed in Erik P. Hoffmann and Robbin F. Laird, *Technocratic Socialism: The Soviet Union in the Advanced Industrial Age* (Durham: Duke University Press, 1985), 161, 222 ff.

6. Anatoly Sobchak, "Uroki Sakharova," *Izvestiia,* December 14, 1992, 2.

7. Adam Michnik, "Liubov Moia," *Izvestiia,* January 24, 1994, 4.

8. Hannes Adomeit, "Soviet Ideology, Risk-Taking, and Crisis Behavior," in *Soviet Foreign Policy: Classic and Contemporary Issues,* ed. Frederic J. Fleron, Jr., Erik P. Hoffmann, and Robbin F. Laird (New York: deGruyter, 1991), 267–68.

9. Cf. Philip Roeder, *Red Sunset: The Failure of Soviet Politics* (Princeton: Princeton University Press, 1994).

10. Cited and discussed in Erik P. Hoffmann, "Political Opposition in the Soviet Union," in *Political Opposition and Dissent,* ed. Barbara McLennan (New York: Dunellen, 1973), 347–48, 377 ff.

11. Jerry Hough, "Rational Choice Theory and Reform of Communist Economies: Evidence from a 1993 Russian Election Study" (paper presented at the national convention of the American Political Science Association, New York City, September 2, 1994), 57–62, and Jerry Hough, "The Russian Election of 1993: Public Attitudes toward Economic Reform and Democratization," *Post-Soviet Affairs* 10 (January–March 1994): 1–37. Also, A. E. Dick Howard, ed., *Constitution Making in Eastern Europe* (Washington, D.C.: Wilson Center Press, 1993).

12. Jan Zielonka, "New Institutions in the Old East Bloc," *Journal of Democracy* 5 (April 1994): 99–104.

13. Viktor Sergeyev and Nikolai Biryukov, *Russia's Road to Democracy: Parliament, Communism, and Traditional Culture* (Hants, England: Elgar Publishing Limited, 1993), 147, 207–8 ff. Cf. Western "congruists" theorists, e.g., Harry Eskstein, *Regarding Politics: Essays on Political Theory, Stability, and Change* (Berkeley: University of California Press, 1992), especially Chapter 5; and Robert D. Putnam, *Making Democracy Work: Civic Traditions in Modern Italy* (Princeton: Princeton University Press, 1993).

14. Walter Laqueur, *Black Hundred: The Rise of the Extreme Right in Russia* (New York: HarperCollins, 1993), 120–22.

15. Gregory Freeze, *From Supplication to Revolution: A Documentary Social History of Imperial Russia* (New York: Oxford University Press, 1988).

16. Peter Juviler, personal correspondence. See Peter Juviler and Bertram Gross, eds., with Vladimir Kartashkin and Elena Lukasheva, *Human Rights for the Twenty-first Century: Foundations for Responsible Hope* (Armonk, N.Y.: M. E. Sharpe, 1993).

17. Donna Bahry, "Society Transformed? Rethinking the Social Roots of Perestroika," *Slavic Review* 52 (fall 1993): 554; see also Frederic J. Fleron, Jr., "Post-Soviet Political Culture in Russia: An Assessment of Recent Emperical Investigations," *Europe-Asia Studies* 48 (March 1996): 225–60.

18. Boris Yeltsin, *The Struggle for Russia* (New York: Times Books, 1994), 126–27.

19. Probably the best English translation is in *Current Digest of the Post-Soviet Press* 45 (no. 45) (December 8, 1993), 4–16. For the official Russian and English versions under one cover, see *Konstitutsiia Rossiiskoi Federatsii: The Constitution of the Russian Federation* (Moscow: Iuridicheskaya Literatura, 1994). And for thoughtful

comparisons of the July and December versions, see American Bar Association Central and East European Law Initiative, *Preliminary Analysis of the Draft Constitution of the Russian Federation* (Washington, D.C.: American Bar Association, December 7, 1993).

20. Sergei Filatov, interview with *Rossiiskie vesti,* translated in *Daily Report: Central Eurasia* (Washington, D.C.: Foreign Broadcast Information Service, September 2, 1994), 17–19.

21. Dmitry Volkov and Aleksei Zubro, "Constitution: Boris Yeltsin's Basic Law," *Segodnia,* November 11, 1993, 1; translated in *Current Digest of the Post-Soviet Press* 45 (no. 45): 2.

22. Boris Yeltsin, Address to the Federal Assembly, Moscow television, February 24, 1994; translated in *Daily Report: Central Eurasia* (Washington, D.C.: Foreign Broadcast Information Service, February 24, 1994), 15, 21.

23. See, for example, Christine Wallich, ed., *Russia and the Challenge of Fiscal Federalism* (Washington, D.C.: World Bank, 1994).

24. Scott Mainwaring and Matthew Shugart, "Juan Linz, Presidentialism, and Democracy: A Critical Appraisal," working paper, July 1993.

25. Larry Diamond, "Three Paradoxes of Democracy," in *The Global Resurgence of Democracy,* ed. Larry Diamond and Marc Plattner (Baltimore: Johns Hopkins University Press, 1993), 106. On the Russian and CIS contexts, see, for example, David Remnick, *Lenin's Tomb: The Last Days of the Soviet Empire* (New York: Vintage Books, 1994); Richard Sakwa, *Russian Politics and Society* (New York: Routledge, 1993); and Karen Dawisha and Bruce Parrott, *Russia and the New States of Eurasia: The Politics of Upheaval* (Cambridge: Cambridge University Press, 1994).

26. Hough, "Rational Choice Theory and Reform of Communist Economies," 61.

27. *Segodnia* report, translated in *Daily Report: Central Eurasia* (Washington, D.C.: Foreign Broadcast Information Service, October 21, 1994), 36–37.

28. Yeltsin, Address to the Federal Assembly, 15–16.

References

Adomeit, Hannes. "Soviet Ideology, Risk-Taking, and Crisis Behavior." In *Soviet Foreign Policy: Classic and Contemporary Issues,* edited by Frederic J. Fleron, Jr., Erik P. Hoffmann, and Robbin F. Laird. New York: deGruyter, 1991.

American Bar Association Central and East European Law Initiative. *Preliminary Analysis of the Draft Constitution of the Russian Federation.* Washington, D.C.: American Bar Association, December 7, 1993.

Bahry, Donna. "Society Transformed? Rethinking the Social Roots of Perestroika." *Slavic Review* 52 (fall 1993): 512–54.

Barry, Donald, and Carol Barner-Barry. *Contemporary Soviet Politics: An Introduction.* 4th ed. Englewood Cliffs, N.J.: Prentice-Hall, 1991.

Brzezinski, Zbigniew. *Out of Control: Global Turmoil on the Eve of the Twenty-first Century.* New York: Scribner's, 1993.

Dahl, Robert. *Democracy and Its Critics.* New Haven: Yale University Press, 1989.

Dawisha, Karen, and Bruce Parrott. *Russia and the New States of Eurasia: The Politics of Upheaval.* Cambridge: Cambridge University Press, 1994.

Diamond, Larry. "Three Paradoxes of Democracy." In *The Global Resurgence of Democracy,* edited by Larry Diamond and Marc Plattner. Baltimore: Johns Hopkins University Press, 1993.

"Dogovor ob obshchestvennom soglasii," *Izvestiia,* April 30, 1994.

Dror, Yehezkel. *Public Policy Reexamined.* New Brunswick, N.J.: Transaction Books, 1983.

Eckstein, Harry. *Regarding Politics: Essays on Political Theory, Stability, and Change.* Berkeley and Los Angeles: University of California Press, 1992.

Elazar, Daniel. *Exploring Federalism.* Tuscaloosa: University of Alabama Press, 1987.

Filatov, Sergei. Interview by *Rossiiskie vesti.* Translated in *Daily Report: Central Eurasia.* Washington, D.C.: Foreign Broadcast Information Service, September 2, 1994.

Fleron, Frederic J., Jr. "Post-Soviet Political Culture in Russia: An Assessment of Recent Empirical Investigations," *Europe-Asia Studies* 48 (March 1996): 225–60.

Fleron, Frederic J., Jr., and Erik P. Hoffmann, eds. *Post-Communist Studies and Political Science: Methodology and Empirical Theory in Sovietology.* Boulder, Colo.: Westview Press, 1993.

Fleron, Frederic J., Jr., Erik P. Hoffmann, and Edward W. Walker. "Whither Post-Sovietology?" *Harriman Institute Forum* 6 (February–March 1993): 2–28.

Freeze, Gregory. *From Supplication to Revolution: A Documentary Social History of Imperial Russia.* New York: Oxford University Press, 1988.

Friedgut, Theodore, and Jeffrey Hahn, eds. *Local Power and Post-Soviet Politics.* Armonk, N.Y.: M. E. Sharpe, 1994.

Hahn, Jeffrey. "Continuity and Change in Russian Political Culture." In *Post-Communist Studies and Political Science: Methodology and Empirical Theory in Sovietology,* edited by Frederic J. Fleron, Jr., and Erik P. Hoffmann. Boulder, Colo.: Westview Press, 1993.

Hoffmann, Erik P. "Political Opposition in the Soviet Union." In *Political Opposition and Dissent,* edited by Barbara McLennan. New York: Dunellen, 1973.

Hoffmann, Erik P., and Robbin F. Laird. *Technocratic Socialism: The Soviet Union in the Advanced Industrial Age.* Durham: Duke University Press, 1985.

———, eds. *The Soviet Polity in the Modern Era.* Hawthorne, N.Y.: Aldine Publishing Co., 1984.

Hough, Jerry. "The Russian Election of 1993: Public Attitudes toward Economic Reform and Democratization." *Post-Soviet Affairs* 10 (January–March 1994): 1–37.

———. "Rational Choice Theory and Reform of Communist Economies: Evidence from a 1993 Russian Election Study." Paper presented at the national convention of the American Political Science Association, New York City, September 2, 1994.

Howard, A. E. Dick, ed. *Constitution Making in Eastern Europe.* Washington, D.C.: Wilson Center Press, 1993.

Huntington, Samuel. *The Third Wave: Democratization in the Late Twentieth Century.* Norman: University of Oklahoma Press, 1991.

Juviler, Peter, and Bertram Gross, eds., with Vladimir Kartashkin and Elena Lukasheva. *Human Rights for the Twenty-first Century: Foundations for Responsible Hope.* Armonk, N.Y.: M. E. Sharpe, 1993.

Kavrus-Hoffmann, Nadezhda. "Changing Social Strata and Election Results in Russia." Paper presented at Russell Sage College, Troy, N.Y., March 22, 1994.

Konstitutsiia Rossiiskii Federatsii: The Constitution of the Russian Federation. Moscow: Iuridicheskaya Literatura, 1994. English translation is in *Current Digest of Post-Soviet Press* 45, no. 45 (December 8, 1993).

Laqueur, Walter. *Black Hundred: The Rise of the Extreme Right in Russia.* New York: HarperCollins, 1993.

Lerner. "The Supreme Court and American Capitalism." *Yale Law Journal* 42 (1932). Quoted in Wallace Mendelson, *The Constitution and the Supreme Court.* New York: Dodd, Mead, 1959.

Lindblom, Charles. *The Intelligence of Democracy: Decision Making through Mutual Adjustment.* New York: Free Press, 1965.

Linz, Juan, and Arturo Valenzuela, eds. *The Failure of Presidential Democracy.* Baltimore: Johns Hopkins University Press, 1994.

Mainwaring, Scott, and Matthew Shugart. "Juan Linz, Presidentialism, and Democracy: A Critical Appraisal." Working paper, July 1993.

Meyer, Alfred. "Observations on the Travails of Sovietology." *Post-Soviet Affairs* 10 (April–June 1994): 191–95.

Michnik, Adam. "Liubov Moia." *Izvestiia,* January 24, 1994.

Miroff, Bruce. *Icons of Democracy: American Leaders as Heroes, Aristocrats, Dissenters, and Democrats.* New York: Basic Books, 1993.

Nathan, Richard P., and Erik P. Hoffmann. "Modern Federalism: Comparative Perspectives and Lessons for the Commonwealth of Independent States and Russia." In *Government Structures in the USA and the Sovereign States of the Former USSR: Power Allocation Among Central, Regional, and Local Governments,* edited by James Hickey and Alexej Ugrinsky. Westport, Conn.: Greenwood Press, 1996, 53–62.

Pain, Emil. "The Breakup of Russia Is No Longer a Problem." *Moskovskie novosti,* June 5–12, 1994. Translated in *Current Digest of the Post-Soviet Press* 46, no. 23 (July 6, 1994).

Powers, Timothy. "The Pen Is Mightier Than the Congress: Presidential Decree Power in Brazil." Paper presented at the COVICO Conference, Albany, N.Y., March 17–20, 1994.

Putnam, Robert D. *Making Democracy Work: Civic Traditions in Modern Italy.* Princeton: Princeton University Press, 1993.

Rahr, Alexander. "Russia's Future: With or Without Yeltsin." *RFE/RL Research Report,* April 29, 1994, 1–7.

Reisinger, William. "Conclusions: Mass Public Opinion and the Study of Post-Soviet Societies." In *Public Opinion and Regime Change: The New Politics of Post-Soviet Societies,* edited by Arthur Miller, William Reisinger, and Vicki Hesli. Boulder, Colo.: Westview Press, 1993.

Remington, Thomas. "Regime Transitions in Communist Systems: The Soviet Case." In *Post-Communist Studies and Political Science: Methodology and Empirical Theory in Sovietology,* edited by Frederic J. Fleron, Jr., and Erik P. Hoffmann. Boulder, Colo.: Westview Press, 1993.

Remnick, David. *Lenin's Tomb: The Last Days of the Soviet Empire.* New York: Vintage Books, 1994.

Riggs, Fred. "Conceptual Homogenization of a Heterogeneous Field: Presidentialism in Comparative Perspective." In *Comparing Nations: Concepts, Strategies, Substance,* edited by Mattei Dogan and Ali Kazancigil. Cambridge, Mass.: Blackwell, 1994.

Roeder, Philip. *Red Sunset: The Failure of Soviet Politics.* Princeton: Princeton University Press, 1994.

———. "Varieties of Post-Soviet Authoritarian Regimes." *Post-Soviet Affairs* 10 (January–March 1994): 61–101.

Rose, Richard. "Postcommunism and the Problem of Trust." *Journal of Democracy* 5 (July 1994), 18–30.

Ruble, Blair. "Local Policy Making: Urban Planning." Paper prepared for the conference "Democratization in Russia: The Development of Legislative Institutions," Harvard University, October 29–30, 1993.

Sakwa, Richard. *Russian Politics and Society.* New York: Routledge, 1993.

———. "Russia, Communism, Democracy." In *Developments in Russian and Post-*

Soviet Politics, edited by Stephen White, Alex Pravda, and Zvi Gitelman. Durham: Duke University Press, 1994.

Sartori, Giovanni. "Constitutionalism: A Preliminary Analysis." *American Political Science Review* 56 (December 1962): 853–64.

Sergeyev, Viktor, and Nikolai Biryukov. *Russia's Road to Democracy: Parliament, Communism, and Traditional Culture.* Hants, England: Elgar Publishing Limited, 1993.

Sharlet, Robert. *The New Soviet Constitution of 1977: Analysis and Text.* Brunswick, Ohio: Kings Court Communications, 1978.

———. *Soviet Constitutional Crisis: From De-Stalinization to Disintegration.* Armonk, N.Y.: M. E. Sharpe, 1992.

———. "Russian Constitutional Crisis: Law and Politics under Yeltsin." *Post-Soviet Affairs 9* (October–December 1993): 314–36.

———. "Citizen and State under Gorbachev and Yeltsin." In *Developments in Russian and Post-Soviet Politics*, edited by Stephen White, Alex Pravda, and Zvi Gitelman. Durham: Duke University Press, 1994.

Shugart, Matthew, and John Carey. *Presidents and Assemblies: Constitutional Design and Electoral Dynamics.* Cambridge: Cambridge University Press, 1992.

Simon, Yves. *Philosophy of Democratic Government.* Chicago: University of Chicago Press, 1951. Reprint, Notre Dame, Ind.: University of Notre Dame Press, 1993.

Skowronek, Stephen. *The Politics Presidents Make: Leadership from John Adams to George Bush.* Cambridge: Harvard University Press, 1993.

Smith, Gordon. *Soviet Politics: Struggling with Change.* 2d ed. New York: St. Martin's Press, 1992.

Sobchak, Anatoly. "Uroki Sakharova." *Izvestiia*, December 14, 1992.

Stepan, Alfred, and Cindy Skach. "Constitutional Frameworks and Democratic Consolidation: Parliamentarianism versus Presidentialism." *World Politics* 46 (October 1993), 1–22.

Sundquist, James L. *Constitutional Reform and Effective Government.* Rev. ed. Washington, D.C.: Brookings Institution, 1992.

———. "The U.S. Presidential System as a Model for the World." Paper presented at COVICO conference, Albany, N.Y., March 17–20, 1994. Also published as Chapter 3 in this volume.

Thompson, Michael, Richard Ellis, and Aaron Wildavsky. *Cultural Theory.* Boulder, Colo.: Westview Press, 1990.

Tolz, Vera. "Problems in Building Democratic Institutions in Russia." *RFE/RL Research Report,* June 17, 1994, 1–7.

Tucker, Robert C. *The Soviet Political Mind: Stalinism and Post-Stalin Change.* Rev. ed. New York: Norton, 1971.

———. *Political Culture and Leadership in Soviet Russia.* New York: Norton, 1987.

Urban, Michael. "December 1993 as a Replication of Late-Soviet Electoral Practices." *Post-Soviet Affairs* 10 (April–June 1994): 127–58.

Volkov, Dmitry, and Aleksei Zubro. "Constitution: Boris Yeltsin's Basic Law." *Segodnia,* November 11, 1993. Translated in *Current Digest of the Post-Soviet Press* 45, no. 45 (December 8, 1993).

Wallich, Christine, ed. *Russia and the Challenge of Fiscal Federalism.* Washington, D.C.: World Bank, 1994.

Yeltsin, Boris. Address to the Federal Assembly, Moscow television, February 24, 1994. Translated in *Daily Report: Central Eurasia.* Washington, D.C.: Foreign Broadcast Information Service, February 24, 1994.

———. News conferences and other leaders' statements in *Daily Report: Central Eurasia.* Washington, D.C.: Foreign Broadcast Information Service, October 4, 1994, October 6, 1994.

———. *The Struggle for Russia.* New York: Times Books, 1994.

Zielonka, Jan. "New Institutions in the Old East Bloc." *Journal of Democracy* 5 (April 1994), 99–104.

Part Three

Limitations of Constitutionalism

10

Democratic Consolidation: Institutional, Economic, and External Dimensions

Diane Ethier

The third wave[1] of democratization raises the question of the viability of new democracies established since 1975 in Southern Europe, Latin America, Asia, Central Europe, and Africa. Due to the numerous studies carried out on this subject during the second cycle of democratization and after, researchers today have at their disposal more precise theoretical tools for evaluating the longevity of new democracies. Yet the comparative analysis of democratic development, in both Western and "peripheral" countries, has demonstrated that the viability of democracies has depended on their stability—that is, their capacity to avoid or resolve the social and political conflicts likely to lead to their replacement by authoritarian regimes (Lipset 1959; Huntington 1965; Linz 1982).

The stability of democracies has been closely associated with their consolidation—the legitimization and institutionalization of democratic values, rules, and procedures by the vast majority of elites and citizens (Rustow 1970; Dahl 1971). This transformation of opinions and attitudes has been linked mainly to the establishment of political institutions favorable to the representation and aggregation of various interest groups. However, many other conditions have been deemed necessary to the democratization of political institutions and culture: the pursuit of economic and social development, the willingness of political leaders to promote democracy, a relatively weak level of politicization and mobilization within civil society, and the demonstration effect of Western democratic models.

Recent evaluations of democratic consolidation in Southern Europe, Latin America, Asia, and Eastern Europe are largely inspired by these approaches. On the whole, they show that only Greece, Spain, and Portugal have succeeded in consolidating their democratic regimes, while the process remains problematic in most countries of the other regions. The democratization of political culture and institutions has simply been much more rapid and deep in Southern Europe than in Latin America, Asia, and Eastern Europe, during the period following the end of democratic transitions (Baloyra 1987; Diamond, Linz, and Lipset 1989; Ethier 1990, 1991; Pridham 1990; Huntington 1991; Higley and Gunther 1992; Mainwaring, O'Donnell, and Valenzuela 1992).

The analysis of the impact of internal and external economic factors on democratic consolidation has not been particularly deep. Now, two new fields of research facilitate the definition of the role of these variables. First, recent studies on the processes of economic adjustment show that the enactment of neoliberal reforms during or immediately after democratic transitions (the Latin American and Eastern European scenarios) constitutes a significant obstacle to democratic consolidation, whereas the achievement of this process before launching economic adjustment (the Southern European scenarios) favors the success of both (Przeworski 1990; Nelson 1990b; Köves and Marer 1991; Bird 1991; Köves 1992; Haggard and Kaufman 1992; Maravall, Pereira, and Przeworski 1993; Bermeo 1994). Second, my own work on the third enlargement of the European Community (EC) shows that the success of democratic consolidation and economic adjustment in Greece, Spain, and Portugal is attributable largely to cultural, institutional, social, and economic transformations driven or imposed by the preparation for and the concretization of entry into the EC, in 1981 for Greece, and 1986 for Iberian countries.

The objective of this study is to delve more deeply into these research findings. I will present the main elements of the theory of democratic consolidation, summarize the main conclusions of recent publications, examine the effects of economic adjustment processes on democratic consolidation, and explain why and how entry into the EC contributed to the success of both democratic consolidation and economic adjustment of Southern Europe.

The Theory of Democratic Consolidation

Studies have shown that, while national independence and the modernization of economic, social, and cultural structures of societies constitute the necessary conditions for the foundation of democratic regimes, their establishment further depends primarily on the achievement of a compromise between the dominant social groups on several issues (Lerner 1958; Lipset 1959; Almond and Coleman 1960; Rostow 1971; Almond 1973). These include the essential rules, procedures, and institutions of modern or polyarchic democracy (Rustow 1970; Dahl 1971; O'Donnell and Schmitter 1986), the free exercise of fundamental rights and liberties, regular elections featuring the secret ballot and universal suffrage, multipartyism, the separation of legislative, judiciary, and executive powers, and the codification of these rules within a constitution.

Rustow (1970) and many other authors after him have insisted that the viability of these minimal or formal democracies has depended on the eventual enlargement of the initial democratic pact to include the entire society (Pridham 1984; Linz 1990; Ethier 1990). The achievement of this large social consensus, guarantor of the stability of the political system, has been equated with democratic consolidation. This expression has been given many different definitions (see Morlino 1986; Pridham 1990a; Hermet 1991), but the most widely accepted associates democratic consolidation with the legitimization and the institutionalization of democratic values and norms, that is, with the acceptance and effective application of these values and norms by a large majority of elites and citizens (Lipset 1959; Rustow 1970; Morlino 1986; Morlino and Montero 1991; Schmitter 1993). Essentially, democratic consolidation therefore implies a profound transformation of the beliefs and behavior of political actors.

Analysis of the conditions of democratic consolidation has revealed that the positive evolution of opinions and attitudes about democracy depends on many factors: the effectiveness of the political system in its capacity to promote the pursuit of economic and social development, a previous positive experience with democracy, a negative memory of the former authoritarian regime, the demonstration or attraction effects of consolidated Western democracies, the achievement of juridical and institutional reforms allowing a deepening of the representation and participation of different interest groups within the political system, and the willingness of the elites to proceed to the democratization of political institutions (Huntington 1984, 1991; Diamond and Linz 1989; Przeworski 1990; Hermet 1991).

The role of external variables, such as the impact of the state's position within the international system on the consolidation of its democratic regime, has received little attention from scholars. Some authors (Huntington 1984, 1991; Diamond and Linz 1989) argue that changes in the international system since 1970—including further industrialization, globalization, and integration of markets, the disappearance of the communist threat, and the greater support given to democracy by the Western powers and international organizations—have favored the establishment and survival of constitutional regimes. But no substantial research has yet tried to analyze the causal relations between global changes and the more, or less, successful processes of democratic consolidation. The effects of internal economic and social variables on these processes have also been neglected, with the majority of studies according a greater importance to political variables, such as characteristics of political institutions, attitudes of decision makers, and level of citizen mobilization and politicization.

The Democratization of Political Institutions

The development of political institutions occupies a predominant place in the literature devoted to democratic consolidation, because the majority of specialists consider the acceptance and effective application of democratic values and rules by the citizens to follow mainly from the enlargement of the participation of various interests in the process of political decision making. This objective can be achieved only by the elimination or the reform of norms, procedures, and institutions that limit this participation to certain groups in formal democracies.

Because of their longevity and great stability, the Anglo-Saxon democracies have served as principal models for the definition of institutional changes favorable to democratic consolidation. These changes include the abolition of control by the army and the bureaucracy over the political system; the elimination of clientelist networks between political elites and various interest groups; improvement of the representation, pluralism, stability, and entrenchment of political parties within civil society; the development of ideological convergence and cooperation between the parties; and the independent organization of interests within civil society and the establishment of formal or informal links between pressure groups and political parties.

The first category of reforms aims at breaking the monopoly of certain particular interests over the political system, while the others try to give institutions representing the popular will (pressure groups, parties, and the legislature) real control over the process of political decision making. There is fairly broad consensus among authors that changes to the party system constitute the most crucial element in the process of democratic consolidation,[2] because the rootedness and the sociological pluralism of the parties determine, through elections, the level of citizen participation in the process of political decision making. The representativeness of parties, as well as the convergence of and capacity for party cooperation, determine the degree of consensus within the society, the stability of governments, and the rationality (in accordance with the general interest) of public policy (Powell 1982; Pridham 1990a: 2–7; Burton, Gunther, and Higley 1992b: 1–38).

Parliamentarism versus Presidentialism

The analysis of institutional changes favoring democratic consolidation has also elicited much debate on the respective merits and weaknesses of parliamentary (British style) and presidential (American style) regimes. The dominant view is that parliamentarism is more likely to encourage democratic consolidation than is presidentialism, because it permits a greater aggregation of interests and greater stability in the political system. Linz 1990 provides an excellent summary of this argument. Presidential regimes, he avers, are less favorable to democratic consolidation because they are founded on a double legitimacy that is potentially in conflict, their political decision-making process is rigid and based on the winner-take-all principle, they are characterized by paradoxes, and their stability is more theoretical than real.

In parliamentary regimes, on the other hand, the executive is held responsible to the parliament, the only body representative of the popular will. In presidential regimes, the executive has fairly broad autonomy compared with the legislature as a whole, because the executive is elected by universal suffrage. This double legitimacy is a potential source of conflict, notably "when the majority of the legislature represents a political option opposed to the one the president represents" (Linz 1990: 53). To the extent that no democratic principle governs a choice between these two legitimacies, "it is therefore no accident that in some such situations in the past, the armed forces were often tempted to intervene as a mediating power" (Linz 1990: 53). The fact that such a scenario has never occurred in the United States is the exception that confirms the rule, and is essentially attributable to the very particular characteristics of the Democratic and Republican Parties—notably their lack of ideological unity and discipline.

The fixed term of the presidential mandate constitutes another problem, because "it breaks the political process into discontinuous, rigidly demarcated periods, leaving no room for the continuous readjustment that events may demand. The duration of the president's mandate becomes a crucial factor in the calculations of all political actors, a fact which is fraught with important consequences."[3]

In other respects, "presidentialism is problematic because it operates according to the rule of 'winner-take-all,' an arrangement that tends to make democratic politics a zero-sum game with all the potential for conflict that such games portend" (Linz 1990: 56). Executive power is not shared among many political forces, as is often the case in multiparty parliamentary regimes. Of course, government coalitions favor cooperation between parties, because incumbents are attentive to the demands and interests of even smaller parties. These, in turn, "retain expectations of sharing power and, therefore, of having a stake in the system as a whole" (Linz 1990: 56). By contrast, the conviction that he possesses independent authority and a popular mandate is likely to incite the president to confront the inevitable opposition to his policies.

The danger inherent in the zero-sum game is compounded by the rigidity of the president's fixed term. Because winners and losers are sharply defined for the entire period of the presidential mandate of four years or more, with no possibility for shifts in alliances, or new elections, tensions and polarization within the political system are exacerbated. In a country like the United States, where the majority of the electorate is centrist, the risks of conflict inherent in this long-lasting monopolization of power are small. They are much greater, by contrast, in less developed societies where socioeconomic inequalities fuel the influence of radical political currents.

In theory, presidential regimes are supposed to favor the independence and objectivity of the executive power in relation to particular interests, by means of numerous provisions designed to limit a president's personal power, such as rules against a second mandate, impeachment procedures, powers of parliamentary advice and consent in presidential nominations, and the independence of the judiciary. In practice, however, presidential regimes favor the development of networks of lobbying and influence between the executive and interest groups and encourage, notably in Hispanic societies, a strong personalization of the presidency.

The argument most often invoked in favor of presidentialism is that this type of regime is more stable than parliamentary regimes since the executive power is not shared and cannot be overturned by parliament. A less superficial analysis of the functioning of these two regimes demonstrates, however, that this argument is quite debatable. Frequent changes of government in certain parliamentary regimes, as in Italy, mask the continuity of the partisan coalitions in power and the game of musical chairs that characterizes each new cabinet. In fact, the stability of the executive power in presidential regimes is a source of conflict and can lead to a crisis of legitimacy, because of the rigidity of the political decision-making process and the winner-take-all principle to which it succumbs (Linz 1990: 64–66).

The Consolidation of New Democracies: Comparative Perspectives

Recent comparative studies reveal that among the democracies established since 1975, only the Greek, Spanish, and Portuguese systems are relatively consolidated today. New democracies of Latin America, Asia, and Eastern Europe remain, to varying degrees, formal, unstable, and fragile (Pridham 1990a; Huntington 1991; Higley and Gunther 1992). This conclusion is based on the observation that during the years following their transitions to democracy the legitimization and institutionalization of democratic values and rules have been much more significant in Southern Europe than in other regions (Baloyra 1987; Diamond, Linz, and Lipset 1989; Mainwaring, O'Donnell, and Valenzuela 1992; Kim and Kihl 1988; Morlino and Montero 1991;[4] Przeworski 1993).

The progress or difficulties in legitimizing and institutionalizing a democracy are related mainly to the scope or limits of the institutional reforms in these different regions. Thus, many works demonstrate that the army's control over the political system has been abolished in Southern Europe, whereas it continues in most Latin American, Asian, and Eastern European states, despite recognition of the independence and supremacy of civil political power in their constitutions.[5] These differences are attributed to various causes: the existence of higher levels of social mobilization in Latin America and Eastern Europe than in Southern Europe (Schmitter 1986; Roniger 1989); a stronger and more long-standing historic claim on political power by the army in Latin America, Eastern

Europe, and Asia than in Southern Europe (Schmitter 1986); the fact that in Southern Europe, acts of repression by the armed forces were less severe than in other regions, which contributed to the easier acceptance by the population of amnesty measures adopted by the new democratic regimes; and membership in NATO, which favored a modernization of military institutions and a purge of their upper hierarchies in Greece, Spain, and Portugal.

Some studies indicate that the reduction in bureaucratic control over political power has been more substantial in Southern Europe (notably in Spain) than in the other regions (Mainwaring, O'Donnell, and Valenzuela 1992; Maravall, Pereira, and Przeworski 1993). This evolution can be attributed to the larger scope of neoliberal economic reforms in Greece, Spain, and Portugal, which has led to the deregulation of the public sector and a reduction in its size. It can also be attributed to changes—decentralization, improvements in the transparency and control of the administrative apparatus—imposed on these three countries by their joining the EC, the completion of the single market, and the realization of European political and economic union.[6]

The autonomy of civil society in relation to the state is one of the principal criteria for democratic consolidation in these different regions. There is broad consensus that this process has seen a more important evolution in Southern Europe than in other regions. The comparison of different studies on the subject (notably Schmitter 1986; Maravall and Santamaria 1986; Diamandouros 1986; Boschi 1990; Touraine 1988; Cotton 1989; and Jackson 1989) shows that basic communities (clans and families), and corporatist and clientelist organizations, have played a less important role in the development of European societies than in Latin American and Asian ones. This has fostered the emergence, even during the period of authoritarian regimes, of public organizations of religious, ethnic, professional, and cultural interests. In Eastern Europe, the difficulties inherent in establishing the autonomy of civil society are attributed to the introversion, apathy, fear, and dependence maintained in public and private life under communist party and state control for more than forty years. They are also tied to the continued control by the state, public organizations, and the parties over the emerging new interest networks (Havel 1985; Lewis 1992; McGregor 1991).

The evolution of the party system is the major theme of studies on the prospects for consolidation of the new democracies. Many of them indicate that the period following 1975–78 has been characterized—as much in Greece as in Spain and Portugal—by a significant increase in the electoral popularity of the centrist parties or the emergence of a two-party system. These are made up of New Democracy and the Panhellenic Socialist Movement (Panellinio Socialistiko Kinema, or PASOK) in Greece, the Spanish Workers' Socialist Party (Partido Socialista Obrero Español, PSOE) and the Popular Alliance in Spain, and the Socialist and Social Democratic Parties in Portugal (Bar 1984; MacLeod 1990; Gladdish 1990; Graham 1992; Featherstone 1990). These changes are attributed to the deepening of ideological, rather than sociological, party pluralism, the latter still being dominated by elites and little implanted into society. They are also related to the decline of extreme left- or right-wing party influence, due to the collapse of their alternatives (socialism and authoritarianism) and to their internal crises, and to the effects of proportional representation electoral systems, which limit the representation of smaller parties. In Spain, the strengthening of bipartisanism is also attributed to the weakening of regional nationalist party influence, following the granting of autonomous status to the regional communities. The succession of majority governments since the beginning of the 1980s in Greece and Spain,[7] and since 1987 in Portugal, and the consensual unification of the elites are thought to be direct consequences of this transformation of party systems (Burton, Gunther, and Higley 1992a).

While, in Southern Europe, the major political parties' lack of deep roots in civil society is compensated for by their ideological pluralism, their links with numerous pressure groups, and the existence of many regional third parties, this is not the case in Latin America and Asia. In these regions, the main national parties represent only the urban classes and are dominated by relatively sectarian and dogmatic ideologies. The absence or weak development of pressure groups accentuates the exclusion of broad social strata from the political system, such as landowners, peasants, the subproletariat, and aboriginal groups. This exclusion only encourages the perpetuation of corporatist and clientelist practices and the existence of radical and violent protest movements—two conditions favoring the maintenance of military control over political power (Ducatenzeiler 1990; Waisman 1989). The poor representativeness and ideological convergence of political parties is accompanied in some countries, including Brazil and the Philippines, by factionalism and organizational instability (Wurfel 1990; Boschi 1990). In many societies, however, such as Colombia, Peru, Chile, Uruguay, Argentina, and South Korea, the party system is dominated by two stable and unified formations

(Gillespie 1990; McClintock 1989; Abugattas 1987; Hartlyn 1989; Joo-Han 1989).

In the Eastern European democracies, the broadening of interest representation and aggregation is impeded by the fact that the many new political groups are generally not deeply rooted within civil society (a phenomenon linked to the absence of autonomous pressure groups), and they display instability, factionalism, and nonpluralist ideological orientations. These weaknesses are, however, more striking in some societies—for example, Poland, Bulgaria, Romania, Albania—than in others, such as former East Germany, Hungary, and the Czech Republic (Berglund and Dellenbrant 1991; Przeworski 1993).

The evaluation of prospects for democratic consolidation does not accord a very important place to the nature of constitutional regimes—be they parliamentary or presidential. This is because the choice of constitutional regime constitutes the final stage of democratic transition and that amendments to constitutions are generally limited and difficult to achieve once democracy has been established.[8] Nevertheless, many authors feel that the constitutional framework chosen can either facilitate (in the case of parliamentarism) or complicate (in the case of presidentialism) the process. Thus, Spain and Greece adopted the parliamentary model, monarchical in the first case, republican in the second, and Portugal opted for an abbreviated semipresidential regime in 1982 and 1988. The choice of presidentialism by the new democracies in Latin America, Eastern Europe, and Asia has been termed by some authors an important determinant of the unequal progress of democratic consolidation (Katsoudas 1987; Linz 1990: 58–60; Bruneau 1990; Liebert and Cotta 1990).

The explanation of differences in democratic consolidation processes does not go very deep. It is also problematic in many respects. Thus, the socioeconomic development gaps between the regions considered are often cited as a factor in their unequal progress toward democratic consolidation. However, a comparison of the evolution of modernization indicators from 1960 to 1987 in Southern Europe, Latin America, and Asia shows that the structural characteristics of certain Southern European countries, especially Greece and Portugal, are very similar to the newly industrialized countries of Latin America and Asia (Ethier 1991).

Moreover, while the level of modernization can be a significant explanatory variable in the case of the poorest Eastern European countries (such as Bulgaria, Albania, and Romania), such is not the case for the industrialized countries of this region (such as former East Germany, the

Czech Republic, Hungary, and Poland). In the case of socialist countries, the level of economic and social development is a less significant variable than the specific (socialist) modalities of development. The culture—modernist or "archaic" (corporatist, populist, nationalist, socialist)—of political leaders, and more generally of the elites, is often held responsible for the depth or limits of democratic consolidation. This type of explanation tends, however, to turn the theory of democratic consolidation into a tautological one, advancing the adoption of liberal democratic values and rules as both cause and consequence of the transformation of political institutions. Understanding the causes of the success (in Southern Europe) or the difficulties (in other regions) of democratic consolidation is also limited by the relative lack of attention to the impact on this process of transformations in the international system, particularly economic transformations. Analysis of the implications for different countries of the two central dynamics of the present evolution of the international economic order—the abandonment of Keynesian economic policies in favor of neoliberal "economic adjustment," and the entrenchment of market integration, by means of multilateral (Uruguay Round of GATT) and regional (European Union, North American Free Trade Agreement, Mercosur) trade liberalization—allows a clearer understanding of the unequal progress of consolidation within new democracies.

Economic Adjustment and Democratic Consolidation

Since the beginning of the 1980s, all countries have been confronted with the need to adopt adjustment programs in order to adapt their economies to the globalization of markets—the primary condition for successfully maintaining or renewing their sustainable economic growth. Economic adjustment, which calls into question the Keynesian dogma of the postwar period in favor of neoliberalism,[9] includes two series of measures. The first are *stabilization* measures—such as increases in interest rates, reduction in public spending, growth of tax load—aimed at curbing inflation and correcting the balance of payments and budget deficits of governments. The second are *structural change* measures designed to increase the freedom and competitiveness of the market—privatization of public enterprises, deregulation of different economic sectors, reduction in the size and improvement in the effectiveness of government administrations, rationalization, modernization, and merging of private businesses, and improvements in professional training. The success of economic adjustment depends on the consistent and sustained application, during a period of ten or more years, of stabilization and structural change measures (Nelson 1990a: 3–4).[10]

Economic adjustment is a process both favorable and unfavorable to democratic consolidation. To the extent that it leads to bureaucratic reform and reduction—improvement in the rationality and transparency of decision-making and recruitment processes, decreases in size, deregulation of public markets, transfer of some powers to local and regional administrations—it favors the elimination of corruption and of clientelist networks, an increase in competition between various interest groups, and the creation of a civil society based on autonomous individuals. By contrast, it generates significant transition costs such as bankruptcies, marked increase in unemployment, decrease in revenues, and growth of the tax burden, which are long lasting and unequally distributed between social groups, economic sectors, and regions (Przeworski 1990). These transition costs lead to conflicts between interest groups and reduce citizen confidence in the effectiveness of the political system—two phenomena that hinder the legitimation and institutionalization of the rules of the democratic game.

Several authors consider the negative effects of economic adjustment more significant than its positive effects; they believe that it is preferable to pursue economic adjustment before democratic transition, or after a phase of consolidation, rather than during either one (Przeworski 1990; Köves and Marer 1991; Haggard and Kaufman 1992; Bermeo 1994; Maravall, Pereira, and Przeworski 1993). The risk of conflict and the weakening of the political system's legitimacy is judged less significant when economic adjustment is undertaken within the framework of a consolidated democracy: the integration of the vast majority of interest groups into the decision-making process leads them to lower their expectations, make compromises, and accept the uncertain outcome of the negotiation characteristic of democratic decision making. The different partners are willing to accept that this negotiation may lead to losses, because they maintain hope for future gains (Whitehead 1988; Przeworski 1990). In nonconsolidated democracies, on the other hand, the exclusion of many social groups from the political decision-making process fosters the criticism, or rejection, of government policies. These risks of mobilization are, however, attenuated when economic adjustment has been achieved within the framework of an authoritarian regime, since the establishment of a democratic regime then takes place in an economic context characterized by the rehabilitation of public finances and by renewed growth.

The comparative evaluation of political context and adjustment success in different countries tends to confirm these hypotheses. In Greece, Spain, and Portugal, where adjustment was undertaken in 1983, after a period of five to eight years of democratic consolidation, the process of economic reform took place in an environment of relative social consensus (Bermeo 1994; Maravall 1993), despite the large scale of these reforms (particularly in Spain and Portugal). By contrast, in most Latin American, Eastern European, Asian, and African countries, which introduced economic adjustment during, or immediately after, their transitions to democracy, it was accompanied by profound controversies and tensions (Köves and Marer 1991; Köves 1992; Kaufman 1990; Haggard 1990; Stallings 1990; Haggard and Kaufman 1992; Przeworski 1993; Pereira 1993; Duquette 1994). In Chile and South Korea, where the main measures of stabilization have been put in place by authoritarian regimes, before democratic transition, the level of conflict or instability in the new political system is lower (Duquette 1994).

It follows from these findings that the majority of the democracies instituted since 1975 are today confronted with a dilemma: how to achieve economic adjustment, a necessary precondition for economic development, without compromising the consolidation of their democracies. The analyses of Przeworski (1990, 1993) show that this dilemma is very difficult to resolve, not only because economic adjustment and democratic consolidation are relatively contradictory processes, but because the options that would allow an escape from this vicious cycle are impracticable. The first option would mean adopting a strategy of gradual adjustment, in order to mitigate the severity of transition costs and to create a political climate more conducive to democratic consolidation. Due to the problems and particular characteristics of their economic systems—size of the public sector, low competitiveness of businesses, high level of inflation and debt, tax evasion—such a choice could not help but aggravate the difficulties faced by new democracies, limiting their chances for legitimation and institutionalization. The second option would be to go ahead with adjustment, while at the same time adopting effective aid programs for social groups, businesses, and regions penalized by the costs of transition; this would mitigate the risk of conflict, thereby creating conditions more favorable to democratic consolidation. However, the application of these measures requires financial resources not available to new democratic states. Furthermore, they cannot count on external assistance, given that such help is now conditional on adopting measures of adjustment, and is not designed to mitigate the costs of transition (Nelson 1992, 1993).

An analysis of the success of democratic consolidation in Southern Europe does demonstrate, however, that there is a third option possible, not previously investigated by researchers: integration within a regional bloc. The fact that Greece, Spain, and Portugal were able to consolidate their democratic regimes before undertaking economic adjustment is due in large part to their membership in the European Community. Examining why this membership has contributed to the success of democratic consolidation and economic adjustment is important: it promotes a better understanding of the rapid and profound political and economic transformations these three countries experienced during the 1980s, and it also alerts us to the extent to which this experience can be exported to other regions.

Regional Integration and Democratic Consolidation: Lessons from Southern Europe

Lawrence Whitehead is one of those rare scholars who has studied the impact of external factors on the process of democratic transition. He has identified three main modes of influence of the international system on democratization: (1) contagion, or diffusion of the democratic experience of other states by the demonstration or attraction effect, (2) control, by one or more foreign states promoting democratic policies, accompanied by positive or negative sanctions, and (3) consent, which refers to "a complex set of interactions between international processes and domestic groups that generated new democratic norms and expectations from below" (Whitehead 1991), a process that in its most advanced form leads to integration within another state or a bloc of states. Philippe Schmitter has introduced a fourth mode of influence into this typology—conditionality—which he describes as "the deliberate use of coercion to promote democracy by attaching specific conditions to the distribution of benefits to recipient countries on the part of multilateral institutions." Schmitter also illuminates a critical timing issue: "regardless of the form that it takes, external interventions will have a greater and more lasting effect upon the consolidation of democracy that upon the transition to it" (Schmitter 1993: 6, 8).

Conditionality of EC Membership

Membership in the EC has been a determining factor in the processes of transition and democratic consolidation in Southern Europe. The economic crisis of the early 1970s reinforced the sentiment of Greek, Spanish, and Portuguese elites that a renewal of growth depended on membership in the EC. The fact that this membership was conditional on democratization of authoritarian regimes, in accordance with the provisions of the Treaty of Rome of 1957 and the Birkelback Report of 1962, contributed greatly to the appeal of democratization within governing coalitions and various opposition groups (Pridham 1990b; Schmitter 1993). The reestablishment of democracy in these three countries allowed membership negotiations to begin. However, the Community notified the three prospective members, particularly by means of the opinion of the European Commission,[11] that these negotiations could not be completed before a certain consolidation of their democratic regimes was achieved (Verney 1990: 207). The goal of the Community was the stabilization of Southern European democracies by solving the problems most likely to threaten their survival.

Although the analysis of this subject is still preliminary, it can be affirmed that four types of reform have been undertaken by the Southern European governments during the years preceding their joining the EC—reform of the armed forces, solution of nationalist problems in Spain, delay of economic adjustment programs, and improvement of social policies. Greece attained membership in 1981, Spain and Portugal in 1986.

In Portugal, the purge in and modernization of the army between 1976 and 1982 was instigated by President António Eanes, and facilitated the abolition of the Council of the Revolution within the framework of the constitutional reform of 1982, and the adaptation of Portuguese defense policy to Community norms the same year (Graham 1992: 29). In Greece, the reform of the military institution took place in 1977 (Veremis 1987); in Spain, the democratization of the army began with membership in NATO in 1982, and continued during the second PSOE mandate (1986–90), after joining the EC. The problem of the claims of different nationalist groups in Spain was in large part resolved by the 1979–82 negotiations on the content of autonomous status, laid out in the 1978 constitution, between Madrid and each of the seventeen regions concerned. Although these negotiations did not put an end to terrorist activities by Basque

Homeland and Freedom (Euzkadi ta Azkatasuna, EtA), they nonetheless allowed the central government to win the support of the majority of the Basque political parties and citizens, which facilitated a new French-Spanish agreement for joint intervention against the EtA (Gillespie 1990: 126–47).

The period following the reestablishment of democracy was characterized by a worsening of the economic problems first appearing in the 1970s—inflation, balance of payments disequilibrium, budget deficits, and low productivity (Hudson and Lewis 1985). Judging that the consolidation of their democratic regimes was a more important objective than the adoption of stabilization and structural change measures, the governments of Southern Europe opted, with the accord of the Community, to maintain their expansionist policies during the 1975–83 period. The increase in public expenditure has been oriented primarily toward the improvement of social programs: universalization of health care systems, democratization of access to education, and augmentation of retirement benefits (Maravall 1993). In Spain, the liberalization of many labor laws was accompanied by an improvement in social benefits for workers, such as sick days, vacations, workplace safety, and health (McElrath 1989).

The reforms flowing from the conditionality of EC membership have no doubt contributed to the growth of the legitimacy of the Southern European democracies. On this point, a study by Morlino and Montero (1991: 32, 38) demonstrates that, in 1985, 61 percent of Portuguese, 70 percent of Spaniards, and 87 percent of Greeks thought that democracy was preferable to all other forms of government. The proportion of citizens with a positive perception of the effectiveness of the democratic regime was 77 percent in Portugal, 75 percent in Spain, and 84 percent in Greece.

Impact of Integration into the EC

It is important to distinguish between the effects produced by the prospect of EC membership and the effects engendered by the concretization of membership.

Concerning the prospective effects, Verney (1990) pointed out that the imminence of membership, and the perception that the process had become irreversible, helped to modify the attitudes of citizens and elites. Sidjanski and Ayberk (1990) showed that one of the principal consequences of the change in behavior of the elites has been the transnationalization of parties and interest groups, which began between 1980 and 1986. The integration of Greek, Spanish, and Portuguese political groups and interest groups into the European lobbying networks, and into federal and nonfederal associations, has largely been motivated by the desire to increase their influence within EC political institutions (Parliament, Commission, committees) and financial organs (structural funds, European Investment Bank). Consequently, the number of Southern European interest groups integrated into European organizations increased between 1975 and 1986 from 2 to 154 in Greece, from 5 to 189 in Spain, and from 0 to 113 in Portugal (Sidjanski and Ayberk 1990: 238). Although this chapter does not deal with the consequences of this transnationalization, we can advance the hypothesis that it has enhanced the ideological and organizational modernization of the parties and interest groups, thus contributing to the stabilization of the party system and the autonomy of civil societies.

EC membership treaties forced Greece, Spain, and Portugal to abolish all obstacles to the free circulation of goods, capital, and labor between their territories and those of the other EC member states. This liberalization of markets required the Southern European governments to accelerate and enlarge the adjustment programs launched in 1983, in the context of the early-1980s recession. However, this change in economic policy direction did not meet with significant protest from the elites and the population at large.[12] Three factors explain the public acceptance and, consequently, the pursuit by governments, of economic adjustment: the existing consolidation of democratic regimes, the economic benefits of EC membership, and the many programs designed to foster economic and social cohesion to which the three new member states had access once they joined the EC.

Membership in the EC has led to a significant increase in foreign investment, especially in Spain and Portugal. This influx of capital sparked an important renewal of domestic consumption, a decrease in unemployment, an increase in government revenues, and a consequent decrease in debt loads (Ethier 1991). These circumstances reinforced the satisfaction of the citizens with membership and their faith in democratic government efficiency, thereby helping the pursuit of economic adjustment concurrent with the entrenchment of legitimacy and the institutionalization of democracy.

Tolerance of adjustment policies can also be linked to the reinforcement of economic and social cohesion policies, concurrent with EC expansion to include Spain and Portugal, and the adoption of the Single European Act in 1986 and the Treaty on European Union in 1991.[13] The EC policies on economic and social cohesion aim at lessening the socio-economic disparities among the regions and the member states through intervention programs designed to aid the least competitive to adapt to the new conditions of competition created by the liberalization of markets. The primary instruments for the implementation of these policies are the European Regional Development Fund (ERDF), the European Agricultural Guidance and Guarantee Fund (EAGGF), the European Social Fund (ESF), the European Investment Bank (EIB), and the European Coal and Steel Community (ECSC).

Unfortunately, as a result of limited financial resources, and ineffective interventions, these institutions were not able to prevent the exacerbation of regional economic disparities between 1960 and 1986. The disparities were greatly amplified by the inclusion of Spain and Portugal; thus, the states with the least-developed regions and highest unemployment rates[14] made their support of the Single European Act and the European Union treaty conditional on a profound reform of the budgets and interventions of these institutions. Consequently, two successive reforms of the structural funds, in 1988 and 1992–93, allowed the poorer regions (all of Greece and Portugal, as well as ten regions of Spain) to benefit from important transfers of different program resources. These transfers promoted (1) development in the less developed regions, (2) conversion of industrial zones in decline, (3) modernization of agriculture, and (4) the professional reintegration of the unemployed. The scope of these programs—and the fact that their design, implementation, and follow-up involved the EC, the central, regional, and local governments, the private sector, and the unions of the target states—contributed to the acceptance by the elites and the population of the costs of transition involved in economic adjustment.[15]

Conclusion

The comparative evaluation of the prospects for consolidation of new democracies demonstrates that, while their viability is not threatened in the short and medium term, their stabilization is problematic, due as much to institutional and cultural factors as to the disruptive effects of economic adjustments. The analysis of the Southern Europe cases, which constitute an exception to this rule, reveals that integration into the European Community has been a determining factor in the combined progress of democratic consolidation and economic adjustment in Greece, Spain, and Portugal during the period following the reestablishment of democracy. This conclusion argues in favor of new enlargements of the EC, particularly for the countries of Eastern Europe. It also raises a number of questions as to the possible political benefits of other regional integration processes, particularly the North American Free Trade Agreement (NAFTA) and the Initiative for the Americas project, on the consolidation of new democracies.

Beyond its very specific character, the dynamic of Europe shows that the regional integration of markets can foster democratic consolidation in three ways: (1) by stimulating demonstration or contagion effects from consolidated democracies, when the regional bloc includes such states, as NAFTA does; (2) by favoring a renewal of investment and growth—circumstances that facilitate the reduction of transition costs inherent in economic adjustment, a major obstacle to democratic consolidation; and (3) by encouraging, when the alliance includes advanced democratic states, a certain harmonization from above of labor legislation and social policies, an important condition for lessening the costs of transition.

Notes

1. According to Huntington 1991 (16–26), modern history (the period that began with the birth of the nation-states) has been characterized by three waves of democratization (1828–1926, 1943–62, and 1975–present) separated by two phases of authoritarianism (1922–42 and 1958–75).

2. Opinion on this question, though, is far from unanimous. Some authors (including Touraine 1988, 1991) believe that the autonomous organization of civil society—the development of pressure groups—is more of a determining factor in the broadening of popular political participation in the political decision-making process. Schmitter's analysis (1986) reconciles the two points of view by specifying that pressure groups can effectively represent the various interests within society only if they maintain formal or informal links with political parties.

3. Linz 1990 cites as an example the replacement of the president, due to death or incapacity during the course of his mandate, which often leads to the nomination of an incompetent successor and the weakening of the executive.

4. Many other studies have also analyzed the democratization of the political culture in Portugal (Heimer, Viegas, and Andrade 1990) and in Spain (Molas 1984; Fishman 1982, 1984; Ibañez and Enrique 1987).

5. The Portuguese Constitution of 1976 is an exception to the rule, since it conceded to the Council of the Revolution, made up of representatives of the army leadership, the power to control many of the decisions of the president of the republic. This provision was abolished, however, as part of the constitutional reform of 1982 (see Bruneau 1990).

6. On this point, see the many works on the impacts of the membership treaties, the Single European Act, and the Treaty on European Union upon the political and economic systems of Greece, Spain, and Portugal (e.g., Alonso 1985; Pellicer 1988; Ruesga 1989; Torres and Fiesola 1989; and Alonso Olea, et al. 1992.

7. This pattern was broken by the election of two successive minority center-right (New Democracy) governments in Greece in 1989, and of a minority socialist (PSOE) government in Spain in 1993.

8. The rejection of parliamentarism during the 1993 Brazilian referendum confirms this rule. The constitutional reforms of 1982 and 1988 in Portugal are not really an exception to this rule. They demonstrate rather that external pressures and conditional policies (notably within the context of regional integrations) can favor the transformation of the state's institutional frameworks.

9. The term neoliberalism refers to a set of theories founded on the critique of Keynesianism and the renewal of neoclassical approaches: monetarist theory, supply-side theory, property rights theory, radical or libertarian liberalism (see Beaud and Dostaler 1993: 129–69). The first two approaches in particular have influenced the reorientation of the economic policies of capitalist countries. This movement was started by the Thatcher and Reagan governments during the 1979–82 recession. It was then generalized, notably due to the influence of American monetary policies, to international financial institutions (IMF, World Bank, etc.) and to other countries. On this point, see Thomas (1990).

10. Nelson (1990a) specifies that measures of stabilization are usually built up over a period of two to five years, whereas structural reform stretches out over a decade.

11. See the Commission of the European Community (1976: 7, 1978: 6).

12. This point must, however, be nuanced in the case of Greece. Opposition to measures of adjustment persisted in the sectors dominated by PASOK—unions, the bureaucracy, and protected national industries. This opposition explains the suspension of measures of adjustment by PASOK during its second mandate, in 1985–90 (see Maravall 1993).

13. The Single European Act was adopted by the Council of Europe in 1986; it was ratified by the parliaments of the member states during 1987, and came into effect in July 1987. The Treaty on European Union, or Maastricht treaty, was adopted by the Council of Europe in 1991; it was ratified by parliamentary approval or referendum in the member states in 1992 and 1993.

14. These countries were France, Germany (due to the West's reunification with the East), Italy, Greece, Spain, Portugal, and Ireland.

15. On the content and implications of the EC structural funds, see Ethier (1993).

References

Abugattas, L. A. 1987. Populism and After: The Peruvian Experience." In *Authoritarians and Democrats*, edited by James Malloy and Michael A. Seligson. Pittsburgh: University of Pittsburgh Press.

Agh, A. 1990. "Société étatique et société civile." *Alternatives non violentes* (September).

Almond, Gabriel A., and James S. Coleman. 1960. *The Politics of the Developing Areas.* Princeton, N.J.: Princeton University Press.

Alonso, Alvarez. 1985. *España en el Mercado Común Del Acuerdo del 70 a la Comunidad de Doce.* Madrid: Espasa Calpe.

Alonso Olea, Manuel, et al. 1992. *España y la Unión Europea: Las Consecuencias del Tratado de Maastrich.* Barcelona: Plaza y Janes.

Baloyra, Enrique. 1987. *Comparing New Democracies.* Boulder, Colo.: Westview Press.

Bar, A. 1984. "The Emerging Spanish Party System: Is There a Model?" *West European Politics* 13 (June): 129–55.

Beaud, Michel, and Gilles Dostaler. 1993. *La pensée économique depuis Keynes.* Paris: Le Seuil.

Berglund, S., and J. A. Dellenbrant. 1991. *The New Democracies in Eastern Europe: Party Systems and Political Changes.* Aldershot and Brookfield, Vt.: Edward Elgar.

Bermeo, Nancy. 1994. "Sacrifice, Sequence, and Strength in Successful Dual Transitions: Lessons from Spain." *Journal of Politics,* 56: 3. 601–27.

Bird, Graham. 1991. *Economic Reform in Eastern Europe.* Aldershot and Brookfield, Vt.: Edward Elgar.

Boschi, Renato R. 1990. "Social Movements, Party System, and Democratic Consolidation: Brazil, Uruguay, and Argentina." In *Democratic Transition and Consolidation in Southern Europe, Latin America, and Southeast Asia*, edited by Diane Ethier. London: MacMillan.

Bruneau, Thomas. 1990. "Constitution and Democratic Consolidation: Brazil in Comparative Perspective." In *Democratic Transition and Consolidation in Southern Europe, Latin America, and Southeast Asia,* edited by Diane Ethier. London: MacMillan.

Burton, Michael, Richard Gunther, and John Higley. 1992a. "Elites and Democratic Consolidation in Southern Europe and Latin America: An Overview." In *Elites and Democratic Consolidation in Southern Europe and Latin America*, edited by John Higley and Richard Gunther. Cambridge: Cambridge University Press.

———. 1992b. "Introduction: Elite Transformations and Democratic Regimes." In *Elites and Democratic Consolidation in Southern Europe and Latin America*, edited by John Higley and Richard Gunther. Cambridge: Cambridge University Press.

Buse, Michael. 1984. *La Nueva Democracia Española: Sistema de Partidos y Orientación del Voto (1967–1983).* Madrid: Únion Editorial.

Commission of the European Community (CEC). 1976. "Report on Membership Application of Greece. Communication of the CEC to the Council—29 January, 1976." *Bulletin of the European Communities.* Supplement February 1976.

———. 1978. "Enlargement of the European Community: General Considerations. Communication of the CEC to the Council—20 April, 1978." *Bulletin of the European Communities.* Supplement January 1978.

Cotton, James. 1989. "From Authoritarianism to Democracy in South Korea." *Political Studies* 37: 244–59.

Dahl, Robert. 1971. *Polyarchy, Participation, and Opposition.* New Haven, CT.: Yale University Press.

Diamandouros, Nikifouros P. 1986. "Regime Change and the Prospects for Democracy in Greece 1974–1983." In *Transitions from Authoritarian Rule: Prospects for Democracy,* edited by Guillermo O'Donnell, Philippe Schmitter, and Lawrence Whitehead. Vol. 1. Baltimore: Johns Hopkins University Press: 138–75.

Diamond, Larry, and Juan C. Linz. 1989. "Introduction: Politics, Society and Democracy in Latin America." In *Democracy in Developing Countries*, edited by Larry Diamond, Juan C. Linz, and Seymour Martin Lipset. Boulder, Colo.: Lynne Rienner.

Diamond, Larry, Juan C. Linz, and Seymour Martin Lipset, eds. 1989. *Democracy in Developing Countries.* Boulder, Colo.: Lynne Rienner.

Ducatenzeiler, Graciela. 1990. "Social Concertation and Democracy in Argentina." In *Democratic Transition and Consolidation in Southern Europe, Latin America, and Southeast Asia*, edited by Diane Ethier. London: MacMillan.

Ethier, Diane. ed. 1990. *Democratic Transition and Consolidation in Southern Europe, Latin America, and Southeast Asia.* London: MacMillan.

———. 1991. "Democratic Consolidation in Southern Europe, Latin America, and Southeast Asia: Comparative Perspectives." *Journal of Developing Societies* 7 (July–October): 195–217.

———. 1993. "The Reform of the European Community's Structural Funds: From the Single Act to Maastricht and After." *International Review of Administrative Sciences* 59 (June): 195–213.

Featherstone, Kevin. 1990. "Political Parties and Democratic Consolidation in Greece." In *Securing Democracy: Political Parties and Democratic Consolidation in Southern Europe,* edited by Geoffrey Pridham. London: Routledge.

Featherstone, Kevin, and Dimitrios Katsoudas, eds. 1987. *Political Change in Greece.* New York: St. Martin's Press.

Fishman, Robert M. 1982. "The Labour Movement in Spain from Authoritarianism to Democracy." *Comparative Politics* 14 (April): 281–306.

———. 1984. "El Movimiento Obrero en la Transición Objectivos Políticos y Organizativos." *Revista Española de Investigaciones Sociologicas* 26 (April–June): 61–113.

Gillespie, E. Charles. 1990. "Models of Democratic Transition in South America: Negotiated Reform versus Democratic Rupture." In *Democratic Transition and Consolidation in Southern Europe, Latin America, and Southeast Asia*, edited by Diane Ethier. London: MacMillan.

Gladdish, Ken. 1990. "Portugal: An Open Verdict." In *Securing Democracy: Political Parties and Democratic Consolidation in Southern Europe,* edited by Geoffrey Pridham. London: Routledge: 104–26.

Graham, Lawrence S. 1992. "Redefining the Portuguese Transition to Democracy." In *Elites and Democratic Consolidation in Southern Europe and Latin America*, edited by John Higley and Richard Gunther. Cambridge: Cambridge University Press.

Gunther, Richard. 1989. "Electoral Laws, Party Systems, and Elites: The Case of Spain." *American Political Science Review* 83 (September): 835–59.

———. 1992. "Spain, the Very Model of the Modern Elite Settlement." In *Elites and Democratic Consolidation in Southern Europe and Latin America,* edited by John Higley and Richard Gunther. Cambridge: Cambridge University Press.

Haggard, Stephen. 1990. "The Political Economy of the Philippines Debt Crisis." In *Economic Crisis and Policy Choice,* edited by Joan Nelson. Princeton: Princeton University Press.

Haggard, Stephen, and Robert Kaufman. 1992. "Economic Adjustment and the Prospects for Democracy." In *The Politics of Economic Adjustment,* edited by Stephen Haggard and Robert Kaufman. Princeton: Princeton University Press.

Hartlyn, Jonathan. 1989. "Colombia: The Politics of Violence and Accommodation." In *Democracy in Developing Countries,* edited by Larry Diamond, Juan C. Linz and Seymour Martin Lipset. Boulder, Colo.: Lynne Rienner.

Havel, Vaclav. 1985. *The Power of the Powerless: Citizens against the State in Central Eastern Europe.* London: Hutchinson Educational.

Heimer, F. W., J. M. L. Viegas, and M. N. Andrade. 1990. "Regime Transition and Consolidation in Portugal: The Subjective Dimension." Paper presented to the International Sociological Association, Twelfth World Congress, Madrid, July 9–13.

Hermet, Guy. 1991. "Présentation: le temps de la démocratie?" *Revue internationale des sciences sociales* 128 (May): 265–75.

Higley, John, and Richard Gunther, eds. 1992. *Elites and Democratic Consolidation in Southern Europe and Latin America.* Cambridge: Cambridge University Press.

Hudson, Ray, and John Lewis. 1985. *Uneven Development in Southern Europe: Studies of Accumulation, Class, Migration, and the State.* London: Methuen.

Huntington, Samuel P. 1965. "Political Development and Political Decay." *World Politics* 17 (April): 386–430.

———. 1984. "Will More Countries Become Democratic?" *Political Science Quarterly* 99 (Summer): 193–218.

———. 1991. *The Third Wave: Democratization in the Late Twentieth Century.* Norman: Oklahoma University Press.

Ibañez, R., and J. Enrique. 1987. *Después de una Dictadura: Cultura Autoritaria y Transición Política en España.* Madrid: Centro de Estudios Constitucionales.

Jackson, Karl D. 1989. "The Philippines: The Search for a Suitable Democratic Solution, 1946–1986." In *Democracy in Developing Countries,* edited by Larry Diamond, Juan C. Linz, and Seymour Martin Lipset. Boulder, Colo.: Lynne Rienner.

Joo-Han, Sung. 1989. "South Korea: Politics in Transition." In *Democracy in Developing Countries,* edited by Larry Diamond, Juan C. Linz, and Seymour Martin Lipset. Boulder, Colo.: Lynne Rienner.

Katsoudas, Dimitrios K. 1987. "The Constitutional Framework." In *Political Change in Greece,* edited by Kevin Featherstone and Dimitrios Katsoudas. New York: St. Martin's Press: 14–34.

Kaufman, Robert. 1990. "Stabilization and Adjustment in Argentina, Brazil, and Mexico." In *Economic Crisis and Policy Choice,* edited by Joan Nelson. Princeton: Princeton University Press.

Kim, Ilpyong J., and Young Whan Kihl, eds. 1988. *The Political Change in South Korea.* New York: Korean PWPA, Inc.

Köves, Andras. 1992. *Central and East European Economies in Transition.* Boulder, Colo.: Westview Press.

Köves, Andras, and Paul Marer. 1991. *Foreign Economic Liberalization: Transformations in Socialist and Market Economies.* Boulder, Colo.: Westview Press.

Lerner, David. 1958. *The Passing of Traditional Society.* Glencoe, Ill.: Free Press.

Lewis, Paul G., ed. 1992. *Democracy and Civil Society in Eastern Europe.* New York: St. Martin's Press.

Liebert, Ulrike, and Maurizio Cotta. 1990. *Parliament and Democratic Consolidation in Southern Europe.* London: Pinter Publishers.

Linz, Juan C. 1982. "The Transition from Authoritarian Regimes to Democratic Political Systems and the Problems of Consolidation of Political Democracy." Paper presented to the International Political Science Association Round Table, Tokyo, March 29–April 1.

———. 1990. "The Perils of Presidentialism." *Journal of Democracy* 4 (winter): 51–69.

Lipset, Seymour Martin. 1959. "Some Social Requisites of Democracy: Economic Development and Political Legitimacy." *American Political Science Review* 53 (March): 69–105.

MacLeod, Alex. 1990. "The Parties and the Consolidation of Democracy in Portugal: The Emergence of a Dominant Two-Party System." In *Democratic Transition and Consolidation in Southern Europe, Latin America, and Southeast Asia,* edited by Diane Ethier. London: MacMillan.

Mainwaring, Scott, Guillermo O'Donnell, and Samuel Valenzuela. 1992. *Issues in Democratic Consolidation. The New South American Democracies in Comparative Perspectives.* Notre Dame, Ind.: University of Notre Dame Press.

Maravall, José Maria. 1993. "Politics and Policy: Economic Reforms in Southern Europe." In *Economic Reforms in New Democracies: A Social-Democratic Approach,* edited by José Maria Maravall, Luis Carlos Bresser Pereira, and Adam Przeworski. Cambridge: Cambridge University Press.

Maravall, José Maria and Juliane Santamaria. 1986. "Political Change in Spain and the Prospects for Democracy." In *Transition from Authoritarian Rule: Prospects for Democracy,* edited by Guillermo O'Donnell, Philippe Schmitter, and Lawrence Whitehead. Baltimore: Johns Hopkins University Press, 1, 71–109.

Maravall, José Maria, Luis Carlos Bresser Pereira, and Adam Przeworski. 1993. *Economic Reforms in New Democracies: A Social-Democratic Approach.* Cambridge: Cambridge University Press.

Mazier, Jacques, and Cécile Couharde. 1991. "Croissance et efficacité des politiques structurelles dans la Communauté économique européenne." *Revue du Marché commun et de l'Union européenne* 350 (September) 604–30.

McClintock, Cynthia. 1989. "Peru: Precarious Regimes, Authoritarian and Democratic." In *Democracy in Developing Countries,* edited by Larry Diamond, Juan C. Linz, and Seymour Martin Lipset. Boulder, Colo.: Lynne Rienner.

McElrath, R. G. 1989. "Trade Unions and the Industrial Relations Climate in Spain." *European Studies* No. 10.

McGregor, James P. 1991. "Value in a Developed Socialist System: The Case of Czechoslovakia." *Comparative Politics* 23 (January): 181–99.

Molas, Luis. 1984. "Sur les attitudes politiques dans l'après-franquisme." *Pouvoirs* 8: 13–23.

Morlino, Leonardo. 1986. "Consolidación Democrática: Definición, Modelos, Hipótesis." *Revista Española de Investigaciones Sociologicas* 35 (July–September).

Morlino, Leonardo, and José R. Montero. 1991. "Legitimacy and Democracy in Southern Europe." Paper presented to the Latin American Studies Association, Sixteenth Congress, Washington, D.C., April 4–6.

Nelson, Joan. 1990a. "Introduction: The Politics of Economic Adjustment in Developing Nations." In *Economic Crisis and Policy Choice,* edited by Joan Nelson. Princeton: Princeton University Press.

———. ed. 1990b. *Economic Crisis and Policy Choice.* Princeton: Princeton University Press.

———. 1992. "Encouraging Democracy: What Role for Conditional Aid?" *Policy Essay* 4 Washington, D.C.: Overseas Development Council.

———. 1993. "Global Goals, Contentious Means: Issues of Multiple Conditionality." Paper presented to the Social Sciences Research Council Seminar on International Dimensions of Liberalization and Democratization, Washington, D.C., April 14–16.

O'Donnell, Guillermo, and Philippe Schmitter. 1986. "Tentative Conclusions about Uncertain Democracies." In *Transitions from Authoritarian Rule: Prospects for Democracy,* edited by Guillermo O'Donnell, Philippe Schmitter, and Lawrence Whitehead. Vol. 4. Baltimore: Johns Hopkins University Press.

O'Donnell, Guillermo, Philippe Schmitter, and Lawrence Whitehead, eds. 1986. *Transitions from Authoritarian Rule: Prospects for Democracy.* 4 vols. Baltimore: Johns Hopkins University Press.

Pellicer, Olga. 1988. "Grecia en la Comunidad Europea: 1981–1988." *Foro internacional* 31 (November-December): 195–223.

Pereira, Luis Carlos Bresser. 1993. "Economic Reforms and Cycles of State Intervention." *World Development* 21 (August): 1337–53.

Powell, G. Brigham. 1982. *Contemporary Democracies: Participation, Stability, and Violence.* Cambridge: Harvard University Press.

Pridham, Geoffrey. ed. 1984. *The New Mediterranean Democracies: Regime Tran-*

sition in Spain, Greece, and Portugal. London: Frank Cass.

———. 1990a. "Southern European Democracies on the Road to Consolidation: A Comparative Assessment of the Role of Political Parties." In *Securing Democracy: Political Parties and Democratic Consolidation in Southern Europe,* edited by Geoffrey Pridham. London: Routledge.

———. 1990b. *Securing Democracy: Political Parties and Democratic Consolidation in Southern Europe,* edited by Geoffrey Pridham. London: Routledge.

Przeworski, Adam. 1990. *Democracy and the Market: Political and Economic Reforms in Eastern Europe and Latin America.* Cambridge: Cambridge University Press.

———. 1993. "Economic Reforms, Public Opinion, and Political Institutions: Poland in the Eastern European Perspective." In *Economic Reforms in New Democracies: A Social-Democratic Approach,* edited by José Maria Maravall, Luis Carlos Bresser Pereira, and Adam Przeworski. Cambridge: Cambridge University Press.

Roniger, Luis. 1989. "Democratic Transition and Consolidation in Contemporary Southern Europe and Latin America." *International Journal of Comparative Sociology* 30.

Rostow, W. W. 1971. *The Stages of Economic Growth: A Non-Communist Manifesto.* Cambridge: Cambridge University Press.

Ruesga, Santos M., ed. 1989. *España ante el Mercado Único.* Madrid: Piramide.

Rustow, Dankart. 1970. "Transitions to Democracy." *Comparative Politics* 2 (April): 337–64.

Schmitter, Philippe. 1986. "An Introduction to Southern European Transitions from Authoritarian Rule: Italy, Portugal, Spain, and Turkey." In *Transitions from Authoritarian Rule: Prospects for Democracy,* edited by Guillermo O'Donnell, Philippe Schmitter, and Lawrence Whitehead. Vol. 1. Baltimore: Johns Hopkins University Press.

———. 1993. "The International Context: Political Conditionality and the Consolidation of Neo-Democracies." Paper presented to the Social Sciences Research Council Seminar on International Dimensions of Liberalization and Democratization, Washington, D.C. April 14–16.

Sidjanski, Dusan, and Ural Ayberk. 1990. *L'Europe du sud dans la Communauté européenne.* Paris: PUF.

Stallings, Barbara. 1990. "Politics and Economic Crisis: A Comparative Study of Chile, Peru and Columbia." In *Economic Crisis and Policy Choice,* edited by Joan Nelson. Princeton: Princeton University Press.

Thomas, Jean-Pierre. 1990. *Les politiques economiques au XXe siécle.* Paris: A. Colin.

Torres, F. S., and B. Fiesola. 1989. "Portugal, the EMS and 1992: Stabilization and Liberalization." European University Institute Working Paper 413, no. 89.

Touraine, Alain. 1988. *La parole et le sang.* Paris: Odile Jacob.

———. 1991. "Qu'est-ce que la démocratie aujourd'hui?" *Revue internationale des sciences sociales* 128 (May): 275–85.

Veremis, Thanos. 1987. "The Military." In *Political Change in Greece,* edited by Kevin Featherstone and Dimitrios Katsoudas. New York: St. Martin's Press.

Verney, Suzannah. 1990. "To Be or Not To Be within the European Community: The Party Debate and Democratic Consolidation in Greece." In *Securing Democracy: Political Parties and Democratic Consolidation in Southern Europe,* edited by Geoffrey Pridham. London: Routledge.

Waisman, Carlos H. 1989. "Argentina: Autarkik Industrialization and Illegitimacy." In *Democracy in Developing Countries,* edited by Larry Diamond, Juan C. Linz, and Seymour Martin Lipset. Boulder, Colo.: Lynne Rienner.

Whitehead, Lawrence. 1986. "'International Aspects of Democratization." In *Tran-*

sitions from Authoritarian Rule: Prospects for Democracy, edited by Guillermo O'Donnell, Philippe Schmitter, and Lawrence Whitehead. Vol. 3. Baltimore: Johns Hopkins University Press: 3–47.

———. 1988. "The Consolidation of Fragile Democracies." Paper presented to a conference of the European Consortium for Political Research.

———. 1991. *The International Context of Regime Transitions in Southern Europe*. Cambridge: Cambridge University Press.

Wurfel, David. 1990. "Transition to Political Democracy in the Philippines." In *Democratic Transition and Consolidation in Southern Europe, Latin America, and Southeast Asia*, edited by Diane Ethier. London: MacMillan.

11

Globalization and the Residual State: The Challenge to Viable Constitutionalism

PHILIP G. CERNY

Introduction

The essence of the constitutional state, and the main practical condition for its viability, lies in the fact that sovereign and autonomous political institutions are capable of deriving legitimacy from a distinct citizenry located in a defined territory. This key relationship is potentially undermined, by definition, by the globalization or transnationalization of political and economic relations in the international system. The international system did not present a fundamental challenge to the state so long as that system was based on states as the basic units or agents in the system—in other words, when the international system was also a "states system." Indeed, in such a context, the international system constituted a bulwark of the constitutional state and the ultimate proof of its sovereignty and autonomy. However, increasing transnational interpenetration, which has always been present to some degree in the international system, has the potential to transform the international system from a true states system into one in which this external bulwark is not only eroded but also fundamentally undermined.

Today, the term globalization is used to represent this process. In this chapter, I will argue that globalization is indeed presenting a growing challenge to viable constitutionalism; however, at the same time, that challenge is not seen as uniform or homogeneous.[1] Indeed, rather than representing a clearly defined transcendence of the state, globalization is a multilayered phenomenon that incorporates the state and sustains many of its ostensible functions, while at the same time altering its very essence and undermining its constitutional foundations.

Globalization is already a widely used conceptual term in international relations and international political economy, but its substance is vague. Its boundaries are unclear, and its constituent elements and multidimensional character have as yet been inadequately explored.[2] Yet, certain broad issues can be discerned, from the empirical problem of identifying "global" structures and processes, to the theoretical question of what globalization means for analyzing a range of far-reaching changes in the contemporary world. The significance of the concept of globalization is potentially paradigmatic. If we are indeed living in a globalizing or even globalized world, whether in a holistic or a more fragmented sense, how might this alter our understanding of such central concerns to the constitutional state as security, collective choice, political obligation, citizenship, legality, or even justice?

The concept of the state itself, an "essentially contested concept" in the terms of philosophical analysis, has played a key role in defining the character of both international relations and domestic political science. The classic statement of this position is found in the first paragraph of Aristotle's *Politics:*

> Observation shows us, first, that every *polis* [or state] is a species of association, and secondly, that all associations are instituted for the purpose of attaining some good—for all men do all their acts with a view to achieving something which is, in their view, a good. We may therefore hold that all associations aim at some good; and we may also hold that the particular association which is the most sovereign of all, and includes all the rest, will pursue this aim most, and will thus be directed to the most sovereign of all goods. This most sovereign and inclusive association is the *polis*, as it is called, or the political association.[3]

Michael Oakeshott described the state (or at least the version found in the Western constitutional tradition) as a "civil association"—an association the sole purpose of which is to enable other, more circumscribed social, political, and economic activities to take place, and which must continue to exist so long as people wish to pursue those other activities. This civil association is seen as distinct from an "enterprise association," which has particular ends and which can be dissolved when those ends are no longer, or unsatisfactorily, pursued.[4] For the study of international relations, the state has constituted the key unit of action, while the interaction of states has been the bottom line, the very object of inquiry. In the study of domestic political science, the constitutional state has encompassed the political system within which agents engage in politics, the very playing field on which the game is played as well as a potentially autonomous collective agent within that field.[5]

In this context, globalization constitutes a fundamental challenge to the analytical primacy of the constitutional state in both international relations and political science. It raises the distinct possibility that the state is not "the most sovereign and inclusive association." It not only suggests that some structures and processes escape the organizational and political primacy of the state, but it also implies that certain key structures and processes are becoming *both more sovereign and more inclusive* than the state. Globalization can thus be defined as the ascendancy of structures and processes that (1) are both transnational and multinational in character (more "inclusive" than the constitutional state), (2) wield more structural power in critical issue areas than the state (more "sovereign" than the state), and (3) are decisionally autonomous of the state.

Globalization occurs at different levels and affects different sectors of political, economic, and social activity unevenly. However, a critical threshold may potentially be crossed when the cumulative effect of globalization in strategically decisive issue areas undermines the general capacity of the state to pursue the "most sovereign of all goods"—the "common good" or, in Oakeshott's rather different formulation, the capacity of the state to be a true "civil association." Even if this threshold is not crossed, however, it is arguable that the state does not remain quite what it was before, and that its role becomes modified, reduced, or otherwise structurally problematic. In this context, what is useful about Oakeshott's formulation, in contrast to Aristotle's, is the way that the former conceives of the alternative form of association, the "enterprise association." This is a rather different phenomenon from Aristotle's substate "household," which is more limited in scope and range.

In a world characterized by increasing globalization, the growth of two intertwined structural trends might be hypothesized. The first of these—the eventual emergence of some sort of overarching global order to replace the anarchy of the states system—might seem more logically obvious, but is more empirically questionable. The second trend, the one addressed in this chapter, is the transformation of the state essentially from constituting a civil association into a more limited form of enterprise association, or perhaps some more complex combination of the two. Something not unlike the latter prospect was always possible in Aristotle's analysis, although this phenomenon was seen as entailing the emergence of essentially corrupt forms of the state, perverted by selfish rulers or predatory groups into tyranny, oligarchy, or mob rule. However, in a globalizing world, the hypothesis of an uneven evolution of the state toward some more limited form of association allows the observer to bring into the analysis a wider range of complex structural developments, internal tensions, and latent contradictions. It is this conceptual thicket—linking uneven globalization with the emergence of a still-embryonic "residual state"—that I propose to enter here in a tentative way.

Certain aspects of the approach taken in this chapter have been rather freely borrowed from the literature on collective choice or collective action. However, the focus of the analysis is on the structural context within which collective action takes place rather than specific processes or outcomes of choice in a given setting. As Michel Crozier and Erhard Friedberg noted in their studies of the sociology of organization in the 1970s, real individual and collective choices are not made in homogeneous or unchanging contexts. Rather, they are always made within specific "structured fields of action."[6] Differently structured fields elicit different strategies and tactics. Furthermore, such fields are themselves made up of complex, multilayered structures that incorporate distinct and often asymmetric structural levels. Finally, of course, their structural form can also change over time. This framework is applied here to the evolution of structured linkages between the state, "domestic" societies and economies, and the international system. In pursuing this overall analysis, I will focus on the changing nature and scale of goods—public goods and private goods—as a basis for political-institutional structure (expanding on Mancur Olson)[7] and on the relationship between specific assets and nonspecific assets as a basis for industrial market structure (expanding on Oliver Williamson).[8] I will argue that changing political economies of scale have fundamentally altered the structured field of action within which the state itself is constituted.

I will then briefly examine certain key structural characteristics of the nation-state as it has been known through most of the nineteenth and twentieth centuries, in both domestic and international politics. This era, I argue, represented a particular—and historically specific—phase of convergence between two analytically distinct but interdependent and empirically intertwined structural fields of action: the bureaucratic state and the Second Industrial Revolution. I suggest that most orthodox conceptualizations of the state or the political system in international relations and political science tend to reify inordinately the structural characteristics of this period. At that point, I will address a central component of the overall argument—the accelerating, if uneven, divergence between the structure of the state itself and the structure of industrial and financial markets in the globalizing world of the "Third Industrial Revolution." Finally, I will address two interwoven questions: How is the structure of the state changing in response to the globalization of political economies of scale, and what tasks are left for the residual state? Throughout the analysis, the changing role and structure of the state are seen as part of a wider process of structural change—as part not only of the uneven globalization of the world economy per se, but also of the transnationalizing of a range of decision-making processes in key public policy issue areas. It is hoped that the framework developed here may help to clarify the nature and the significance of globalization for both international relations and political science.

The Evolution of Political and Economic Structures: A Framework for Analysis

The development of the modern state and the growth of capitalism involve a complex process of interaction, a dialectic of synergy and tension, between crosscutting structural forms. Within each complex structural formation, linkages and tensions between politics and economics, and between market and hierarchy, cut across each other in complex ways. The modern nation-state, which has been at the core of the development of both domestic political science and international relations in the twentieth century, represents one such complex form. However, the evolution of the nation-state has also reflected the uneven development of these different dimensions of structure. Central to these developments are political economies of scale, in which particular political structures appear to be more or less efficient in, for example, stabilizing, regulating, controlling, or facilitating economic activities. In the late twentieth century, such political economies of scale have been shifting dramatically. A range of key economic issues today reflects the *differentiation* of economic structures both upward to the transnational and global levels and downward to the local level, with significant consequences for the structure of the state.

Goods, Assets, and Political Economies of Scale

It is fundamentally mistaken to assume, as is common in much of the political economy literature, that state structures are essentially hierarchical and bureaucratic, while economic structures are based essentially on market exchange.[9] On the contrary, both are complex compounds of market and hierarchy. Furthermore, the specific characteristics of each market-hierarchy mix as found in a particular place at a particular time, are also the outcome of the interaction of politics and economics in a distinct matrix. This latter distinction becomes increasingly crucial as scale shift occurs, given that political structures (centered on the state) and economic structures (centered upon firms and sectors) appear as separate institutions in more complex societies. Thus, evolution of political economic structures results from the interaction of independent changes along each dimension (market-hierarchy and politics-economics), and from complex feedback effects that occur as the consequence of that interaction.

Approached in this way, conceiving of the state as the highest form of political association or as an ongoing manifestation of "civil association" appears to be fragile. For a state to approximate this ideal role would require that it have the real and effective organizational capacity to shape, influence, and control designated economic activities—that is, to stabilize, regulate, promote, and facilitate economic activity generally, as well as to exercise other forms of politically desired or structurally feasible control over more specific, targeted processes of production and exchange. By real and effective, I mean in such a way as to enable economic agents to produce goods as efficiently as possible—given available resources and factors of capital, the current state of economic and technological knowledge, and so forth. Of course, it has been all too often the case in human history that such activities have been carried out in spite of the state rather than because of it. This is particularly true of predatory and parasitic states, although it could of course be argued, as Thomas Hobbes did, that at times even such states provide a certain basic stability that might be socially or economically preferable to the chaos of a Hobbesian state of nature or the ravages of continual external warfare. Nevertheless, the function of the state as a civil association is historically problematic—and, I would argue, time-bound—rather than given. This problematic was manifested in a particularly central way in the "modern" capitalist state as it developed through the nineteenth and much of the twentieth centuries; furthermore, the equation is today undergoing fundamental change in the context of globalization.

The core of this problematic—the complex interaction of political and economic structures and of market and hierarchy—lies in the character of the different kinds of material and nonmaterial resources and values that are needed or desired by individuals and by society, that is, in the different kinds of goods or assets (including services) produced and exchanged, whether through the state or through nonstate economic mechanisms. It is standard, in different contexts, to start from a distinction between two main polar types of goods or assets. The best-known distinction of this sort in political science and international relations is Olson's contrast between the notion of public goods, which are indivisible in crucial ways and from the use of which specific people cannot be easily or effectively excluded, on the one hand, and private goods, which are divisible and excludable, on the other. In between, and deriving from the interaction of, these polar types, stands a range of crucial intermediate categories of semipublic or quasi-private mixed goods.[10]

A second and more recent distinction, found primarily in institutional economics, is the one Williamson makes between specific assets and nonspecific assets.[11] This distinction is based on two dimensions. The first dimension, which needs little elaboration here, is that of technological economies of scale in production, distribution, or exchange; this means that the value of the entity kept as a whole would in theory be far more valuable than its breakup price. The second dimension is that of transaction costs—those costs incurred in the process of attempting to fix an "efficiency price" for an asset and actually to exchange it for another, substitute asset. A specific asset is essentially an asset for which there is no easily available substitute—its exchange involves either high transaction costs or large economies of scale, or both. Therefore, efficiency prices and ready markets may be difficult or even impossible to find.

The significance of these distinctions is that different types of goods or assets are said to be more or less efficiently provided through different structural forms or institutions, rather than simply through abstract economic processes. Such a broadly structural-institutional approach can, in theory, be applied either to the narrowly political sphere or to the narrowly economic sphere—or to the complex structural relations cutting across the two spheres, as is the case both in collective action or public choice theory and in this chapter. Williamson refers to these different structural forms quite straightforwardly as "market" and "hierarchy"; for Olson, public goods cannot be efficiently provided through a market, for there will always be "free riders" who escape paying their fair share of the costs of providing such goods and thereby load extra costs onto others. Only authoritative structures and processes (the state) make it possible for costs to be efficiently recuperated from the users of public goods. On the other hand, of course, private goods can be most efficiently provided through market mechanisms, as public provision would create monopolistic effects, raising costs, and misallocating resources.

In analogous fashion, for Williamson, specific assets—those difficult or impossible to trade efficiently on a market, because they are characterized by technological economies of scale or high transaction costs—are also more efficiently organized and managed authoritatively, through hierarchy. Of course, for Williamson the authoritative unit he is considering is not the state but the firm. Such authoritative allocation is done through long-term contracting (keeping the same collaborators) and decision making by managerial fiat (integration, merger, cartel, etc.) rather than through the short-term, "recurrent contracting" of marketable, easily substitutable, nonspecific assets. Whereas efficient regulation of the market for the latter requires merely post hoc legal adjudication through contract law and the courts, the former requires increasing degrees of proactive, institutionalized governance in the allocation of resources and values. The most extreme form of efficient hierarchy is found in the natural monopoly, but various different kinds of structural integration—distinct mixes of market and hierarchy—may be judged to suit particular mixes of specific and nonspecific assets.

In the context of the relationship between political and economic structures then, the sort of legitimate, holistic political authority that both Aristotle and Oakeshott would consider characteristic of the *polis* or state is actually a reflection of an (Olsonian) commitment to provide public goods efficiently, or of the (Williamsonian) presence of extensive specific assets as embodied in people (human capital), "immobile factors of capital" such as infrastructure, or the promotion of certain types of large-scale integrated industrial processes. Of course, traditional conceptions of the state also extend to other specific factors, especially the defense of national territory, the protection and inculcation of a common culture, national ideology or constitutional norms, the preservation of collective unity in the face of "the other," and the maintenance of a widely acceptable and functioning legal system. These tasks and activities, in Williamson's terms, would normally be more efficiently carried out through predominantly hierarchical institutions—a classic conundrum for public decision making in a liberal democracy.[12]

However, as both Olson and Williamson point out in different ways, the core of political conflict and intellectual debate does not so much revolve around generally accepted categories of public goods and specific assets on the one hand,[13] or indisputably private goods and nonspecific assets on the other, as around the provision of goods and assets that fall between the two poles. In this context, political power is an epiphenomenon not only of the requirements of constructing differentiated, relatively efficient structures within which to provide public goods and to minimize transaction costs in the maintenance of specific assets, but also of managing the system of producing and exchanging nonspecific assets and private goods. This system itself constitutes a public good and forms the essence of viable constitutionalism.

Scale Shift in the Evolution of Political-Economic Structures

In the real world, how such complex political-economic structures develop is mainly through a continuing process of bricolage or tinkering. Broad constitutional change usually emerges in response to more ideological and directly political pressures and concerns. Indeed, the historical weakness of attempts to design viable constitutions reflects the normal lack of focus of constitution builders on the structural characteristics of the political-economic matrix. Occasional paradigmatic change does occur, however, when the gap between the requirements for providing both public goods and private goods widens beyond the capacity of the institutional structure to reconcile the two over the medium to long term, although these shifts are usually not constitutional changes in the narrow sense. Such major transformations are reflected in historical changes of scale—or what are here called political economies of scale—in the society and economy. Changes in political economies of scale can be most easily summed up by comparing the differences between small-scale and large-scale societies in a schematic if highly oversimplified way.

At one end of the spectrum, then, the smaller the scale of an economy, the more the public and the private are likely to overlap and coincide; they thereby become inextricably intertwined through the same, all-embracing social structures in a quasi-automatic fashion; these social structures in turn influence and shape the structure of the overall system. Such mechanisms and institutions remain relatively undifferentiated. The outstanding exemplar of how this management system works can be seen in the role of kinship as studied by anthropologists. The nature of subsistence and early surplus production and reproduction in small, relatively isolated—mainly village—communities usually leads to the emergence of a single, relatively homogeneous political and economic power structure, in which economic and political power are all part of the same more or less hierarchical system.[14]

In contrast, however, the larger the structural scale of an economy (perhaps national, regional, or global), the more some of what previously seemed to constitute public goods or specific assets in a smaller-scale context are in effect transformed into private goods or nonspecific assets, and a new structured settlement must be found through bricolage. Sociological theorists have long identified structural differentiation as the core process of the development of societies,[15] and analogous processes of political and economic differentiation are the key to understanding how political economies of scale shift over time. As Raymond Cohen and Elman Service have pointed out, this was true of the early emergence of state-like structures in agricultural societies, whether the early state emerged as the result of predation or power grabbing by a single group, on the one hand, or from the development of a more "organic" (Durkheimian) division of labor, on the other.[16] Later, as Douglas North among others has argued, the modern state, whatever its specific historical origin, developed not only from the need to provide appropriate levels of new and more broadly defined public goods but also in order to create appropriate conditions for stabilizing and promoting rapidly expanding market processes.[17] These structural innovations originally developed in order to enable postfeudal societies to survive and compete in the fierce military and economic struggles of that period, as embryonic state societies evolved through dynastic consolidation to absolutism, mercantilism, and eventually industrial capitalism.[18]

In effect, the central process leading to the development of the modern capitalist nation-state involved a complex shift of both political and economic structures—structures increasingly differentiated from each other, as well as internally differentiated between market and hierarchical forms—to a broader scale. For a whole series of reasons, some accidental, some linked through similar logics of structural development, each set of structures eventually converged at the level—on the scale—of the nation. Increasing interaction, through both economic competition and military conflict, between states was a crucial part of this process of convergence. In order to foster the expanding provision of private goods, the development of national markets and national production processes was promoted by otherwise quite different types of states.

In this process, states themselves came to undertake a range of general social, economic, and political functions—notably stabilization of the social order, promotion of a national culture, the establishment (and defense) of more clearly defined territorial borders, increased regulation of economic activities, and the development and maintenance of a legal system to enforce contracts and private property. The expansion of these general functions of the state was, of course, closely linked to the demand for constitutional forms of government. However, states also increasingly took on a range of narrower, more specific functions such as public works, promotion and protection of particular industries, the development of monopolies, building infrastructure, and the like. In doing this, agents of the nation-state came to exercise a certain, if variable, amount of control over capital within its borders in order to reconcile profitmaking with the increase of national wealth.

More important for the argument here, however, is the way in which specific historical, structural changes in technology, production, and finance can be seen to feed into the process of scale shift. The development of the nation-state in the late nineteenth and early twentieth centuries was inextricably intertwined with the emergence of the so-called Second Industrial Revolution.[19] The scenario is perhaps familiar enough in itself, but its significance for the argument here lies in the contrast between this Second Industrial Revolution state and the later era of globalization and the "Third Industrial Revolution."

The Second Industrial Revolution is associated with the development of advanced forms of mass production, the increasing application of science and scientific methods both to production processes and to management techniques, and the expansion of technological economies of scale—often called "Fordism." This era—along with the emergence of the Second Industrial Revolution state—is generally acknowledged to have taken off with the expansion of railroad systems from small lines to national networks. In the United States, oligopolistic firms, heavily subsidized by the federal government (mainly through land grants), emerged as the core of the new heavy industrial capital, as America in the 1880s became the world's largest industrial producer. In other newly industrializing countries of the day—not only in Europe and later in Japan, but to a greater or lesser extent throughout the world as emerging states sought to industrialize—a new industrial state (or a more or less successful version thereof) took a more direct role in tying its economies and societies together with these "bands of steel." The steel industry, and later chemicals, automobiles, and a wide range of other large-scale heavy industries grew up, generally in highly favorable political and bureaucratic conditions. Central to this era was the development of large-scale "finance capital," whether under the wing of the state (as Lenin and Rudolf Hilferding used the term) or in a more freewheeling liberal environment, as in the United States.[20] Along with these developments came national-scale processing and packing industries, integrated distribution systems centered first on the railroad and later on roads and motor vehicles, and the emergence of chains of large wholesale and retail firms. The rise of the modern corporation and modern scientific management were part and parcel of this era.[21]

In this environment, state promotion of industrial development unified the nation-state and created conditions for an intensification of national economic competition. In the United States, with its huge domestic market, this process involved relatively less direct state intervention, whereas in Germany and Japan the state was at the heart of large-scale capital. Max Weber's conception of modern forms of social organization—the development of large-scale political and economic bureaucracies[22]—as well as Karl Marx's belief that the end result would be a top-heavy monopoly capitalism shored up by the state, were essentially Second Industrial Revolution theories. Britain's decline was inextricably intertwined with its inability to develop much beyond the structures of a First Industrial Revolution state (a status that it had never really had to share).[23] The subsequent development of the Second Industrial Revolution state can be traced forward to the intense national competition of the 1930s, most strikingly embodied in the rise of fascism and Stalinism. Indeed, it has been argued that this worldwide scale shift in political-economic structures made possible what Karl Polanyi called "the great transformation"[24]—from the First Industrial Revolution's attempt to establish a worldwide self-regulating market to the corporatist, social democratic, national welfare state that germinated in the 1930s, and became the dominant form after World War II and during the long boom from the early 1950s to the early 1970s.

In the Second Industrial Revolution state, then, both political and economic structures converged on an increasingly centralized model concerned with an increasing range of specifically economic functions: promoting and maintaining large-scale mass production industries, providing the requisite levels of regulation and demand management to ensure, in particular, that their extensive specific assets would not be undermined by economic downturns, and creating not only mass markets but also a disciplined work force (increasingly union organized, except where these were banned in order to enforce even more direct forms of labor discipline) to keep the factories humming.

From an early point, of course, a fundamental bifurcation occurred *within* the process of scale shift between distinct models of Second Industrial Revolution political-economic structures: on the one hand, an open, relatively liberal, free-trading model in the tradition of Adam Smith and David Ricardo, and on the other, a closed, relatively bureaucratic-authoritarian, autarchic model, in the tradition of Alexander Hamilton and Friedrich List. Significant aspects of this bifurcation remained after the defeat of the capitalist autarchic empires in World War II.[25] However, the fact that the open model became hegemonic at an international level through the political and economic dominance of the United States opened the way for greater eventual globalization.

The Increasing Differentiation of Political and Economic Structures

This account of the convergence of the political and economic structures of the Second Industrial Revolution is, of course, a schematic oversimplification. The first problem with such an account is that it does not take much notice of tensions and contradictions *within* the political-economic structures of the Second Industrial Revolution; indeed, such tensions and contradictions, an inherent part of increasing structural differentiation, have been present virtually from the start of the state development process. The second problem is that such a formulation cannot anticipate new developments that would create pressures for fundamental structural change beyond the Second Industrial Revolution model. The rest of this section will briefly address the first problem. The remainder of the chapter will examine how the interaction of existing structural tensions and new pressures for change—both of which (but especially the latter) have been inextricably intertwined with the process of globalization—has created a disjunction between political and economic structures, and between market and hierarchy, to which the state, in broader historical terms, is only just beginning to adjust. Instead of a broad convergence of politics and economics, and of market and hierarchy, then, there has been an increasing divergence along both of these axes since the high water mark of the Second Industrial Revolution model after World War II.

The tensions and contradictions embedded in the long-term state development process—and therefore in the Second Industrial Revolution state, too—were of two kinds: endogenous and exogenous. On the endogenous level, the principal economic pressures derived from the competition of different fractions of capital and increasingly differentiated processes of production and consumption. The competition of capitals was not so much between real capitalist firms as it was between sectors rooted in different asset structures and producing and marketing different types of goods. Large-scale production sectors characterized by high levels of specific assets, especially natural monopolies and sectors producing capital goods, were best placed to benefit structurally from state promotion and procurement and from centralized structures of public and private finance capital. Small-scale sectors characterized primarily by nonspecific assets were structurally oriented toward other small producers and final consumers and found their relationships with the state or with high finance nonexistent, irrelevant, or threatening to their markets. The United States was probably the only country that, because of the size of its home market, could effectively cater to both sectors through its political-economic structures.

The outcome of these issues in different countries was partially determined through various distinct forms of class-state interdependence that evolved over time, as described by Pierre Birnbaum.[26] At the same time, however, the tension between these economic sectors was interwoven with political and ideological clashes across a range of social and economic groups supporting different forms of authoritarianism and democracy—the major political form of tension in the constitutional development of the nation-state. Because of both types of tension—economic and political—the control span of the state qua hierarchy was continually under challenge, even in the most outwardly authoritarian of states, and failures of hierarchy to work efficiently were commonplace.

More important in the long run, however, was the interaction of these endogenous tensions with exogenous ones. On the exogenous level, the principal forms of tension were those between the nationalization of warfare and the gradual but uneven internationalization of civilian production and exchange. Until World War I, this tension was contained for the newly emerging great powers—Germany, Japan, and the United States—by the convergence characteristic of the Second Industrial Revolution model described earlier. The dynamics of economic competition and those of military rivalry were not so different with regard to many key issues, and the nation-state constituted the predominant (although not the only) organizational unit for both activities.[27] The international economic instability of the 1920s and the Great Depression of the 1930s, however, represented a fundamental loss of control by states, both authoritarian and liberal, over international economic processes.[28] The immediate result was, of course, the rise of more intensely authoritarian autarchic empires and the withdrawal of even liberal states behind trade barriers as states tried to recapture hierarchical control over their economic processes. That the results of this process may have had a silver lining can perhaps be seen in Polanyi's *Great Transformation.* However, other tensions would eventually undermine that transformation too.

The history of capitalism even in the era of the Second Industrial Revolution was one of internationalization even if not yet one of globalization. Britain's relatively free-trading empire, increasingly reinforced (and later replaced) by America's deepening foreign policy tradition of the Open Door,[29] created productive financial and trade links that, although often backed by the state, drew the Second Industrial Revolution state out of its national shell and into an international web of linkages. As Germany attempted to recreate state economic and political power through Nazism, *Lebensraum*, and the New Order, as Japan pursued the expansion of the Greater East Asia Co-Prosperity Sphere, and as Britain retreated behind Imperial Preferences, the internationalists, who were in the ascendancy in the Roosevelt administration in the mid-to-late 1930s,[30] developed the aim of establishing an arms-length, increasingly multinational, free-trading system after the war.[31] At the same time, the outcome of World War II fundamentally altered the nature of warfare, shifting its scale from nation-state–based multipolar confrontation to permanent bipolar alliances and integration into mutually exclusive socioeconomic systems. The character of American hegemony after the war, based on multilateral international economics and integrated defense systems, helped to ensure that the system that developed was not dependent upon the continuance of American hegemony per se for its survival. Basically, free trade managed to outlive the recession and the new protectionism of the 1970s and endured even after America's relative decline and predatory behavior had perhaps hastened the demise of the Bretton Woods system. Meanwhile, Charles de Gaulle's attempt in the 1960s to revive the notion of purely national, nonintegrated defense had petered out even before his exit from power.[32]

Thus, although political consciousness remained overwhelmingly national, both security and economic structures, especially the latter, became increasingly internationalized. In this way, the later stages of the Second Industrial Revolution, which paradoxically came to full flower in the long boom from the early 1950s to the early 1970s, also saw the growth of tensions leading to the decay of the Second Industrial Revolution state, the "modern" capitalist nation-state of social and political theory, economic history, classical Marxism, and the like. By the time John Kenneth Galbraith published *The New Industrial State* in the late 1960s,[33] the relatively monolithic political-economic "technostructure" he depicted was already out of date. But that decay did not result merely from the contradictions within the preexisting system. It also involved the interaction of those contradictions with a new phase of scale shift in both the national and international economy. The shift of the world economy to a global scale in trade and finance and to the Third Industrial Revolution in terms of production structures has created new sources of divergence and differentiation between political and economic structures, and between market and hierarchy. The efficient provision of both public and private goods, specific and nonspecific assets, became highly problematic in this new environment, leading at first to political polarization and later to attempts to "reinvent government." It is in this context that I will now turn to globalization, the changing structure of collective action, and the emergence of the residual state.

Globalization, Economic Differentiation, and the Structure of Collective Action

The economic structure of the world today is not only in the process of changing rapidly; it has already changed dramatically since the 1950s. Globalization has altered the scale of the "structured field of action" in which the relationship between the provision of different kinds of goods and assets is shaped. Much of what constituted public goods in the Second Industrial Revolution are either no longer controllable by the state because they are transnational in structure, or have essentially become private goods in a wider world marketplace. The Third Industrial Revolution has also profoundly altered the structure of both public and private goods and specific and nonspecific assets through a process of differentiation within production processes and through the segmentation of markets. The globalization of finance has increasingly divorced finance capital from the state. In this context, political control, stabilization, regulation, promotion, and facilitation of economic activities have become increasingly fragmented. From international regimes[34] to local pressures and subaltern forms of resistance,[35] new "circuits of power" are emerging,[36] not so much to challenge the state as to overlap with it, cut across it, and fragment it.

Globalization and the Scale of Public Goods

The most important dimension of convergence between political and economic structures in the Second Industrial Revolution state was the dominance of national-level organizational apparatuses in each sphere and the development of sophisticated forms of organized interpenetration cutting across the two spheres. Expanding national bureaucracies continually took on new social and economic tasks, while national capital found that the national state provided a congenial and appropriate framework around which to organize. Political consciousness and growing demands from below emerged and consolidated through (even if sometimes in opposition to) the playing field of the national constitutional state. Even Marxist proletarian internationalism, especially under the revisionist influence of Lenin,[37] became increasingly focused, in both theoretical and organizational terms, on taking power and creating socialism by means of appropriating the apparatuses of the state—the dictatorship of the proletariat eventually transmogrifying into Stalin's "socialism in one country." In this context, public goods were perceived by all interested parties as national-level phenomena, even when they were externalized through formal—or later, increasingly informal—imperial expansion. Such perceptions have been crucial in forming the way the modern state has been conceptualized, and they persist to the present day.

These public goods have been essentially of three kinds.[38] The first involved the establishment of a workable market framework for the ongoing operation of the system as a whole, which I call regulatory goods. This included the establishment and protection of private (and public) property rights, a stable currency system, the abolition of internal barriers to production and exchange within the national market, the standardization of a range of facilitating structures such as a system of weights and measures, a legal system to sanction and enforce contracts and adjudicate disputes, a regulatory system to stabilize and coordinate economic activities, a system of trade protection, and various facilities that could be mobilized to counteract system-threatening market failures, such as "lender of last resort" facilities and emergency powers.

Public goods of the second kind involved the development of various specific (direct or indirect) state-controlled or state-sponsored activities of production and distribution (called here productive/distributive goods). These have included full or partial public ownership of certain industries, the direct or indirect provision of infrastructure and public services from sewerage and urban planning to military and diplomatic support for firms operating overseas, direct or indirect involvement in finance capital (including publicly owned or state-sponsored long-term credit banks), and, most obviously, public subsidies of myriad kinds.

The third kind of public goods were what can be called redistributive goods, the provision of which resulted from the expanding political and public policy demands of emerging social classes, economic interests, and political parties. These demands evoked state responses both in the context of attempts to build national solidarity in relatively authoritarian systems, as in Bismarck's Germany, and as the result of pressures exercised through liberal democratic parties and pressure groups. Redistributive goods have included direct health and welfare services, employment policies, systems for corporatist bargaining, environmental protection, and the like—indeed, the main apparatus of the national welfare state. Clearly, the provision of all three of these kinds of goods was inextricably intertwined with the converging structures of the national economy and the nation-state, and rested on the interweaving of large-scale specific assets between bureaucratic structures and the structures of capital.

The provision of all three of these categories of public goods, however, has become problematic for national states to supply or foster, directly or indirectly, in a globalizing world. Regulatory goods are an obvious case. In a world of relatively open trade, financial deregulation, and the increasing impact of information technology, property rights are increasingly difficult for the state to establish and maintain. Cross-border industrial espionage, counterfeiting of products, and copyright violations have made the multilateral protection of intellectual property rights a focal point of international disputes and a controversial cornerstone of the Uruguay Round negotiations. International capital flows, and the proliferation of offshore financial centers and tax havens, have made the ownership of firms and their ability to internally allocate resources through transfer pricing and the like increasingly opaque to national tax and regulatory authorities. Traditional forms of trade protectionism are both easily bypassed and counterproductive. Currency exchange rates and interest rates are set in rapidly globalizing marketplaces, and governments attempt to manipulate them often at their peril; as Margaret Thatcher has been aptly quoted, "You can't buck the markets." Legal rules are increasingly easily evaded, and attempts to extend the legal reach of the national state through the development of "extraterritoriality" are ineffective and hotly disputed.

Finally, the ability of firms, market actors, and competing parts of the national state apparatus itself to defend and expand their economic and political turf through activities such as transnational policy networking and "regulatory arbitrage"—the capacity of industrial and financial sectors to "whipsaw" the state apparatus by pushing state agencies into a process of competitive deregulation, or what economists call "competition in laxity"—has both undermined the control span of the state from without and fragmented it from within.[39] It must of course be emphasized that real or potential inefficiencies in the provision of regulatory public goods have much wider ramifications than merely for the provision of public goods per se, because they constitute the framework within which private goods as well as other public goods are provided in the wider economy and society. Indeed, the provision of regulatory public goods by the national state is inextricably intertwined with constitutionalism.

Perhaps a more familiar theme in the public goods literature, however, has been the impact of globalization on the capacity of the state to provide productive/distributive public goods. The most visible aspect of this impact has been the crisis of public ownership of strategic industries and the wave of privatization that has characterized the 1980s and 1990s. Once again, there are both political and economic scale factors at work. At one level, such industries are no longer perceived as "strategic"—that is, as core industries without national control of which a national economy would become both structurally and, indeed, militarily weak. The steel, chemicals, railroad, motor vehicle, aircraft, shipbuilding, and basic energy industries were once seen as the core set of strategic industries.

The internationalization of these industries—with foreign investment going in both directions—has made even high-technology industries producing components for weaponry fundamentally internationalized. Economists today tend to dismiss orthodox national security arguments for the restriction of foreign direct investment in many militarily sensitive areas of, for example, research and development or even the production of weapons components.[40] At the same time, at another level, the state is regarded as structurally inappropriate for this task. Public ownership is now widely regarded as so economically inefficient—the "lame-duck syndrome"—as to render counterproductive its once-perceived benefits of permitting national planning, providing employment, or increasing social justice. Third World countries, too, have increasingly rejected "delinkage" and import substitution industrialization and embraced export promotion industrialization—thereby imbricating their economies even more closely with the global economic order—as the best way to counter neocolonialism.[41] And even where public ownership has been expanded or maintained, its ostensible rationale has been as part of a drive for international competitiveness and not as an exercise in national exclusiveness, as in France in the early 1980s.[42]

The same can be said for more traditional forms of industrial policy, such as state subsidies to industry, public procurement of nationally produced goods and services, or trade protectionism. The core of the current public and academic debates on issues of industrial policy is precisely whether it is possible, given the internationalization of production and distribution, for governments to have any "efficient" role in the industrial policy arena. Monetarist and private sector supply-side economists, of course, deny that the state has ever been in a position to intervene in these matters in a truly efficient way; they also argue that the possibility of playing such a role in today's globalized world has utterly evaporated in the era of "quicksilver capital" flowing across borders.[43] However, even social liberal and other relatively interventionist economists nowadays regard the battle to retain the very idea of the "national economy" to be lost, and view states as condemned to tinker around the edges.[44]

The outer limits of effective action by the state in this environment are usually seen to comprise its capacity to promote a relatively favorable investment climate for transnational capital by providing a circumscribed range of public goods or specific assets, described as immobile factors of capital. Such potentially manipulable factors are often thought to include human capital (the skills, experience, education, and training of the work force); infrastructure (from public transportation to high-tech information highways); support for a critical mass of research and development activities; the basic public services necessary for a good quality of life for those working in middle- to high-level positions in otherwise footloose (transnationally mobile) firms and sectors; and the maintenance of a public policy environment favorable to investment (and profit making) by such companies, whether domestic or foreign-owned. I have elsewhere called this mixture the competition state,[45] but here it forms the core of what I refer to, perhaps more pessimistically, as the residual state.

Finally, of course, globalization has had a severe impact, both direct and indirect, on the possibility for the state efficiently to provide redistributive public goods. Corporatist bargaining and employment policies are breaking down everywhere, although somewhat unevenly, in the face of international pressure for wage restraint and flexible working practices. Although developed countries have generally not found it possible to reduce the overall weight of the welfare state in the economy, there has been a highly significant transformation in the way that welfare funds are being spent. There has been a shift in both political emphasis and funding in many countries from the maintenance of freestanding social and public services to the provision of unemployment compensation and entitlement programs. This shift has, of course, been increasingly necessary in financial terms as the latter have ballooned as a consequence of industrial downsizing, increasing inequalities of wealth, the aging of the population in industrial societies, and so on, thereby tending to crowd out funding for other services. Lastly, the most salient new sector of redistributive public goods, environmental protection, is particularly threatening to the structural capacity of the national state. Environmental problems are particularly transnational in character; air and water pollution or the rape of natural resources do not respect borders.[46] Therefore, in all three of the principal categories of public goods, the increased provision of which characterized the consolidation of the Second Industrial Revolution state, globalization has undercut the structural capacity of the national state in all but a few areas.

The Third Industrial Revolution and the State in the Changing Global Context

Particularly central to this transformation, however, has been not merely the changing scale of public goods per se, but the changing technological and institutional context in which *all* goods are increasingly being produced and exchanged. The so-called Third Industrial Revolution is characterized by several profound and far-reaching structural changes that have been major factors in the globalization of economic structures. As the character of public goods is less controllable by the national state, so the character of the mix of specific and nonspecific assets in industrial production and finance has shifted in even more complex ways. States and policymakers are increasingly having to experiment with new policy structures and techniques—what in the United States has been called reinventing government—in order to cope with the fragmentation of the structural environment.

The Third Industrial Revolution has a wide range of characteristics, but the ones most relevant to our concern with scale shift include five trends in particular, each of which is inextricably bound up with the others. The first is the development of flexible manufacturing systems, and their spread not only to new industries but to older ones as well. The second is the changing hierarchical form of firms (and bureaucracies) to what has been called lean management. The third is the capacity of decision-making structures to monitor the actions of all levels of management and of the labor force far more closely through the use of information technology, and thereby to use such methods as performance indicators far more widely. The fourth characteristic is the segmentation of markets in a more complex consumer society. Finally, the Third Industrial Revolution has been profoundly shaped by the emergence of increasingly autonomous and global financial markets and institutions.

The issue of flexible manufacturing systems has been at the heart of the new comparative and international political economy over the past decade and a half. Given the huge amount of fixed capital advanced industrial states had inherited from the various phases of the Second Industrial Revolution (and Britain from the first)—some of it having been built as recently as the 1950s and 1960s—a large amount of restructuring, or what Joseph Schumpeter called creative destruction of fixed capital stock, would be required before the next phase of capital investment could take off. Analyses were similar for Europe and the United States. The legacy of Second Industrial Revolution industries led businesspeople in what were rapidly becoming top-heavy sectors to look to the state for increasing relief and protection. The first reaction of the state, still shaped by the experiences and characterized by the structures of Second Industrial Revolution bureaucracies, was to attempt to take industry under its wing again in the traditional way. But the more open international environment developing since World War II simply made such measures increasingly counterproductive. International competition from flexible, high-tech economies like Japan and some other newly industrializing countries[47]—whose governments promoted such flexibility—seemed to turn decline into a vicious circle.

Flexible production itself requires not an integration, but a differentiation, of both distinct stages of the production process and of increasingly complex and variable production line tasks themselves. Rather than being managed authoritatively through the command structures of a hierarchical firm, flexible production is organized through a range of processes characterized by what Williamson would call recurrent contracting. These processes include increased subcontracting (rather than direct control) of the manufacturing and supply of peripheral components of the production process, increasingly autonomous labor and management teams charged with evolving more efficient ways of carrying out their particular tasks ("intrapreneurship," Japanese-style quality circles, etc.), and the shortening of process and product cycles in both technological and organizational terms—including "just in time" procurement of parts supplies and the ability to switch both machines and workers from product to product and from task to task.

This structure obviously requires not merely a work force both flexible and highly trained (a potential problem in itself), but also the latest in high-technology production techniques such as robots, reprogrammable machine tools, and computerized production lines. These types of production facilities have been thought to require a range of new conditions to work efficiently, including such factors as the availability of "green field" sites—away from the decaying fixed capital and unionized work forces of the Second Industrial Revolution industries in the Rust Belt—and proximity to other similarly structured industries. In such locations, cross-fertilization between the experiences of workers and managers, the development of product improvements in related fields, and the learning curve of process innovation can create a virtuous circle or synergy among flexible firms. The electronics industry was the example, and Silicon Valley in California was the exemplar. Furthermore, such developments were not great respecters of borders, and flexible production has been identified as a crucial element in the internationalization of production and of competition.

The implications of this trend have been analyzed at several levels since the late 1970s and early 1980s, especially by political scientists, political economists, and sociologists on the center-left (and some on the right, too) in the United States and Europe. John Zysman, anticipating much of the later literature, demonstrated how the attempt by the French government in the 1970s to promote the development of the electronics industry (through the Plan Calcul), in the same way that it had in earlier years successfully promoted the Second Industrial Revolution industries of oil and steel, failed because of the different structures of the industries involved.[48] Several authors, including Robert Reich, argued in the early 1980s that restructuring the U.S. economy would require a thorough-going change not only in the organization of industry and of the state, but also in the economic and political culture of the country.[49]

Zysman and Laura Tyson's *American Industry in International Competition* examined the challenges to competitiveness in a range of key industrial sectors and diagnosed a lack of flexibility as the main problem.[50] They suggested that a proactive state should be able to develop a capacity to manipulate the structure of competitive advantages held by different industrial sectors in order to promote and facilitate the necessary adjustment processes. Michael Piore and Charles Sabel's *The Second Industrial Divide* examined the experience of craft production in Europe, and argued that the flexible specialization exhibited there also had lessons for American adjustment. These approaches were also reflected not only in sociological analysis, partly influenced by sea changes in neo- and post-Marxism, but in certain trends in economic analysis too, from the more radical Regulation School in France to the new institutional economics of Williamson and others in the United States. The rapid development of post-Fordist social and economic structures has been analyzed extensively across the social sciences.[51]

The right, especially in the Reagan and Thatcher years, spoke much the same language about the need for flexible structures; this neoliberal right believed, however, that deregulation and market forces rather than proactive industrial policy constituted the only way to achieve this. Indeed, their distrust of state power in general was rooted in their opposition to, and skepticism of, the capacity of the state—essentially the Second Industrial Revolution state, which in their view could never change its spots—to efficiently intervene at all. It must be noted, however, that certain groups within the right rejected the neoliberal analysis, not in favor of the welfare state as such, but in terms of a more active, pro-business industrial policy approach; politicians such as Michael Heseltine in Britain and observers like Chalmers Johnson in the United States were particularly prominent in their opposition to neoliberal orthodoxy.

Closely linked with the development of more flexible production processes was the question of the structure of firms themselves. In addition to experimenting with new forms of differentiation outside the core firm (as with subcontracting), managerial theorists focused on the flexibilization of the bureaucratic layers of the firms themselves. This did not simply require the firing of layers of cadres, although downsizing has become an increasingly central feature of the change. It also required altering the consciousness of managers themselves. Although management literature has always been filled with exhortations to such qualities as excellence, the emphasis in the scientific management era of the Second Industrial Revolution was on the efficient division of responsibilities among individuals who were highly skilled at discrete tasks.

In the Third Industrial Revolution, by contrast, two sorts of individuals became the totems of the new excellence: brilliant innovator-managers such as Steven Jobs or William Gates, who could single-handedly envision and construct new processes and products from outside the established structures (the entrepreneurs); and the leaders of autonomous teams *within* large but increasingly flexible organizations who could change the direction of those institutions (the intrapreneurs). "Lean, mean management" became the buzzwords of the new industrial structures. Even IBM, which had long attempted to incorporate the new structures piecemeal without relinquishing the base it had built up in its Second Industrial Revolution–style managerial hierarchy and its secure and reliable workforce, has eventually had to adjust—both by dramatically increasing subcontracting and, more recently, by extensive downsizing. In Williamson's terms, what had previously been built up as specific assets, from a skilled and loyal work force to large-scale mass production facilities—and which had been prized as such—were increasingly being destroyed or transformed into nonspecific assets that could be exchanged on the market. The extent of the restructuring of firms and production processes in the developed world and in the Third World alike has been dramatic, and, of course, such firms are psychologically as well as materially better prepared and more eager to participate in world markets.

At the heart of these processes of flexibilization of both production processes and firms themselves has been the explosive development of information technology. Olson argued that one of the key factors that made collective action difficult in large groups (this issue being the main focus of his book) was the inability of large groups to monitor the behavior of members who might be tempted (or determined) to free ride—that is, to use public goods without paying their share of the costs. The rapid development of electronic computer and communications technology has, of course, transformed this problem. The establishment of computer networking has established a form of control that could not have been dreamed in the Second Industrial Revolution, and it is bridging one of the oldest institutional conundrums in history and theory, that between centralization and decentralization.

In this context, the ability to coordinate centralized and therefore coherent strategic decision making, with decentralized and therefore innovative and cutting-edge operational decision making, was for Williamson the central predicament in setting up the organizational structure of the firm, in determining the most efficient relationship between market and hierarchy. Today, workers and lower-level managers are increasingly left on their own to learn how to carry out their tasks more productively and competitively; however, at the same time, a more discreet but more powerful Orwellian Big Brother—mainly in the form of accountants and other financial managers—is watching them like hawks from a distance through their ever more complex and flexible information networks. This capacity to monitor seemingly autonomous activity also bridges the gap between public and private goods, enabling central decision makers to harness the initiatives of peripheral managers and workers to the wider aims of the seemingly more amorphous organization. This monitoring capability also leaps national borders and brings firms, markets, and consumers into a single, global production process in an increasing number of sectors.

But these aspects of the Third Industrial Revolution—flexibilization of production, firm structure, and monitoring—are only part of the picture. They represent the supply side of the equation. The other side is the development of ever more complex consumer societies of advanced capitalism and the resulting segmentation of markets. This reflects the convergence of two developments. The first is the technological capacity to produce flexibly—the capacity of business to produce at the appropriate scale, however multilayered. The second, however, is the increasing differentiation of the class system in advanced capitalist societies.

In the Second Industrial Revolution, workers in particular, but the middle classes too, could expect to buy only fairly standardized products—widely referred to in the United States today as the one-size-fits-all approach. This was partly because the growing factories were technologically capable of (and usually limited to) long-run, large-scale production, and partly because social mobility meant that many were first-time buyers who were glad to get whatever product was available. The term Fordism, as applied to the Second Industrial Revolution, derived not only from Henry Ford's contribution to mass production techniques, but also from his statement about his first major success, the Model T: "You can have any color you like, as long as it's black."

However, with the end of the 1960s in the advanced capitalist world, more and more of these first-time markets were becoming saturated. Much of the long boom had grown out of burgeoning first-time markets for such products as white goods (refrigerators, washing machines, etc.) or television sets. Customers coming back a second time aiming to buy new models, however, demanded higher specifications and greater choice. Differentiating demand and flexible supply, then, converged on market segmentation—producing a wider range of variations on a particular product or set of products, with each variation targeted to a particular subset of consumers. This process was inextricably intertwined with globalization, as it created consumer demand for foreign-produced goods, and it forced firms to internationalize, too. These pressures now apply to the provision of public goods by governments as well.

The final characteristic of the Third Industrial Revolution is the growing significance of global finance and financial markets.[52] Karl Polanyi, writing in 1944, argued that the "great transformation" was a deep-rooted social reaction to the instability and inequities inherent in the attempt during the nineteenth century to establish a worldwide self-regulating market under the hegemony of British-led, but essentially transnational, *haute finance*.[53] The abstract nature of finance—the link with trade in commodity gold having been broken in the 1930s—makes trading in financial instruments virtually instantaneous. Indeed, John Maynard Keynes believed that financial markets were too easy to play, too readily divorced from the "real economy," for socially and economically necessary production to take place. The financial regulatory reforms of the 1930s, especially those of the New Deal in the United States, and the financial arrangements incorporated into the Bretton Woods system after World War II, were intended to control speculative financial flows (blamed by many for the Great Depression) and to ensure that finance was channeled into productive investment.

But in the period since the 1950s, and especially since the breakdown of Bretton Woods in 1971–73, finance has once again become globalized, with newly deregulated markets increasingly absorbing money from the real economy.[54] Indeed, finance embodies all of the other characteristics of the Third Industrial Revolution described above. In product terms, it has become the exemplar of a flexible industry, trading in notional and infinitely variable financial instruments. Financial innovation has been rapid and far-reaching, affecting all parts of the industry and shaping every industrial sector.[55] Furthermore, product innovation has been matched by process innovation. Management structures have evolved a long way from the traditional staid world of domestic banking, and traders and other financial market actors and firms are expected to act like entrepreneurs (or intrapreneurs) as a matter of course. The expansion and globalization of the financial services industry in recent years has been virtually synonymous with the rapid development of electronic computer and communications technologies, which transfer money around the world with the tap of a key.[56] The ownership and transfer of shares and other financial instruments are increasingly recorded only on computer files, without the exchange of paper certificates (what the French call "dematerialization"), while a "paper trail" can always be printed out for financial controllers, auditors, or regulators (in principle, at least).[57] With the increasing globalization of production and trade, market demand for financial services products is continually segmenting, too.

But probably the most important consequence of the globalization of financial markets is their increasing structural hegemony in wider economic (and political) structures and processes. In a more open world, financial balances and flows are increasingly dominant—with the volume of financial transactions variously estimated as totaling twenty to forty times the value of merchandise trade. Exchange rates and interest rates, essential to business decision making as well as to public policymaking, are increasingly set in world markets. In addition, as the trade and production structures of the Third Industrial Revolution go through the kinds of changes outlined earlier, they will be increasingly coordinated through the application of complex financial controls, rapidly evolving accounting techniques, financial performance indicators (because nonfinancial performance measures are more and more complex and difficult to apply in a globalizing world), and the like. These strictures are, of course, equally applicable to a range of organizations, including government bureaucracies. In this context, the globalization of production and trade and the globalization of finance reinforce each other—

with, however, the global financial tail increasingly wagging the real economy dog. Financial markets epitomize, in Williamson's terms, the structural ascendancy of almost purely nonspecific assets over specific assets in the global economy.

To summarize then, the structural changes embedded in the Third Industrial Revolution have turned the convergence of, and synergy between, political and economic structures characteristic of the Second Industrial Revolution into a rapidly expanding process of structural differentiation, leading to a structural dissonance to which states are attempting in an awkward and piecemeal way to adapt. To take this point several steps further, it can be argued that the economic and political world of the Third Industrial Revolution increasingly revolves around a central paradox. On the one hand, globalization would seem at first glance to entail the shift of the world economy to an even larger structural scale. This perception of globalization was what misled observers a decade or two ago to misinterpret the significance of multinational corporations, which were seen as involving the worldwide integration of specific assets.[58] While some firms in some sectors, and some problems like environmental pollution, do partially approximate this model of a relatively homogeneous "upward" shift in scale, for the most part economic restructuring has involved a more complex process, leading in a very different direction. For the second face of globalization entails the undermining of the public character of public goods and of the specific character of specific assets—that is, the privatization and marketization of the political economic structure itself. These processes, in turn—especially as represented in the globalization of financial markets—lead to the whipsawing of states between structural pressures and organizational levels they cannot control.

In this context, economic globalization contributes not only to superseding of the state by a homogeneous global order, but to the splintering of the existing political order, too. Indeed, globalization leads to a growing disjunction between the democratic, constitutional, and social aspirations of people—which are still shaped by, and understood through, the frame of the territorial state—on the one hand, and the dissipating possibilities of genuine and effective collective action through constitutional political processes, on the other. Certain possibilities for collective action through multilateral regimes may increase,[59] but these operate at least once removed from democratic or constitutional control and accountability; they are also vulnerable to being undermined by the anarchic nature of the international system. New nodes of economic power are crystallizing that, in their own partial domains, are in effect more sovereign than the state. What, then, are the limits and possibilities of what is left for the state in a globalizing economic order?

The Residual State: Constitutionalism in a Segmented World Economy

We have been accustomed for so long to telling the story of how the modern state gradually expanded its social and economic functions that it is cognitively dissonant to describe how those functions are being increasingly constrained in the contemporary world. Governments, mired in embedded financial orthodoxy, are constantly straining to do more for less. Nevertheless, despite the globalization of economic structures, the constitutional state, of course, retains great political, social, and psychological significance for its citizens. At the same time, states still retain a significant range of vital political and economic functions at both domestic and international levels—and some of these have actually been strengthened by globalization. In this context, policy wonks everywhere are seeking to reinvent government, that is, to restructure the state so that it can play *new* roles in the future.

In general, however, my argument is that while the state retains a crucial role in the political-economic matrix of a globalizing world, its holistic and overarching character—as reflected in Aristotle's "most sovereign and inclusive association" or Oakeshott's "civil association"—has been fundamentally compromised. Shifting—and differentiating—political economies of scale are creating a growing plurality of structures and processes to provide different sorts of public goods and to perform a range of what were once state functions. Nevertheless, a combination of constitutional legitimacy and the fact that the state retains a range of residual functions—some of which have actually been reinforced by globalization—means that existing landmarks are no longer sufficient. The state today is, therefore, a potentially unstable mix of civil association and enterprise association—of constitutional state, pressure group, and firm—with state actors, no longer so "autonomous,"[60] feeling their way uneasily in an unfamiliar world. Furthermore, the evolution of state structures and of political economies of scale is continuing, and there is no guarantee that the current mix of politics and economics, and of market and hierarchy, will persist in its present form.

The Continuing Salience of the Gemeinschaft *State*

The primary significance of the constitutional state as a social structure lies not merely in its practical functioning as a framework for particular economic and social activities—that is, with regard to its role as a provider of goods (public and private) or as a manager of assets. It also has the more symbolic social function of embodying the sense that people have of belonging to a particular social unit. In the terms used by Ferdinand Tönnies, the strength of any social unit derives from its particular mix of *Gesellschaft* and *Gemeinschaft,* the former representing the practical functions and the latter being a form of organic emotional-psychological bonding similar to that found in extended families and village societies. The modern nation-state became the central structure of modern society not only because of the convergence of political economies of scale, but also because it embodied what Florian Znaniecki has called a "national culture society."[61] In this context, the challenge of globalization affects a range of classical issues, including political obligation, the nature of community, the viability of constitutions, and the democratic accountability of state actors not merely for their own actions but for the state of the nation. Can this role of the state continue in the sort of globalizing world I have just described?

If it is suggested that this sort of sociopsychological function is a necessary part of human existence, as is the case in much social and political philosophy, then the question can be reformulated in two parts: First, will the residual state be able to maintain this *gemeinschaftlich* bond in spite of the circumscription of its *gesellschaftlich* functions; and second, is there an alternative structural form that could evolve into a repository for this sort of social belonging? The first question is difficult to answer. As the state is likely to retain a range of key political and economic functions despite (and partly because of) globalization, then the decay of *gemeinschaftlich* loyalty will be uneven, and in relatively stronger states this decay will proceed more slowly than in economically weaker states.

For example, if Reich is correct in his analysis in *The Work of Nations,*[62] then economic globalization is likely to lead to two kinds of socioeconomic stratification. The first is between a relatively large class of "symbolic analysts" (managers, technicians, researchers, intellectuals) consisting of about 20 to 40 percent of the population in advanced societies, and a low-paid service sector covering most of the rest—advanced societies having lost much of their labor-intensive production to the Third World. The second stratification is between those countries that, because of their infrastructure, education systems, workforce skills, and quality-of-life amenities (immobile factors of capital), have also been able to attract mobile, footloose capital of a highly sophisticated kind (employing lots of symbolic analysts engaging in high-value-added activities), and those countries that have to depend on low-wage, low-cost manufacturing or agricultural production. If the developed trilateral states of the United States, Europe, and Japan (along with perhaps some others) are better able to provide these advanced facilities, then *gemeinschaftlich* loyalty in those states may erode more slowly or perhaps even stabilize.

On the other hand, mobile international capital may well destabilize less favored states, whose already fragile governmental systems will be torn by groups attempting to recast those *gemeinschaftlich* bonds through claims for the ascendancy of religious, ethnic, or other grassroots loyalties. We are all aware of the revival of nationalism in the world today, but this nationalism is not of the state-bound, nineteenth-century variety; it is more elemental, and leads to the breakup of states rather than to their maintenance. Max Singer and Aaron Wildavsky have characterized this bifurcation of the world as leading to the differentiation between zones of peace and zones of turmoil—although they believe that in the long run there will be a tendency for the zones of turmoil to converge with the zones of peace, given increasing world trade, international communication, and the spread of prosperity gradually, if unevenly, outward from the core.[63] At the same time, however, it is not inconceivable that growing inequalities could lead to the opposite process, with the zones of peace gradually eroding, too. A linked scenario might be the emergence of an uneven patchwork more akin to neofeudalism. However, whether such scenarios prove to be realistic may depend far more on how the residual state adapts to carrying out its new, circumscribed range of political and economic functions than on vague, even more unrealistic, attempts to relocate *gemeinschaftlich* loyalties to equally problematic new levels.

The Residual State as a Continuing Structural Force in the Global Era

If we want to look for an alternative way of conceiving of the residual state, probably the best place to look is at American state governments. These governments have never been able to claim more than a partial loyalty from their inhabitants, and their power over internal economic and social structures and forces has been limited indeed. The way in which they have been increasingly required to operate over the course of the past two centuries in an open continental market, without there being such a thing as state citizenship (only residence, alongside the free movement of persons within the United States as a whole), is reflected increasingly in what other countries are facing in the globalizing world economy. Nevertheless, they do—like countries, provinces, and regions in other countries—foster a sense of identity and belonging that can be quite strong. In economic policy matters they represent the essence of what I have called the competition state. Their taxing and regulating power has been seriously constrained in many spheres by the expansion of the weight and the legal prerogatives of the federal government. However, at the same time, their ability to control development planning, to collect and use the tax revenues they do impose (as well as offering tax incentives and subsidies), to build infrastructure, to run education and training systems, to enforce law and order, and the like, give states a capacity to influence the provision of immobile factors of capital in significant ways. In Olson's and Williamson's terms, the state still has a major role to play in the provision of certain crucial types of public goods and the management of a range of significant specific assets, even if it must do so in a context where its authoritative power is weak and circumscribed.

The main focus of the competition state in the world—in a way that is partly analogous to the focus of state governments in the United States—is the promotion of economic activities, whether at home or abroad, that will make firms and sectors located within the territory of the state competitive in international markets. (The question of foreign or domestic ownership is highly problematic here; Reich argues that ownership is far less important than the ability to attract capital, whether domestic or foreign, that will invest in high-value-added activities and provide jobs for domestic workers.)[64] In this process, however, the state to some extent becomes an agent of its own transformation from civil association to enterprise association. Rather than offering public goods or other services that cannot be efficiently provided by the market—in other words, rather than acting as a "decommodifying" agent where market efficiency fails—the state is drawn into promoting the commodification or marketization of its own activities and structures (including the internal fragmentation of the state itself).

The state has always to some extent been a promoter of market forces rather than a purely hierarchical or public organization; this marketizing quality is especially inherent in the concept of regulatory public goods explained earlier. But there is a difference between promoting market activities as a general public good and being transformed into a market-based organization per se. There is a crucial threshold somewhere here, beyond which the cumulative structural trends involving the progressive commodification of the state lead to a difference in kind rather than merely in degree. This difference in kind lies in the Olsonian and Williamsonian thresholds between public and private goods and between specific and nonspecific assets. For it is in the transformation of the predominant mix of goods from public dominated to private dominated, or the transformation of the predominant mix of assets from specific to nonspecific, that in turn transforms the state from a primarily hierarchical, decommodifying agent into a primarily market-based, commodifying agent. In this context, I suggest that the key to understanding how and when that threshold is approached and crossed can be found in the development of globalization. In a globalizing world, the state, by increasingly promoting the transnational expansion and competitiveness of its industries and services abroad and in increasingly competing for inward investment—and in transforming society itself (as well as its own role in society) to prioritize that objective—in effect becomes a critical agent, perhaps the most critical agent, in the process of globalization itself.

This paradoxical situation, in which the competition state maintains itself and undermines itself at one and the same time by focusing on one central public role—promoting competitiveness—while shedding many of its other traditional public roles, is paralleled by developments at the multilateral level. In order to pursue policy goals beyond the control span of the state, of course, a network of international and transnational regimes has grown up, some with more general and some with more circumscribed jurisdictions. It has been increasingly suggested for some time now within international relations that such regimes, where they are successful in fulfilling their tasks—and even if they are sometimes essentially intergovernmental bodies—have increasingly been developing the capacity to operate more autonomously of the states that have established and maintained them.[65] In this context, the very constitutional position of such regimes is inherently problematic, given the anarchical character of the international system—with the most crucial issue being that it becomes virtually impossible to establish clear or even operational lines of democratic accountability in such a situation.

Clearly the shift of decision-making power in a globalizing world is differentiating along several dimensions—not merely downward to domestic firms and markets or into different corners of the splintered state, but also upward to international markets and firms and to a range of more or less functionally specialized international bodies. In this context, the scenario of constitutional decay and fragmentation becomes at the same time both more and less plausible. It becomes more plausible because no one structure or closely interwoven set of structures is actually hegemonic in a political sense; not only are strategic issues difficult to resolve, but conflicts can undermine the cohesion of the different decision arenas. However, it becomes less plausible if looked at in the context of the sort of pluralist theory that has been so influential in domestic political science and political sociology. When analyzed in this light, it might be hypothesized that crosscutting conflicts and overlapping webs of affiliations may prove better at stabilizing global society in the long run than any attempt to resolve them authoritatively. In a globalizing world, we are increasingly dealing with predominantly private goods and nonspecific assets; in this context, authoritative forms of allocation of values and resources may be inherently less efficient than market forms, if we are to believe Olson's collective action theory or Williamson's transaction cost analysis. Many political sociologists have, of course, argued in the past that the stability and viability of constitutional democracy depend less upon formal democratic accountability and more upon the peaceful competition of a plurality of groups with overlapping memberships. Resituating this problematic at a global or transnational level, the residual state would not simply erode or decay, but would remain a key building block (among others) in this multilateral web—a role that would be increased and reinforced, rather than undermined, by the process of globalization.[66]

Reinventing Government: New Roles for the Residual State

At the same time that the state faces changes in the way people perceive it in sociological terms, and in the way it has maintained certain functions still critical even in a more differentiated international and domestic context, the search is on to find new ways for it to function and new roles for it to play. The most important changes have been analogous to the changing structures of production and distribution in the Third Industrial Revolution. The attempt to make the state more flexible has moved a long way over the past decade or so, not only in the United States and Britain—where deregulation, privatization, and liberalization have evolved furthest—but also in a wide range of other countries in the First and Third Worlds (and later in the Second World, too). Some of these changes have already become controversial not only because they have challenged tested ways of making and implementing public policy or confronted important cultural values, but because their prescriptions can be tested only at the risk of failure. Privatization and deregulation are particularly important in this context, because they involve the increasing interweaving of the domestic economy and the global economy. In particular, they introduce the possibility of what I have elsewhere called regulatory arbitrage. Regulatory arbitrage refers to a situation in which different state bodies get pressured into what economists call competition in laxity. This is where the state's response to economic pressures becomes increasingly one of adjusting levels of regulation and intervention downward so as not to lose competitive advantage vis-à-vis states with looser regulation or greater market freedom for businesses—especially footloose, mobile, transnational capital.

Beyond privatization and deregulation, probably the most extensive experiment in the United States and the United Kingdom has been the subcontracting out of public and social services. Regarding garbage collection, prisons, or the running of state-financed schools, the state has attempted to replace hierarchical systems with recurrent contracting. As with private firms, too, what has seemed to make such innovations realistic has been the possibility of vigilant performance monitoring (especially using new information technology), and the application of highly targeted financial controls. Closely linked to subcontracting is the attempt to introduce internal markets into previously hierarchical organizations. In Britain, it is being made possible for recently privatized electricity suppliers—thought by many economists to be as near as you can get to a technological "natural monopoly," given the expense of laying parallel cables and the like—to compete on price in each others' geographical areas by requiring each of them to sell a certain amount of their electricity to industries (and eventually to private consumers) at prices set by their competitors. The structural division of the U.K.'s National Health Service into suppliers and purchasers of services is perhaps a better-known example, mainly because it has been more politically controversial given the salience of the NHS to the *gemeinschaftlich* ideology of the postwar welfare state and of the Labour Party; nevertheless, the

Labour Party announced it will attempt only to reverse some, and not all, of these changes should it come to power.

Some of the packages of proposals to reinvent government go much farther, of course, by calling for a new entrepreneurialism (and intrapreneurialism?) in the far reaches of government and the public sector. Although leading American advocates of the process (who are close to the Clinton administration) believe that these reforms can be carried out in a way that is consistent with center-left, social-liberal principles,[67] the fact remains that the most extensive experimentation with these kinds of measures is that carried out by the Thatcher government in Britain in the 1980s. Although these policies are not the direct result of the globalization processes that are the focus of this chapter, they are inextricably intertwined with the organizational changes we have been addressing here. These have their root cause in structural changes in the predominant mixes of goods and assets—changes that have been part and parcel of globalization and of complex shifts in the political economies of scale characteristic of an interpenetrated, Third Industrial Revolution world.

Conclusions: Constitutional Viability and the Changing Logic of Collective Action in a Globalizing World

This chapter started by suggesting that the process of globalization has fundamentally transformed the structural context of collective action, and thereby the nature of the constitutional state, in the contemporary world. I have argued that globalization has undermined the sovereign and inclusive character of the political association (according to Aristotle) and the character of the state as a civil association (Oakeshott), especially in the way that those conceptualizations have been understood and applied in the context of the modern, Second Industrial Revolution nation-state. In the Second Industrial Revolution state, collective action games were played out on a structured field in which economies of scale in both political and economic structures converged on a particular matrix of market and hierarchy, of public and private goods.

The process of change since the Second Industrial Revolution, however, has not been homogeneous. The combination of internal tensions within the Second Industrial Revolution system, especially in the interwar period and after World War II, and fundamental shifts in political economies of scale that came with economic internationalization and the complex technological and organizational changes of the Third Industrial

Revolution, has created a new matrix—a new, more complex set of political economies of scale—in which the role of the state is changing dramatically. Rather than globalization simply leading to the emergence of a more clearly defined and homogeneous global order, it has instead been characterized by the increasing differentiation of both economic and political structures. Globalization is an inherently heterogeneous phenomenon, and entails a fundamental shift in the mix of goods and assets—from public to private, and from specific to nonspecific—in ways that undermine crucial aspects of the public and constitutional character of the state.

These changes threaten the very nature of the constitutional state as a sovereign, inclusive political association and as a civil association. Against this background, the state is increasingly being transformed into a complex mix of civil and enterprise association, the "residual state," rooted in the competition state. On the one hand, the state does retain a certain hold over national consciousness and constitutional legitimacy, and its residual functions are still central both to the globalization process and to carrying out a range of crucial political, economic, and social functions. On the other hand, however, just how far state structures will have to be transformed if they are not to be eroded further is not yet clear. The commodified state may well be in the process of becoming a predominantly enterprise association, with key civic, public, and constitutional functions becoming increasingly vestigial. At the same time, the future stability of the international system presents a problematic picture. Globalization does not mean that the character of the international system is any less anarchic, as is said in international relations theory; it merely changes the structure of that anarchy from one comprising relations between sovereign states to one comprising relations between what Susan Strange has called "transnational structures."[68] Whether the state will, despite its changing roles, remain a key element in a stabilizing, multilateral web of levels and institutions, or whether its decay will exacerbate a trend toward instability, is not yet entirely clear. What is clear is that we are only now in the first stages of a complex worldwide evolutionary process that will transform the state and affect the viability of constitutionalism for a long time to come.

Notes

1. The notion that transnational interpenetration is not homogeneous is essential to the concept of complex interdependence as developed in Robert O. Keohane and Joseph S. Nye, Jr., *Power and Interdependence* (Boston: Little, Brown, 1977), but the implications of the growing heterogeneity of transnational structures for domestic and

international politics are more thoroughly explored in Susan Strange, *States and Markets: An Introduction to International Political Economy* (London and New York: Hinter and Basil Blackwell, 1988). Strange's analysis is explicitly based on the identification of the discrete and dissimilar structural conditions and dynamics characteristic of distinct "transnational structures" in security, finance, production, and knowledge (called "primary structures"), as well as on distinguishing a range of "secondary structures."

2. For a consideration of some definitional problems, see Robin Brown, "The New Realities: Globalization, Culture, and International Relations," paper presented to the annual meeting of the British International Studies Association, University of Swansea, December 14–16, 1992.

3. *The Politics of Aristotle,* edited and translated by Ernest Barker (New York: Oxford University Press, 1962), 1.

4. Cf. Josiah Lee Auspitz, "Individuality, Civility, and Theory: The Philosophical Imagination of Michael Oakeshott," *Political Theory* 4, no. 3 (August 1976): 261–352; and Michael Oakeshott, "On Misunderstanding Human Conduct: A Reply to My Critics," ibid., 353–67.

5. These issues are examined at more length in Philip G. Cerny, *The Changing Architecture of Politics: Structure, Agency, and the Future of the State* (London and Newbury Park, Calif.: Sage Publications, 1990), especially Chapter 4.

6. Michel Crozier and Erhard Friedberg, *L'acteur et le système: Les contraintes de l'action collective* (Paris: Éditions du Seuil, 1977).

7. Mancur Olson, *The Logic of Collective Action* (Cambridge: Harvard University Press, 1971).

8. Oliver E. Williamson, *Markets and Hierarchies* (New York: Free Press, 1975), and *The Economic Institutions of Capitalism* (New York: Free Press, 1985).

9. Cerny, *The Changing Architecture of Politics,* especially Chapter 3.

10. Olson, *The Logic of Collective Action.*

11. Williamson, *Markets and Hierarchies,* and *Economic Institutions of Capitalism.*

12. A classic statement of the predicament of how stability and effectiveness in democratic systems may depend on authoritarian institutions and processes is found in Harry Eckstein's *A Theory of Stable Democracy*, reprinted in Eckstein, *Division and Cohesion in Democracy: A Study of Norway* (Princeton: Princeton University Press, 1966); see also Giovanni Sartori, *Democratic Theory* (New York: Praeger, 1965).

13. The identification of specific assets, Williamson points out, is more widely accepted where technological economies of scale are concerned; transaction cost analysis, which adds a significantly new dimension to Williamson's argument, is less easily quantifiable and less accepted by neoclassical economists (who attribute a much larger role in the structural consolidation of firms to monopolistic behavior).

14. It could even be suggested that by basing society for political and economic reasons around an extended kinship structure, the range of what Hirsch calls "positional goods" (those goods that can be used only by a small number of people, such as standing on the top rung of a ladder or, in this case, occupying a patriarchically determined position of power in a kinship hierarchy) might therefore also be constrained and controlled in one virtual "natural monopoly of power." See Fred Hirsch, *Social Limits to Growth* (London: Routledge and Kegan Paul, 1976).

15. See Peter M. Blau, ed., *Approaches to the Study of Social Structure* (New York and London: Free Press and Open Books, 1975).

16. Raymond Cohen and Elman R. Service, eds., *Origins of the State: The Anthropology of Political Evolution* (Philadelphia: Institute for the Study of Human Issues, 1985), especially 2–17.

17. Douglas C. North, *Structure and Change in Economic History* (New York:

Norton, 1981), especially Chapter 3, "A Neoclassical Theory of the State." Cf. Perry Anderson, *Lineages of the Absolutist State* (London: New Left Books, 1974).

18. A similar analysis, although expressed in less social-theoretical language, is developed in Paul Kennedy, *The Rise and Fall of the Great Powers: Economic Change and Military Conflict From 1500 to 2000* (London: Unwin Hyman, 1988).

19. Although the changing scale of industrial production is seen usually as the core of these structure changes, it must not be forgotten that in some countries, especially the United States (which had become the world's largest agricultural producer even before the Second Industrial Revolution), the development of large-scale farming techniques in grain production and cattle ranching, for example, had already begun to alter the scale economies of agriculture.

20. See Philip G. Cerny, "Money and Power: The American Financial System from Free Banking to Global Competition," in *Markets*, ed. Grahame Thompson, vol. 2 of *The United States in the Twentieth Century* (London: Hodder and Stoughton, 1994); and Ron Chernow, *The House of Morgan: An American Banking Dynasty and the Rise of Modern Finance* (New York: Simon and Schuster, 1990).

21. For an insightful analysis of these developments, see Robert B. Reich, *The Next American Frontier* (New York: Times Books, 1983), Part 2.

22. Max Weber, *Economy and Society*, 2 vols., ed. Guenther Roth and Claus Wittich (Berkeley and Los Angeles: University of California Press, 1978).

23. Eric J. Hobsbawm, *Industry and Empire* (Harmondsworth, England: Penguin, 1969).

24. Karl Polanyi, *The Great Transformation: The Political and Economic Origins of Our Time* (New York: Rinehart, 1944).

25. Cf. Andrew Shonfield, *Modern Capitalism: The Changing Balance of Public and Private Power* (London and New York: Oxford University Press, 1965), and John Zysman, *Governments, Markets, and Growth: Financial Systems and the Politics of Industrial Change* (Ithaca: Cornell University Press, 1983).

26. Pierre Birnbaum, *La logique de l'État* (Paris: Fayard, 1982).

27. In particular, powerful international forces persisted in finance, and multinational corporations, increasingly American in origin, were growing in size and significance on the world scene.

28. This general loss of control was perhaps even more significant than the loss of hegemonic control addressed by Kindleberger (which was a key symptom of the broader phenomenon, nonetheless); see Charles P. Kindleberger, *The World in Depression, 1929–1939* (London: Allen Large, Penguin Press, 1973).

29. A now classic analysis of the history of American foreign policy in terms of the Open Door approach is William Appleman Williams, *The Tragedy of American Diplomacy* 2d ed. (New York: Dell, 1972).

30. See Lloyd C. Gardner, *Economic Aspects of New Deal Diplomacy* (Boston: Beacon Press, 1971).

31. E. F. Penrose, *Economic Planning for the Peace* (Princeton: Princeton University Press, 1953).

32. See Philip G. Cerny, *The Politics of Grandeur: Ideological Aspects of de Gaulle's Foreign Policy* (Cambridge: Cambridge University Press, 1980), especially Chapters 7–9.

33. John Kenneth Galbraith. *The New Industrial State* (Harmondsworth, England: Penguin, 1967).

34. See Stephen Krasner, ed., *International Regimes* (Ithaca: Cornell University Press, 1983).

35. T. V. Sathyamurthy, "Indian Peasant Historiography: A Critical Perspective on

Ranajit Guha's Work," *Journal of Peasant Studies* 18, no. 1 (October 1990): 90–144.

36. The concept of circuits of power, and their increasing fragmentation in the contemporary world, was developed by Michel Foucault; see Foucault, *Power/Knowledge: Selected Interviews and Other Writings, 1972–1977*, ed. Colin Gordon (New York: Pantheon Books, 1980). Foucault's analysis is one of the many strands of postmodernist thought.

37. V. I. Lenin, *Imperialism, the Highest Stage of Capitalism* (1917; reprint, Moscow: Progress Publishers, 1978), and *State and Revolution* (1918; reprint, New York: International Publishers, 1932).

38. I am borrowing freely here from Theodore Lowi's three categories of public policy—distributive, regulatory, and redistributive—as developed in "American Business, Public Policy, Case Studies, and Political Theory," *World Politics* 16, no. 4 (July 1964): 677–715, and *The End of Liberalism: Ideology, Polity, and the Crisis of Public Authority* (New York: Norton, 1969).

39. For an analysis of regulatory arbitrage in the financial sector, see Philip G. Cerny, ed., *Finance and World Politics: Markets, Regimes, and States in the Post-Hegemonic Era* (Cheltenham, England, and Brookfield, Vt.: Edward Elgar, 1993), especially Chapters 3 and 6.

40. See Edward M. Graham and Paul R. Krugman, *Foreign Direct Investment in the United States* (Washington, D.C.: Institute for International Economics, 1989), Chapter 5.

41. Cf. Nigel Harris, *The End of the Third World* (Harmondsworth, England: Penguin, 1986), and Stephan Haggard, *Pathways from the Periphery: The Politics of Growth in the Newly Industrializing Countries* (Ithaca: Cornell University Press, 1990).

42. Philip G. Cerny, "State Capitalism in France and Britain and the International Economic Order," chapter 10 in *Socialism, the State, and Public Policy in France*, ed. P. G. Cerny and M. A. Schain (London and New York: Pinter and Methuen, 1985).

43. Richard B. McKenzie and Dwight R. Lee, *Quicksilver Capital: How the Rapid Movement of Wealth Has Changed the World* (New York: Free Press, 1991).

44. Probably the best-known protagonist in this field is Robert B. Reich; see Reich, *The Work of Nations: Preparing Ourselves for Twenty-first-Century Capitalism* (New York: Knopf, 1991).

45. Cerny, *Changing Architecture of Politics*, especially Chapter 8.

46. See Angela Liberatore, "Problems of Transnational Policymaking: Environmental Policy in the European Community," in "The Politics of Transnational Regulation: Deregulation or Reregulation," ed. P. G. Cerny, Special Issue of the *European Journal of Political Research* 19, nos. 2 and 3 (March–April 1991): 281–305.

47. Especially those following the path of export promotion industrialization.

48. John Zysman, *Political Strategies for Industrial Order: Market, State, and Industry in France* (Berkeley and Los Angeles: University of California Press, 1977).

49. Cf. Reich, *Next American Frontier*, and S. M. Miller and Donald Tomaskovic-Devey, *Recapitalizing America: Alternatives to the Corporate Distortion of National Policy* (Boston and London: Routledge and Kegan Paul, 1983).

50. John Zysman and Laura d'Andrea Tyson, *American Industry in International Competition* (Ithaca: Cornell University Press, 1983).

51. See Ash Amin, ed., *Post-Fordism: A Reader* (Oxford and New York: Basil Blackwell, 1994), especially the editor's introductory essay.

52. For a more extensive treatment of these issues, see Cerny, ed., *Finance and World Politics*, especially Chapter 3.

53. Polanyi, *The Great Transformation*, Chapters 1 and 2.

54. Roy E. Allen, *Financial Crises and Recession in the New Global Economy*

(Cheltenham, England, and Brookfield, Vt.: Edward Elgar, 1994), and *Studies in International Political Economy,* Brookfield, Vt.: Edward Elgar, 1994).

55. See Richard D. Crawford and William W. Sihler, *The Troubled Money Business: The Death of an Old Order and the Rise of a New Order* (New York: HarperBusiness, 1991).

56. The implications of technological change in the financial services industry are examined in Susan Strange, "Finance, Information, and Power," *Review of International Studies* 16, no. 3 (July 1990): 259–74.

57. The collapse several years ago of the Bank of Credit and Commerce International and the conviction of leading traders like Ivan Boesky and Michael Milken show, however, that the temptation to defraud, and the capability of keeping it hidden for a long time, still exists.

58. A more complex and sophisticated analysis of multinational corporations—how they work, how they interact with each other, and how they interact with states—can be found in John Stopford and Susan Strange (with John S. Henley), *Rival States, Rival Firms: Competition for World Market Shares* (Cambridge: Cambridge University Press, 1991).

59. See Friedrich Kratochwil and Edward D. Mansfield, eds., *International Organization: A Reader* (New York: HarperCollins, 1994).

60. For a consideration of the problem of state "autonomy" and the different approaches taken to it in the neo-Marxist, neo-Weberian, and neopluralist debates of the 1980s, see Cerny, *Changing Architecture of Politics,* especially Chapter 4.

61. Ferdinand Tönnies, *Community and Association* (East Lansing: Michigan State University Press, 1957; originally published as *Gemeinschaft und Gesellschaft,* 1887); Florian Znaniecki, *Modern Nationalities: A Sociological Study* (Westport, Conn.: Greenwood Press, 1973; originally published 1952).

62. Reich, *The Work of Nations,* Part 3 and 243–51.

63. Max Singer and Aaron Wildavsky, *The Real World Order: Zones of Peace/ Zones of Turmoil* (Chatham, N.J.: Chatham House Publishers, 1993).

64. Reich, *The Work of Nations,* 252–61.

65. Cf. J. G. Ruggie, J. A. Caporaso, S. Weber, and M. Kahler, "Symposium: Multilateralism," Special Issue of *International Organization* 46, no. 3 (summer 1992): 561–708; and Robert W. Cox, "Multilateralism and the World Order," *Review of International Studies* 18, no. 2 (April, 1992): 161–80. See also Krasner, *International Regimes,* and Kratochwil and Mansfield, *International Organization.*

66. This is my argument in Philip G. Cerny, "Plurilateralism: Structural Differentiation and Functional Conflict in the Post–Cold War World Order," *Millennium: Journal of International Studies* 22, no. 1 (spring 1993): 27–51.

67. Especially David Osborne and Ted Gaebler, *Reinventing Government: How the Entrepreneurial Spirit Is Transforming the Public Sector, from Schoolhouse to Statehouse, City Hall to the Pentagon,* (Reading, Mass.: Addison-Wesley, 1992).

68. Strange, *States and Markets.*

References

Allen, Roy E. *Financial Crises and Recession in the New Global Economy.* Cheltenham, England: Aldershot, Hants, 1994.

———. *Studies in International Political Economy.* Brookfield, Vt.: Edward Elgar, 1994.

Anderson, Perry. *Lineages of the Absolutist State.* London: New Left Books, 1974.

Aristotle. *The Politics of Aristotle.* Edited and translated by Ernest Barker. New York: Oxford University Press, 1962.

Amin, Ash, ed. *Post-Fordism: A Reader.* Oxford and New York: Basil Blackwell, 1994.

Auspitz, Josiah Lee. "Individuality, Civility, and Theory: The Philosophical Imagination of Michael Oakeshott." *Political Theory* 4, no. 3 (August 1976): 261–352.

Birnbaum, Pierre. *La logique de l'État.* Paris: Fayard, 1982.

Blau, Peter M., ed. *Approaches to the Study of Social Structure.* New York and London: Free Press and Open Books, 1975.

Brown, Robin. "The New Realities: Globalization, Culture, and International Relations." Paper presented to the annual meeting of the British International Studies Association, University of Swansea, December 14–16, 1992.

Cerny, Philip G. *The Politics of Grandeur: Ideological Aspects of de Gaulle's Foreign Policy.* Cambridge: Cambridge University Press, 1980.

———. "State Capitalism in France and Britain and the International Economic Order." Chapter 10 in *Socialism, the State, and Public Policy in France,* edited by P. G. Cerny and M. A. Schain. London and New York: Pinter and Methuen, 1985.

———. *The Changing Architecture of Politics: Structure, Agency, and the Future of the State.* London and Newbury Park, Calif.: Sage Publications, 1990.

———. "Plurilateralism: Structural Differentiation and Functional Conflict in the Post–Cold War World Order." *Millennium: Journal of International Studies* 22, no. 1 (spring 1993): 27–51.

———. "Money and Power: The American Financial System from Free Banking to Global Competition." In *Markets,* edited by Grahame Thompson, vol. 2 of *The United States in the Twentieth Century,* London: Hodder and Stoughton, 1994.

———. ed. *Finance and World Politics: Markets, Regimes, and States in the Post-Hegemonic Era.* Cheltenham and Brookfield, Vt.: Edward Elgar, 1993.

Chernow, Ron. *The House of Morgan: An American Banking Dynasty and the Rise of Modern Finance.* New York: Simon and Schuster, 1990.

Cohen, Raymond, and Elman R. Service, eds. *Origins of the State: The Anthropology of Political Evolution.* Philadelphia: Institute for the Study of Human Issues, 1985.

Cox, Robert W. "Multilateralism and the World Order." *Review of International Studies* 18, no. 2 (April, 1992): 161–80.

Crawford, Richard D., and William W. Sihler. *The Troubled Money Business: The Death of an Old Order and the Rise of a New Order.* New York: HarperBusiness, 1991.

Crozier, Michel, and Erhard Friedberg. *L'acteur et le système: Les contraintes de l'action collective.* Paris: Éditions du Seuil, 1977.

Eckstein, Harry. *A Theory of Stable Democracy.* Reprinted in *Division and Cohesion in Democracy: A Study of Norway,* edited by Harry Eckstein. Princeton: Princeton University Press, 1966.

Foucault, Michel. *Power/Knowledge: Selected Interviews and Other Writings, 1972–1977.* Edited by Colin Gordon. New York: Pantheon Books, 1980.

Galbraith, John Kenneth. *The New Industrial State.* Harmondsworth, England: Penguin, 1967.

Gardner, Lloyd C. *Economic Aspects of New Deal Diplomacy.* Boston: Beacon Press, 1971.

Graham, Edward M., and Paul R. Krugman. *Foreign Direct Investment in the United States.* Washington, D.C.: Institute for International Economics, 1989.

Haggard, Stephan. *Pathways from the Periphery: The Politics of Growth in the Newly Industrializing Countries.* Ithaca: Cornell University Press, 1990.

Harris, Nigel. *The End of the Third World.* Harmondsworth, England: Penguin. 1986.

Hirsch, Fred. *Social Limits to Growth.* London: Routledge and Kegan Paul, 1976.

Hobsbawm, Eric J. *Industry and Empire.* Harmondsworth, England: Penguin, 1969.

Kennedy, Paul. *The Rise and Fall of the Great Powers: Economic Change and Military Conflict From 1500 to 2000.* London: Unwin Hyman, 1988.

Keohcane, Robert O., and Joseph S. Nye, Jr. *Power and Interdependence.* Boston: Little, Brown, 1977.

Kindleberger, Charles P. *The World in Depression, 1929–1939.* London: Allen Large, Penguin Press, 1973.

Krasner, Stephen, ed. *International Regimes.* Ithaca: Cornell University Press, 1983.

Kratochwil, Friedrich, and Edward D. Mansfield, eds. *International Organization: A Reader.* New York: HarperCollins, 1994.

Liberatore, Angela. "Problems of Transnational Policymaking: Environmental Policy in the European Community." In "The Politics of Transnational Regulation: Deregulation or Reregulation," edited by P. G. Cerny, Special Issue of the *European Journal of Political Research* 19, nos. 2 and 3 (March–April 1991): 281–305.

Lowi, Theodore. "American Business, Public Policy, Case Studies, and Political Theory." *World Politics* 16, no. 4 (July 1964): 677–715.

———. *The End of Liberalism: Ideology, Polity, and the Crisis of Public Authority.* New York: Norton, 1969.

McKenzie, Richard B., and Dwight R. Lee. *Quicksilver Capital: How the Rapid Movement of Wealth Has Changed the World.* New York: Free Press, 1991.

Miller, S. M., and Donald Tomaskovic-Devey. *Recapitalizing America: Alternatives to the Corporate Distortion of National Policy.* Boston and London: Routledge and Kegan Paul, 1983.

North, Douglas C. *Structure and Change in Economic History.* New York: Norton, 1981.

Oakeshott, Michael. "On Misunderstanding Human Conduct: A Reply to My Critics." *Political Theory* 4, no. 3 (August 1976): 353–67.

Olson, Mancur. *The Logic of Collective Action.* Cambridge: Harvard University Press, 1971.

Osborne, David, and Ted Gaebler. *Reinventing Government: How the Entrepreneurial Spirit Is Transforming the Public Sector, from Schoolhouse to Statehouse, City Hall to the Pentagon.* Reading, Mass.: Addison-Wesley, 1992.

Penrose, E. F. *Economic Planning for the Peace.* Princeton: Princeton University Press, 1953.

Polanyi, Karl. *The Great Transformation: The Political and Economic Origins of Our Time.* New York: Rinehart, 1944.

Reich, Robert B. *The Next American Frontier.* New York: Times Books, 1983.

———. *The Work of Nations: Preparing Ourselves for Twenty-first-Century Capitalism.* New York: Knopf, 1991.

Ruggie, J. G., J. A. Caporaso, S. Weber, and M. Kahler. "Symposium: Multilateralism." Special Issue of *International Organization* 46, no. 3 (summer 1992): 561–708.

Sartori, Giovanni. *Democratic Theory.* New York: Praeger, 1965.

Sathyamurthy, T. V. "Indian Peasant Historiography: A Critical Perspective on Ranajit Guha's Work." *Journal of Peasant Studies* 18, no. 1 (October 1990): 90–144.

Shonfield, Andrew. *Modern Capitalism: The Changing Balance of Public and Private Power.* London and New York: Oxford University Press, 1965.

Singer, Max, and Aaron Wildavsky. *The Real World Order: Zones of Peace/Zones of Turmoil.* Chatham, N.J.: Chatham House Publishers, 1993.

Stopford, John, and Susan Strange (with John S. Henley). *Rival States, Rival Firms: Competition for World Market Shares.* Cambridge: Cambridge University Press, 1991.

Strange, Susan. *States and Markets: An Introduction to International Political Economy.* London and New York: Hinter and Basil Blackwell, 1988.

———. "Finance, Information, and Power." *Review of International Studies* 16, no. 3 (July 1990): 259–74.

Tönnies, Ferdinand. *Community and Association.* East Lansing: Michigan State University Press, 1957. Originally published as *Gemeinschaft und Gesellschaft,* 1887.

Weber, Max. *Economy and Society.* 2 vols. Edited by Guenther Roth and Claus Wittich. Berkeley and Los Angeles: University of California Press, 1978.

Williams, William Appleman. *The Tragedy of American Diplomacy.* 2d ed. New York: Dell, 1972.

Williamson, Oliver E. *Markets and Hierarchies.* New York: Free Press, 1975.

———. *The Economic Institutions of Capitalism.* New York: Free Press, 1985.

Znaniecki, Florian. *Modern Nationalities: A Sociological Study.* Westport, Conn.: Greenwood Press, 1973. Originally published in 1952.

Zysman, John. *Political Strategies for Industrial Order: Market, State, and Industry in France.* Berkeley and Los Angeles: University of California Press, 1977.

———. *Governments, Markets, and Growth: Financial Systems and the Politics of Industrial Change.* Ithaca: Cornell University Press, 1983.

Zysman, John, and Laura d'Andrea Tyson. *American Industry in International Competition.* Ithaca: Cornell University Press, 1983.

Index